Benjamin G. Wold

Women, Men, and Angels

The Qumran Wisdom Document *Musar leMevin* and
its Allusions to Genesis Creation Traditions

Mohr Siebeck

BENJAMIN G. WOLD, born 1974; 2000 MA Jerusalem University College; 2002–2003 doctoral exchange student in Tübingen; 2004 Ph.D. University of Durham; Postdoctoral Fellow, University of Durham, Department of Theology and Religion.

ISBN 3-16-148691-9
ISSN 0340-9570 (Wissenschaftliche Untersuchungen zum Neuen Testament, 2. Reihe)

Die Deutsche Bibliothek lists this publication in the Deutsche Nationalbibliographie; detailed bibliographic data is available in the Internet at *http://dnb.ddb.de*.

© 2005 Mohr Siebeck, Tübingen, Germany.

The book was printed by Gulde-Druck in Tübingen on non-aging paper and bound by Buchbinderei Held in Rottenburg/N.

Printed in Germany.

Wissenschaftliche Untersuchungen
zum Neuen Testament · 2. Reihe

Herausgeber / Editor
Jörg Frey

Mitherausgeber / Associate Editors
Friedrich Avemarie · Judith Gundry-Volf
Martin Hengel · Otfried Hofius · Hans-Josef Klauck

201

When Asked Who Is Your Neighbour
Tim and Kay Winn Have Responded:

הגר אתכם ואהבת לו כמוך (Lev 19.34)

Acknowledgements

This monograph is a revision of my doctoral thesis submitted to the Department of Theology and Religion, Durham University, England. I am grateful to Professor Jörg Frey for accepting my manuscript for publication in the WUNT 2 series.

The ideas for this research began in the course of lengthy discussions with my Doktorvater, Loren Stuckenbruck, as we traveled with his son Hanno in Israel during the summer of 2000. Loren's gifted expertise and patient concern in the years that followed made my research and writing personally very fruitful. Loren has been not only a world-class supervisor, but a friend and colleague as well. I am thankful for my years of study in the historic city of Durham among so many exceptional scholars.

Tim and Kay Winn of the Lampstand Foundation provided me with scholarships throughout my studies. If it were not for their philanthropy and graciousness I would not be where I am today. It is with deep gratitude that I dedicate this book to them.

Robert Hayward and Rabbi Robert Ash facilitated the post-doctoral fellowship that I presently have. I am thankful for their confidence and generosity in inviting me to this position at the Centre for Jewish Studies at Durham University, Department of Theology and Religion. The research time made possible by the fellowship has allowed me to make revisions to this work and enjoy two more beautiful years in Durham. The staff at St. Mary's College have been outstanding hosts to me during this time as well.

Several others deserve recognition. Steve Notley first introduced me to early Judaism and was both a teacher and mentor during my studies in Israel. In addition, Randall Buth, Hanan Eshel, and Hannah Safrai were for me significant instructors who have left a lasting impact. At Eberhard-Karls Universität Tübingen, Professor Hermann Lichtenberger warmly received me, provided opportunities to present my research, and co-supervised me during this year abroad. The faculty and staff at the Theologicum in Tübingen provided me a friendly and welcoming environment in which to study. Thank you.

I would especially like to thank two friends. Floyd Plemmons has been an exceptional friend since we first met in Jerusalem. The experiences we have shared together -- travels, adventures and many an all night conversation -- have meant more to me then I can express here. Saya Nagafuji, whom I first met in the Internationales Sprachprogramm in Tübingen, has been a close friend during the last years of my studies. Saya deserves the credit for much of my German language acquisition, and without her I doubt I would be able to utter more than a simple Dankeschön.

Most of all I would like to acknowledge deepest gratitude to my family: my mother, my father, Rease, Teckla, and Jasara. Through the sometimes tumultuous ups and downs of the last years, their love and support, so often from the other side of the globe, meant more to me than they will ever know. It is my hope that this publication not only makes a contribution to understanding an aspect of Judaism in the Graeco-Roman Period, but also serves as an explanation of what it is I have been doing during the last few years.

Durham, Easter 2005   Benjamin G. Wold

Table of Contents

CHAPTER 1. Review of Research and Remaining Issues................................... 1
  1. Introduction.. 1
  2. General Information on the Document.. 2
  3. History of Research.. 4
  4. Issues Addressed in Recent Publications.. 7
    4.1 Provenance... 7
    4.2 The Relationship to the 'Sectarian Community'....................... 8
    4.3 The Meaning of רז נהיה... 20
    4.4 Language of Poverty... 24
    4.5 Reconstruction... 30
    4.6 Angelology.. 38
  5. Issues Raised and Resolved... 40
  6. Suggestions for Remaining Tasks.. 41

CHAPTER 2. Non-Explicit Use of Biblical Traditions: Methodology for
             Identification.. 43
  1. Introduction.. 43
  2. Non-Explicit Traditions in the New Testament.............................. 49
  3. Non-Explicit Traditions in the Pseudepigrapha.............................. 62
  4. Non-Explicit Traditions in the *Hodayot* and Dead Sea Scrolls........ 65
  5. Biblical Interpretation in Qumran Wisdom Texts........................... 71
  6. Synthesis of Approaches and Criteria... 77
  7. Conclusion.. 79

CHAPTER 3. Identification of Allusions to Genesis Creation Accounts..... 81
  1. Introduction.. 81
  2. Presentation of Fragments.. 82
    2.1 4Q415 2 i + 1 ii.. 82
    2.2 4Q415 2 ii.. 85
    2.3 4Q416 1... 89
    2.4 4Q416 2 iii... 91
    2.5 4Q416 2 iv... 95
    2.6 4Q417 1 i... 97

  2.7 4Q418 69 ii... 103
  2.8 4Q418 77... 104
  2.9 4Q418 81 + 81a... 106
  2.10 4Q418 126 i-ii... 108
  2.11 4Q418 177 (& 178)... 109
  2.12 4Q418 178... 111
  2.13 4Q418 206... 111
  2.14 4Q418a 16b + 17... 112
  2.15 4Q423 1, 2 i.. 113
  2.16 4Q423 5... 120
 3. Conclusions... 121

CHAPTER 4. Angelology and Anthropology.. 124
 1. Introduction.. 124
 2. 4Q417 1 i lines 15-18... 124
  2.1 Armin Lange... 125
  2.2 Torleif Elgvin... 128
  2.3 George J. Brooke.. 130
  2.4 John J. Collins.. 131
  2.5 Matthew J. Goff.. 135
  2.6 Harrington and Strugnell... 137
  2.7 Summary and Translation of 4Q417 1 i lines 15-18........................ 138
  2.8 Philo, Genesis 1.26 and 4Q417 1 i lines 15-18.............................. 141
  2.9 Targums on Genesis 1.26 and 4Q417 1 i lines 15-18........................ 147
  2.10 Rabbinic Literature on Genesis 1.26 and 4Q417 1 i lines 15-18.......... 147
  2.11 Genesis 1.26 Traditions and Conclusions on 4Q417 1 i lines 15-18...... 148
 3. Angelic Reference in 4Q416 2 iii.. 149
  3.1 Translating the Term אדנים... 150
  3.2 Interpreting the Term נדיבים.. 155
 4. Indefatigable Angelic Models.. 157
  4.1 4Q418 55... 157
  4.2 4Q418 69... 158
 5. Reconstruction and Identification of 4Q418 81.............................. 161
  5.1 Armin Lange... 163
  5.2 Torleif Elgvin... 166
  5.3 Harrington and Strugnell... 167
  5.4 Eibert J. C. Tigchelaar.. 169
  5.5 Crispin Fletcher-Louis.. 170
  5.6 Loren T. Stuckenbruck.. 173
  5.7 Summary of 4Q418 81... 178
 6. Conclusions... 180

CHAPTER 5. Women, Wives and Daughters... 183
  1. Introduction.. 183
  2. Allusions to Genesis 1-3 and the Creation of Women................................ 185
    2.1 4Q416 2 ii-iv.. 185
      2.1.1 Menaham Kister on 4Q416 2 ii line 21.. 192
      2.1.2 Elgvin on 4Q416 2 ii line 21... 194
      2.1.3 Harrington and Strugnell on 4Q416 2 ii line 21............................. 194
      2.1.4 1 Peter 3.7... 196
    2.2 4Q417 1 i lines 8-12... 197
    2.3 4Q415 2 ii.. 199
    2.4 Synthesis of References to the Origin/Separation of the Female................. 202
    2.5 Male Dominion Over the Female.. 203
    2.6 4Q423 1, 2 i and 1Q26 1.. 204
    2.7 Summary... 206
  3. Women and Angels.. 206
  4. 'Cover Your Shame'... 208
    4.1 Occurrences of 'Shame' in Other Early Jewish Literature....................... 208
    4.2 Occurrences of 'Shame' in *Musar leMevin*...................................... 214
    4.3 Conclusions Concerning 'Shame'... 224
  5. Remaining Fragments about Women... 226
    5.1 4Q415 11... 226
    5.2 4Q415 9... 230
    5.3 4Q418 126 i-ii.. 232
  6. Conclusions.. 234
  7. Excurses: Implications for the New Testament.. 235

CHAPTER 6. Conclusions.. 241

Bibliography... 246

Index of References.. 262

Index of Authors.. 281

Index of Subjects... 284

Note on Policy

The majority of representations of Hebrew reconstructions of *Musar leMevin* are taken from DJD 34. Any alterations to DJD 34 are footnoted. On the few occasions that the Hebrew is taken from Tigchelaar's reconstruction this is noted as well. English translations of *Musar leMevin* are mine unless otherwise indicated. Most diacritical markings are not included in the representation of the Hebrew fragments.

CHAPTER 1

Review of Research and Remaining Issues

1. Introduction

Among the documents discovered in the caves around Khirbet Qumran was a previously unknown sapiential composition. Since its discovery, this document has been discussed under a variety of titles or designations: מוסר למבין ('instruction for an understanding one'), Sapiential Work A, 4QInstruction, Instruction and 4Q415ff. Since the publication of the document in the *Discoveries in the Judaean Desert* (DJD 34) series in 1999 the work has been discussed simply as 4QInstruction with greater regularity.[1] This document survives, however, not only in materials from Cave 4 (4Q415-418, 423) but also from Cave 1 (1Q26); therefore, it would be accurate to refer to the composition as a whole without cave designation. Furthermore, the use of the title *Instruction* becomes pedantic as the document is concerned in large part with sapiential *instruction*. In light of these considerations, the Hebrew title *Musar leMevin* will be the title used throughout the present study.[2]

This work will be focused upon issues of reception with a particular emphasis on the use and influence of creation traditions as derived from Genesis in *Musar leMevin*. The significance of traditions related to Genesis 1-3, both explicit and non-explicit usages, will be identified and explored in relation to the document as a whole. Traditions stemming from the creation account in Genesis often appear to be the basis for framing both anthropologic and angelic conceptions in the document. In addition, other motifs (e.g. רז נהיה) in *Musar leMevin* may be better understood in light of a sustained investigation of these traditions. Relations between the addressees, fellow humankind, angels as well as issues pertaining to women and marriage are each significant themes that will be addressed.

---

[1] J. STRUGNELL, D. J. HARRINGTON, T. ELGVIN (eds.), *Discoveries in the Judaean Desert XXXIV: Sapiential Texts Part 2, 4QInstruction (Mûsār lᵉMēvîn): 4Q415ff. with a Re-edition of 1Q26 by John Strugnell and Daniel J. Harrington, S. J., and an edition of 4Q423 by Torleif Elgvin, in Consultation with Joseph A. FITZMYER, S. J.* (Oxford: Clarendon Press, 1999).

[2] 'Sapiential Work A' was a working title that was never intended to be a permanent designation. The frequent use of '4QInstruction' elsewhere is not accurate in the context of speaking about a document as a whole but rather manuscripts.

The purpose of this chapter is first to introduce the document *Musar leMevin* and its characteristics, then to review selected scholarly contributions to studying it. Issues and controversies surrounding current discussions on the document, such as provenance, reconstruction, and the nature of instruction will be the focus of attention. After this assessment considerations of some tasks that await research will be made.

2. General Information on the Document

Manuscripts. An introduction to the document *Musar leMevin* that offers a number of generally agreed upon observations may be provided. Nevertheless, detailing any sort of broad picture will be impossible at this point. Regarding issues of palaeography, for instance, it may be uncomplicated to note that manuscripts evidence scribal hands that date to between the late 1st century BCE and early 1st century CE.[3] However, that six manuscripts of this document were found in Caves 1 and 4 is not a straightforward matter; it remains uncertain how many manuscripts are preserved among the fragments from Cave 4. In particular, the manuscript designated '4Q418' may actually consist of more than two manuscripts, and 4Q424, not usually counted among the six manuscripts, may also be a copy of *Musar leMevin*. Thus it is more accurate to say, by way of introduction, that there were at least six manuscripts of *Musar leMevin* discovered in the two caves. Furthermore, the materials disclose that the document originally consisted of between approximately 23 and 30 columns, making it one of the lengthier documents among the Dead Sea Scrolls. The combination of these facts indicate the likelihood of the work's importance and popularity, generally, at least during the Herodian period: (1) fragments were found in Caves 1 and 4; and (2) a number of manuscripts, at least six in number, were discovered. With these considerations in mind, it can be further noted that *Musar leMevin* is a sapiential document written in Hebrew, extant in hands that date to about the turn of the Common Era, and was a significant and substantial document within the Qumran library.

Extent of Fragments. Observations made in relation to the material fragments, the largest and most significant as well as the vast number of

---

[3] According to the editors of *DJD XXXIV* 4Q416 and 4Q418 are written in a hand that is transitional between Hasmonean and early Herodian. 4Q418a is early Herodian or perhaps even late Hasmonean. 4Q415 and 4Q417 display early Herodian script while 4Q423 represents a middle to late Herodian hand and 1Q26 is somewhere between early or middle Herodian. ELGVIN argues that all copies are Herodian. 4Q416 is the youngest, written in an early Herodian hand, while 4Q423 and 1Q26 are the oldest, written in a middle Herodian hand. See ELGVIN, 'Reconstruction of Sapiential Work A (*),' in *RevQ* 16 (1995): 559-80. The document almost certainly has an earlier provenance that palaeographic analysis reveals.

smaller and more obscure fragments, serve to introduce *Musar leMevin* further. The largest single fragment is 4Q416 2 i-iv; even here, most of the lines of these columns are incomplete and less than half are preserved from margin to margin. Column iii is the best preserved with 20 lines extant in relatively good condition. The adjoining column ii is the next best preserved with 22 lines, all of which are incomplete. 13 lines of column iv are extant, but only from the left margin to the middle of the column. Only 7 lines of the bottom left corner of column i survive while the top 17 lines on the right of the column survive as a separate fragment. The 18-line fragment of 4Q416 1 is particularly important as it has a wide margin on the right that appears to be the beginning of the scroll. Another of the larger fragments is 4Q417 1 i; it survives in 27 lines of which lines 7-18 are preserved from margin to margin. 4Q417 2 i is a large fragment as well with 28 extant lines. Other larger fragments are 4Q418 55 (12 lines), 4Q418 69 (15 lines), 4Q418 81 (20 lines), 4Q418 103 (9 lines), 4Q418 126 (17 lines), 4Q418 127 (7 lines), and 4Q423 1, 2 (9 lines). Not a single column of *Musar leMevin* survives in full, and the overwhelming majority of fragments do not even preserve a complete line. The smaller fragments number to over 400 and range in size from several incomplete lines down to single letter fragments. Just under 300 of these fragments have been assigned to '4Q418'.

Addressee(s). *Musar leMevin* is written primarily as a work addressed to a single individual (2nd person address); as the Hebrew title implies, it is directed at one who is told to understand (ואתה מבין), understands (מוסר למבין), and at times simply 'you' (ואתה see 4Q418 81). It does, however, contain a third person masculine address at one point (4Q416 1) and, surprisingly, at another point it has an address in the second person feminine (4Q415 2 ii). There are also a number of occurrences of second person masculine plural suffixes throughout the document (see for example לבבכמ]ה or עיניכמה in 4Q417 1 i 27).

The author(s) of the composition are concerned with financial transactions and family matters, but these concerns are placed within the framework of an eschatological and cosmological context. *Musar leMevin* has elements of an apocalyptic worldview that emphasises pursuit of the knowledge of good and evil, creation, angelology, a division of humanity and conceptions of future judgement and vindication for the righteous.[4] Especially important in the document is the frequent and variously termed command to pursue (פרש, לקח, הביט, דרש, בין, אוזן) the רז נהיה (approximately 28 occurrences), a phrase used to refer to an esoteric revelation that is the source of wisdom. One final note is the document's emphasis on the addressee's poverty. This alone

---

[4] See both J. J. COLLINS in *Apocalyptic Imagination* (New York: Crossroads, 1984) and more recently, M. J. GOFF, *The Worldly and Heavenly Wisdom of 4QInstruction* (STDJ 50; Leiden: Brill, 2003) pp. 80-115.

is apparent from the frequent use of the term מחסור ('lacking'; 'poverty'), which occurs approximately 26 times throughout *Musar leMevin*.

The various issues raised and scholarly contributions to reading and reconstructing *Musar leMevin* will be summarised below. A review of these topics will aid in setting the exploration of 'intertextual' occurrences within the framework of present scholarship. Issues such as the social setting of *Musar leMevin*, its relationship to other early Jewish literature, genre, and occurrences of unique motifs will precede the examination of the influence of creation traditions.

3. History of Research

The document *Musar leMevin* has only been the subject of study in any noticeable way since the mid-1990's. The first reasonably accessible transcription of the manuscripts became available to the academic community in Wacholder and Abegg's *Preliminary Edition* in 1992.[5] John Strugnell had originally been given the rights to publish the manuscripts. As was the case with a large number of documents the Wacholder editions were followed by the relatively rapid production of critical editions in the DJD series. The nine-line fragment of 1Q26 was first published in DJD I in 1955[6] and was re-edited in DJD 34. To date, there are a growing number of articles that give particular attention to *Musar leMevin*.[7] In addition, several monographs have devoted

---

[5] B. Z. WACHOLDER and M. G. ABEGG (eds.), *A Preliminary Edition of the Unpublished Dead Sea Scrolls: The Hebrew and Aramaic Texts from Cave 4* (Washington, D.C.: Biblical Archaeology Society, 1991-1992): 44-154.

[6] D. BARTHÉLEMY and J. T. MILIK, *DJD I: Qumran Cave 1* (Oxford: Clarendon, 1955).

[7] J. K. AITKEN, 'Apocalyptic, Revelation and Early Jewish Wisdom Literature,' in P. J. HARLAND and R. HAYWARD (eds.), *New Heaven and New Earth: Prophecy and the Millennium. Essays in Honour of Anthony Gelston* (SVT 77; Leiden: Brill, 1999) pp. 181-93; J. E. BURNS, 'Practical Wisdom in 4QInstruction,' in *DSD* 11 (2004): 12-42; J. J. COLLINS, 'In the Likeness of the Holy Ones: The Creation of Humankind in a Wisdom Text from Qumran,' in D. W. PARRY and E. ULRICH (eds.), *The Provo International Conference on the Dead Sea Scrolls: Technological Innovations, New Texts, and Reformulated Issues* (Leiden: Brill, 1999) pp. 609-18; 'Wisdom Reconsidered, in Light of the Scrolls,' in *DSD* 4 (1997): 265-81; T. ELGVIN, 'Admonition Texts from Qumran Cave 4,' in J. J. COLLINS et al. (eds.), *Methods of Investigation of the Dead Sea Scrolls and the Khirbet Qumran Site: Present Realities and Future Prospects* (New York: New York Academy of Sciences, 1994) pp. 179-96; 'Early Essene Eschatology: Judgment and Salvation According to *Sapiential Work A*,' in D. W. PARRY and S. D. RICKS (eds.), *Current Research and Technological Developments* (STDJ 20; Leiden: Brill, 1996) pp. 126-65; 'The Mystery to Come: Early Essene Theology of Revelation,' in Th. L. THOMPSON, F. H. CRYER (eds.), *Qumran Between the Old and New Testament* (JSOTSupp 290; Sheffield: Sheffield Academic Press, 1998) pp. 113-50; 'The Reconstruction of Sapiential Work A,' in *RevQ* 16 (1995): 559-80; 'Wisdom, Revelation, and Eschatology in an Early Essene Writing,' in *SBLSP* 34 (1995): 444-63; 'Wisdom and Apocalypticism in the Early Second Century BCE: the Evidence of 4QInstruction,' in L. H.

considerable attention to *Musar leMevin*[8] and a few monographs focus on the document exclusively. Eibert Tigchelaar's volume addresses, comprehensively, the reconstruction and sequencing of fragments of the

---

SHIFFMAN, E. TOV and J. C. VANDERKAM (eds.), *The Dead Sea Scrolls Fifty Years After their Discovery: Proceedings of the Jerusalem Congress 1997* (Jerusalem: Israel Exploration Society, 2000) pp. 226-47; 'Wisdom With and Without Apocalyptic,' in D. K. FALK, F. GARCÍA MARTÍNEZ and E. M. SCHULLER (eds.), *Sapiential, Liturgical and Poetical Texts from Qumran: Proceedings of the Third Meeting of the International Organization for Qumran Studies Oslo 1998* (Leiden: Brill, 2000) pp. 15-38; J. FREY, 'The Notion of Flesh in 4QInstruction and the Background of Pauline Usage,' in D. K. FALK, F. GARCÍA MARTÍNEZ and E. M. SCHULLER (eds.), *Sapiential, Liturgical and Poetical Texts from Qumran: Proceedings of the Third Meeting of the International Organization for Qumran Studies Oslo 1998* (Leiden: Brill, 2000) pp. 197-226; M. J. GOFF, 'Reading Wisdom at Qumran: 4Qinstruction and the Hodayot,' in *DSD* 11 (2004): 263-88; G. IBBA, 'Il "Libro dei Misteri" (1Q27, F. 1): Testo escatologico,' in *Henoch* 21 (1999): 73-84; D. J. HARRINGTON, 'The *Rāz Nihyeh* in a Qumran Wisdom Text (1Q26, 4Q415-418, 423),' in *RevQ* 17 (1996): 549-53; 'Ten Reasons Why the Qumran Wisdom Texts are Important,' in *DSD* 4 (1997): 245-54; 'Wisdom at Qumran,' in E. ULRICH and J. C. VANDERKAM (eds.), *The Community of the Renewed Covenant: the Notre Dame Symposium on the Dead Sea Scrolls* (Notre Dame: University of Notre Dame Press, 1994) pp. 137-52; 'Two Early Jewish Approaches to Wisdom: Sirach and Qumran Sapiential Work A,' in *JSP* 16 (1997): 25-38; 'The Qumran Sapiential Texts in the Context of Biblical (OT and NT) and Second Temple Literature,' in L. H. SCHIFFMAN, E. TOV and J. C. VANDERKAM (eds.), *The Dead Sea Scrolls Fifty Years After their Discovery: Proceedings of the Jerusalem Congress 1997* (Jerusalem: Israel Exploration Society, 2000) pp. 256-62; A. LANGE, 'Wisdom and Predestination in the DSS,' in *DSD* 2 (1995): 340-54; E. PUECH and A. STEUDEL, 'Un nouveau fragment de manuscrit 4QInstruction (XQ7 = 4Q417 ou 418),' in *RevQ* 19 (2000): 623-27; M. MORGENSTERN, 'The Meaning of בית מולדים in the Qumran Wisdom Texts,' in *JJS* 51 (2000): 141-44; J. E. SMITH, 'Another Look at 4Q416 2 ii.21, a Critical Parallel to First Thessalonians 4:4,' in *CBQ* 63 (2001): 499-504; J. STRUGNELL, 'The Sapiential Work 4Q415ff. and pre-Qumranic Works from Qumran: Lexigraphic Considerations,' in D. W. PARRY and E. ULRICH (eds.), *The Provo International Conference on the Dead Sea Scrolls: Technological Innovations, New Texts, and Reformulated Issues* (Leiden: Brill, 1999) pp. 595-608; E. J. C. TIGCHELAAR, 'The Addressees of 4QInstruction,' in D. K. FALK, F. GARCÍA MARTÍNEZ and E. M. SCHULLER (eds.), *Sapiential, Liturgical and Poetical Texts from Qumran: Proceedings of the Third Meeting of the International Organization for Qumran Studies Oslo 1998* (Leiden: Brill, 2000) pp. 62-78. M. KISTER, 'A Qumranic Parallel to 1Thess 4:4? Reading and Interpretation of 4Q416 2 II 21,' in *DSD* 10 (2003): 365-70; B. G. WOLD, 'Re-examining an Aspect of the Title Kyrios in Light of 4Q416 2 iii,' in *ZNW* 95 (2004): 149-160; 'Towards a Reconstruction of 4Q416 2 ii line 21: Comments on the Reconstruction of Menahem Kister,' in *DSD* 12 (2005): 205-11.

[8] J. J. COLLINS, *Jewish Wisdom in the Hellenistic Age* (Edinburgh: T & T Clark, 1997); D. J. HARRINGTON, *Wisdom Texts from Qumran* (New York: Routledge, 1996); C. H. T. FLETCHER-LOUIS, *All the Glory of Adam: Liturgical Anthropology in the DSS* (Leiden: Brill, 2002); A. LANGE, *Weisheit und Prädestination: Weisheitliche Urordnung und Prädestination in den Textfunden von Qumran* (Leiden: Brill, 1995); C. M. MURPHY, *Wealth in the Dead Sea Scrolls and in the Qumran Community* (Leiden: Brill, 2001).

document.[9] Another monograph, devoted exclusively to *Musar leMevin*, is to be published in the near future by Torleif Elgvin as a broadly reworked version of his Ph.D. dissertation.[10] Another noteworthy contribution to *Musar leMevin* is Armin Lange's work which devotes considerable time discussing, among other texts, 4Q417 1 i. John Collins's and Daniel Harrington's books on sapiential literature are pedagogical and introductory in nature and are thus not devoted to an in-depth analysis of the document. Catherine Murphy dedicates a chapter of her book on poverty and wealth in the Dead Sea Scrolls to *Musar leMevin*, a topic that is prominent in the document. Among Elgvin's publications is an article that addresses a reconstruction and sequencing of the fragments as well as several articles which address issues of the document's provenance. Several articles from the 1998 Tübingen Symposium are another recent contribution to studies on *Musar leMevin*.[11] The Orion Center of the Hebrew University held a symposium in 2001 where sapiential literature from the Dead Sea Scrolls was the focus of the call for papers. Among the papers presented were several works specifically about *Musar leMevin*, all of which are due to be published soon.[12] Even more recently a colloquium was held at the Catholic University of Leuven where a number of papers were presented on the document.[13]

---

[9] E. J. C. TIGCHELAAR, *To Increase Learning for the Understanding Ones: Reading and Reconstructing the Fragmentary Early Jewish Sapiential Text 4QInstruction* (Leiden: Brill, 2002).

[10] T. ELGVIN, *An Analysis of 4QInstruction* (Ph.D. dissertation, Hebrew University, 1997).

[11] C. HEMPEL, A. LANGE and H. LICHTENBERGER (eds.), *The Wisdom Texts from Qumran and the Development of Sapiential Thought* (Leuven: Peeters, 2002). Articles specifically written on *Musar leMevin* include: TIGCHELAAR, 'Towards a Reconstruction of the Beginning of 4QInstruction: 4Q416 Fragment 1 and Parallels'; H. NIEHR, 'Die Weisheit des Achikar und der musar lammabin im Vergleich'; G. J. BROOKE, 'Biblical Interpretation in the Wisdom Texts from Qumran'; L. T. STUCKENBRUCK, '4QInstruction and the Possible Influence of Early Enochic Traditions: an Evaluation'; D. J. HARRINGTON, 'Two Early Jewish Approaches to Wisdom: Sirach and Qumran Sapiential Work A'; C. HEMPEL, 'The Qumran Sapiential Texts and the Rule Books'; J. DOCHHORN '«Sie wird dir nicht ihre Kraft geben»: Adam, Kain und der Ackerbau in 4Q423 2 3 und Apc Mos 24'; J. FREY, 'Flesh and Spirit in the Palestinian Jewish Sapiential Tradition and in the Qumran Texts: An Inquiry into the Background of Pauline Usage'.

[12] The Sixth International Symposium; *Sapiential Perspectives: Wisdom Literature in Light of the Dead Sea Scrolls Proceedings of the Sixth International Symposium of the Orion Center, 20-22 May*, G. STERLING and J. J. COLLINS (eds.) (Leiden: Brill, forthcoming); papers presented on *Musar leMevin*: J. J. COLLINS, 'The Eschatologizing of Wisdom in the Dead Sea Scrolls'; D. DIMANT, 'Mussar La-mevin (4QInstruction) – a Sectarian Wisdom'; T. ELGVIN, 'Priestly Sages? The Milieus of Origin of 4QMysteries and 4QInstruction'; L. H. SCHIFFMAN, 'Halakhic Elements in the Sapiential Texts'; B. G. WRIGHT, 'The Categories of Rich and Poor in the Qumran Sapiential Literature'.

[13] F. GARCÍA MARTÍNEZ (ed.), *Wisdom and Apocalypticism in the Dead Sea Scrolls* (BETL 168; Leuven: Peeters, 2003); papers presented on *Musar leMevin*: É. PUECH, 'Apports des Textes Apocalyptiques et Sapientiels de Qumrân: À l'eschatologie du Judaïsme Ancien';

I am aware of at least two Ph.D. dissertations recently published on *Musar leMevin*.[14]

4. Issues Addressed in Recent Publications

Most of the activity surrounding *Musar leMevin* has centred on a number of areas: (1) theological motifs; (2) similarities and differences with other sapiential literature; and (3) the relationship of this document to the other literature of early Judaism and, especially, the 'sectarian community'. The last mentioned has been one of the more controversial of these issues. In particular, discussion has been focused on the translation and interpretation of particular phrases and concepts within *Musar leMevin*. Less prominent, but of great significance, has been the endeavour to reconstruct the manuscripts and sequence columns. The following is a review of scholarship on these issues by topic. The purpose here will be to: (1) summarise conclusions which have been reached on basic issues; (2) highlight continuing issues of contention; and (3) identify previously unexamined areas for further study.

4.1 Provenance

Musar leMevin, as scholars have observed since the beginning of research on the document, contains practical wisdom instruction alongside eschatological and apocalyptic motifs. This combination receives considerable attention by Lange in his book *Weisheit und Prädestination* in which he attempts to relate *Musar leMevin* to other previously unknown documents from Qumran (*Instruction on the Two Spirits* and the *Book of Mysteries*). Harrington has compared and contrasted the approaches to wisdom in *Musar leMevin* and Sirach[15] and provides a general introduction to the former in his book.[16] In his more recent articles Harrington places *Musar leMevin* in the context of biblical and early Jewish literature.[17] Collins, in *Jewish Wisdom in the Hellenistic Age*, introduces the document and its character briefly against the backdrop of almost every conceivable wisdom document known from early

---

C. COULOT, 'L'image de Dieu dans les écrits de sagesse 1Q26, 4Q415-418, 4Q423'; J. J. COLLINS, 'The Mysteries of God: Creation and Eschatology in 4QInstruction and the Wisdom of Solomon'; D. J. HARRINGTON, 'Wisdom and Apocalyptic in 4QInstruction and 4 Ezra'.

[14] GOFF, 'The Worldly and Heavenly Wisdom'; D. J. JEFFERIES, 'Wisdom at Qumran: A Form-Critical Analysis of the Admonitions in 4QInstruction' (Gorgias Dissertations NES 3; Piscataway: Gorgias Press, 2002). GOFF also published an article from his dissertation 'The Mystery of Creation in 4QInstruction,' in *DSD* 10 (2003): 163-86.

[15] HARRINGTON, 'Two Early'.

[16] HARRINGTON, *Wisdom Texts*.

[17] HARRINGTON, 'The Qumran'.

Judaism.[18] In a more recent article Collins addresses wisdom as a literary
category and situates *Musar leMevin*, taking its unusual characteristics into
account, within that literary form.[19] There, Collins challenges previously held
notions of what characterises a wisdom composition and attempts to offer a
developmental history of wisdom. The editors of DJD 34, Elgvin,
Stuckenbruck and Tigchelaar all consider *Musar leMevin's* relationship to *1
Enoch*.[20] The esoteric and apocalyptic nature of wisdom in *Musar leMevin* is
often contrasted with that of other more typical sapiential documents, most
frequently Sirach. Elgvin views *Musar leMevin* as a conflation of two literary
layers: (1) an older traditional sapiential work and (2) a later apocalyptic
layer.[21] Elgvin's view dramatically alters *Musar leMevin's* place and
provenance within early Jewish wisdom compositions and will be discussed
below.

4.2 The Relationship to the 'Sectarian Community'

The issue of *Musar leMevin's* relationship to compositions of the Qumran
group has been the focus of numerous discussions. Some scholars who have
written about *Musar leMevin* have made their position known in this regard
while others have spent considerable time defending the nuances of their
particular view. Relating *Musar leMevin* to the Qumran community and other
documents in early Judaism has helped to narrow the milieu in which the
document is interpreted. Several approaches have been employed to place this
composition in both its social as well as literary context. The basic initial
question has been whether or not *Musar leMevin* should be regarded as a
sectarian document. A sub-question in this regard is the identity of the
addressees and their social setting. It is most conceivable that the author(s) of
the document provide instruction with various people in mind.[22]

---

[18] COLLINS, *Jewish Wisdom.*

[19] COLLINS, 'Wisdom Reconsidered,' and, 'Wisdom, Apocalypticism and Generic
Compatibility,' in L. G. PERDUE, B. B. SCOTT and W. J. WISEMAN (eds.), *In Search of
Wisdom. Essays in Memory of J. G. Gammie* (Lousville: Westminster, 1993): 165-85.

[20] *DJD XXXIV*, pp. 34-35; ELGVIN, 'Analysis'; STUCKENBRUCK, '4QInstruction';
TIGCHELAAR, *To Increase Learning.*

[21] ELGVIN, 'Wisdom and Apocalypticism,' p. 226. HEMPEL, 'The Qumran Sapiential
Texts,' pp. 281-83; considers that it is conceivable that the work is composite and is
comprised of traditional sapiential material together with other parts from a community in
early Judaism, though not the *Yahad*. However, she notes a close link between the abstract
(theological) and practical instruction (e.g. 4Q416 2 iii 20-21) which can not be easily
separated. If the document is indeed a composite work, she argues, the two types of material
are closely interwoven.

[22] TIGCHELAAR also argues 'that *Instruction* consists of different sections directed to
varying addressees'; see *To Increase Learning*, p. 236 and 'The Addressees'. The various
singular, plural, masculine and feminine addresses indicate different intended audiences. In
addition, there may be multiple classes as well, such as priestly and non-priestly categories.

Before considering the relationship of *Musar leMevin* to the so-called 'Essene', or Qumran community, it is necessary to question what criteria are used to evaluate the inclusion or exclusion of a document to this group. In an article concerned mainly with providing such criteria for determining sectarian works, Lange sets forth and evaluates standards that have been suggested for excluding and including documents to this classification.[23] This work is valuable for organising criteria to evaluate the origin of manuscripts that may otherwise not have appeared in conjunction with one another. Although some of Lange's criteria are debatable or perhaps rigid in conception, critical interaction between them and discussions surrounding the provenance of *Musar leMevin* will be beneficial.

There are numerous manuscripts represented in the texts from Qumran preserving various theological and ethical positions. Some manuscripts predate the settlement at Qumran and the Essene inhabitants and, therefore, it is clear that many of the texts found at Qumran do not have an Essene origin. In his article, Lange summarises the numerous attempts that have been made to differentiate and categorise documents from the Qumran library. He gleans from these suggestions a streamlined list for evaluating potential Essene works. However, the redactional activity of the Essenes complicates the issue, since there are documents that could be understood as originating with the Essene's in addition to those that were likely adopted and reworked by the Essenes. This issue leads one to question which documents should be assigned as strictly originating from the settlement at Qumran and, therefore, used as a foundation for investigating criteria for determining Essene texts. Lange allows for the *Pesharim*, which are only known from the Qumran Library, and manuscripts of *Serekh haYahad* to be associated with the community. These two text groups serve as the point of departure for evaluating forms and themes to be associated with the Essenes and the basis for developing these criteria of exclusion and inclusion. Lange's list of criteria have been modified, summarized and translated below. They will serve as a guide to appraise the relationship of *Musar leMevin* to other sectarian works as well as evaluate the conclusions others have made about this relationship.

---

[23] LANGE, 'Kriterien essenischer Texte,' in J. FREY and H. STEGEMANN (eds.) *Qumran kontrovers: Beiträge zu den Textfunden vom Toten Meer* (Bonifatius: Paderborn, 2003) pp. 59-69. The use of the title 'Essene' is problematic and as LICHTENBERGER discusses should be discussed in relation to the Qumran community: '"Essener" und "essenisch" sollen hier auf die antiken Berichte, "Qumrangemeinde" und "qumranisch" auf die Texte von Qumran bezogen werden,' LICHTENBERGER, *Studien zum Menschenbild in Texten der Qumrangemeinde* (SUNT 15; Göttingen: Vandenhoeck & Ruprecht, 1980) p. 14. C. HEMPEL, 'Kriterien zur Bestimmung „essenischer Verfasserschaft" von Qumrantexten,' pp. 71-88 in the same collection as LANGE'S article also discusses the subject of 'Essenes' and is cautious relating this group to the sectarian Qumran group. See also LANGE and LICHTENBERGER, 'Qumran,' in *TRE* vol. 28 (1997) pp. 45-79.

Exclusive Criteria:

(1) *Pesharim* and *Serekh haYahad* only use the tetragrammaton when quoting and it appears typically in paleo-Hebrew letters. A free use of the tetragrammaton is not observed. The latest work that uses it is the book of Daniel and the book of *Jubilees*. The use of the tetragrammaton in the *Pesharim* and *Serekh haYahad* is similar to the use elsewhere in the literature from the middle of the 2nd c. BCE. The *Pesharim* and *Serekh haYahad* also avoid using אלהים and one seldom finds אדוני and אל ישראל. Therefore, a free use of the tetragrammaton excludes a document from being classified as Essene.

(2) 1QpHab xi 4-8 describes the Wicked Priest's persecution of the Teacher of Righteousness on Yom Kippur. In all likelihood the Essenes used a different calendar and celebrated holidays on different days than the priests in the Jerusalem Temple. This is confirmed by 4Q259. At the end of the Community Rule the calendrical text 4Q*Otot* is numbered 4Q319 and, yet, belongs to 4Q259. This document is concerned with one of several calendars that attest a 364-day-solar-calendar in which the year is divided into 12 months each with 30 days with a total of 52 weeks. The 364-day-calendar is older than the Essene movement. One can find similar systems in the book of *Jubilees* and Enochic Literature. Presumably, any document that does not at least attempt to reconcile calendrical issues with the Essenes, such as the 354-day-lunar-calendar, should be excluded.

(3) Every text that is identified as Essene based upon other criteria is written in Hebrew. An Aramaic, Greek or Nabatean text is, therefore, certainly not Essene.

(4) Since the Damascus Document produced the point of origination of the Essene community about 150 years BCE, one must finally consider any document produced before this time as either not Essene or at least proto-Essene.

Inclusive Criteria:

(1) According to *Pesharim* and *Serekh haYahad* Essene texts use a typical terminology, which reflects an Essene self-understanding. For example, they refer to themselves with phrases such as: עצת היחד ('Council of the Community'), אנשי היחד ('men of the community'), עדת היחד ('Gathering of the Community') and הברית ('the Covenant'). However, these designations cannot serve as a criterion of exclusion since the Essenes could have taken them over from others. Within the category of 'terminology' should be included the central characters of the Essene movement: the Teacher of Righteousness, Seeker of the Torah, Wicked Priest, Man of Lies, Men of Mockery, Seekers of Smooth Things, and Lion of Wrath.

(2) The *Pesharim* reflect a critical distance from the Jerusalem Temple and its priesthood. The Essenes were apparently upset because of non-Zadokite high priests and a false calendar and, therefore, considered the Jerusalem Temple to be unclean. The Essenes then understood their community to be a spiritual human temple in which their liturgical worship was considered sacrificial.

(3) This distance to the Jerusalem Temple corresponds in the *Pesharim* and *Serekh haYahad* to a clear understanding that the Pharisees and Jerusalem priests abandoned the Torah. Adherence to the Torah, according to Essene opinion, is only possible within their community through the revelation of the Teacher of Righteousness. This key hermeneutical role of the Teacher of Righteousness is evident from his title: דורש התורה ('Seeker of the Torah'). The Essene followers designated themselves as: עושי התורה ('Doers of the Torah').

(4) The worldview of the Essenes is shaped from a cosmic and ethical dualism, in which anyone who is not Essene has been predestined to perish in an eschatological judgement.

Both spheres belong to humans and angelic beings and both stand under the rule of angelic beings. When the eschaton breaks forth Belial and his followers will be destroyed and those obedient to the *Yahad* will be saved.

(5) An important criterion that has not been considered for a while is the question of an Essene *Halakha*. That is, the Sabbath does not begin with the sunset, but rather even earlier when beams of sunlight are still visible on the horizon. Radical Torah observance shapes the Essene Sabbath *Halakha*; for instance, one does not help an animal give birth on the Sabbath, nor rescue someone with a tool who has fallen in water on the Sabbath.

(6) One might consider the processing or quoting of an Essene Text as indicating an Essene origin. However, this would presuppose that the *Yahad* wrote texts that were only read and received by them, which is difficult to either prove or disprove. Therefore, the reception of Essene Texts should be considered only as additional indication that a work was composed by the *Yahad*.

(7) A problematic consideration is the use of orthography and morphology (i.e. writing conventions) as a criterion for determining an Essene text. A special school of scribes who knew a specific writing style, whether it be an idiolectic orthography or morphology, only demonstrates that a manuscript was copied in the Essene Community. An Essene or even Qumran idiolect appears to be improbable and should not be used as a criterion to identify Essene Texts.

Lange cautions that one should not identify a text as Essene based upon only one of the above inclusive criteria (e.g. community terminology). Clearly, the more inclusive criteria that apply to a text the more the likelihood increases that it is in fact Essene. However, if even one of the exclusive criteria are true of a given document, one may determine that it is not Essene.

Before considering how others evaluate *Musar leMevin's* relationship to sectarian literature Lange's criteria may be summarily applied to the document. Based upon the above four criteria *Musar leMevin* can not be excluded from a sectarian, or Essene, provenance. Although, dating the document is difficult since palaeography only indicates the period of transmission and not composition. There is no reason not to conjecture that *Musar leMevin* was written in whole or part earlier than 150 BCE. However, there are few grounds upon which *Musar leMevin* should be included among the theorised sectarian documents. There are points to be raised concerning typical terminology, but the obvious vocabulary cited by Lange is not used. The document gives no clear indication of an estrangement from the Jerusalem Temple and its priesthood. There is no mention of Torah or the Teacher of Righteousness either. Humanity is divided into two categories and a type of dualism is embedded in the theology of the document. Angelology also plays an important role, however, further research is needed to understand it in the document. Dualistic notions and angelic beings in *Musar leMevin* are quite dissimilar from *Sefer haMilhamah* and do not necessarily locate the document closer to the sectarian community.

A number of scholars have discussed the similarities and dissimilarities between *Musar leMevin* and documents thought to originate from the Essene sectarian milieu. Harrington addresses the location of the document in relation to the Qumran community in several ways, though he places most emphasis on the particular topics addressed in the preserved portions of the document.[24] He notes that *Musar leMevin* devotes considerable attention to addressing commercial transactions (e.g. loans and deposits), social relations (e.g. superiors and inferiors), and family matters (e.g. wife, parents, in-laws). He argues that these subjects assume a setting in which the addressees are living outside of the community described by the *Serekh haYahad* or a monastic setting generally. It is thus not so simple, writes Harrington, to define the community behind *Musar leMevin* as narrowly or rigidly as the *Serekh haYahad's* descriptions.

In general agreement, a more expanded list of documents of the Qumran group drawn upon for comparison are the *Serekh haYahad* (1QS)[25], the *Hodayot* (1QH[a]), *Sefer haMilhamah* (1QM)[26], *Habakkuk Pesher* (1QpHab), *Messianic Rule* (1QSb) and *Damascus Document* (CD-A; CD-B; 4Q266-273). Among this short list of foundational documents is the *Damascus Document*, which shares some non-monastic elements with *Musar leMevin*. Harrington notes that there were different ways of being an Essene and there are different ways in which to reconcile the incongruities between the documents. Harrington first suggests, therefore, that *Musar leMevin* may reflect a pre-Qumranic phase in the community's history (2nd century BCE or earlier). He also raises the possibility that *Musar leMevin* could have been composed for a branch of the Essene or Qumran movement that was living outside of the monastic movement.[27] Though popular at Qumran, *Musar leMevin* may not have been directly related to the community (analogous to the Enochic traditions).

It is not, by Harrington's own admission, as simple as relating the topics addressed in *Musar leMevin* to what we know of the community from the sectarian corpus listed above. There are similarities between *Musar leMevin* and, especially, the *Serekh haYahad* and the *Hodayot* that align them rather closely. The unusual phrase רז נהיה appears almost nowhere outside of *Musar leMevin*, only in the *Book of Mysteries*[a] (1Q27 1 i line 4; 4Q299-300 lines 3-4 300; and similar expressions רזי אור, רזי תושי, רזי, כול רז (רוית) and the *Serekh haYahad* (1QS xi 3-4).[28] There are also verbatim overlaps between *Musar*

---

[24] HARRINGTON, *Wisdom Texts from Qumran*, pp. 41, 84-86; 'Two Early Jewish Approaches,' pp. 25, 37.

[25] Also 4Q*Serekh haYahad*[a-j] (4Q255-264); and 5Q11.

[26] Also 4Q*Milhamah*[a-g] (4Q491-496; 4Q285).

[27] In accord with the likely hypothesis, based upon Josephus description of the Essenes, of celibate and married sectaries.

[28] As HEMPEL has pointed out, the רז נהיה only occurs in the context of a hymn in 1QS xi and this hymn is missing in one of the cave 4 manuscripts of *Serekh haYahad* (4Q259). Therefore, it is likely that the hymn originally existed independently and was later added.

leMevin and the *Hodayot* (cf. e.g. 4Q418 55 10; 1QH^a x 27-28).[29] Beyond these and other linguistic similarities *Musar leMevin* and the Qumran group share ideas concerning eschatological judgement and some dualistic language.[30] The different social settings assumed in the documents, however, complicate these similarities. In the end, the theory that reconciles these incongruities for Harrington is that *Musar leMevin* represents the intellectual and religious heritage of a movement larger than the Essenes.[31]

Strugnell approaches the subject of *Musar leMevin's* provenance based upon lexigraphical considerations. He did so first in an article and, a few years later, published selected portions in the introduction to DJD 34.[32] The following is a summary of both publications.[33] In his analysis Strugnell addresses the frequency and infrequency of sectarian vocabulary in *Musar leMevin* and, on most occasions, derives frequency through comparison to usage or non-usage in traditional Hebrew wisdom compositions. In his article Strugnell lists frequency of vocabulary in one of two ways: (1) infrequent vocabulary in *Musar leMevin* that is more common in 1Q-11Q; and (2) frequent vocabulary that is more sparsely applied in 1Q-11Q. This examination suggests that *Musar leMevin* differs markedly from traditionally understood sectarian works from the Qumran Caves in its relatively high number of foreign words and in its lack of terms and expressions characteristic of the Qumran corpus. In both presentations Strugnell has arranged the lexical frequency according to topic in order to make transparent the significance of the occurrences of vocabulary (purity and impurity, Torah, the community, doxological language, dualism, etc.). For the sake of brevity they have been listed below in alphabetical order[34]:

Relating *Musar leMevin* to the Qumran group based upon the occurrence of the mystery in both documents is, then, undermined. See HEMPEL, 'The Qumran Sapiential Texts,' pp. 284-85.

[29] 4Q418 55 line 10 '[*all their hidden mysteries.* Ac]cording to their knowledge they (i.e. men) *will* receive honour, one man *more than* his neighbor (ולפ]י דעתם יכבדו איש מרעהו), And according to each one's understanding *will* his glory *be* increased'; and 1QH^a x 27-28 ולפי דעתם יכבדו איש מרעהו ('and according to their knowledge they will be honoured, one from his neighbour').

[30] See *DJD XXXIV*, pp. 28-29.

[31] HARRINGTON, *Wisdom Texts*, p. 85.

[32] STRUGNELL, 'The Sapiential Work 4Q415*ff.* and pre-Qumranic Works,' and *DJD XXXIV*, pp. 22-30.

[33] At the time the article was written STRUGNELL did not have access to an 11Q concordance and thus his frequency statistics were of only 1-10Q. In *DJD XXXIV* the frequency numbers have been updated with 11Q included. Also, the article includes substantially more 'frequent vocabulary' than the DJD volume.

[34] The numbering system (00:00) places 1Q-11Q number of occurrences in digits to the right of the colon while the digits left of the colon represent the occurrences in *Musar leMevin*. So, for instance, '(0:140) תורה' means that the term Torah never occurs in *Musar*

Infrequent Vocabulary in Musar leMevin:

אור (3:149)	ישר-יושר (0:44)	ענו (0:11)
אלוהים (1:341)	ישראל (0:362)	ענוה (0:17)
גורל (2:91)	מצוה (3:48)	פלא (6:241)
היחד (0:98)	מקדש (0:96)	פשע (2:68)
הרבים (0:66)	נדה (2:66)	צדקה-צדיק (3:136)
חושך (0:76)	נפלא (1:43)	קהל (0:43)
חסד (3:109)	עדה (0:134)	קודש (13:306)
טהרה (1:170)	עליון (0:36)	רע-רשע (3:118)
טמאה (1:216)	עם (0:226)	תבונה (0:frequent)
יהוה (0:174)	עני (0:19)	תורה (0:140)

Abnormally Frequent Vocabulary in Musar leMevin:

אביון (6:28)	חכמה (10:37)	רז נהיה (32:1)
אמת (41:223)	כבוד (18:296)	רצון (17:97)
בינה (15:63)	מבונה (6:0)	רש (11:5)
גבורה (18:296)	מוסר (4:12)	שוה (10:7)
דל (1:6)	מחסור (28:2)	שחר (11:20)
הבין (25:50)	משקל (7:12)	שכל (8:40)
המשיל (18:7)	נחלה (35:47)	שקד (10:3)
השכיל (10:71)	נשמר (7:13)	תמיד (11:34)
התבונן (12:21)	פקודה (16:20)	
חיים (18:55)	רז (30:81)	

Strugnell concludes that features traditionally viewed as marks of a sectarian work are conspicuously lacking in the vocabulary of *Musar leMevin*. However, the significant overlap between the document and the sectarian Qumran corpus signifies a relationship between the two. Strugnell suggests three possible relationships for *Musar leMevin* and this corpus. First, it could be related in an ideological or chronological way to the sectarian corpus (e.g. 1QH[a], 1QS, 1QM, and perhaps *4QShirShabb*). Given his preference for the other alternatives (below), Strugnell concludes otherwise. Second, it is a pre-Qumranic document that came from an earlier but related sect or group (e.g. 11QT, according to Schiffman *et al.*). Third, it may merely represent a general non-sectarian and post-exilic Jewish background (e.g. as CD xiff., *4QWords of the Luminaries*[a-c], or 11QPsalms[a]). Based on these lexicographic considerations Strugnell argues that the third option is the most likely. No

---

leMevin while it occurs 140 times in traditionally understood sectarian compositions considered by STRUGNELL.

lexicographic evidence compels one to regard *Musar leMevin* as a sectarian composition.[35]

More specifically in terms of the social provenance of *Musar leMevin*, Harrington and Strugnell raise various possibilities.[36] They list the following options: (1) the work does not need to be confined to or to originate from the Qumran group; (2) it represents a wider non-celibate branch of the Essene movement mentioned by Josephus; (3) it should be associated with the foundational pre-Qumranic phase of a Jewish movement; or (4) it is a general offshoot of Jewish wisdom groups. It is the fourth option that Strugnell and Harrington regard as the most plausible alternative.

Lange reaches not dissimilar, though more specific, conclusions. In his work *Weisheit und Prädestination* he views *Musar leMevin* as 'nichtessenisch und protoessenisch'. Lange suggests a framework of compositions that evidence the idea of a pre-existent sapiential order. These compositions, in an ideological framework are *Musar leMevin*, *Book of Mysteries* (1Q27; 4Q299-301) and the *Instruction on the Two Spirits* (1QS iii 13-iv 26).[37] These documents develop the idea of a pre-existent order of creation that regulates the world, history and the fate of human beings. This theology, concludes Lange, was later adopted by the *Yahad*, and can therefore be termed 'pre-Essene'. The Essene documents that Lange identifies as having subsequently adopted the theology are 1QH[a] i, CD ii 2-13, 4Q180 1 1-15 (*Ages of Creation A*), and 1QpHab vii 5-14.[38]

Like Strugnell and Harrington, Collins, in a review of wisdom literature found at Qumran, appears to be in favour of a more general origin for *Musar leMevin*.[39] Collins posits the existence of a number of groups who had varying

---

[35] HEMPEL, 'The Qumran Sapiential Texts,' considers three terminological (רז נהיה, Book of Hagi, the *Maskil*) similarities found in Qumran sapiential works, especially the *Book of Mysteries*, *Musar leMevin*, and Rule Books. While no clear relationship is defined, she concludes: 'The most interesting and fascinating result of the above discussion, to my mind, is the presence of a number of overlapping terms and ideas between the material that describes organizational matters in the Rules and the sapiential texts as was the case particularly with the Book/Vision of Hagi.' pp. 294-95.

[36] *DJD XXXIV*, pp. 21-22.

[37] LANGE, *Weisheit*, p. 130 writes 'Aus diesen Parallelen darf geschlossen werden, daß die Zwei-Geister-Lehre aus den Kreisen stammt, die auch 4QSap A und Myst hervorgebracht haben. Jedoch stellt sie zumindest gegenüber 4QSap A eine Weiterentwicklung dar, die die schon in diesem Text angelegten dualistischen Tendenzen stärker betont und das eschatologische Moment von Myst ausbaut'. See also 'Wisdom and Predestination,' pp. 340-43.

[38] Elsewhere LANGE has argued that *Musar leMevin*, along with the *Book of Mysteries*, should be situated in the cultic environment of the Jerusalem Temple; LANGE, 'In Diskussion mit dem Tempel: zur Auseinandersetzung zwischen Kohelet und weisheitlichen Kreisen am Jerusalemer Tempel,' in A. SCHOORS (ed.), *Qohelet in the Context of Wisdom* (Leuven: Peeters, 1998) pp. 113-60, see esp. pp. 126-28.

[39] COLLINS, 'Wisdom Reconsidered,' pp. 271-76, 280-81.

notions of wisdom and drew upon different traditions. Though these groups would have invariably agreed and disagreed on issues, it is not apparent that the author(s) of *Musar leMevin* were segregated. Sectarian divisions, argues Collins, are not well attested before the first century BCE. Furthermore, wisdom cannot be identified with a single worldview, as not all groups agreed on the curriculum of wisdom; wisdom was a polyvalent concept. Thus one should be cautious in attributing wisdom to one particular worldview or in using it as an antithesis for other viewpoints in Judaism. The apocalyptic perspective of wisdom compositions found at Qumran provide a foundation for *Musar leMevin* just as well as the this-worldly mindset of traditional biblical wisdom. It is not necessary to view apocalyptic wisdom as sectarian.[40]

Elgvin's approach to *Musar leMevin* is more controversial. He has often called *Musar leMevin* an 'early-Essene' document[41] and goes into most detail on its relationship to the sectarian community in two of his articles.[42] Elgvin's thesis is that *Musar leMevin* is a conflation of two literary stages that he conceives of as a 'proto-Essene' community layer over an older wisdom composition. These conflated literary layers are: (1) the older layer of traditional sapiential admonitions; and (2) the younger apocalyptic portion. Elgvin sees a lack of literary unity in the composition between longer discourses containing apocalyptic thought and shorter admonitions that reflect traditional wisdom. These shorter portions of wisdom do not strictly correspond to sectarian or *Yahad* ('Essene') theology; rather, they promote knowledge based on reason (as in wisdom from the Hebrew Bible or in Sirach). The longer apocalyptic portions, by contrast, appeal to the 'mystery to come' (רז נהיה) and to divine mysteries revealed only to an elect community. The tension between traditional Near Eastern and biblical wisdom, on the one hand, and the eschatological and cosmological portions, on the other, leads Elgvin to conclude that they must be conflated layers. Elgvin associates one layer as reflecting a 'proto-Essene' composition. What Elgvin views as an original incompatibility between eschatological and

---

[40] One may question whether special revelation is indicative of a sectarian milieu, see COLLINS, *Jewish Wisdom*, p. 128. Special revelation, such as that found in Enochic literature or in Qumran sapiential works, should not be seen to represent a stream of Judaism separated or distinct from a Torah loyal group. Although there is no mention of the Torah in *Musar leMevin*, its centrality is unquestionable. Furthermore, although similarities exist between Enochic literature and *Musar leMevin* (e.g. angels, revelation, cosmology, dualism) one should take caution in relating the two to the same or similar communities. See, for example, G. Boccaccini, *Beyond the Essene Hypothesis: The Parting of the Ways between Qumran and Enochic Judasim* (Eerdmans: Grand Rapids, 1998).

[41] ELGVIN writes this in the introduction of the document in 'Reconstruction' and again in 'Early Essene Eschatology,' 'Wisdom, Revelation, and Eschatology in an Early Essene Writing'.

[42] ELGVIN, 'Wisdom and Apocalypticism,' and 'Wisdom With and Without Apocalyptic'.

cosmological motifs and sapiential instruction brings him to the conclusion that an earlier form of *Musar leMevin* was interpreted at a later stage.

In Elgvin's view *Musar leMevin*, in its interpolated form, is 'pre-Essene'. The bulk of his argument rests in ideas concerning a remnant community in the document and the evolution of the concept in later Essene writings. *Musar leMevin* deals with ideas related to the elect who he sees as an end-time community and the author as a participant in that community. The phrases associated with the community according to him are: אנשי רצון ('men of good pleasure'), מטעת עולם ('eternal planting'), נוחלי ארץ ('inheritance of the earth'), and פתח מקור ('open a fountain'); all of which are found in 4Q418 81. Elgvin suggests that *Musar leMevin* generated much of this terminology; for example, in the case of the phrase מטעת עולם[43] he is quite clear that the interpolator of *Musar leMevin* coined it. In turn, Elgvin argues that *Musar leMevin* provided the foundation for certain concepts and technical terms eventually borrowed by the Essenes or Qumran community (hence the designation of *Musar leMevin* as 'pre-Essene'). Elgvin argues that the metaphor מטעת עולם, used for the righteous community, later became essential to the self-understanding of the *Yahad*. Elgvin's analysis remains problematic. His location of *Musar leMevin* in relation to sectarian literature does not carefully define which compositions in early Judaism he considers to be sectarian, especially which documents are to be assigned to the so called '*Yahad*'.

Elgvin concludes his discourse on conceptions of a righteous community in *Musar leMevin* by comparing them with similar conceptions in the works of *1 Enoch* and *Jubilees*.[44] While this is certainly appropriate for the subject of shared phraseology in the documents, it does not bring *Musar leMevin* any closer to the category of 'pre-Essene'. By associating *Musar leMevin* with *1 Enoch* and *Jubilees*, he does not clearly define the relationship between these three documents or their chronological progression.[45] No clear explanation is offered, for example, for the relationship of *1 Enoch* literature or *Jubilees* to the Essenes and how one should situate them in relation to a 'pre-Essene' group. It seems that perceived shared self-conceptions central to *Musar leMevin* and later sectarian compositions are the foundation upon which Elgvin identifies the document.

Two problems are potentially resolved by Elgvin's hypotheses. First, if *Musar leMevin* presupposes a social context that is not monastic, assuming

---

[43] P. TILLER, 'The "Eternal Planting" in the Dead Sea Scrolls,' in *DSD* 4 (1997): 312-35; discusses the phrase in *Musar leMevin* along with its occurrence elsewhere in early Jewish literature.

[44] ELGVIN, 'Wisdom With and Without,' pp. 29-30.

[45] For an evaluation of the relationship between *Musar leMevin* and *1 Enoch* both STUCKENBRUCK in '4QInstruction' and Tigchelaar, *To Increase Learning*, pp. 212-16, question ELGVIN's hypothesis.

that the Qumran community was monastic, Elgvin is able to assign those admonitions to an earlier traditional sapiential layer. Second, in regard to lexicographic considerations, the term יחד as a noun is absent from *Musar leMevin*. However, Elgvin attempts to construct essential community or *Yahad* conceptions that derive from *Musar leMevin* and therefore served as precursors to the sectarian community. However, the weakness of Elgvin's theories consists in unsubstantiated claims. In particular, except for observations of eschatologised wisdom there is, in my opinion, no compelling evidence for the existence of two layers of composition in *Musar leMevin*. Issues of redaction and source criticism, especially given the number of manuscripts available, will certainly be revisited by scholars of *Musar leMevin* for some time to come. Although Elgvin's forthcoming monograph may produce further evidence to substantiate his view of the provenance of *Musar leMevin*, the description of the document as 'pre-Essene' is at present not convincing.

A way forward is suggested by Tigchelaar in a brief article that attempts to place *Musar leMevin* on the 'social and religious map of the last centuries BCE'.[46] The purpose of his article is to explore to whom the composition was directed and the context in which it was written. Noting that an answer to this question will only, if ever, be available through a more thorough investigation of both *Musar leMevin* and documents from the period, Tigchelaar makes three observations. First, *Musar leMevin* is clearly distinct from works considered sectarian in its concern with family matters, financial affairs and a lack of any explicit reference to a particular community. Second, there are parallels between *Musar leMevin* and both sectarian and non-sectarian compositions. He cautions, however, that *Musar leMevin* may be a composite or, alternatively, a document that consists of layers of redacted material. Third, the work is addressed to 'one who understands'; this could refer to anyone in society, not only to a professional sage.[47] The composition seems to admonish people from all levels of society. Thus Tigchelaar elsewhere concludes that, 'the lack of any reference to a sectarian group, community, or practice, suggests that the composition is not sectarian, but of a more general nature'.[48]

---

[46] TIGCHELAAR, 'The Addressees,' pp. 74-75.

[47] GOFF, *The Worldly and Heavenly*, pp. 227-28 concludes that the 'The Dead Sea sect is not a good model for understanding the group behind 4QInstruction'.

[48] TIGCHELAAR, *To Increase Learning*, pp. 247-48. Whereas TIGCHELAAR considers the document to be directed at various addressees, GOFF disagrees: 'The elect status of the addressee suggests a sectarian milieu. But the nature of the group to which 4QInstruction is devoted is substantially different from the Dead Sea sect.' It is conceivable to me that the document is addressed to people from a broad spectrum of society, both female and male, but who are part of the faith community. GOFF emphasises the 'elect' status of the addressees

By contrast, Devorah Dimant, in her forthcoming article from the Orion Symposium, argues that *Musar leMevin* is a sectarian composition.[49] The sectarian character of the work, she argues, is indicated by the frequent terminological and ideological links with distinctive sectarian works such as the *Serekh haYahad* and the *Hodayot*. The paper presented by Dimant focuses on 4Q416 1 and emphasises parallels between this column and sectarian works. It is difficult from Dimant's work in its present form to ascertain the precise relationship that suggested parallels have between *Musar leMevin* and the sectarian compositions. Dimant's original argument for *Musar leMevin's* origins will certainly be received with some scepticism.

In summary, there are currently three views on the relationship of *Musar leMevin* and the Qumran sectarian compositions. (1) Strugnell and Harrington prefer to regard the document as a general offshoot of wisdom literature. Lange views *Musar leMevin* as a 'non-Essene' document that was formative for particular sapiential concepts that were adopted by later 'Essene' compositions. The views of Strugnell, Harrington, Lange, and Collins are quite similar in their conclusions, even if they do differ on how they arrived at their conclusion and certain nuances of their argumentation. (2) Elgvin argues that *Musar leMevin* existed in two layers, an earlier portion and a later portion which is the product of 'pre-Essene' author(s). (3) Finally, Dimant has suggested that *Musar leMevin* as a whole is a sectarian wisdom composition, though her work has yet to be published in full.[50]

The working presupposition here is that *Musar leMevin* is a variation of 'traditional' sapiential literature, similar to the conclusion reached by Strugnell and Harrington. Conceptions of judgement, reward, angels, metaphorical language and particular expressions of mysterious wisdom in the document are some such variations on 'traditional' sapiential compositions. *Musar leMevin*, then, represents a single genre that combines elements of wisdom with themes associated with apocalyptic literature.[51] The unusual combination of apocalyptic and sapiential motifs in the document may also, at times, nuance a seemingly traditional wisdom motif. The absence of significant lexicographic similarities, the assumed social context, and the role

---

throughout his monograph, however, this elect status should not be mistaken for a 'sectarian' designation.

[49] DIMANT, '4QInstruction (mussar la-mevin) – A Sectarian Wisdom,' (unpublished, five page abstract).

[50] VERMES, *Complete Dead Sea Scrolls in English*, p. 402 states *Musar leMevin* is "unquestionably sectarian" and that it uses terminology similar to CD and 1QH. JEFFERIES, *Wisdom at Qumran*, p. 59 considers the provenance of *Musar leMevin* to be from the Qumran Community.

[51] GOFF, *The Worldly and Heavenly*, is concerned primarily with the relationship of wisdom and apocalyptic in *Musar leMevin*. His work is particularly helpful in setting the document in relation to other early Jewish literature.

of apocalyptic expressions in the literature of early Judaisms are a few reasons *Musar leMevin* may be located in a broader Jewish milieu. While *Musar leMevin* divides humanity into two basic categories and uses language at times found in wide cross-sections of early Jewish literature including documents from Qumran, such factors do not warrant the claim that the document has an Essene provenance or was later interpolated by an Essene group.

4.3 The Meaning of רז נהיה

The phrase רז נהיה, which occurs about 30 times in *Musar leMevin*, is a prominent motif of the document. The addressee is told to give ear to (גלה אוזן), understand (בין), seek (דרש), gaze (הביט), take (לקח), and distinguish (פרש) the רז נהיה. The expression רז נהיה, by contrast, occurs very rarely among the other Dead Sea Scrolls[52] while varying forms of רז, usually in a construct, occur with relatively greater frequency.[53] Several scholars have addressed the use of this phrase in *Musar leMevin*.[54]

In a short article Harrington explores the phrase רז נהיה exclusively.[55] He notes the unique use of the phrase in *Musar leMevin* and divides his discussion of the term רז נהיה into two basic issues: (1) the expression itself; and (2) its function in particular texts. Harrington first analyses the two words of the expression and their occurrences elsewhere. Important observations concerning the word רז are: (1) It is a Persian loanword; (2) it appears in Daniel (2.18, 19, 27, 30, 47, 4.6) and elsewhere in the Dead Sea Scrolls; and (3) the familiar translation 'mystery' is entirely adequate. With regard to the term נהיה, Harrington considers the following: (1) The expected vocalisation of נהיה with a masculine singular noun in construct is the masculine singular *niphal* participle to be vocalised as *nihyeh*. Moreover, (2) the word has the potential of either a future (so Milik, Harrington, Strugnell) or past sense (so Wacholder, Eisenman-Wise, Martínez). As a construct phrase there is no definite article, but the meaning always takes a definite sense.

The second part of Harrington's discussion centres on the occurrences of the phrase רז נהיה in *Musar leMevin* and elsewhere. In the majority of cases

---

[52] 1Q27 1 i 4 'ונפשמה לוא מלטו מרז נהיה'; 1QS xi 3-4 'הביטה עיני ואורת לבבי לברז נהיה'; 4Q300 lines 3-4 300; ELGVIN argues for a reading of the phrase in 4Q413 (Composition Concerning Divine Providence) lines 4-5 in his article 'Mystery to Come'.

[53] 1QS ix 18 'ויכן להשכילם בז פלא'; 1QHᵃ ix 21 'כיא גליתה אוזני לרז פלא', xv 26 'ורזי פל[א]['ת]כה'; 4Q491 8-10 i 12 (4QMᵃ) 'השכלתני באמתכה ומדי פלאכה'; 4Q299 3 ii 15 'תומכי רזים או]'; 4Q300 8 5 'וברזי עד'; 4Q300 1 ii 2 'כול רז וחבלי' (Book of Mysteries).

[54] See AITKEN, 'Apocalyptic,' pp. 186-93 for a comparison of explicit and implicit divine revelation in *Musar leMevin* and Ben Sira/Sirach. Aitken observes that, 'for Ben Sira, as for the author of *Sapiential Work A* [i.e. *Musar leMevin*], creation and history are the sources for revelation and the understanding of God's plan'.

[55] HARRINGTON, 'Rāz Nihyeh'.

the expression is preceded by the preposition -בּ but it is not clear whether it is used in a local sense ('in' or 'on') or an instrumental sense ('by'). On occasions the רז נהיה stands alone and once is preceded by the preposition -מ. Harrington considers the content of the רז נהיה by examining occurrences of its use in the document. The occurrences chosen are:

(1) Study the *rz nhyh* [מחשבותיכה רז נהיה], and understand all the ways of truth, and all the roots of iniquity shalt thou contemplate (4Q416 2 iii 14).

(2) Gaze in/by the *rz nhyh* [הבט ברז נהיה], and understand the birth-time of salvation, and know who is to inherit glory and iniquity (4Q417 1 i 10-11 [DJD 34 = 4Q417 2 i]).

(3) Gaze in/by the *rz nhyh* [הבט *vacat* ברז נהיה], and know the inheritance of everything that lives (4Q418 2 i 18 [DJD 34 = 4Q417 1 i])

(4) ... the *rz nhyh* [רז נהיה[   ]], and understand the generations of man (4Q418 77 2).

(5) and understand in/by the *rz nhyh* [וקח ברז נהיה] the weight of the times and the measure (4Q418 7 4; translation uncertain).

(6) Thou shalt not know what is allotted to it [i.e. *rz nhyh*], and in righteousness shalt thou walk [התהלך וברז נהיה דרוש מולדיו ואז תדע נחלתו ובצדק תתהלך] (4Q416 2 iii 9[-10]).

(7) [the one who applies himself to studying the *rz nhyh*] shalt know to discern between good and evil (4Q417 2 i 7 [DJD 34 = 4Q417 1 i 7-8]).

(8) meditate in/by the *rz nhyh* [הגה וברז נהיה] by night and investigate it continually (4Q417 2 i 6 [4Q417 1 i 6]).

(9) as he (= they) uncovered thy ear by the *rz nhyh* [ברז נהיה], honour thou them [i.e. your parents] (4Q416 2 iii 18).[56]

Harrington concludes from these parallel phrases that רז נהיה carries associations with the knowledge of righteousness and iniquity and has an eschatological connotation. Furthermore, the one who applies himself to the רז נהיה can expect certain rewards. It seems to be a body of teaching concerning behaviour and eschatology and is likely an 'extra-biblical compendium'. As such it is analogous to: (1) the *Maskil's* instruction in 1QS iii 13-iv 26; (2) the *Book of Meditation* (1QSa i 6-8); or (3) perhaps even the *Book of Mysteries* (1Q27; 4Q299-301) with which it is already associated by the phrase רז נהיה.

Lange takes a different view in the focus of his analysis of רז נהיה in *Musar leMevin* (primarily 4Q417 1 i). Lange translates the phrase as 'Geheimnis des Werdens' thus excluding an eschatological connotation.[57] Lange makes it clear elsewhere that this meaning is to be distinguished from 'the mystery of being' (i.e. the translation of R. Eisenman and M. O. Wise).[58] For him, the

---

[56] HARRINGTON, 'Rāz Nihyeh,' p. 552; summarized and altered from HARRINGTON's original form.

[57] LANGE, *Weisheit*, pp. 91-92.

[58] LANGE, 'Wisdom,' p. 341. R. EISENMAN and M. WISE, *The Dead Sea Scrolls Uncovered* (Dorset: Element Books Ltd., 1992).

רז נהיה refers to the pre-existent order of creation without necessarily referring to history.[59]

Elgvin has also been a major contributor to the discussion concerning the meaning of רז נהיה in *Musar leMevin*. In one article published in 1994 Elgvin provides much of the preliminary background information that Harrington does, but includes Wernberg-Møller and Licht's discussions of the meaning and temporal aspects of רז נהיה in 1QS xi in light of 1QS iii 15 and CD ii 10 (where the term נהיה occurs).[60] Both Wernberg-Møller and Licht understand the phrase רז נהיה and והווא עולם as parallel expressions. For Licht, therefore, it is the mystery of the universe, the provisional ruler of the universe and possibly the mystery of the future. Elgvin also reviews a proposal of Milik[61] who understands the רז נהיה as 'the mystery to come' or 'the mystery which is about to come into being'. Elgvin finds such a translation appealing; however, the difficulty in understanding the phrase רז נהיה as future when it is clearly used in a context referring to the past (4Q418 123 ii 3-4) discourages such a reading. Elgvin concludes, here, that the רז נהיה is the mystery of God, revealed to the men of the community; it is perhaps an alternative expression for the knowledge of God and, as such, may be translated as 'the mystery of being'.

In a 1997 publication Elgvin goes into greater detail and retracts his earlier conclusion.[62] Elgvin concludes here that the רז נהיה is a comprehensive word for God's mysterious plan for creation as a whole, humanity and the redemption of the elect. He considers it best to understand the phrase as 'mystery to come' with an eschatological connotation, rather than as 'mystery of being'. Elgvin's resolution of the occurrence of רז נהיה in 4Q418 123 ii lines 2-8 is part of what makes his change of translation possible. More importantly, Elgvin notes passages where it is far more difficult to reconcile the translation 'mystery of being' with a given context. The clearest instances of an eschatological connotation are, in his opinion, in 4Q417 2 i lines 10-12 and 4Q417 1 i lines 1-14. Elgvin elaborates on the use of the רז נהיה in *Musar leMevin* by considering the remaining occurrences in the document. He states that it serves as the starting point for instructing the enlightened how they should walk in everyday life (e.g. 4Q416 2 iii 13 21 in the admonition to honour father and mother). So, for instance, the result of living one's life according to principles of רז נהיה will be the production of abundant crops (4Q423 3, par. 1Q26 2). Finally, Elgvin emphasises that רז נהיה is not to be

---

[59] LANGE, *Weisheit*, p. 60, writes that the רז נהיה "bezeichnet somit ein Phänomen, das ethische, historische, nomistische, eschatologische und urzeitliche Komponenten in sich vereinigt."

[60] ELGVIN, 'Admonition Texts,' pp. 189-90.

[61] *DJD I*, pp. 101-2.

[62] ELGVIN, 'Wisdom and Apocalypticism,' pp. 232-36.

identified with the Mosaic Torah. Though not strictly an apocalyptic work, *Musar leMevin* does contain in רז נהיה one apocalyptic element that connects the revelation of divine mysteries with salvation (4Q417 2 i 10-11). *Musar leMevin*, Elgvin concludes, has integrated traditional wisdom into an apocalyptic framework. Thus Elgvin is able to maintain his two-stage theory.

Collins dedicates a few pages not so much to how the phrase רז נהיה should be translated than to its function in *Musar leMevin*.[63] Collins cites the various ways the phrase has been translated ('the mystery that is to come'; 'the mystery of existence'; and 'the mystery that is to be') and chooses to give it a future sense in *Musar leMevin* as 'the mystery that is to be'. The content of 'the mystery that is to be' can only be gleaned from a few passages; especially important is 4Q417 2 i lines 10-12 ('gaze on the רז נהיה and understand the birth-time of salvation, and know who is to inherit glory and iniquity'). Collins infers from these lines that 'the mystery that is to be' is concerned with eschatological salvation and judgement. Even more important for the discussion is 4Q417 1 i lines 7-17,[64] where the רז נהיה: (1) is associated with creation (ll. 8-9); (2) speaks of truth and iniquity as well as wisdom and foolishness with an obvious parallel to 1QS iii-iv (ll. 7-8); and (3) distinguishes between 'a people of spirit' and 'a people of flesh' (ll. 16-17). According to Collins' assessment, the רז נהיה seems to embrace the divine plan that spans from creation to the eschatological judgement. The eschatological connotation of the phrase should be understood as resulting from marvellous mysteries (of creation) becoming clear in the end. If the addressee studies the mystery he can know God's glory and the mysteries of God's acts (4Q417 1 i 13). Moreover, the רז נהיה encompasses the coming and going of the periods (4Q418 123 ii 2-8) as well as anything that happens in life (e.g. a life of poverty or wealth). Collins, here, clearly limits the eschatological aspects of the רז נהיה within the framework of God's acts in creation.

Collins concludes his discussion with a note of caution regarding one of Harrington's suggestions. Harrington suggested that the mystery is an actual 'body of teaching' distinct from the Torah, as perhaps works such as the *Instruction on the Two Spirits* or the *Book of Meditation* (the book of 'Haguy' or 'Hagi'). Collins thinks, however, that it may not be identified simply with the contents of a single writing, but with a subject matter to which each of the writings refers.

Speculation about a more precise understanding of רז נהיה in *Musar leMevin* remains. The theme of creation pervades most of the discussion surrounding its interpretation. While issues of possible translations of the

---

[63] COLLINS, 'Wisdom Reconsidered,' pp. 272-74.
[64] COLLINS uses the earlier, pre-*DJD XXXIV*, designation for the fragment '4Q417 2 i', which was changed by the editors to '4Q417 1 i'.

phrase are limited, it may be possible to develop an approach to the רז נהיה which considers more broadly the theme of creation throughout *Musar leMevin*.

4.4 Language of Poverty

The insistence, assumption, or eventuality expressed by the author(s) of *Musar leMevin* regarding the addressee's (מבין) state of poverty or lacking (e.g. 4Q415 6 2, 4Q416 2 iii 12, 4Q418 177 5) has attracted considerable attention. *Musar leMevin* emphasises poverty far more than wealth and uses diverse vocabulary to do so (wealth: הון, עשר; poverty: אביון, דל, מחסור, עני, ריש). The most prominent term for 'poverty' in *Musar leMevin*, as mentioned previously, is מחסור. This term occurs approximately 26 times in the document.[65] Five publications to date focus on exploring this motif. Murphy has recently published a major monograph on the subject of wealth and poverty in the Dead Sea Scrolls and devotes a chapter to *Musar leMevin*.[66] Goff dedicates a chapter of his dissertation to 'poverty' in the document.[67] Wright has presented a paper at the Orion Conference concerned exclusively with categories of rich and poor in Qumran sapiential literature.[68] Tigchelaar, in his article on the addressees of *Musar leMevin*, surveys the characterisation of the addressee as poor as well.[69] Aitken is another who briefly touches upon the theme.[70] Their contributions assist in understanding this motif, however, there is still more to be said about this topic.

Murphy concludes, after a careful and systematic examination of the document, that *Musar leMevin* is typical among sapiential treatments of wealth elsewhere (i.e. proper behaviour within the socio-economic hierarchy regardless of fluctuating position, standard advice on commercial transactions, and matters relating to agricultural production). She notes, however, these exceptions.[71] The first anomaly is the cosmological introduction of the work that sets otherwise typical wisdom sayings within an eschatological framework where God is presented as the ultimate benefactor whom humans serve. The cosmological preface to the agricultural section (4Q423) is slightly different in that it places the special status of the wise farmer within an exegesis of Genesis 1-3 that correlates special knowledge of the elect with the productive Garden of Genesis 2. The second anomaly is the

---

[65] In 4Q415 9 9; 4Q416 1 6; 2 ii 1; 2 ii 20; 2 iii 2; 4Q417 2 i 17; 2 i 19; 2 i 21; 2 i 24; 2 ii + 23 3; 2 ii + 23 25; 4Q418 7b 7; 14 1; 16 3; 81+ 81a 18; 87 6; 88 5; 97 2; 107 3; 122 i 7; 126 ii 13 (2x); 127 1; 159 ii 5; 240 3; 12 1.

[66] MURPHY, *Wealth*, pp. 163-209.

[67] GOFF, *The Worldly*, pp. 127-67.

[68] WRIGHT, 'The Categories'.

[69] TIGCHELAAR, 'Addressees,' pp. 69-71.

[70] AITKEN, 'Apocalyptic,' pp. 184-85.

[71] MURPHY, *Wealth*, pp. 206-7.

integration of legal and eschatological material in a sapiential composition. Third, she observes that the coexistence in *Musar leMevin* of prosaic advice derived from universal human experience and appeals to special revelation (e.g. רז נהיה) as the ultimate tool for discernment is very rare in sapiential literature.

Murphy notes generally that there was in Judaism a struggle with the perception of inadequate divine provision for human needs. Poverty, in such instances, was not a condition to be revelled in as if this were the goal, since it is negative and alienates a person from others and God. By contrast, in *Musar leMevin* poverty has restorative and redemptive qualities. The virtuous person is advised to offer charity, not to shame the poor, and to avoid debt, while the slave is counselled on how to behave so that his status might become more like that of a son (4Q416 2 ii 7-15). Redemption is something occasionally realised through human channels, but the sages ultimately await divine judgement when God will redeem those whose worth is established.

Murphy observes that there is no specific condemnation of the rich in *Musar leMevin*, nor is there an expectation of their destruction. The emphasis throughout the document is rather on 'lacking' and 'poverty'. Hardly any sayings preserve admonitions to avoid the dangers of wealth or unjust gain. There are no critiques of sudden wealth, no instruction on the behaviour of a benefactor, no advice against covetousness, and no explicit advocacy of widows and orphans – all themes that might have been expected in a sapiential context. Wealth is respected in *Musar leMevin*, but it is no longer expected. The addressee is to pursue wisdom even in the circumstance of poverty and to understand that wealth is not gained by merit but by mysterious, divine dispensation.

The *Sitz im Leben* envisaged by Murphy is one where the addressees are employed in a variety of occupations, though farming would have been predominant. The document presumes an audience that struggles regularly with their own difficult financial circumstances that result in the pooling of resources, charity and when need be the taking of loans. The one resource that the recipients of *Musar leMevin* have that sets them apart from others is special divine revelation and the consolation of the רז נהיה.

Murphy devotes a portion of her work to the metaphorical use of some commercial terminology in *Musar leMevin*. The implications of these metaphors on conceptions of poverty have more significance than Murphy and others have observed. She begins with the terms *'ephah* and *sheqel* which are frequently used terms in *Musar leMevin* and observes, along with Strugnell and Harrington, that the 'surrounding context suggest only a metaphorical use of this terminology' (e.g. 4Q418 126 ii 3-4).[72] Murphy comments on other 'language of commercial exchange' that is used

---

[72] MURPHY, *Wealth*, pp. 171-72.

metaphorically, such as פקודה which can mean 'punishment', 'visitation' or the economic sense 'deposit'. 4Q418 126 ii line 6 reads 'to repay (להשיב) vengeance to the masters of iniquity, and punishment (פקודת) with re[compense…]' and Murphy suggests it could read as if 'God were returning the deposit of iniquity'. She further comments: 'the fact that the wicked are contrasted not to the righteous (the natural antonym) but to the poor may be governed by the dominant economic symbolism, but it is also possible that the dominant economic symbolism is governed by the nature of crimes being judged'.[73]

A third option which she does not consider here is that poverty, which is by no means an ideal, is a metaphorical description that implies, at times, lacking in a manner unrelated to material need or debt. Murphy also discusses the term 'inheritance' (נחלה) as it is metaphorically employed in *Musar leMevin*. The term is used variously as (1) perhaps 'one's progeny or symbolically as one's portion in the present or eschatological Israel' (4Q415 2 i + 1 ii 5-6); (2) metaphorically for what God has given the sage in the present (4Q416 3 2); (3) abstract gifts of truth (4Q416 4 3); (4) holiness (4Q418 234 1); (5) the 'inheritance of Adam' (4Q418 251 1); or (6) even life itself (4Q418 88 8 cf. 4Q418 172 5-13).[74] Another possible term used metaphorically is 'storehouse' (אוצר) to describe either divine or human stores (4Q418 237 3).

Perhaps most important in Murphy's chapter on *Musar leMevin* are the conclusions she draws about the social context of the addressees and the Qumran community. The worldview expressed by the document allows one to infer a relatively open economic and social organisation that is at odds with the consensus view of the Qumran community. She suggests two options to reconcile the evidence. First, *Musar leMevin* could be ascribed to a pre-sectarian context. Second, *Musar leMevin* could lead one to think that the Qumran community should be reconceived as less centralised and somewhat more engaged in the surrounding world. She considers both these suggestions likely on grounds of the popularity of the work at Qumran and the absence of specifically sectarian vocabulary.[75]

Murphy briefly discusses the common construction in *Musar leMevin* אביון אתה 'you are poor' (4Q416 2 ii 20; 2 iii 2; 2 iii 8; 2 iii 12; 4Q418 9 13; 148 ii 4; 177 5; 249). She comments that this phrase is:

…customarily followed by a reference to social superiors, such as kings (מלכים) or princes (נדיבים). The consistent contrast in such passages to individuals with greater social capital

---

[73] MURPHY, *Wealth*, p. 172.

[74] MURPHY, *Wealth*, pp. 173-74.

[75] MURPHY, *Wealth*, p. 209, It is not entirely clear whether MURPHY suggests the possibility that *Musar leMevin* has its provenance in the 'sectarian community'.

suggests that a real economic statement is being made here about the maven's social location.[76]

In the instance of the addressee being called poor followed by a referent to kings, Murphy cites 4Q415 6 line 2: אביון א[ת]ה ומלכ[ים. Taken literally and reading the *waw* as 'and', this could imply that the addressees are composed of two groups simultaneously: rich (kings) and poor. It might also be taken metaphorically and the *waw* taken as 'but'. Murphy does not fully detail, however, that the occurrence of statements of poverty followed by references to 'nobles' (נדיבים) is more frequent in *Musar leMevin*. 4Q416 2 iii, for instance, contains two such statements that the addressee is 'needy' (ll. 2, 8, 12) followed by a statement in line 11 that 'with the nobles (נדיבים) He has seated you and over a glorious heritage'. In the following line, directly after this statement to the addressee that he is seated among the 'nobles', there occurs a reminder that he is needy (l. 12).

Whatever being 'seated among the nobles' implies, it is not likely a reference to a monetary reality. The final instance of the poor being set in a context with social superiors occurs also in 4Q418 177 line 5: אתה רש ונדיבים. There is nothing convincing, it will be argued below, that these references (4Q415 6; 4Q416 2 iii; 4Q418 177) strengthen the case that an economic statement is being made here. To the contrary, the suggestion that the addressee is both impoverished and/but a noble or seated among the nobles suggests another reading entirely. A case may be made for these occurrences being read metaphorically or perhaps anthropologically.

Wright analyses the occurrences of language of wealth and poverty in *Musar leMevin* and then compares the situation of the addressees with that of Ben Sira's students.[77] Wright's conclusion is that the addressees of *Musar leMevin* are in a dissimilar social setting than the students of Ben Sira. The addressees in *Musar leMevin* belong to a social stratum that can be essentially categorised as poor. The students of Ben Sira are being trained for official administrative capacities while the addressees of *Musar leMevin* are not being instructed for any official capacity. Whereas Ben Sira addresses issues of the wealthy class, *Musar leMevin* does not even mention a class of rich people. The lack of any reference to a wealthy class in *Musar leMevin* begs the question whether the addressees are in some way isolated from them.[78] The addressees of *Musar leMevin* are constantly on the brink of falling into abject poverty or indentured servitude, which are concrete social realities. Wright notes that evidence indicates that the addressee is in a troublesome economic

---

[76] MURPHY, *Wealth*, p. 187.

[77] WRIGHT, 'The Categories,' pp. 26-28.

[78] WRIGHT does not consider the references to 'kings' and 'nobles' in this regard. The repeated observation that literal wealth and wealthy ones are of no concern to the author(s) of *Musar leMevin* is further indication that poverty language is used unusually.

situation that is ongoing and precarious. Wright is also not inclined, rightly, to view poverty in the document as an ideal value, though he does note the oddity of 4Q416 2 ii lines 20-21 ('Do not esteem yourself highly for your poverty when you are (anyway?) a pauper, lest you bring into contempt your (own) way of life').

Wright does not systematically address every occurrence of poverty in *Musar leMevin*. Nevertheless, the conclusions that he draws are valuable for understanding concepts of wealth and poverty in *Musar leMevin*, especially the comparisons drawn with Ben Sira. His discussion, however, is by no means an exhaustive treatment of the subject. Wright, for instance, does not comprehensively consider the apocalyptic context and metaphorical nature of language in the document that might at times affect an interpretation of 'poverty' or 'lacking'. Nor does he resolve unusual references such as 'according to the poverty of their host' (4Q416 1) or 'so as to fill] up all the deficiencies of his אוש' (4Q416 2 ii 1). Both of these references call into question the straightforward notion of poverty as strictly material.

Tigchelaar, in his treatment on the poverty of the addressee in *Musar leMevin*, is very brief.[79] While he raises several questions regarding the formula 'you are poor' in the document, the major contribution of his discussion is his suggestion that the formula could be read as conditional, 'if (when) you are poor'. Tigchelaar argues that phrases that explicitly describe the addressee as poor are limited and only envisage the possibility that the addressee may become poor. Tigchelaar's suggestion is appealing and plausible; it would make some sense of 4Q416 2 iii where the addressee could presently be seated among the nobles and is simply being warned of the eventuality of poverty. However, if the author(s) warns against the possibility of impoverishment, why are exhortations regarding the dangers of wealth absent from the document? Furthermore, if the addressee is presently seated with the 'nobles' then why is debt and credit a significant motif in *Musar leMevin*? Reconciling occasions where poverty is found in conjunction with these 'nobles' (4Q415 6 2; 4Q418 177 5) in 4Q416 2 iii, a column with three statements that the addressee is poor, can only be done if poverty is a present reality and not an eventuality.

Goff contributes a chapter of his monograph to the discussion of poverty in *Musar leMevin* as well. His conclusions are similar to Murphy's except she 'focuses more on the financial teachings of 4QInstruction than its depiction of poverty'.[80] Goff structures his presentation of poverty in the document in relation to the addressee's elect status. The addressee's poverty, on the one hand, appears to be contrary to his favoured status. On the other hand, poverty

---

[79] TIGCHELAAR, 'The Addressees,' pp. 69-71.
[80] GOFF, *The Worldly*, p. 129.

is used to teach them about their elect status.[81] Goff envisions poverty in the document as a component of the economic situation of the addressees. However, their elect status (e.g. 4Q416 2 iii 11-12) is used to assert a type of heavenly wealth (e.g. 'inheritance').[82] The emphasis in *Musar leMevin* on indebtedness 'is portrayed as a loss of one's spirit', which Goff associates with 'glory' and 'inheritance'.[83]

Economic poverty, argues Goff, is contrasted with two types of wealth: (1) a heavenly inheritance; and (2) a worldly indebtedness to a creditor. Goff recognises that the poverty of the addressee in the document is a hallmark of the composition, and the *Leitmotif* 'you are poor' (4Q415 6 2; 4Q416 2 ii 20; 4Q416 2 iii 2, 8, 12, 19) is without parallel in literature from the period. In addition, he advocates a reading of 4Q416 2 iii lines 11-12 and the term נדיבים ('nobles') as a reference to angelic beings and heavenly wealth.[84] He concludes that the addressee's 'poverty is clearly material'.[85] However, his conclusion should be challenged on the basis of the following observations. First, if wealth and inheritance are portrayed as both worldly and heavenly a case can be made that poverty is used with disparate connotations as well. Second, it is unknown who the readers or hearers of the document were and an insistence that they were all suffering from varying degrees of financial hardship and *need to be reminded of it* is implausible. Finally, 4Q416 2 iii is the column with the single most references to poverty and, as I will discuss in chapter four, contains several references to angelic beings providing a context for poverty that cannot be categorised straightforwardly as economic.

Aitken is alone in stating that the poverty motif in *Musar leMevin* 'seems to play an eschatological role'.[86] He notes the trend in the post-exilic period of emphasising the role of poverty in future speculation. Haggai 1.6 describes the impoverished situation of the post-exilic community saying 'those that earn wages. . .earn them to put into a bag with holes'. The Targum to Haggai translates צְרוֹר נָקוּב meaning 'bag with holes' with the Aramaic word מאירתא meaning 'curse' which elucidates the impoverished state of those who return. The Hebrew word מארה develops the semantic range that includes poverty (see Vulgate and LXX of Deut 28.20; Prov 28.27 and *Peshitta* on Deut 28.20). In an explanation of this possible motif of poverty Aitken writes:

The Targum to the Minor Prophets, which is certainly post-70 C.E. in its final composition but probably contains earlier traditions, expresses an interest in the life that the righteous will

---

[81] GOFF, *The Worldly*, p. 127.

[82] GOFF, *The Worldly*, p. 150.

[83] GOFF, *The Wordly*, p. 164.

[84] GOFF, *The Worldly*, p. 150. Independently from GOFF I reached similar conclusions in ch. 4 that נדיבים is a reference to angelic beings.

[85] GOFF, *The Worldly*, p. 167.

[86] AITKEN, 'Apocalyptic,' p. 184.

enjoy in a new world (e.g. Targum to Hab. 3:2; Mic. 7:14) once the present order has been disbanded, and at Hag. 1:6 it may be attempting to underscore the former state from which the righteous will be delivered. In the book of Malachi a series of blessings and curses are uttered (3:6-12) before the writing down of those who fear the Lord (3:13-21) and before the prediction of the day of the Lord (3:22-24). God has already threatened to send a מארה upon the priests (Mal. 2:2), and then He declares in 3:9 that the whole nation is cursed with a מארה (Vulgate again translates as *penuria*) "because you are robbing me". There may be an irony implied in the prophet's words if God is going to deprive those who are depriving Him, but certainly throughout this section there is an alternation between deprivation and reward.[87]

Aitken points to the allusion to Malachi 3:16 in 4Q417 1 i lines 15-16 to the 'book of remembrance' and the apocalyptic overtones of this fragment. If the author of *Musar leMevin* was familiar with this use of מארה and its emphasis on poverty as a 'prelude to the Lord's deliverance' then the motif of poverty might be understood in this context. Aitken cites 4Q416 2 iii lines 9-12 where God is said to lift the head of the addressee out of poverty and place him in a glorious inheritance. He also notes 4Q418 126 lines 1-10 which describes a future judgement by God where the good and wicked will be separated and the 'poor' will be vindicated while the 'lords of iniquity' will be punished.[88] Aitken refers also to the *Epistle of Enoch* where the 'poverty of the addressee is implied' within an apocalyptic context and is promised restitution in the life to come. *Contra* Tigchelaar, Aitken finds the impoverished state of the addressee emphasised throughout *Musar leMevin*: he is repeatedly reminded of his poverty.[89]

On the one hand, Murphy, Wright, Tigchelaar and Goff notice particular oddities of the theme of poverty in *Musar leMevin* and attempt to reconcile it, in varying degrees, to a more traditional sapiential use. Aitken, on the other hand, describes a possible alternative for reading some references in an esoteric eschatological manner. An exploration of this motif in conjunction with the use of other possible traditions at play in *Musar leMevin* is needed. The possibility that poverty in *Musar leMevin* is used with connotations that should be understood outside of a literal impoverished social condition have yet to be fully explored.

4.5 Reconstruction

The task of reconstructing *Musar leMevin* began with the efforts of Strugnell and Milik in the 1950's. DJD 34 is the result of their combined efforts as well as Harrington and Elgvin who joined in more recent years.[90] The contribution of DJD 34 to a reconstruction of the document *Musar leMevin* will be

---

[87] AITKEN, 'Apocalyptic,' p. 185.
[88] AITKEN, 'Apocalyptic,' p. 184.
[89] AITKEN, 'Apocalyptic,' p. 184.
[90] *DJD XXXIV*, p. xi.

reviewed below. Besides DJD 34, Tigchelaar, Elgvin as well as Steudel and Lucassen have proposed a sequencing of selected fragments. Tigchelaar's contribution to the reconstruction of *Musar leMevin* is the most substantial and in many ways serves as a supplement to DJD 34.

One of the primary tasks of reconstruction is assigning fragments to manuscripts. DJD 34 has divided the fragments under the manuscript designations 4Q415 (4QInstruction^a), 4Q416 (4QInstruction^b), 4Q417 (4QInstruction^c), 4Q418 (4QInstruction^d), 4Q418a (4QInstruction^e), 4Q418c (4QInstruction^f), 4Q423 (4QInstruction^g), and 1Q26 (1QInstruction). Among the manuscript designations 4Q418a and 4Q418c[91] the number of manuscripts preserved by these two designations has been disputed. As Strugnell and Harrington write in the introduction to 4Q418a, 'the principal problem posed by 4Q418a is whether the fragments of 4Q415, 4Q418, and 4Q418a are to be divided among two manuscripts or three [i.e. 4Q418a may be simply 4Q418]'.[92] They add as well that Elgvin may be right in separating 4Q418 1, 2, 4, 286, and 296 into a fourth manuscript. In the case of 4Q418c, Strugnell and Harrington argue on the basis of skin surface, column height and orthography that it represents a distinct manuscript of *Musar leMevin*. The total number of possible manuscripts suggested in DJD 34 could total up to nine, if Elgvin's suggestion is accepted.

Material reconstruction has been another important undertaking by Strugnell and Harrington in DJD 34 and more recently by Tigchelaar. Material reconstruction has taken the form of assigning smaller fragments to a larger fragment (i.e. unconnected fragments are associated with one another) which are then designated, for example, fragments 2, 2a, 2b, 2c. At times, material reconstruction is questionable and the designation appears, for instance, as fragments 7b + 199 (?) + 64 (?) + 66 (?).

The identification of parallels and overlaps between fragments is another valuable method for reconstructing a document. Strugnell and Harrington have identified a number of overlaps, which may be conveniently listed below:

4Q415 1–4Q418 167	**4Q418 1**–4Q416 1	**4Q418 81**–4Q423 8 1-4
4Q418a 15 (?)		
4Q416 1–4Q418 1-2, 2a,	**4Q418 2**–4Q416 1	*4Q418 167*–4Q415 11
b, and c		

---

[91] 4Q418b is not thought to be part of *Musar LeMevin*. It is distinguished with what is thought to be a quotation of Ps 107; *DJD XXXIV*, p. 497.

[92] *DJD XXXIV*, p. 475.

4Q416 2 ii–4Q417 2 ii 4Q418 8, 21, 22 4Q418a 19	**4Q418 7**–4Q417 2 i 4Q417 2 i	**4Q418 188**–4Q423 9 1-4 **4Q418a 11**–4Q417 1 i 21-24
4Q416 2 iii–4Q417 2 ii 26 4Q418 9-10	**4Q418 8**–4Q416 2 ii 2-13 4Q417 2 ii 3-17 4Q418a 19 1-4	**4Q418a 22**–4Q417 2 i 12-16 4Q423 3 1Q26 2 2-4
4Q416 2 iv–4Q418 10 5-10	**4Q418 9**–4Q416 2 iii 2-17	**4Q423 4**–1Q26 1
4Q417 1 *i*–4Q418 43, 44, 45 4Q418a 11	**4Q418 10**–4Q416 2 iii 17-2, iv 1 1-14	**4Q423 8**–4Q418 81 1-5
4Q417 1 ii–*4Q418* 123 I	**4Q418 43, 44, 45 i**–4Q417 1 i 2-22	**4Q423 9**–4Q418 188 1-8
4Q417 2 i–4Q416 2 i 4Q418 6(?), 7, 26, 27, 64(?), 66(?), 199(?) 4Q418a 22	**4Q418 69**–4Q417 5 1-5 **4Q418 77**–4Q416 7 1-3	**1Q26 1**–4Q423 4 **1Q26 2**–4Q423 3 2-4

The obvious contribution of these identifications is the creation of composite texts, which Strugnell and Harrington have constructed. Tigchelaar devotes half of his monograph to analysing overlaps and suggests several new additions and readings. Since *Musar leMevin* is in such a poor state of preservation with very few full lines entirely extant, such identifications of overlaps have made it possible to restore a number of lines more fully (e.g. 4Q416 2 ii).

Elgvin has published a useful suggestion for sequencing fragments of *Musar leMevin*, which will be examined below.[93] Hartmut Stegemann's methods for material reconstruction are the basis of Elgvin's work.[94] Steudel and Lucassen, who also draw on Stegemann's methods, have proposed a sequencing of fragments as well, but have not published the results outside of

---

[93] ELGVIN, 'The Reconstruction,' pp. 579-80. The table below adapts Elgvin's section subtitled 'Survey of Contents'. The brief content sketches of fragments are intended to provide a flow of subject matter through the document. Aspects of the summaries will be discussed and defended in later chapters.

[94] H. STEGEMANN, 'Methods for the Reconstruction of Scrolls from Scattered Fragments,' in L. H. SCHIFFMAN (ed.) *Archaeology and History in the Dead Sea Scrolls. The New York University Conference in Memory of Yigael Yadin* (JSPSup 8; JSOT/ASOR Monographs 2; Sheffield: JSOT Press, 1990) pp. 189-220.

the contribution of a table in DJD 34.[95] The table prepared below is a synopsis of the two sequences as found in Elgvin's article and Steudel and Lucassen's reconstruction found in DJD 34. Below, the idea of Elgvin's summary of the contents has been borrowed, adapted and applied to Steudel and Lucassen's reconstruction. The intent is to view the results of sequencing for understanding the document *Musar leMevin* from a narrative approach.

T. Elgvin (Putative column 4Q416)	*A. Steudel & B. Lucassen (Putative column 4Q418)*
I)	I) 4Q418 1, 2 (top); parallel 4Q416 1, 2 – The cosmos is established and ordered; dominion is given and by it iniquity is condemned. 4Q418 213 (middle)
II.17-21) 4Q417 III i 1-5 –	II) 4Q418 43 (top); parallel 4Q417 1 i – Meditation on creation, exhortation to understand existence, Vision of Haguy/Book of Memorial, human fashioning, division of humanity.
III.1-20) 4Q416 III (4Q416 2 i) = 4Q417 III 6-27 – Addressees relation to fellow man: needs, property, loans. Exhortation to understand: existence, salvation, inheritance. God and poverty.	III)
III.21-IV.3) 4Q416 2 i 21-ii 3 – God's nourishment of humanity including the 'spirit of flesh'.	
IV.3-18) 4Q416 2 ii 3-18 – Description of demeaning one's spirit and being shamed, elect status of the addressee (servant, son, chosen one).	IV)
IV.18-V.3) 4Q416 2 ii 18 – iii 3 – Live a decent and humble life without luxury.	
V.3-6) 4Q416 2 iii 3-6 – Rules on borrowing.	V)
V.6-8) 4Q416 2 iii 6-8 – Assertion the	

---

[95] *DJD XXXIV*, pp. 18-19.
[96] In Elgvin's sequencing he uses this title and describes the content as 'eschatological'.

addressee is poor, living to be remembered
after death.

V.8-15) 4Q416 2 iii 8-15 – Insistence on
poverty, seated among the 'nobles',
investigation of origins and glorifying one's
creators.

V.15-VI.13) 4Q416 2 iii 15 – iv 13 –   VI)
Reflection on creation and instruction about
one's wife.

VI.17-VIII 15) 'Eschatological discourse'[96]

VI.17-20) 4Q416 4 – rejoicing in an
inheritance.

VII.2-7) 4Q416 1 2-7 – The cosmos is   VII) 4Q418 7 (bottom); parallels
established and ordered, dominion is given.   4Q416 2 i and 4Q417 2 i – Addressees
VII.8-10) 4Q416 1 8-10 – Iniquity is   relation to fellow man: needs,
condemned by the dominion of the heavens.   property, loans. Exhortation to
                                                    understand: existence, salvation,
                                                    inheritance. God and poverty.

VII.11-16) 4Q416 1 11-16 – Prediction of the
judgement on the 'spirit of flesh'.

VII.16-19) 4Q416 1 16-19 –

VIII.9-15) 4Q416 3 – Lot of all beings is from   VIII) 4Q418 8 (top) parallels 4Q416 2
God and exhortation to not rest until evil has   ii and 4Q417 2 ii – Description of
ended.   demeaning one's spirit and being
                                                    shamed, elect status of the addressee
                                                    (servant, son, chosen one) and
                                                    exhortation not to sell one's glory or
                                                    inheritance.

IX)   IX) 4Q418 9 (bottom) 4Q416 2 iii –
                                                    Assertions that addressee is poor,
                                                    seated among the 'nobles'; exhortation
                                                    to know one's origin and honour your
                                                    creators.

X) 4Q417 IX (= 1 i)[97] – Meditation on   X) 4Q418 10 (top) parallel 4Q416 2 iv
creation, exhortation to understand existence,   – Reflection of creation and

---

[97] ELGVIN, 'The Reconstruction,' p. 569 writes that '4Q417 frg. 2 represents cols. IX and X of the same scroll' and that similar wear patterns are visible on frg. 2 (see PAM 42.578)'. *DJD XXXIV* numbers these fragments 4Q417 1 i and ii. which is a fragment preserving portions of two columns that are designated IX (4Q417 1 i) and X (4Q417 1 ii) by ELGVIN.

Vision of Haguy/Book of Memorial, human fashioning, division of humanity.	instruction about one's wife.
XI) 4Q417 X (= 1 ii) – Worship God and seek wisdom.	XI) 4Q418 55 (bottom) – Angels pursue and watch over knowledge; humanity is lazy and individually honoured according to their knowledge.
XII)	XII) 4Q418 207 + 69
XIII)	XIII) 4Q418 69 ii + 128 (bottom) parallel 4Q417 5 –
XIV)	XIV) 4Q418 128 ii (bottom)
XV) 4Q418a XVII, 4Q418 81 – The gifts and responsibilities of the elect. XVI)	XV) 4Q418 81 + 103 (bottom) – The gifts and responsibilities of the elect. XVI) 4Q418 103 ii (bottom)
XVII)	XVII) 4Q418 127 (top)
XVIII)	XVIII)
XIX)	XIX)
XX) 4Q418a XXIII, 4Q418 55 – Angels pursue and watch over knowledge; humanity is lazy and individually honoured according to their knowledge.	XX)
XXI)	XXI)
XXII) 4Q423 1, 2 i – Genesis 2-4 re-written, addressees described as farmers in an Eden like garden.[98]	XXII)
XXIII) 4Q418 127 – A warning: if you are disobedient you will experience trouble and death. God gave everybody their portions, and will test them with scales of righteousness.	XXIII-XXX)

The most noteworthy differences between the two reconstructions have to do with the estimated length of 4Q418. Elgvin has suggested that the manuscript

---

[98] STEUDEL and LUCASSEN do not locate 4Q423 1, 2 i, however, TIGCHELAAR agrees with ELGVIN in locating it near the end of the document, see TIGCHELAAR'S sequencing below.

4Q418 originally consisted of twenty-three columns,[99] while Steudel and Lucassen estimate that there were at least thirty columns.[100] Another difference is Elgvin's placement of 4Q416 1 in column vii rather than at the beginning of the document as argued by Steudel – Lucassen and Strugnell – Harrington. The degree to which sequencing varies is apparent above.

Tigchelaar's contribution[101] is the most extensive work on the reconstruction of *Musar leMevin*, beside DJD 34, to date. The first part of the book is devoted primarily to the following tasks: (1) introducing the document *via* a history of its reconstruction, (2) offering reconstructions of individual manuscripts (he identifies eight: 4Q415, 416, 417, 418*, 418, 418a, 423 and 1Q26) and (3) discussing a reconstruction and sequencing for the document *Musar leMevin*.

Tigchelaar delineates between fragments formerly designated 4Q418 and 4Q418a as representing three manuscripts rather than two and a repair sheet (consisting of three fragments: 1, 2, 2b). On the basis of palaeographic, physical, and textual evidence Tigchelaar concludes that the repair sheet must be interpreted as a separate manuscript which he designates 4Q418*.[102] Reconstruction of manuscripts is provided from personal consultation of fragments and overlap of fragments. Particularly helpful are transcriptions of overlaps with indication of each fragment by way of font style. Tigchelaar's reconstructions offer a number of variant readings (i.e. omissions, additions, substitutions) from DJD 34. The final chapter of part one is devoted to reconstructing the sequence of *Musar leMevin*.

Tigchelaar defines the aim of reconstructing a composition as, 'an absolute or relative placement of preserved fragments in their respective manuscripts, or in relation to fragments of other manuscripts.'[103] Whereas Elgvin bases his reconstruction upon 4Q416 and Steudel and Lucassen upon 4Q418, Tigchelaar's putative column is 4Q418a. The most likely relative order of the preserved fragments of 4Q418a is: [??] – 12 – 11 – 10 – 9 [??] – 22 – [?] – 19 – 18 – 17 – 16+14 – 15+13 – [??] – 8 – 7 – 6 – 5 – 4 – 3 –2 – 1 – [??] while 20+21 have not be placed.[104] Using overlaps with 4Q418a Tigchelaar is able to sequence a number of important fragments from other manuscripts. On this basis 4Q417 1 i is located in the first few columns of the document (overlaps 4Q418a 11) and is followed several columns later by 4Q417 2 i (overlaps 4Q418a 22) and the 4Q417 2 ii (overlaps 4Q418a 19). 4Q423 5 (overlaps

---

[99] ELGVIN, 'The Reconstruction,' p. 580.

[100] *DJD XXXIV*, p. 19.

[101] TIGCHELAAR, *To Increase Learning*.

[102] TIGCHELAAR, *To Increase Learning*, p. 64.

[103] TIGCHELAAR, *To Increase Learning*, p. 155.

[104] TIGCHELAAR, *To Increase Learning*, p.157, explains that the, 'siglum [??] means that fragments of one or more revolutions of the scroll may be missing. . .[?] means that one (but no more) fragment of one revolution of the scroll may be missing'.

4Q418a 3) is situated among the final columns of *Musar leMevin*. Tigchelaar's sequencing may be provided for comparison with Elgvin, Steudel and Luccasen:

Wad	Frags.	Overlaps	Overlaps
	4Q418a [??]		
B 4	4Q418a 12		
B 3	4Q418a 11	=4Q417 1 i 21-24	=4Q418 43-45
B 2	4Q418a 10		
B 1	4Q418a 9 2		=4Q416 4 1 ?
	4Q418a [??]		
	4Q418a 22 1-5	=4Q417 2 ii 19-21	=[4Q416 2 i 7-10]
	4Q418a [?]		
D 5	4Q418a 19 1-4	=4Q417 2 ii 19-21	=4Q416 2 ii 14-16
D 4	4Q418a 18 1-4		=4Q416 2 iv 3-7
D 3	4Q418a 17		
D 2	4Q418a 16		
D 1	4Q418a 15	=4Q415 11	=4Q418 167a + b
	4Q418a [??]		
A 8	4Q418a 8	=4Q415 6 ?	
A 7	4Q418a 7		
A 6	4Q418a 6		
A 5	4Q418a 5		
A 4	4Q418a 4		=4Q418 103 ii
A 3	4Q418a 3	=4Q423 5	
A 2	4Q418a 2		
A 1	4Q418a 1		
	4Q418a [??][105]		

On the basis of the large right hand margin of 4Q416 1, rather than overlaps with 4Q418a, Tigchelaar agrees with all but Elgvin in locating 4Q416 1 as the first column of the document. In reconstructing and sequencing documents,

---

[105] TIGCHELAAR, *To Increase Learning*, p. 158.

Tigchelaar repeatedly emphasises that much of the task is uncertain and approximate.

A great deal of work towards a more complete reconstruction of *Musar leMevin* has been accomplished. While some new overlaps may be identified as the task of textual reconstruction of *Musar leMevin* continues, new theories regarding the sequencing of larger fragments may be possible. Furthermore, taking into account the sequencing of fragments may help to understand better the theology of the document. For instance, 4Q416 1 likely introduces the document and there is a high probability that 4Q423 fragments are to be located near the end. If the document opens with reflection on the creation and ordering of the cosmos and concludes with a section that re-writes Genesis 2-4 describing the addressee as a farmer in an Eden like garden; the importance of creation narratives for the document as a whole increases.

4.6 Angelology

In comparison with other documents from the Qumran Library, *Musar leMevin* has been available for study for a much shorter period of time. It is not surprising, therefore, that contributions to the study of angelic beings[106] and angelology have been unable to take into account important references that occur in *Musar leMevin*.[107] However, considering the importance of this document for understanding angelology in early Judaism, more recent assessments of the subject will need to take it into account. Kevin Sullivan recently published a monograph that broadly considers angelology in early

---

[106] STUCKENBRUCK, "'Angels" and "God": Exploring the Limits of Early Jewish Monotheism,' in L. T. STUCKENBRUCK and W. E. S. NORTH (eds.) Early Jewish and Christian Monotheism (JSNTSS 263; London/New York: T & T Clark International, 2004) p. 46, distinguishes between 'angels' and 'angelic beings': 'It is thus important to recognize from the outset that, despite the focus of the present discussion, a study of "angels" should not be isolated within the broad spectrum of ideas regarding mediation in Jewish antiquity. Other categories of mediator figures with which divine activity was associated have been identified and discussed, categories that cannot be completely distinguished from either "angelic beings" on the one hand or, in some cases, from one another, on the other hand. A listing of these illustrates how fluid a typology of mediator figures can actually be: divine attributes (e.g. Logos, Sophia, Glory); patriarchal personages (e.g. Enoch, Jacob, Moses); priestly and royal figures in the literature (e.g. the idealized monarch and high priest); and eschatological ideal figures (e.g. 'Messiah', 'Son of Man', Melchizedek).' See HURTADO, *One God, One Lord: Early Christian Devotion and Ancient Jewish Monotheism* (Edinburgh: T&T Clark, 1998) pp. 17-92.

[107] Most noteworthy is M. DAVIDSON, *Angels at Qumran: A Comparative Study of 1 Enoch 1-36, 72-108 and Sectarian Writings from Qumran* (Sheffield: JSOT Press, 1983). Davidson is not clear in defining what a 'sectarian' document is and includes a fairly broad range of compositions in this category. *Musar leMevin* is unknown to DAVIDSON in this monograph.

Judaism and the New Testament and does not discuss *Musar leMevin* at all.[108] Among the publications on *Musar leMevin*, aspects of angelology are discussed in relation to the interpretation of specific passages, however, a more comprehensive and sustained examination may be helpful.

Crispin Fletcher-Louis discusses angelic references in *Musar leMevin* in light of what he considers to be a wide-spread theology of angelmorphology in early Judaism.[109] He conceives of a sweeping phenomenon in the literature of the period where righteous individuals have the rights, privileges, and status of angels. Certain individuals, such as Simon the High Priest, Moses, Enoch, and Noah are elevated to an even more exalted status where they are included 'within the grammar of God's own life, embodying *his* Glory and receiving the honour (and worship) otherwise reserved for him'.[110] Fletcher-Louis attempts to find a matrix or pre-figuration for Christology in the study of angelology and anthropology in the literature of early Judaism. With this in mind, Fletcher-Louis is able to find traces of angelmorphology in a large collection of documents found in the Qumran Library.[111] As concerns *Musar leMevin*, several columns significant for understanding angelic beings in the document (e.g. 4Q417 1 i and 4Q418 81) are found to fit into Fletcher-Louis' angelmorphic scheme. Fletcher-Louis' analysis of selected passages and his conclusions are not persuasive.[112]

A number of passages have been discussed as relating to angelic beings. For instance, Collins suggested that 4Q417 1 i lines 15-18 allude to the creation of a segment of humankind in the likeness of the 'holy ones' identified as angels.[113] Some observations have been made on a number of other angelic references, or possible references, in 4Q416 2 iii; 4Q418 55, 69,

---

[108] K. P. SULLIVAN, *Wrestling with Angels: A Study of the Relationship Between Angels and Humans in Ancient Jewish Literature and the New Testament* (AGAJU 55; Leiden: Brill, 2004).

[109] The term 'angelmorphology' is fairly new and comes from the notion that exalted human beings can take on or become like angelic beings. Studies of angelmorphology have been carried out primarily by scholars of the New Testament looking for earlier formulations that might elucidate studies in Christology. See L. HURTADO, *One God, One Lord*; C. A. GIESCHEN, *Angelmorphic Christology: Antecedents and Early Evidence* (Leiden: Brill, 1998); C. FLETCHER-LOUIS, *Luke-Acts: Angels, Christology and Soteriology* (Tübingen: Mohr Siebeck, 1997).

[110] FLETCHER-LOUIS, *All the Glory*, p. 135.

[111] FLETCHER-LOUIS' *All the Glory*, has been critically reviewed by a number of scholars: G. J. BROOKE, *JSOT* 27 (2003): 167-68; K. P. SULLIVAN, *CBQ* 65 (2003): 256-58; J. J. COLLINS, *JSJ* 34 (2003): 73-79; M. GOFF, *JBL* 122 (2003): 165-175; and C. A. NEWSOM, *DSD* 10 (2003): 431-35.

[112] FLETCHER-LOUIS, *All the Glory*, p. 183 makes a number of assumptions about *Musar leMevin*, for instance, his reading of 4Q418 81 assumes the addressee to be a priest in a community that is estranged from the Jerusalem Temple. He is also insistent that the 'holy ones' are not angelic beings but rather members of the community.

[113] COLLINS, 'In the Likeness'.

and 81. A more comprehensive analysis of the angelology of *Musar leMevin* and the relationship of different addressees to angelic beings is needed. It may be seen that the addressee has a venerative attitude towards angels beyond what has been suggested from 4Q418 81 line 1 ('He opened your lips, a spring, to bless the holy ones; and you, like an eternal spring, praise['). Indeed, if Collins is correct that 4Q417 1 i has in mind creation in the likeness of angels there may be other streams of this thought elsewhere in the document.

5. Issues Raised and Resolved

A review of the above literature demonstrates both the exceptional progress of scholars for an understanding of *Musar leMevin* as well as evidence of the disunity among them on how to interpret the document. The basic questions that have been raised are as follows. First, while *Musar leMevin* clearly conceives of wisdom in language and conceptions similar to other wisdom literature (e.g. Ben Sira), much can be learned from points of dissimilarity between *Musar leMevin* and other such documents. Second, the dissimilarities in *Musar leMevin* from biblical and non-biblical wisdom literature, its unique use of vocabulary, and its possible popularity in the library at Qumran raise questions regarding its relationship to other literature, traditions, and the community of Qumran. Third, phrases such as רז נהיה as well as the abundant terminology and references to the impoverished have attracted much attention and have been the focus of debate as to how they both should be interpreted in relation to the theology of the document. Fourth, the task of reconstructing this poorly preserved document has been and remains a foundational endeavour. The large majority of fragments have been assigned, without objection, to their manuscripts. Also, a large number of overlaps have been identified and valuable composite texts constructed. Several sequences for the fragments of *Musar leMevin* have been proposed with significant variants between them. Finally, Fletcher-Louis has addressed issues of angelology and anthropology. Other scholarly contributions, to be reviewed in chapter four, raise issues related to angelic beings in the document as well. These works demonstrate, among other things, that a variety of interpretative issues must be resolved in order to begin forming conclusions on angelology and anthropology. In the case of Fletcher-Louis, one is able to see the significance an interpretation of the relationship between angels and addressees has not only on this document but also, for instance, on early Christology and related concerns.

6. Suggestions for Remaining Tasks

The reconstruction of the document *Musar leMevin* is one of the most crucial tasks that remains. The two methods used at present to reconstruct the document are: (1) material reconstruction (the so called 'morpho-phthiseo-critical' analysis), and (2) textual reconstruction. Another (possible) method for reconstructing the document may be an analysis of intertextual occurrences in the document. In identifying the use of other traditions, the reconstruction of certain lines and phrases may be reproduced with greater certainty. In addition, it is generally assumed at present that *Musar leMevin* is a loosely structured composition, similar to other wisdom literature, and does not necessarily preserve a logical progression or presentation of ideas. This assumption can be questioned. It may be possible to identify a coherent structure, perhaps limited, to the document's presentation of concepts that will aid in the sequencing of some fragments.

The identification of biblical and non-biblical traditions, explicit and non-explicit, in *Musar leMevin* will hopefully yield insights to topics previously addressed. A systematic analysis of the use of Genesis creation traditions may result in a clarification, for instance, of the terms רז נהיה, נדיבים or מחסור. In the case of language that refers to poor and needy the identification of such traditions will elucidate some of the more unusual occurrences of the concept in *Musar leMevin*. The contributions at present are valuable, but a broader attempt that employs a new methodology may prove beneficial.

Theological motifs in *Musar leMevin* that need to be addressed to a greater extent are anthropology, angelology and cosmology. 4Q416 1, likely the first column of the manuscript, provides a cosmological introduction. The influence of cosmological motifs throughout the document need further exploration; for instance, the way in which the pursuit of mysterious revelation is related to cosmology. The author(s) may also conceive of a portion of humanity having a relationship to angelic beings. It is worth inquiring whether conceptions of poverty and revelation are related to anthropology generally, or perhaps even angelology. *Musar leMevin* is concerned on a number of occasions with the female and even addresses a female in one instance (4Q415 2 ii). No comprehensive treatment of women in *Musar leMevin* has yet been produced. A point of departure for exploring these themes is the identification of allusions to traditions from Genesis, which, I propose, are foundational for many such conceptions in the document.

In conclusion, the task of identifying the use of biblical and non-biblical traditions in *Musar leMevin* may well be significant for reconstructing (and perhaps ordering columns of) the document, clarifying debated concepts and phrases, and ultimately situating more precisely *Musar leMevin* among the literature of the library from Qumran and early Jewish literature generally. Various streams of tradition related to creation in Jewish literature from the Graeco-Roman period will hopefully be elucidated as well. Two initial tasks first present themselves: (1) a methodology for identifying allusions should be formulated; and (2) possible allusions to Genesis 1-3 traditions should be identified and adjudicated.

CHAPTER 2

Non-Explicit Use of Biblical Traditions: Methodology for Identification

1. Introduction

Discussions of non-explicit use of biblical traditions in the documents from Qumran are, at present, few in number. In the use of the phrase 'non-explicit' such terms as 'allusion' and 'echo' spring to mind. These terms are loosely used in scholarship and frequently misused when applied in exegesis. It is with good reason that the present discussion on the non-explicit use of traditions is relatively undeveloped as it is often rather problematic even to define the terms 'allusion' or 'echo'. Once defined, it is with even greater difficulty that a series of criteria or tests are developed for adjudicating the likelihood of an occurrence. Most often, the tendency of scholars is to make unsupported claims that one text is alluding to another without the degree of caution here desired. Thus, it is important to attempt to broaden the present discussion of the non-explicit use of biblical traditions. The document *Musar leMevin* uses, it appears, a great number of biblical traditions non-explicitly and a formulated approach for identifying these uses is necessary if one is to ascertain the role of Genesis 1-3 in the document.

The term 'allusion', unlike 'quotation', is subject to a lack of precision. It is not surprising, therefore, if biblical scholars have used the word liberally, perhaps even as a default that denotes everything that does not come under the category of quotation. The present task, therefore, is to ask what basis there may be for making the claim that one text is alluding to another. Answering such a question is not a straightforward matter; there are only a handful of scholars who, in referring to an 'allusion', attempt at the same time to offer criteria underlying their choice of the term. This allowance for vagueness does not result in precision when describing a wide variety of intertextual[1]

---

[1] J. A. SANDERS, 'Intertextuality and Canon,' in S. L. COOK and S. C. WINTER (eds.), *On the Way to Nineveh* (Atlanta: Scholars Press, 1999) p. 316; states that the term 'intertextuality' is used with three basic senses: (1) interrelation of blocks of text in close proximity; (2) the function of older literature cited or in some way alluded to in later literature; and (3) the interrelation of text and reader. S. MOYISE, 'Intertextuality and the Study of the Old Testament in the New Testament,' in S. MOYISE (ed.), *The Old Testament in*

resonances, sometimes inconsistent in nature, to one and the same expression.[2] Is it possible to attain a more technical understanding of allusion, or is one to accept that confusion or amorphous generalisation is inherent to the term? For example, on the one hand, there can be cases in which an 'allusion' is indisputable as such, while, on the other hand, non-explicit references to other documents or sources seem little more than conjecture. For the sake of clarity in this study, it is thus necessary to formulate a definition that emerges from an analysis of problems encountered in *Musar leMevin* than to abandon the expression altogether or to use it without sufficient transparency. Therefore, the ensuing discussion, with reference to the contiguous areas of study (New Testament, early Jewish sources, and other Dead Sea documents), will attempt to delineate 'allusions' within the wider context of intertextuality and early Jewish exegesis.[3]

To further complicate the discussion about the use or reception of scripture in *Musar leMevin* and other Jewish literature from the Graeco-Roman period is defining what is meant by 'scripture'. Is the use of the term 'scripture' anachronistic if used in the present discussion? For instance, the Law, Prophets and Writings are clearly important and authoritative, however, they took various forms. An example of this are the fifteen 'non-biblical' psalms discovered in the caves around Qumran, six were previously known (e.g. Psalm 154, Syriac Ps. 2, 11Q5 xviii) and nine are new (e.g. 11Q5 xix 'Plea for Deliverance', xxvii 'Davids Composition'[4]; 11Q11 'Songs Against Demons'; and 4Q88 viii 'Apostrophe to Zion', ix 'Eschatological Hymn', x 'Apostrophe to Judah'[5]). There is nothing to indicate that these Psalms were not considered canonical by some Jewish communities.[6] Another issue is the acceptance of other works as authoritative. The book of *Jubilees* is cited as authoritative on at least two occasions (4Q228 9 introduces a citation with 'כן כתוב'; see also

---

the New Testament: Essays in Honour of J. L. North (JSNTSup 189; Sheffield: Sheffield Academic Press, 2000) pp. 14-41, offers three influences between 'text and subtext': (1) Intertextual Echo, the influence of the old upon the new; (2) Dialogical Intertextuality, the influence of the old and the new upon each other; and (3) Postmodern Intertextuality, the influence of all other texts, especially those known to the reader.

The term 'intertextual' will be used in this chapter to denote the occurrence of earlier literary traditions upon later writings; see SANDERS' point (2) and MOYISE'S point (1).

[2] So, for instance, in the case of *Musar leMevin* there is little consensus for the identification of the allusion to either Seth/Sheth in 4Q417 1 i 15-17.

[3] See M. FISHBANE, *Biblical Interpretation in Ancient Israel* (Oxford: Clarendon Press, 1988) for a general introduction to practices of Jewish exegesis.

[4] *DJD XXIII.*

[5] *DJD XVI.*

[6] One might consider that the LXX establishes canonical psalms, however, we cannot speak of *the* Septuagint or use it to establish what works were canonical for an array of communities. In fact, the author of the Lords Prayer in Matthew's Gospel may have considered a 'non-canonical' psalm such as 11Q5 xix as authoritative.

CD xvi 2-4) and suggests it may have held a scriptural status by some communities. The importance of re-written biblical texts generally is not fully understood and it is conceivable that they had an authoritative role. There is also the well-known reference to Enoch in Jude 14, which indicates the respect of this tradition by the author. One might point to many other indications that various communities adopted Enochic traditions and held them to be authoritative.

One cannot speak straightforwardly about the use of scripture in relation to 'allusion', to do so is to speak about the formation of canon, the shape of individual books and to conceive of a monolithic Judaism rather than a number of diverse Jewish traditions.[7] Therefore, it is more accurate to speak of a variety of biblical traditions, which include authoritative compositions that are no longer considered to be 'scripture' ('Old Testament'[8], Hebrew Bible, etc.).[9] Discovering non-explicit uses of biblical traditions, it will be argued, is at times dependent on shedding the notion of the use of scripture. This is not to debate that traditions are derived from biblical documents, but that in order to discover allusions one must look for the earliest preceding

---

[7] 'Allusion' suggests 'reception', one cannot read an ancient literary work in search of allusions without taking into account that an interpretive process has already occurred in creating the allusion. Interpretive actions are influenced by a literary and social milieu.

[8] The use of the designation 'Old Testament' as a vague designation for Jewish traditions that an author would have deemed to be authoritative is unacceptable. It is inherently biased terminology, as are 'B.C.' and 'A.D.', it suggests conclusions of canon formation and it promotes the exclusion of traditions that adapted biblical materials. Furthermore, it is a confessional designation that is not transferable to theological conversations on works that are not part of the New Testament. For a discussion of this terminology see R. B. HAYS and J. B. GREEN, 'The Use of the Old Testament by New Testament Writers,' in J. B. GREEN (ed.) *Hearing the New Testament: Strategies for Interpretation*, (Grand Rapids: Eerdmans, 1995), 223–25. It is preferable to speak of 'biblical traditions' since it is sufficiently broad to include documents preserved in the Masoretic Tradition as well as literature that knows traditions similar to it.

[9] H. H. D. WILLIAMS, III, *The Wisdom of the Wise: The Presence and Function of Scripture within 1 Cor. 1:18-3:23* (AGAJU 49; Leiden: Brill, 2001) pp. 15-16, makes a clear distinction between 'intertestamental literature' and 'Scripture'; however, it should be noted that portions of the Hebrew Bible are themselves 'intertestamental' compositions. He cites more than ten significant contributions of reading Paul's use of biblical traditions in 1 Cor 1-3 in light of Jewish literature from the Graeco-Roman period and concludes: 'While many of the insights of the these investigations can be gleaned for this present study, further attention must be paid to the Scripture texts that have influenced the contemporary ideas of much early Jewish literature.' The distinction between scripture and interpretive traditions used authoritatively is not clear in this context. Books in the Hebrew Bible interpret other books in the Hebrew Bible written at earlier periods (e.g. the Garden of Eden is alluded to in Ezek). The contention here is not that a tripartite grouping of scriptural documents were/were not accepted in Judaisms of the period, but that multiple forms of the tradition existed. Furthermore, when speaking about allusion we are interested in the literary world of an author. Whether one studies 2nd c. BCE Hebrew Texts or NT compositions, authoritative traditions beside the Hebrew Bible (or LXX), written and oral, exert significant influence.

referent. A wide variety of biblical traditions may be identified as referents for allusions and would have been considered authoritative and formative for our author(s).

Scholarship on the use of biblical traditions at Qumran has focused mainly on categories of explicit citation[10], introductory formula[11], 'pesher'[12], anthology[13], and re-written Bible.[14] Similarly, in New Testament scholarship the vast number of works that study intertextuality are concerned primarily

---

[10] For a general introduction to the use of scripture in writings from Qumran, see G. VERMES: 'The Qumran Interpretation of Scripture in its Historical Setting,' in VERMES, *Post-Biblical Jewish Studies* (Leiden: E. J. Brill, 1975) pp. 37-49.

[11] D. I. BREWER, *Techniques and Assumptions in Jewish Exegesis before 70 CE* (Tübingen: J.C.B. Mohr [Paul Siebeck], 1992); W. H. BROWNLEE, 'Biblical Interpretation in the Dead Sea Scrolls,' in *BA* 14 (1951): 54-76; F. F. BRUCE, *Biblical Exegesis in the Qumran Texts* (London: Tynedale Press, 1959); M. FISHBANE, 'Use, Authority and Interpretation of Mikra at Qumran,' in M. J. MULDER and H. SYSLING (eds.), *Mikra: Text, Translation, Reading and Interpretation of the Hebrew Bible in Ancient Judaism and Early Christianity. Compendia Rerum Iudaicarum ad Novum Testamentum.* II. 1 (Philadelphia: Fortress Press, 1988) pp. 339-77; J. A. FITZMYER, 'The Use of Explicit Old Testament Quotations in Qumran Literature and in the New Testament,' in *NTS* 7 (1960-1): 297-33; M. H. GOTTSTEIN, 'Bible Quotations in the Sectarian Dead Sea Scrolls,' in *VT* 3 (1953): 79-82; F. L. HORTON, 'Formulas of Introduction in the Qumran Literature,' in *RevQ* 7 (1969-71): 505-14; J. L. KUGEL, *In Potiphar's House: The Interpretive Life of Biblical Texts* (Cambridge, MA: Harvard University Press, 1990); *Traditions of the Bible: A Guide to the Bible As It Was at the Start of the Common Era* (Cambridge, MA: Harvard University Press, 1999); M. R. LEHMANN, 'Midrashic Parallels to Selected Qumran Texts,' in *RevQ* 3 (1961-62): 545-51; B. M. METZGER, 'The Formulas Introducing Quotations of Scripture in the New Testament and the Mishnah,' in *JBL* 70 (1951): 297-307; B. J. ROBERTS, 'Bible Exegesis and Fulfillment in Qumran,' in P. R. ACKROYD and B. LINDARS (eds.), *Words and Meaning: Essays Presented to David Winton Thomas* (Cambridge: University Press, 1968) pp. 195-207; E. SLOMOVIC, 'Towards an Understanding of the Exegesis in the Dead Sea Scrolls,' in *RevQ* 7 (1969-71): 3-15; J. C. TREVER, 'The Qumran Covenanters and Their Use of Scripture,' in *Per* 39 (1958): 127-38; S. WEITZMAN, 'Allusion, Artifice, and Exile in the Hymn of Tobit,' in *JBL* 115 (1996): 49-61; P. WERNBERG-MØLLER, 'Some Reflections on the Biblical Material in the Manual of Discipline,' in *ST* 9 (1955): 40-66.

[12] G. J. BROOKE, 'Qumran Pesher. Towards the Redefinition of a Genre,' in *RevQ* 10 (1979-81): 483-503; A. FINKEL, 'The Pesher of Dreams and Scriptures,' in *RevQ* 4 (1963-4): 357-70; M. FISHBANE, 'The Qumran Pesher and Traits of Ancient Hermeneutics,' in *PWJCS* 6 (1977) I: 97-114; L. I. RABINOWITZ, 'Pesher/Pittaron: Its Biblical Meaning and Significance in the Qumran Literature,' in *RevQ* 8 (1972-75): 219-32; J. A. SANDERS, 'Habakkuk in Qumran, Paul and the Old Testament,' in *JR* 39 (1959): 232-44.

[13] G. J. BROOKE, *Exegesis at Qumran: 4QFlorilegium in its Jewish Context* (JSOTSup 29, Sheffield: Sheffield Academic Press, 1985).

[14] J. H. CHARLESWORTH, 'The Pseudepigrapha as Biblical Exegesis,' in C. A. EVANS and W. F. STINESPRING (eds.), *Early Jewish and Christian Exegesis: Studies in Memory of William Hugh Brownlee* (Atlanta: Scholars Press, 1987) pp. 139-52; B. N. FISK, *Do You Not Remember: Scripture, Story and Exegesis in the Rewritten Bible of Pseudo-Philo* (JSPSup 37; Sheffield: Sheffield Academic Press, 2001).

with the explicit use of the Hebrew Bible and Septuagint.[15] Discussions of allusions within biblical, early Jewish, and New Testament studies are much fewer in number and among them only some develop a clear methodology for approaching the issue.[16] In the case of the Apocalypse of John, non-explicit biblical traditions are used quite densely and yet discussions regarding approach and methodology for identifying such usages are almost non-existent.[17] Study of the use of non-explicit traditions in the Dead Sea Scrolls has centred almost exclusively on the *Hodayot* while there is almost complete silence with respect to the other documents. Due to the paucity of contributions that concern themselves with understanding anything less than formal citations of traditions, any scholarship that seeks to develop an approach to identifying non-explicit traditions should be considered.

The word 'allusion' alone suggests an ambiguity that renders the discussion of occurrences difficult to pursue along lines of categorical paradigms. Therefore, a large extent of scholarship that attempts to define and

---

[15] See for example H. ANDERSON, 'The Old Testament in Mark's Gospel,' in J. M. EFIRD (ed.), *The Use of the Old Testament in the New and Other Essays: Studies in Honor of W. F. Stinespring* (Durham: Duke University Press, 1972) pp. 280-306; J. C. BECKER, 'Echoes and Intertexuality: On the Role of Scripture in Paul's Theology,' in C. A. EVANS and J. A. SANDERS (eds.), *Paul and the Scriptures of Israel* (JSNTSup 83; Sheffield: Sheffield Academic Press, 1993) pp. 64-9; M. BLACK, 'The Theological Appropriation of the Old Testament by the New Testament,' in *SJT* 39 (1986): 1-17; R. L. BRAWLEY, *Text to Text Pours Forth Speech: Voices of Scripture in Luke-Acts* (Bloomington: Indiana University Press, 1995); C. A. EVANS, 'Listening for Echoes of Interpreted Scripture,' in C. A. EVANS and J. A. SANDERS (eds.), *Paul and the Scriptures of Israel* (JSNTSup, 83; Sheffield: Sheffield Academic Press, 1993) pp. 47-51; M. P. MILLER, 'Targum, Midrash and the Use of the Old Testament in the New Testament,' in *JSJ* 2 (1971): 29-82; C. D. STANLEY, *Paul and the Language of Scripture: Citation Technique in the Pauline Epistles and Contemporary Literature* (Cambridge: Cambridge University Press, 1992).

[16] B. S. ROSNER, for instance, does not develop a conversation concerning Paul's use of non-explicit references to earlier traditions, he simply understands Paul's use of 'scripture' to be simply implicit and instinctual ROSNER, *Paul, Scripture and Ethics: a Study of 1 Corinthians 5-7* (Leiden: Brill, 1994) p. 17.

[17] R. LONGENECKER, *Biblical Exegesis in the Apostolic Period* (Grand Rapids: Eerdmans, 1975) pp. 12, 57 writes in his introduction that the authors of the NT used 'biblical materials' in an 'allusive' manner and later adds that 'the distinction between a direct quotation and an allusion is of course notoriously difficult' and can be 'somewhat arbitrary'. However, outside of these brief comments no discussion on 'allusion' is forthcoming. The NT composition with arguably the most allusions to biblical traditions, is the Johannine Apocalypse. In fact, there is no formal citation of an earlier tradition anywhere in the book. MOYISE, in his study of *The Old Testament in the Book of Revelation* (Sheffield: Sheffield Academic Press, 1995), never develops the conversation further than identifying and arguing for specific occurrences in the apocalypse. A recent contribution within NT scholarship that addresses a methodology for identifying non-explicit uses of biblical traditions comes from S. SHUM, *Paul's Use of Isaiah in Romans* (WUNT2 156; Tübingen: Mohr Siebeck, 2002) pp. 5-11; SHUM interacts with R. HAYS' (see below) criteria of identification but does not develop a methodology beyond these.

describe occurrences of allusions has resorted to analogies in order to further the discussion. As an attempt is made in this study to clarify the nature and function of non-explicit intertextual occurrences in *Musar leMevin*, it will become apparent that analogy is often one of the few ways by which to communicate or illustrate usage. So, for instance, many elements of the genre of the *Hodayot* are not shared by *Musar leMevin*; one important similarity does exist however: both documents formulate theological conceptions largely on the basis of non-explicit occurrences of a tradition.

The works within New Testament studies that address non-explicit biblical traditions will also be explored below in search of a viable methodology. It should be noted that there is an all too frequent tendency within New Testament scholarship to make facile claims about the occurrence of an allusion.[18] Furthermore, in the case of non-explicit use of biblical traditions the field of possible referents available to ancient writers may be articulated more accurately. The form of a tradition as it appears in a later text may be an allusion to several layers or streams of a tradition which, though ultimately derived from a biblical source, have acquired an independent life of their own and are also now in some way a 'biblical tradition'. There is often a failure to recognise the literary life of a tradition outside of the scriptural canon that often circulated for hundreds of years. Identifying the strands of independent growth and variation are indispensable if one wishes to determine more precisely the nature of an intertextual occurrence.

Musar leMevin may know a tradition that adapts, re-writes, or interprets a biblical source and formulates various theological constructions on a document that is several steps removed from the biblical text *per se*. The document will be studied from a history of reception approach that seeks to discover various streams of a tradition as well as to understand the motivation behind particular interpretations.

The task of identifying non-explicit uses of a biblical tradition in *Musar leMevin*, as opposed to explicit citations, is complicated by the occurrence of re-written and/or paraphrased portions of Genesis 1-3 in the document. It is not appropriate to speak of occurrences of 'quotations' in the book of *Jubilees* as the document more accurately re-writes the biblical books of Genesis and the beginning of Exodus. In the case of at least one column of *Musar leMevin* (4Q423 1, 2 i), there is the occurrence of a paraphrased account, or perhaps re-written narrative, of the Garden of Eden. In such instances, designations

---

[18] See for instance C. A. KIMBALL, *Jesus' Exposition of the Old Testament in Luke's Gospel* (JSNTSup 94, Sheffield: Sheffield Academic Press, 1994) pp. 47-48, who comments on allusions in Luke: '...the works that list OT citations and allusions in the NT do not agree completely on definitions or on the identification of such references in Luke and the NT. Even the editions of the two standard Greek texts do not agree. The UBS3 text lists 24 Lukan references as OT quotations and does not deal with allusions. The NA26 text italicizes 31 references as quotations and lists 525 allusions (inclusive of the 31 quotations).'

such as 'allusion' or 'quotation' may be inadequate and inaccurately describe the manner in which a tradition is being used. It may be that an examination of Genesis creation traditions will uncover other columns in the document that paraphrase Genesis 1-3 rather than use it explicitly.

2. Non-Explicit Traditions in the New Testament

Since its publication, Richard Hays' book *Echoes of Scripture in the Letters of Paul* has been frequently cited in discussions concerned with the use of biblical traditions in the New Testament.[19] Hays is one of the first to apply scholarship on intertextuality in English literature to the realm of the New Testament's use of non-explicit citations of biblical sources. Thus, an analysis of Hays' proposed methodology and a critical examination of the approach he applies to identifying and discussing non-explicit uses of biblical sources will serve as a point of departure for identifying similar occurrences in *Musar leMevin*.

An analysis of Hays' discourse on intertextuality as developed for application in English poetry as analogous and helpful for understanding Jewish literature from the Graeco-Roman period is significant. Hays recognises that research on literary allusion and echo is far more developed and widespread in the academia of English poetry than that in biblical scholarship. He attempts to adopt research into the theory behind intertextual studies in English literature in order to understand and illuminate the nature of Paul's use of non-explicit biblical sources. Hays' work is important because it seeks to develop and refine approaches to non-explicit citations to a greater degree than scholars have previously attempted. The benefits of his approach will be evaluated below and at the end of this chapter criteria developed in discussions about allusions in English literature as adopted by Hays will be further evaluated.

Notably, Hays begins his methodological discussion by briefly rejecting the category of 'midrash', which he regards as neither helpful nor pertinent.[20] Part of his criticism is due to the generic meaning of the word midrash and the inaccuracy of applying it to almost any exegetical activity in either Jewish or Christian compositions. Hays also criticises notions that suggest rabbinic midrashic compositions as the background for understanding Pauline thought.

---

[19] R. HAYS, *Echoes of Scripture in the Letters of Paul* (New Haven: Yale University Press, 1989).

[20] HAYS, *Echoes of Scripture*, pp. 10-14.

It should be, he argues, that Paul is more accurately seen as the background for midrash and not *vice versa*.[21]

While such criticisms should serve as words of caution, they forget the aim any approach should seek: a wider conversation with related literary phenomena that can further elucidate our discourse on intertextual occurrences. The dismissal, or minimising, of nearly contemporary relatives of the New Testament canon is puzzling especially when it stands juxtaposed to suggested conversation partners like Alexander Pope, Yeats, or Milton. The term midrash certainly can be used to cover over a 'multitude of exegetical sins,' but it can be used responsibly and cautiously as one of the closest relatives to early Jewish compositions. Furthermore, one might observe that there are interpretative practices in documents from Qumran that resemble later midrashic practices. There are peshers, for instance, that are not always restricted to one work (e.g. 4Q171).[22] It is widely recognised that the interpretive rules known as *middot*, which are defined in later Rabbinic literature, are at play in much earlier literature. An important aspect of midrash is the style of organising scriptural citations. It is not always clear what organising principles are at work in newly discovered documents from Qumran or whether the closest relative is indeed midrash. There are, in fact, several works from the Qumran library that have been designated as midrashim (4Q249 *'Midrash Sefer Moshe'*; 4Q174, 177 *'Eschatological Midrash'*).

More importantly, Hays' aim is to apply intertextual approaches that have developed within literary criticism on English poetry to the letters of Paul in hopes of illuminating scriptural allusions and citations therein.[23] Whereas for Paul, Hays argues, the canon of scripture is the Law, Prophets and Writings, elsewhere the body of traditions, or canon, for intertextual reflection include Spenser, Shakespeare, Milton, Wordsworth, Stevens and so forth. He begins this exploration by citing the works of Julia Kristeva and Roland Barthes who define intertextuality as: *the study of the semiotic matrix within which a text's acts of signification occur.* This definition of intertextuality shapes Hays' approach to Paul and he deduces his intent to go beyond the historical-critical

---

[21] Whether midrash is the background for Paul or Paul for midrash is not necessarily relevant. The well-known occurrence in 1 Cor 10.4 'for they drank from the supernatural Rock *which followed them*, and the Rock was Christ' is a non-biblical tradition preserved also by midrashic sources and serves to elucidate Paul's use of a tradition. See *Midrash Sifra Numbers* 11.21; B. Talmud *Shabbath* 35a, *Avot* 5.6, *Sukka* 3a-3b; *Midrash Numbers Rabbah* 19.25-26; *T. Sukka* 3.11; and *T. Onqelos Numbers* 21.17.

[22] See P.W. FLINT, *The Dead Sea Scrolls and the Book of Psalms* (STDJ 17; Leiden: Brill, 1997).

[23] HAYS, *Echoes of Scripture*, p. 15.

approach, which seeks genetic and causal explanations in order to focus rather on describing the 'system of codes or conventions that the texts manifest'.[24]

Hays argues that the semiotic matrix for Paul is clearly Israel's scripture. The scriptures are a source of symbols and metaphors that are deeply imbedded in Paul's mind and 'condition his perception of the world'. For Hays, Paul's use of scripture is viewed progressively less as an exegetical or expository occurrence and more of a poetical usage.[25] The difference between an authoritative source, such as biblical texts, and an influential literary milieu, are distinctions that are never quite spelled out by Hays. Furthermore, the importance of speaking broadly of traditions that influenced a Jewish author of the period that were brimming with biblical codes and conventions should take a more central role in Hays' semiotic matrix.

Another influential factor in Hays' approach is John Hollander who has written on echoes of biblical traditions in Milton's Paradise Lost. Hollander, as cited by Hays, seeks to 'consider a way of alluding that is inherently poetic rather than expository, and makes a new metaphor rather than learned gestures'.[26] Hollander also uses the terms 'revisionary power,' 'allusive echo,' and 'new figuration' when describing the natural distortion that occurs in intertextual echo. It is the task of those who study literary echo first to identify an echo and, second, to give account of the new figurations generated by them. Hays appeals to an example provided by Robert Alter to illustrate this task. In the example below are Yeats' quatrain, 'The Nineteenth Century and After' in parallel with Matthew Arnold's 'Dover Beach'. These texts are used to illustrate an 'allusive echo':

Yeats	Matthew Arnold
Though the great song return no more There's keen delight in what we have: The rattle of pebbles on the shore Under the receding wave.	The Sea of Faith Was once, too, all the full, and round earth's shore Lay like the folds of a bright girdle furled. But now I only hear Its melancholy, long, withdrawing roar, Retreating. . .

---

[24] HAYS, *Echoes of Scripture*, p. 15.

[25] HAYS, *Echoes of Scripture*, p. 24, summarises Paul's use of scripture in the statement: 'Paul's citations of Scripture often function not as proofs but as tropes: they generate new meanings by linking the earlier text (Scripture) to the later (Paul's discourses) in such a way as to produce unexpected correspondences, correspondences that suggest more than they assert'.

[26] HAYS, *Echoes of Scripture*, p. 19.

Hays, as both Hollander and Alter, uses this illustration as an instance where Arnold's work is described as 'recollection' and not 'citation'. There is no case for quotation or allusion here, but rather echo. One of the properties of echo in this illustration is that allusive echo at times may operate as a diachronic trope. Diachronic trope is a phrase substituted with 'transumption' and 'metalepsis' by Hollander. These three terms are used to describe an instance when a 'literary echo links the text in which it occurs to an earlier text, the figurative effect of the echo can lie in the unstated or suppressed (transumed) points of resonance between the two texts'.[27] Allusive echo, Hays explains, is the instance of an interplay between two texts when text B is best understood with a knowledge of text A. This allusive echo, or metalepsis, 'places the reader within a field of whispered or unstated correspondences.' Hays borrows from Hollander the term 'resonance' and speaks with the phrases 'internal resonances' or 'cave of resonant signification.' Here Hays replaces Kristeva and Barthes' 'semiotic matrix' with Hollander's 'cave of resonant signification' to emphasise once again that it is to scripture one must turn in order to understand the literary influence on Paul.

Hays uses Philippians 1.19 as a point of departure to illustrate how echoes of biblical sources function in Paul's epistles. In this discussion the distinction between echo and allusion is placed on a scale with quotation on one end, progressing to allusion and then echo. The difference between the terms is the 'semantic distance between the source and the reflecting surface'.[28] The greatest difficulty is when an echo nears 'vanishing point,' that is when the reader is no longer able to determine whether there is an echo or not. Hays offers criteria for identifying echoes, a term here identified with 'intertextual fusion that generates new meaning,' which he entitles *The Locus of Echo: Five Options*. These five options are composed to answer questions regarding claims of intertextual meaning. The purpose of listing these is to highlight the importance of distinguishing the fine line between the task of identifying a non-explicit occurrence and understanding the role of the hermeneutical event in deciphering the occurrence.

(1) The hermeneutical event occurs in Paul's mind. Claims about intertextual meaning effects are valid where it can credibly be demonstrated that Paul intended such effects.
(2) The hermeneutical events occur in the original readers of the letter. Claims about intertextual meaning effects are valid where it can credibly be demonstrated that the Philippians would likely have perceived such effects.
(3) The intertextual fusion occurs in the text itself. (In this case, we cannot properly speak of a hermeneutical event.) We have not access to the author or to the original readers; we have only the text. Consequently, assertions about Paul's intention are intelligible only as statements about the implied author, and assertions about 'the Philippians' are intelligible only

---

[27] HAYS, *Echoes of Scripture*, p. 20.
[28] HAYS, *Echoes of Scripture*, p. 23.

as statements about the implied reader. Implied author and implied reader are epiphenomenona of the text's rhetoric. Consequently, claims about intertextual meaning effects are valid where it can credibly be demonstrated that they are in some sense properties of the text's own rhetorical or literary structure.

(4) The hermeneutical event occurs in my act of reading. Claims about intertextual meaning effects are valid if I say so. In other words, the perception of intertextual effects has emerged from my own reading experience, and no further validation is necessary.

(5) The hermeneutical event occurs in a community of interpretation. Claims about intertextual meaning effects are valid where it can credibly be demonstrated that they conform to the hermeneutical conventions of a particular community of readers. (Such communities can, of course, be variously composed and disposed: the church, the guild of biblical scholars, the guild of literary critics, the readers of this book – and each of these communities is, of course, fractured into various schismatic schools and sub-communities).[29]

Hays' intention is to hold these criteria together in creative tension rather than systematically apply them. In the process of developing an approach to identifying and discussing intertextual occurrences, the hermeneutical event as a tool for deciphering the likelihood of a citation may be raised. In embracing these five options Hays acknowledges one key hermeneutical axiom: there is an 'authentic analogy...between what the text meant and what it means'.[30] Hays, as the reader, may detect the echoes similarly to the first century audience, being informed and moulded by scripture himself. For him, hermeneutics plays a significant role in his approach to identifying allusions in Paul's writings. Asking questions regarding where the hermeneutical event takes place is important to consider and will be returned to.

Hays does not fully express an important element of detecting literary allusions and echoes. There are elements of a reading mechanism that go beyond familiarity with the Hebrew Bible (or LXX). The way in which we read is as critical as opposed to pre-critical readers. The better read one is in the literature of the period the closer one comes to the thought world of the author. The reader is able to make progressively more connections to similar vocabulary, themes and arguments. The reading mechanism is not just about being informed about the content of a biblical tradition, but being inducted into an entirely different way of reading itself. Entering into a different way of interacting with a written tradition, free of parameters built by modern readership, is as important as familiarity with the Hebrew Bible. Present day concerns, such as 'original meaning', logical progression and grouping ideas around our own themes are not the concerns of early Jewish interpreters. In addition, a modern reader is not immersed in the linguistic or cultural world of the audience and has no way of evaluating the difference between 'scriptural' language that has become common place speech and 'scripture' itself.

---

[29] HAYS, *Echoes of Scripture*, pp. 26-27.
[30] HAYS, *Echoes of Scripture*, p. 27.

Hays provides a list of criteria that he uses when identifying the presence and meaning of scriptural echoes in Pauline epistles. This summary represents critically developed criteria that may assist us to find an interplay between earlier traditions in a later work.[31]

(1) Availability. Was the proposed source of the echo available to the author and/or original readers?

(2) Volume. The volume of an echo is determined primarily by the degree of explicit repetition of words or syntactical patterns, but other factors may also be relevant: how distinctive or prominent is the precursor text within Scripture, and how much rhetorical stress does the echo receive in Paul's discourse?

(3) Recurrence. How often does Paul elsewhere cite or allude to the same scriptural passage?

(4) Thematic Coherence. How well does the alleged echo fit into the line of argument that Paul is developing? Is its meaning effect consonant with other quotations in the same letter or elsewhere in the Pauline corpus? Do the images and ideas of the proposed precursor text illuminate Paul's argument?

(5) Historical Plausibility. Could Paul have intended the alleged meaning effect? Could his readers have understood it?

(6) History of Interpretation. Have other readers, both critical and pre-critical, heard the same echoes? The readings of our predecessors can both check and stimulate our perception of scriptural echoes in Paul.

(7) Satisfaction. With or without clear confirmation from the other criteria listed here, does the proposed reading make sense? Does it illuminate the surrounding discourse? Does it produce for the reader a satisfying account of the effect of the intertextual relation?[32]

Hays suggests these guidelines for detecting intertextual occurrences without intending that they serve as strict principles for identifying allusions or echoes. Hays speaks of the 'spontaneous power' of 'intertextual conjunctions' that throw 'sparks' and 'fragments of flame on their rising heat'. Hays concludes that any identification and interpretation of scriptural echoes which seeks to understand Paul's intention is a matter of historical speculation. Scriptural echoes are acts of figuration, and the figures used may be read and understood differently by later recipients of Paul's letters. Paul's non-explicit use of scripture, as categorised by Hays, is poetic on the one hand and a source from which he derives word plays or invents new meaning for familiar phrases on the other.[33]

From the outset, Hays writes admiringly of the extensive work that has been accomplished in intertextual studies in English literature. A poetic composition's echo of its 'semiotic matrix' may indeed be a new way of speaking about the influence of biblical documents on Paul's compositions, however, how valuable is that discussion for the study of intertextuality in

---

[31] For the sake of brevity, HAYS explanatory comments that follow each category have been edited here.

[32] HAYS, *Echoes of Scripture*, pp. 29-31.

[33] HAYS, *Echoes of Scripture*, p. 33.

Jewish literature from the Graeco-Roman period? One contribution of turning to English poetry for approaching early Jewish literature are the lists of criteria that may be further adopted for locating allusions in Jewish literature from the Graeco-Roman period. While the nuances of some of these criteria could be debated, it is clear that the lists provided by Hays are a helpful step forward.

One of the major points that Hays returns to repeatedly is the influence of scripture on Paul. It is precisely on this point that the proximity of the analogy between Paul and English poetry can deteriorate. There is no doubt that an analogy can be drawn between Arnold's use of Yeats and Paul's use of Deuteronomy, but they are significantly distant relatives. The discussions underway in the field of English literature may be relevant for interpreting Paul and asking general hermeneutical questions, but the degree of their relevance is limited. Hays' approach is rather lop-sided in that it makes much use of a number of works on the subject in English literature, but does not fully recognise the character and difference of authoritative hagiographic Jewish literature that received biblical traditions over a relatively long period of time.

Intertextuality in English literature is certainly germane in a discussion of the use of traditions in early Judaism, but caution should be taken in evaluating where the contribution lies. Hays views Paul through a more confessional approach that conceives of the task at hand as better understanding the use of the Old Testament in the New Testament. Thus, his analogies with English literature are attempted in a synthetic paradigm that conceives of Paul ('b') poetically assimilating scripture ('a') into a theological composition. Hays has since responded to similar criticisms and emphasised that Paul was in dialogue with other interpreters of the scriptures.[34] However, the reason for adapting a tradition non-explicitly differs for Jewish writers in the Graeco-Roman period than, say, for Yeats. There is less interest in a poetic interface as, for instance, adapting an authoritative tradition to support a theological idea or agenda. The degree to which a tradition is used, at times and in some early Jewish literature, has more to do with how well the earlier tradition avails itself within, perhaps, an exhortation, cosmological treatise or theological precept.

Hays' work has been well received by the world of New Testament scholarship as a significant contribution in hermeneutics and Pauline exegesis.[35] But to what extent can Hays' work be said to provide the basis for

---

[34] R. HAYS, 'On the Rebound: A Response to Critiques of *Echoes of Scripture in the Letters of Paul*,' in C. A. EVANS and J. A. SANDERS (eds.) *Paul and the Scriptures of Israel* (JSOTSup 83; Sheffield: Sheffield Academic Press, 1993) pp. 70-73.

[35] R. E. CIAMPA, *The Presence and Function of Scripture in Galatians 1 and 2* (WUNT2 102; Tübingen: Mohr Siebeck, 1998) pp. 24-25; K. H. JOBES, 'Jerusalem, our Mother: Metalepsis and Intertextuality in Gal. 4:21-31,' in *WTJ* 55 (1993): 299-320. See also reviews

a methodology and approach to the larger task of interpreting early Jewish literature, specifically *Musar leMevin*? Hays' application of his own guidelines is not to be questioned nor is the value of the conclusions drawn from his careful reading of selected Pauline passages. Indeed, for the present study, Hays' seven tests of non-explicit use of a tradition offer an embarkation point for developing an approach to *Musar leMevin*. Moreover, the contribution of English literature for expressing a hermeneutical event in an intertextual occurrence appears to be significant. However, in the process of formulating a history of reception approach it may be questioned whether there is anything more in English literature besides an eloquent vocabulary for the formation of the current discussion.

Francis Watson has adopted elements of Hays work that warrant mention here. On the basis of the brief article Hays wrote in response to criticism he received, Watson envisages biblical interpretation by Paul as a 'three-way conversation'.[36] The three conversation partners described by Watson are: (S) Scripture; (P) Pauline texts; and (J) non-Christian Jewish texts. In what way can this three-way conversation be applied to documents outside of the New Testament, particularly *Musar leMevin*? As discussed throughout, there is no clear distinction between 'scripture' and 'Jewish [hagiographic] texts'. Furthermore, it would be methodologically unsound to speak of a three way conversation between: (S) 'scripture'; (J) 'Jewish texts'; and (M) *Musar leMevin*, since the distinction between scriptures and Jewish texts is ambiguous. Watson adopts Hays' recent language of a 'conversation' between Paul and his two other sources. However, one may question the appropriateness of 'conversation' language since it implies listening to the *message* of another text. While it is not helpful to dismiss this language, in the case of re-written Bible it is less a conversation as it is a creative adaptation of *components* of another literary work. In seeking to describe the appropriation and growth of traditions in early Jewish literature distancing our own exegetical tradition and style of reading from that of other earlier readers of Jewish literature is important. The approach to Jewish literature from the Graeco-Roman period by Pauline scholarship is beneficial in advancing a scholarly approach, but caution should be taken in developing categories that may not be applicable more broadly.

Watson writes that 'to interpret is always to interact with a text, and it is also to be *constrained* by a text'.[37] The task of interpretation always needs a subject or it would cease to be interpretation. What does it mean to be

_____

by C.A. EVANS in *CBQ* 53 (1991): 496-98 and C.L. STOCKHAUSEN in *JBL* 52 (1992): 155-157. B. D. SOMMER, 'Exegesis, Allusion and Intertextuality in the Hebrew Bible: A Response to Lyle Eslinger,' in *VT* 46 (1996), p. 484, n. 9, criticises the usefulness of some of HAYS' seven criteria.

[36] F. WATSON, *Paul and the Hermeneutics of Faith*, (London: T & T Clark, 2004) pp. 3-5.

[37] WATSON, *Paul and the Hermeneutics*, p. 4, italics his.

'constrained' by a text? Not only is there a radical difference between the exegetical practices of pre-critical and critical readers, but also the presuppositions, assumptions and traditions an interpreter brings to the text alter the meaning of 'constraint'.[38] In comparison with modern readers pre-critical readers are not constrained (e.g. by contradiction; narrative flow) by a text, at least not in the way that we may be constrained. Interpretive forms such as pesher and re-written Bible are foreign practices for modern readers. Ancient writers often did not think in the same categories modern readers do. Attempts to understand pre-critical modes of construction by way of a critical methodology have their place; however, shedding our critical approach could bring us into closer alignment with the ancient reader.[39] Many authors derive significance for traditions by altering them, adding to them, removing them from their literary context, narrowing their focus, and creating anthologies that are not necessarily thematic or chronological.

Since in many respects ancient readers interpreted biblical traditions differently from modern readers, the identification of non-explicit traditions cannot be conceived of as a relationship between scripture and *Musar leMevin*. Doing so would be to assume that we find the same traditions when we read the Hebrew Bible as the author(s) of *Musar leMevin* would have. Without the companionship of other early Jewish exegetical traditions and hermeneutical approaches of early Jewish readers, the biblical traditions are not visible to us in the same way they were to a reader (or hearer) of the period. Therefore, in the case of allusions as opposed to citations one cannot make a clear distinction between scripture and tradition.

In addition to Hays, Dale Allison in his work on Matthew's typology of Moses has a helpful discussion for determining the occurrence of a non-explicit tradition.[40] Allison's criteria may be compared with Hays. In seeking to identify allusions Allison presents two sets of guidelines that serve to narrow the probability of an intertextual occurrence. The first list provided addresses the issue concerning the various ways one text can be linked to another. Allison's six suggestions are summarised here:

---

[38] See S. FISH, *Is There a Text in This Class* (Harvard: Harvard University Press, 1980).

[39] Perhaps 'emic' and 'etic' language could be more broadly adapted to how intertextuality is discussed in biblical studies. Emic constructs being accounts, descriptions, and analyses expressed in terms of the conceptual schemes and categories that are regarded as meaningful and appropriate by the members of the culture under study. An emic construct is correctly termed 'emic' if it is in accord with the perceptions and understandings deemed appropriate by the insider's culture. Etic constructs are expressed in terms of the conceptual schemes and categories that are regarded as meaningful and appropriate by the community of scientific observers. An etic construct is correctly termed 'etic' if it is in accord with the epistemological principles deemed appropriate by science (i.e. precise, logical, comprehensive, replicable, and observer independent).

[40] D. C. ALLISON, *The New Moses: A Matthean Typology* (Edinburgh: T & T Clark, 1993).

(1) Explicit statement. An author can circumvent ambiguity by straightforward comparison.
(2) Inexplicit citation or borrowing. Texts can be dug up and transplanted without acknowledgment.
(3) Similar circumstances. An event may be intended to recall another circumstantially like it.
(4) Key words or phrases. One may dress up a story with the words of another that is like it and well known.
(5) Similar narrative structure. The structure of a text can itself be allusive.
[For example:]

1 Kings 19	Mark 1
Elijah appears	Jesus appears
Elisha is at work	The disciples are at work
The call to discipleship	The call to discipleship
Elisha follows Elijah	The disciples follow Jesus

(6) Word order, syllabic sequence, poetic resonance. The rhythm or meter of sentences as well as the patterns of words and syllables can be imitative in order to allude.[41]

While points (1) and (2) are easily identified and adjudicated, points (3) through (6) raise usages that may not always be substantiated so easily. For instance, *similar circumstances* may be taken as an allusion when in fact it is a common place event. *Key words and phrases*, if in broad use, may be identified as an allusion instead of normal patterns of speech. Therefore, the more rare or detailed the occurrence with the proposed subject of the allusion, the more likely the allusion is intended.

The second list that Allison provides sets forth six ways that non-explicit occurrences or allusions may be identified. Allison rightly cautions that diligent searching can always uncover resemblances between two texts and there is a struggle with how to determine which similarities are meaningful. A controlling method for identifying allusions is not altogether possible because there is always an element of intuition and sense perception that play a role in the task. The guidelines Allison provides for identifying or eliminating an allusion are intended to be broad in approach. They are summarised as follows:

(1) Chronological Relationship. One text can only allude to or intentionally recall another prior to it in time.
(2) Significance. Probability will be enhanced if it can be shown (on other grounds) that a passage's proposed subtext belongs to a book or tradition which held some significance for its author.
(3) Similar Circumstance. In the absence of explicit citation or clear unacknowledged borrowing, a typology [allusion] will not be credible without some combination of devices (3) – (6); see above.

---

[41] ALLISON, *New Moses*, pp. 19-20.

(4) Prominence. A type should be prominent. A proposed typology [allusion] based on Moses and the exodus owns an initial plausibility, whereas one requiring knowledge of Ittai, the Philistine commander (2 Samuel 15), does not.

(5) Precedence. An alleged typology [allusion] has a better chance of gaining our confidence if its constituent elements have been used for typological construction in more than one writing.... Precedence enhances probability.

(6) Unusual imagery and uncommon motifs. Two texts are more plausibly related if what they share is out of the ordinary.[42]

While the nuances of several of Allison's criteria are different than those of Hays, the two lists are remarkably similar. Hays' seventh criterion, that of satisfaction, is noticeably lacking in Allison's list. The criterion of satisfaction is considered by Hays to be the most important test of an allusion or echo. This test answers questions such as: 'does the proposed reading make sense?' or 'does it produce for the reader a satisfying account of the effect of the intertextual relation?'.[43] Hays' seventh test is difficult because it raises issues surrounding the intent of intertextuality, a topic that Allison addresses in the conclusion of his work. The perception of what a text meant and what it means, the hermeneutical event, are intrinsic to the criterion of 'satisfaction'. Allison's list avoids the contentious and difficult terrain of using the hermeneutical event as a criterion for identifying an allusion.

In his treatment on typology in Matthew, Allison states that the gospel writer did not 'trumpet all his intentions' nor did he 'instruct us about his literary methods'.[44] Matthew is not a self-contained entity, but rather a piece of a larger work that demands to be read in the context of other texts. The reader must be actively engaged in the act of understanding what the gospel presupposes from the biblical sources. The density of the allusions in the gospel cannot be reduced to being verbal inflations; rather they are highly significant utterances. Like *11QMelchizedek*, an eschatological midrash, the author uses single words or sentences that purposefully lead the reader into the possibility of multiple interpretations. Furthermore, the audience that Matthew had in mind when writing were equipped far better than modern readers to understand these occurrences. Allison draws on the analogy of the famous hymn by Augustus Montague Toplady 'Rock of Ages':

Rock of Ages, cleft for me,
Let me hide myself in Thee!
Let the water and the blood,
From Thy riven side which flowed,
Be of sin the double cure,

---

[42] The presentation of these six points has been slightly modified from ALLISON's presentation for the sake of brevity. *New Moses*, pp. 21-22.

[43] HAYS, *Echoes of Scripture*, p. 31.

[44] ALLISON, *New Moses*, p. 284.

Cleanse me from its guilt and power...

The complexity of this analogy displays the clever interplay of multiple allusions in one text.[45] This 'catena of allusions', discusses Allison, draws upon: (1) John 19.34 for the image of water and blood flowing from the side of Jesus; (2) the 'Rock' as Jesus is an equation spelled out in 1 Corinthians 10.4; (3) the idea of being hidden in the cleft of a rock is from Exodus 33.22; and (4) finally the possibility of water flowing from a rock could be from Exodus 17 and Numbers 20. It is not to be assumed that the intended audience would have recognised and understood every allusion, but the compactness of the allusions serves to encourage and increase the knowledge of the audience. In the case of Matthew, 'the focus upon moral instruction, the habit of topical presentation, and the ubiquity of mnemonic devices...when taken together, strongly suggest [catechetical intent]'.[46] The use of Jewish scripture in Matthew, then, has a parallel with the use of tradition in the hymn 'Rock of Ages'. The ultimate goal in mind of both compositions is to stimulate interest in the Bible with carefully planted allusions that would be recognised by the audience.

Svend Holm-Nielsen, in his work on the *Hodayot*, raises a relevant issue that should be noted in connection to what Allison proposes here. It is important to distinguish between the extraction of texts from a biblical source and a simple application of terminology that was current in the community and drawn in the distant past from the Bible.[47] The work of a composer embodies and reflects a creative process that synthesises information with a complexity that at times may deliberately include allusions while, at other times a natural linguistic and cultural heritage with no thought of another text or tradition.

Whether the conclusion suggested by Allison that 'stimulating interest in the Bible' was one of the primary intents of Matthew's allusions is correct, it nonetheless appeals to the hermeneutical event. The intention of an author using biblical traditions could be manifold. It is not entirely persuasive, for

[45] ALLISON, *New Moses*, p. 1, states in the introduction of the book: '...there are at least three types of intertextuality: borrowing which alludes to no subtext, borrowing which alludes to a series of subtexts, and borrowing which alludes to or cites a specific subtext'.

[46] ALLISON, *New Moses*, pp. 285-87.

[47] Another underlying issue related to this question is whether an allusion or citation is intended to remind the readers or hearers of the context of the earlier text. The answer to this question for HAYS would appear to be that it is generally not intended to do so. On the issue of context see G. K. BEALE, *The Right Doctrine from the Wrong Texts? Essays on the Use of the Old Testament in the New* (Grand Rapids: Baker, 1994); D. I. BREWER, *Techniques and Assumptions*, p. 167; J. CAMPBELL, *The Use of Scripture in the Damascus Document 1-8, 19-20* (BZAW 228; Berlin: Walter de Gruyter, 1995) p. 207; C. H. DODD, *According to the Scriptures: The Sub-structure of New Testament Theology* (London: Nisbet, 1953) pp. 126-27.

instance, that Matthew's intent was to stimulate interest as much as to use the authority of biblical traditions to convince his audience about the truthfulness of his message. The possibility that one may recognise an allusion based upon the hermeneutical event or perceived authorial intent is difficult. However, one must recognise that as subjective as it may be, it is a tool (or interpretive reality) that cannot be discarded.

Also reasonable to consider is that a test of satisfaction, as Hays has termed it, may easily be passed when in fact the allusion was actually haphazard and has no clear referent. Hays formulates the test of satisfaction further in asking whether 'the proposed reading offers a good account of the experience of a contemporary community of competent readers'.[48] In the case of a didactic work rich in allusions, it is unknown whether or not a proposed allusion was designed to compel the reader to learn, explain what they presently read, or form an authoritative voice that might compel the addressee to act in a certain way. In the case of establishing an allusion that may in fact be misidentified, it is easy to conceive that a satisfactory explanation could be provided for an allusion that is otherwise unsupportable. Questions about the hermeneutical event stimulate dialogue and could be useful in identifying streams of non-explicit traditions in a composition.

Drake Williams writes on the purpose and function of scripture in the New Testament and describes three guiding principles for investigating 'indirect dependence on Scripture'.[49] Williams study focuses generally on the use of biblical traditions in 1 Corinthians 1-3 including both explicit and non-explicit occurrences. The assumption of his work is that the content of the scriptures is the current 'Hebrew Bible'.[50] His first and second principles reveal the difficulty of conceiving of the task of identifying allusions as a use of scripture. His principles may be summarised as follows:

(1) Traits common to the scripture text must correspond with a text in early Jewish literature for indirect dependence to have occurred. This may concern a particular theme, a distinct word, or a distinct phrasing that may show a relationship between Scripture and early Jewish literature.
(2) 'Safety in Numbers', a broad survey of literature from Palestinian and Diaspora Judaism will help confirm the existence of common thematic knowledge that could have influenced Paul's use of a particular scriptural text.
(3) Indirect dependence provides less clarity than direct dependence. Texts where indirect dependence is considered will be examined following texts where direct dependence can be

---

[48] HAYS, *Echoes of Scripture*, pp. 31-32.
[49] WILLIAMS, *The Wisdom of the Wise*, pp. 30-31.
[50] WILLIAMS, *The Wisdom of the Wise*, p. 22 he writes: 'For this study, the current Hebrew Bible will be the working assumption for the contents of the Scriptures, which is customary for the field of Paul's use of Scripture.'

established. Indirect dependence of a scripture text may help further support traditions where direct dependence can be established.[51]

The first two principles taken together reflect that the first concern is to find allusions to early Jewish exegetical traditions. The third principle is one found in the criteria above: in a context where a citation or more explicit use of a tradition occurs, the use of less explicit traditions may be better substantiated.

The conversation in New Testament studies about the use of scripture is well developed and useful for an examination of *Musar leMevin*. The principles and criteria developed by others for determining the likelihood of an allusion, or helping to evaluate the significance of an allusion, will be revisited at the end of this chapter alongside other contributions.

3. Non-explicit Traditions in the Pseudepigrapha

Dimant offers a valuable contribution to the discussion of allusions to biblical traditions that occur in the Apocrypha and Pseudepigrapha.[52] Her work on allusions and intertextual occurrences has been carried out in relation to non-biblical and early Jewish literature. Dimant defines an allusion as: *a device for the simultaneous activation of two texts, using a special signal referring to the independent external text. These signals may consist of isolated terms, patterns and motifs taken from the independent text alluded to.*[53] The two types of allusions in the 'Apocrypha' and 'Pseudepigrapha' are allusions to either isolated verses or to a running biblical text. Dimant's discussion is broken into these two categories and several examples are provided.

Dimant uses Wisdom of Solomon as a source for her examples of isolated allusions. The opening verses of 1.1-15 and 6.1-21 are two passages in Wisdom of Solomon that are 'linked' by style, words and subject, forming a concentric chiasmus. These passages are further linked by biblical allusions and include words from Psalm 2.10 (LXX). Dimant suggests that Psalm 2 is selected by the author because it urges kings and judges to exercise wisdom, an indirect polemic against Hellenistic theories of kingship. The example of Psalm 2.10 is presented solidly as an allusion on the basis of linguistic and

---

[51] WILLIAMS, *The Wisdom of the Wise*, pp. 30-31.

[52] D. DIMANT, 'Use and Interpretation of Mikra in the Apocrypha and Pseudepigrapha', in M. J. MULDER and H. SYSLING (eds.), *Mikra: Text, Translation, Reading and Interpretation of the Hebrew Bible in Ancient Judaism and Early Christianity. Compendia Rerum Iudaicarum ad Novum Testamentum*, II 1 (Philadelphia: Fortress Press, 1988) pp. 379-419. See also K. W. NIEBUHR, *Gesetz und Paränese: katechismusartige Weisungsreihen in der frühjüdischen Literatur* (WUNT2 28; Tübingen: Mohr Siebeck, 1987) pp. 167-231.

[53] DIMANT, 'Use and Interpretation,' p. 410.

conceptual overlap between the two works. A more discrete example of an allusion is to Proverbs 8.15 and is identified on the basis of similar ideas, style and general tenor. Proverbs 8.15 asserts that through wisdom the kings of the earth rule and judges judge. This concept forms a large part of the discourse of the first nine chapters of Proverbs and converges thematically and stylistically in Wisdom of Solomon 1-6. These two examples (Psalms and Proverbs) illustrate two procedures of biblical allusion. First, one employs a specific and characteristic word or phrase from the original to the 'affinity of context'. Second, a method is used that plays on accumulating less defined elements that are reminiscent of the original.[54] Criteria set forth may be summarised as follows: (1) shared linguistic elements; (2) shared concepts or themes; and (3) shared style.

One other device used when one text alludes to an earlier that Dimant discusses, which incidentally occurs quite seldom in Wisdom of Solomon, is the patterning of the new text on the syntactical structure of the old. Wisdom of Solomon's allusions (chs. 1-6) are usually taken from different contexts and coalesced into a new unity. Within different contexts a distinction should be made of the actual function there and the literary setting, since the same allusion can be used in different places for different purposes.[55]

The second type of allusion discussed by Dimant is one that occurs in relation to a running text. Such occurrences are an act of modelling the new text from the biblical text. This modelling is identified by the new text adopting the original motif, terms, and short phrases from the biblical source. Allusions of this kind often provide explicit reference to their source somewhere in the new context.[56] There is a wider literary purpose in the case of allusions to a running biblical text. For instance, a 'pseudonymic attribution' is established when a systematic attribution of a biblical account occurs. Also, a system of allusions is frequently used to create a stylistic analogy with a biblical motif or text. Dimant notes the importance of recognising that imitating biblical style is done for literary or exegetical purposes. In purely stylistic usages biblical elements usually retain only general characteristics and do not point to one specific context whereas elements used for exegetical purposes are always rooted in a specific context.[57]

Pseudepigraphy is, then, a type of allusion in itself. Such an allusion draws mainly from one or two texts and uses them to create new biblical forms or genres. This is the case in early Judaism with prayers that know psalms or testaments using Genesis 49 and Deuteronomy 31-34. Similarly, in narrative

---

[54] DIMANT, 'Use and Interpretation,' p. 412.
[55] DIMANT, 'Use and Interpretation,' p. 415.
[56] DIMANT, 'Use and Interpretation,' p. 415-16.
[57] DIMANT, 'Use and Interpretation,' p. 416.

compositions that are either re-written Bible or free narrative, various biblical
stories function as a model. In the examples that Dimant provides, the concern
is with occurrences of motifs used both with and without characteristic
phraseology. When phrases are used it enhances the referential value of a
motif. Less clear when one reads Dimant's work is whether it is possible to
establish an allusion when phraseology does not occur in a new context.[58] The
notion of pseudepigraphy as allusion is essential for the identification of non-
explicit uses of traditions in *Musar leMevin*. As traditions develop from Bible
to re-written Bible, compositions that know both may be using a more explicit
use of a tradition (i.e. one not found in the MT or LXX) rather than a non-
explicit use of a biblical text.

Dimant uses the book of Tobit as an example of an allusion based upon the
reworking of biblical models and motifs. Tobit, some have observed, evokes
motifs from Genesis and Job. A similarity of key motifs attached to the
characters in Tobit and Job as well as to the character Tobit himself, who
follows a sequence derived from Job, indicates that Job serves as a model
throughout the book. Dimant outlines the following:

Motifs	*Job*	*Tobit*
The hero is pious and righteous	1:1, 8	1:6-12, 16-17
He is prosperous	2:3	2:2-5
He is deprived of his possessions	1:2-3	1:13
He is crippled by illness	1:14-19	1:15-20
His wife works for others	2:7-8	2:9-10
He is provoked by his wife	31:10	2:11-14
	2:9 (LXX)	
He prays and wishes to die	3 *et passim*	2:1-6
His final vindication and		
restitution of health and wealth	42:11-15	14:2-3
He dies in his old age, blessed		
with offspring and wealth	42:16-17	14:11-12[59]

These affinities of Tobit with Job are important because they display a
prolonged and recurring allusion. The narrative is not taken over or reworked
by Tobit and is independent of Job. This use by Tobit of biblical motifs is
different from re-written Bible or pseudepigraphy and is, thus, an example of
'free narrative' wherein a Job-like plot has been re-created. The referential
value occurs in the coincidence of motifs as well as a few terms and leads to a
comparison of the two narratives.[60]

In conclusion, Dimant contrasts the purpose of explicit and implicit uses of
biblical sources:

---

[58] DIMANT, 'Use and Interpretation,' p. 417.
[59] DIMANT, 'Use and Interpretation,' p. 418.
[60] DIMANT, 'Use and Interpretation,' p. 419.

[Explicit usage is:] employed in rhetorical contexts, namely in various types of discourse, and for various rhetorical purposes. The uses in compositional functions occur in all types of contexts and genres. In explicit rhetorical uses the biblical elements stand for the divine authority and are presented as such. In implicit compositional uses biblical elements are part of the materials forming the texture of the composition. Authors employing biblical elements in this way aim at re-creating the biblical models and atmosphere, and identify themselves with the biblical authors.[61]

In terms of genre, *Musar leMevin* is dissimilar from both Tobit and *Wisdom of Solomon* in several respects. Tobit for the most part is a narrative interspersed with prayers and thanksgiving hymns. The *Wisdom of Solomon* may fit under the general category of sapiential literature but it is somewhat proverbial and uses a type of metre as well. The analogy between these works and *Musar leMevin* is helpful but they are not *verbatim* examples that illustrate what may occur here. The contribution of Dimant in discussing the non-explicit use of tradition for *Musar leMevin*, therefore, is the general observation that a system of allusions is used frequently to create an analogy with a biblical motif or narrative(s). In the case of *Musar leMevin*, the use of Genesis 1-3 appears to be analogous at times to such a system of allusion. If *Musar leMevin* is seen to re-write creation narratives to provide a biblical atmosphere, and identify with biblical authors the purpose would likely be to reinforce authority.

4. Non-Explicit Traditions in the *Hodayot* and DSS

In his monograph on the *Hodayot*, Holm-Nielsen dedicates a considerable discussion to identifying the use of biblical traditions within the document.[62] While Bonnie Kittel has subsequently criticised Holm-Nielsen for his description and, often, identification of the *Hodayot's* use of biblical traditions, his work and discussion remain valuable. Research into the non-explicit usage of biblical traditions in the *Hodayot* serves as an excellent point of departure for discussing similar occurrences in *Musar leMevin*. This is due to a few basic similarities: (1) the discussion on the subject of allusions in the *Hodayot* has been addressed whereas for other documents from the Qumran library this is not the case; and (2) the *Hodayot* is undoubtedly using a great deal of biblical tradition in an almost exclusively non-explicit way; and (3)

---

[61] DIMANT, 'Use and Interpretation,' p. 419. Allusion, according to this definition, is used to give the author the same voice and authority as a biblical author.

[62] S. HOLM-NIELSEN, *Hodayot: Psalms from Qumran* (Aarhus: Universitetsforlaget, 1960). See also GOFF, 'Reading Wisdom at Qumran'.

the *Hodayot* knows and makes much use of a number of traditions that are 'non-canonical'.

A number of difficulties arise in identifying and discussing the *Hodayot's* use of biblical traditions. First, Holm-Nielsen considers the struggle of identification in terms of the *Hodayot's* 'paraphrased use of an Old Testament text'.[63] For example, the New Testament, unlike the *Hodayot*, often draws attention to another source with an introductory phrase or statement. In the cases when the New Testament author does not draw attention to the use of a biblical source, most often the citation is of a known biblical tradition. However, in the *Hodayot*, even when two sentences are 'quoted' from the Hebrew Bible, they are not word for word.

Second, there are a vast number of cases in which it is obvious or highly probable that the author had more than one biblical passage in mind. In such cases it is difficult to determine whether the author was aware of quoting or citing these sources. If the context from which it is presumed a quotation derived is examined, it becomes clear that the author paid little or no attention to the context of the biblical source.[64] The similarity between the two texts often lies in the single expression or word alone. The usage of a biblical expression is often so circumstantial and has so little bearing on the new context that it can hardly be reckoned among the cases of an 'actual use of Scripture' and has 'no theological content'.[65]

Third, even when there is an agreement of terms and phrases between the *Hodayot* and a biblical source, it cannot be presumed that a quotation can be identified. Rather, it may be that certain vocabulary and language are permanent phrases, stereotyped expressions, or customary terminology that originated from the biblical tradition but existed in the everyday language of the time and therefore not an intertextual occurrence. Holm-Nielsen observes that within a religious sphere, where special terminology is used, this could easily be the case. It is not uncommon to find the same expression in a number of contexts in the *Hodayot* as well as elsewhere in the Dead Sea Scrolls. There is no way to know, definitively, whether the author is extracting texts from a biblical source or simply applying a terminology that was current in the community which derived from biblical sources at some previous point.[66]

Holm-Nielsen characterises the application of biblical traditions in the *Hodayot* as an attempt to form an original poetic composition by the knitting together of borrowed material. He defines the application as follows:

---

[63] HOLM-NIELSEN, *Hodayot*, p. 302.
[64] HOLM-NIELSEN, *Hodayot*, p. 302.
[65] HOLM-NIELSEN, *Hodayot*, pp. 303-4.
[66] HOLM-NIELSEN, *Hodayot*, p. 303.

'the authors did not have as their object the authorisation of their work as canonical writing by the use of the Old Testament [as compared with the New Testament], but rather the creation of original poetry in an Old Testament style and, by means of the use of the Old Testament in this poetry, the expression of the relationship between God and the community, and between God and the community's individual member.'[67]

The use of a biblical source here is dissimilar to, say, a pesher or midrash in that the authors had no intention of selecting from the biblical source, but of making use of it. The *Hodayot* is not attempting to authorise a definitive interpretation of a biblical passage; rather, it takes the biblical source for granted and 'cultivates a theology' on that basis.

Holm-Nielsen observes the *Hodayot's* use of biblical sources and questions the significance of such usages. He raises the matter of whether the biblical documents, which the authors of the *Hodayot* used in their compositions, possess a significance at all in themselves or whether the significance derives from when texts were first placed in a definite historical context. Stated another way, Holm-Nielson asks if the expressions were simply suitable for giving the mood of the poem as the intention of the present author.[68] While these questions are, to a large extent, rhetorical, they provide the opportunity for Holm-Nielsen to differentiate further between the use of a biblical document in *pesharim*, where the use is there conditioned by history, and the *Hodayot* where theology is in mind.[69] The expressions and words of psalm literature should be taken first as abstract rather than concrete, as illustrations and symbols rather than portrayals of historical occurrences.

From a 'technical viewpoint' Holm-Nielsen notes that among biblical books, the *Hodayot* uses some books more than others. The biblical psalms are clearly the most often used tradition in the *Hodayot*, but their use there is not always transparent. It is not always possible to determine which text the author is referring to and some usages may be indirect. The author could be unconsciously quoting or using a biblical source, a phenomenon noted previously. Holm-Nielsen identifies Psalm 104 as a particularly important Psalm that is used with a frequency that is indicative of its popularity. Other Psalms that have portrayals of misery are also quite popular (e.g. Ps 22, 31, 42).[70] Outside of the Psalms, prophetic books, mainly Isaiah, rank second in

---

[67] HOLM-NIELSEN, *Hodayot*, p. 305. Canonical implies authoritative. The *Hodayot* sought to be authoritative and cannot so easily be made distinct from a New Testament composition by this rational.

[68] The description of the use of biblical sources as 'poetic' in the *Hodayot* is different than Paul using biblical traditions poetically. While Paul is undoubtedly using sources poetically at times, adding texture to his works, Paul's compositions are primarily epistles whereas the *Hodayot* are hymnal. Hays applies discussions about English poetry to Pauline epistles and, therefore, produces a description of allusions and echoes functioning poetically.

[69] HOLM-NIELSEN, *Hodayot*, p. 306.

[70] HOLM-NIELSEN, *Hodayot*, p. 309.

importance. Outside of a few rare examples, the hymns do not use biblical narratives. This is due to the nature of the composition, its purpose clearly is not to admonish or indoctrinate but form poetic expressions of thanksgiving and lament in regard to those who keep the Law and those who do not.[71] Furthermore, Genesis 1-3 stands out as important in the *Hodayot* for use of portraying humanity as corrupt in the present world. The community, in its use of Genesis 1-3, understands itself as existing as a 'reincarnation of the paradise of old'.[72]

Holm-Nielsen describes two types of hymns that use biblical sources differently. First, there are hymns that have close contact with the community in a 'technical' way. The use of biblical sources by these hymns is more sporadic and haphazard. The second type is those psalms which concern themselves with the experience of the individual within the community. In the first category it is possible to speak of 'standard quotations' (e.g. Ps 2, Is 28.11, Hos 14.14). In the second category the use of biblical sources is less consistent between the hymns and they have less in common.[73]

In his concluding remarks on the *Hodayot's* use of biblical sources Holm-Nielsen states that the authors were quite free in their use of the sources. It is clear that terminology that had an origin in biblical sources was being used in the daily life of the community. Holm-Nielsen is not convinced, however, that there is evidence that the authors availed themselves of anthologies or testimonies due to the widely divergent nature of 'Old Testament' usage. If anthologies had been employed it would be expected that some combinations of biblical sources would reoccur. The *Hodayot*, then, should be considered an independent working of biblical traditions by authors who had good knowledge of it.[74]

Holm-Nielsen does not formulate guidelines by which the use of biblical traditions can be identified, but clearly articulates highly pertinent questions to ask of a document that employs non-explicit biblical sources. For instance, are suspect non-explicit citations in *Musar leMevin* dependant on more than one biblical passage? To what extent does the author of *Musar leMevin* pay attention to the context of the biblical source? Is the author of *Musar leMevin* extracting texts from a biblical source or simply applying a terminology that was current in the community and drawn in the distant past from the Bible? Similarities and issues raised by the *Hodayot* serve to place *Musar leMevin's* use of biblical sources in parallel with a relative document.

---

[71] HOLM-NIELSEN, *Hodayot*, p. 311.

[72] HOLM-NIELSEN, *Hodayot*, p. 312. This description of an Eden account is significant for the use of Gen 1-3 in *Musar leMevin*.

[73] HOLM-NIELSEN, *Hodayot*, pp. 313-14.

[74] HOLM-NIELSEN, *Hodayot*, p. 315.

In the process of seeking to define terminology that is both accurate and descriptive of an author's use of biblical traditions, Kittel's excursus on this topic is well-worth examining.[75] In her evaluation of Holm-Nielsen's work, Kittel criticises Holm-Nielsen's use of inaccurate terminology in referring to biblical citations. When identifying a quotation it is imperative to define what, exactly, constitutes a 'quotation' of a biblical tradition in early Jewish literature. In the case of Holm-Nielsen's terminology the phrases 'allusion to,' 'derived from,' and 'inspired by' are intermingled in his observations of biblical traditions and the composition of the *Hodayot*. Whereas Holm-Nielsen, according to Kittel, views the psalms of the *Hodayot* as 'mosaics of Old Testament quotations', she rightly views the psalms as original compositions which imitated biblical style and idiom.

This conflict between the technique of the author(s) of the *Hodayot* in using biblical traditions provides the impetus for an examination by Kittel of Holm-Nielsen and Carmignac's terminology and use of the word 'quotation'.[76] In the first of four observations she states that most 'quotations' consist of only one or two words and often the words quoted in the *Hodayot* appear in different parts of the verse cited. Second, both Holm-Nielsen and Carmignac admit frequently that among these one and two word quotations the context and meaning of the words often change considerably. Third, it is often the case that a 'quotation' is actually a reoccurring biblical idiom that cannot be identified with any one particular chapter and verse. Finally, the quotations conjugate the verb quoted differently in the *Hodayot* than biblical tradition and form varying syntactical relationships as well. Kittel concludes these four observations by disqualifying Holm-Nielsen and Carmignac's identifications of quotations as inaccurate since a quotation is generally understood to be the repetition of a passage verbatim.

These criticisms of the identification of quotations by Kittel produce a need to define more clearly not only the term 'quotation', but also the use of Hebrew Bible in the *Hodayot* in ways other than might be termed quotation. The following observations will help delineate between quotations and allusions in *Musar leMevin*. Kittel analyses biblical idioms in the *Hodayot* (ii 20-30) and differentiates between four usages of borrowing from the biblical sources. First, a quotation or allusion is used to recall a particular passage to the addressee(s). Second, literary forms from the Hebrew Bible are imitated by the use of standardised phrases in the appropriate places. Third, within certain genres or theological motifs characteristic imagery and metaphor can

---

[75] B. P. KITTEL, *The Hymns of Qumran* (SBLDS 50; Chico: Scholars Press, 1981) pp. 48-52.
[76] J. CARMIGNAC, *Les texts de Qumran: traduits et annotés* (Paris: Letouzey et Ané, 1961).

be identified. Finally, it is often the case that thoughts are expressed in a manner consistent with biblical language and terminology.

Kittel argues that it is not possible to assign every phrase of a psalm into one of the above four categories. However, these categories serve to differentiate between the classifications 'quotation' and original material. While she elaborates on issues specific to the language of the *Hodayot*, she also addresses the identification of 'allusions' in the paragraphs that follow. Quotations, by definition, must consist of several words and appear with little variation from the original, but allusions are a much broader category. The term 'allusion' may be used to refer to a loose quotation or to a veiled hint. An allusion, Kittel explains, must refer to a single passage and the context and meaning should, within her study of the *Hodayot*, 'converge on a single text' or must have 'incomplete convergence reinforced by surrounding references to the same passage'.

Kittel provides two examples of allusions to illustrate her principles. The first allusion she identifies as ותשוך בעדי which is an expression that occurs in the *Hodayot* (ii 21) and Job 1.10 (שַׂכְתָּ בַעֲדוֹ). The identification of this first allusion is made using the criteria that Kittel describes as an usage that 'converges on a single text'. The idiom occurs three times elsewhere in the Hebrew Bible, occurring once as √סוך, meaning 'to hedge up' or more generally indicates the obstructing of something. Only in Job 1.10 is שוך used in the sense of protecting something (i.e. God has 'hedged up' Job from evil) and is therefore a unique use of the idiom in the Hebrew Bible. In the *Hodayot* (ii 21) the author thanks God for protecting or 'hedging me up' from death, thus employing the idiom with the same distinct meaning as Job 1.10. Though different pronominal suffixes are used and שוך is conjugated differently, Kittel argues that this is an allusion to the Job passage since the idiom is used with the same distinct meaning and similar context.

The second illustration of an allusion identified by Kittel occurs in the *Hodayot* vii 6-25. The identification of this second allusion is made using the criterion that Kittel described as 'incomplete convergence reinforced by surrounding references to the same passage'. Several expressions in the hymn seem to indicate a use of Zechariah 3 where Joshua the High Priest is the subject. There is, writes Kittel, an 'incomplete convergence' (i.e. it does not fit the criteria of the former allusion): some idioms are changed slightly and some use different meanings than those found in Zechariah 3. The proposed allusions in the hymn are scattered throughout and leave some doubts as to the veracity of the identification. However, she argues, the number of references and sufficient contextual indications show that Zechariah 3 is 'certainly' in the background of the author's thought.

Thus Kittel provides two ways of identifying allusions. The first type of allusion is one that converges on a single text but does not conjugate words identically, however, it does use a *similar distinct meaning* and *similar context*. The second type of allusion is one that does not converge on a single text, but *surrounding references to the same passage reinforce it*. Moreover, the number of suspect allusions and contextual indications within the document verify the certainty of an allusion.

Kittel's definition and identification of an allusion is strict and precise. However, while her caution is warranted and criteria helpful, much more can be said about the probability of an occurrence of a non-explicit use of a tradition. The two types of allusions delineated here are measured by standards that mark allusions of greater certainty, but the application of a broader number of guidelines may allow a measure of greater probability and sustainable speculation.

5. Biblical Interpretation in Qumran Wisdom Texts

George Brooke is the sole contributor to the use of biblical traditions in Qumran Wisdom texts.[77] He addresses fairly extensively issues pertaining to the use of biblical sources in *Musar leMevin*. Brooke offers well-developed and descriptive categories that assist in moving the conversation about biblical interpretation in *Musar leMevin* forward. While Brooke does not address 'allusion' terminology specifically, he does discuss genres and methodologies of various sapiential works represented among the Dead Sea documents. Brooke's aim is to speak broadly about the use of biblical sources in Jewish sapiential literature. In his discussion, identification of allusions are, on occasion, taken for granted. Brooke's work provides an appropriate beginning for the discussion of the use of biblical sources in *Musar leMevin*.

Brooke singles out five ways in which scriptural traditions are used in relation to various genres. They are as follows: (1) wisdom as biblical poetry, (2) wisdom as halakhah, (3) wisdom as parenesis, (4) wisdom as narrative exegesis, and (5) wisdom as pesher. In his discussion of these different usages Brooke cites examples that range from nearly explicit citations (e.g. 'honour your father and mother' in 4Q416 2 ii 21) to non-explicit uses of scripture (e.g. 'Enosh/enosh' and 'Seth/Sheth' in 4Q417 1 i 16).

In Brooke's first category, *wisdom as biblical poetry*, he addresses the 'atomistic' character of poetical presentations of wisdom in sapiential documents from Qumran. In the case of these compositions there is rarely an 'overall grand narrative' or 'systematic ethic'. Within this genre, writes Brooke, the primary use of biblical sources is in the form of 'allusory

---

[77] G. J. BROOKE, 'Biblical Interpretation,' pp. 201-20.

anthologisation' of biblical traditions.[78] The author may select from a number of sources, at times unaware of the source, and create a new arrangement. This particular explanation by Brooke is reminiscent of Holm-Nielsen's description of the psalms of the *Hodayot* noted above. According to Brooke, the hearers or readers were not required to be able to identify the sources of each phrase, but some would certainly have discerned what was taking place. What happens, generally, is that new compositions have been formed from 'old favourites'. Brooke's description of such compositions is similar to the view that Kittel criticises when she speaks of scholars who have a 'low view of the creativity and originality of the poet [of the *Hodayot*] who modelled his work so clearly after biblical compositions'.[79] The use of non-explicit traditions within poetry are the most difficult to identify and substantiate. Kittel, in my opinion, is too rigid in her evaluation of the influence of earlier traditions on the poetic authors. The more a document is embedded with recognisable biblical traditions, the better one may determine that less explicit allusions in the same composition have had influence.

Brooke cites an example of the above 'allusory anthologisation' in the *Book of Mysteries'* (1Q27; 4Q299-301) use of Qohelet. Brooke refers to an example by Lange of allusions in the *Book of Mysteries* to Qohelet (Qoh 6.8-11 in 1Q27 1 ii 3; Qoh 5.5 in 1Q27 6 2-3).[80] Lange's example of allusion is based largely upon the occurrence of similar terms and similar genre (wisdom):

1Q27 ii

(3) מה הוא היותר ל[

(3) how/what is it better to/than

Qohelet 6

(8) כי מה יותר לחכם מן הכסיל מה לעני יודע להלך נגד החיים
(11) כי יש דברים הרבה מרבים הבל מה יתר לאדם

(8) what advantage for the wise one than the fool, what is there for someone poor, knowing to go before the living
(11) because there are many things increasing vanity, what more is there for a man?

---

[78] BROOKE, 'Biblical Interpretation,' p. 208 writes: 'The primary use of scripture in many wisdom compositions is allusory anthologisation of traditions. The wisdom authors many not always be aware of their sources, but they pluck the best flowers from a number of sources and put them together in a new arrangement which has a fresh attractiveness for the reader or hearer.'

[79] KITTEL, *Hymns*, p. 48.

[80] LANGE, 'In Diskussion mit dem Tempel,' in A. SCHOORS (ed.) *Qohelet in the Context of Wisdom* (BETL 136; Leuven: Peeters, 1998); pp. 125-26; and BROOKE, 'Biblical Interpretation,' p. 208. Lange considers similarities between the *Book of Mysteries* and *Musar leMevin* in a short excursus, pp. 127-34.

1Q27 6

(2) [שיהמה [י]כפר על שגנ○○○○ל]
(3) [עד עולם לפניו לכפר הן]

(2)] it will atone for errors [
(3)]forever before him to atone[

(5) אל תתן את פיך לחטיא את בשרך ואל תאמר לפני המלאך כי שגגה היא

(5) do not let your mouth cause your flesh to sin and do not say before an angel that it is an error

In the first instance, the combination of מה and יותר ('what advantage' or 'what more') form the association between the two works. In the second instance, Lange considers that שגגה ('inadvertent sin' or 'error') is a theme taken up in both the *Book of Mysteries* and *Musar leMevin* (4Q417 2 ii בלוא צוה נבונות בשר תשגכ]ה; 'without his commanding the understanding of flesh, y[ou] lead astray[').[81] It is the occurrence of similar terminology in both Qohelet and the *Book of Mysteries* that allows Lange to identify these allusions. Although Lange does not raise possible similarities of context in his identification of the allusion in 1Q27 ii, this issue may be considered. 1Q27 ii is a fragmentary 11 line fragment, however, only a few words survive in the best preserved lines. From lines 4-5 one might summarise the content as concerned with the doing of good or evil (l. 4) and success as related to wealth (l. 5). One might even infer that this subject is related to effort or toil, especially if one translates line 3 as 'what advantage is there'. It is hard to conceive, in this example, that context helps establish the non-explicit use of Qohelet in 1Q27 ii simply because there is not enough left of the fragment to understand the content. 1Q27 6 is much smaller than 1Q27 ii and only the above portions of lines 3-4 are truly readable.

There is a great deal of similarity between the *Book of Mysteries* and *Musar leMevin*. Both compositions, as Brooke discusses, are picking from a number of biblical sources. In the case of *Musar leMevin* one might assume that some traditions are used more frequently, such as other sapiential compositions and Genesis creation traditions. The more one recognises recurring motifs and language, especially between two closely related works, such as the *Book of Mysteries* and *Musar leMevin*, the more one may be convinced of an allusion or relationship with another biblical tradition.[82]

---

[81] LANGE, 'In Diskussion,' p. 126 he however writes: 'Neben diesen beiden Belegen könnte lediglich noch ein weiterer, aus dem in Frage kommenden Zeitraum bekannter Weisheitstext die [שגגה] thematisiert haben, der [*Musar leMevin*].'

[82] TIGCHELAAR, 'Wisdom and Counter-Wisdom in 4QInstruction,' unpublished paper presented at the University of Durham, Seminar for the Study of Judaism in Late Antiquity (7 March 2005). He suggested a number of intertextual occurrences between *Musar leMevin*,

In Brooke's second category, *wisdom as halakhah*, the use of some biblical traditions in contexts where life instruction occurs can be regarded as halakhic exegesis. Halakhic wisdom is described as taking two forms. The first form is described as an imitation of biblical models that applies various principles from Torah, or scripture generally, and not specific and individual rulings or statutes. The second form of halakhic wisdom takes individual rulings from the Torah and interprets it. Brooke provides three examples of the second category all of which are important to discuss as they are taken from *Musar leMevin*.

The first example of a halakhic use of scripture is from 4Q416 2 ii line 21 where one could read 'and also do not curse the vessel of your bosom'. Following Strugnell, Brooke seeks to view this passage as extending the positive commandment of the Decalogue, 'honour your father and mother,' to include one's wife. Brooke notes that most legal interpretations of this type are formed with two passages juxtaposed and asks the question whether this is so in *Musar leMevin*. Brooke proposes the possibility that the occurrence of the phrase 'wife of your bosom' is in a context where one's wife is listed with a number of relations (excluding parents) who could lead the addressee into idolatry. The phrase 'wife of your bosom' occurs in Deuteronomy 13.7 and 28.54 in a context where a disobedient man denies food to his brother, wife and children. Brooke notices that the only relative in this context who is not a blood relation is the wife and that *Musar leMevin* (4Q416 2 ii 21) contains a legal interpretation that rules whether one should honour his wife similarly among these relations.[83]

The second example of a halakhic use of a biblical source is in 4Q418 103 ii lines 7-9 where it reads 'Lest it form something of mixed kinds like a mule, And (lest) thou become as one who we[ars *sha'atnez*], made of wool and flax, And (lest) thy toil be like (that of) one who plo[ughs] with ox and a[s]s [to]geth[er], And (lest) moreover thy crops b[e for thee like] (those of) one who sows diverse kinds, and of one who takes the seed and the full *growth* and the yi[eld of] the [vineyard *together*], to be set apa[rt (for the sanctuary)'.[84] Brooke views this passage as the juxtaposition of two biblical verses to form a legal understanding of different kinds of mixtures. The first scriptural passage that 4Q418 103 ii lines 7-9 use is Leviticus 19.19 which reads, 'You will not let your animals breed with a different kind; you will not sow your field with two kinds of seed; nor will you put on a garment made of two different materials'. The second passage that Brooke envisages as

---

Mysteries and other biblical traditions. For instance, 4Q418 222+221+220 has the phrase אביעה רוחי ('I will pour out my spirit'); he suggested that this is an intertextual occurrence and is found in Prov 1.23; Ben Sira 16.25; and 4Q301 1 1.

[83] BROOKE, 'Biblical Interpretation,' pp. 209-10.

[84] BROOKE, 'Biblical Interpretation,' p. 210.

juxtaposed to Leviticus is Deuteronomy 22.9, 'You will not sow your vineyard with a second kind of seed, or the whole yield will have to be forfeited, both the crop that you have sown and the yield of the vineyard itself'.

Brooke's third example of a halakhic use of biblical tradition is from 4Q416 2 iv lines 6-9, 'over her spirit he has set you in authority so that she should walk in your good pleasure, and let her not make numerous vows and votive offerings; turn her spirit to your good pleasure. And every oath binding on her, to vow a vow, annul it according to a (mere) utterance of your mouth; and at your good pleasure restrain her from performing [...]'.[85] This passage from *Musar leMevin* is understood by Brooke to be a simplification and clarification of a more extensive vow from Numbers 30.6-15. In the *Damascus Document* 16.10-12 a passage very similar to 4Q416 2 iv lines 6-9 occurs and uses Numbers similarly. The scope of defining and locating this referent may be expanded to other early Jewish traditions and take into account surrounding allusions to Genesis.

Brooke's third category, *wisdom as parenesis*, is a category that uses historical circumstances recorded in biblical sources for the purpose of exhortation. Brooke describes two ways such references are usually made: (1) as markers that give the reader a sense of identity (e.g. 4Q185 i 13-15 'remember the miracles he performed in Egypt'); and (2) as primary examples used to encourage a particular way of behaviour in the audience.

Brooke's fourth category, *wisdom as narrative exegesis*, is the most relevant category for the present discussion as we seek to develop language to address *Musar leMevin's* use of traditions. Brooke defines this use of scriptural sources as one that, 'is not explicit, but depends upon the hearer's or reader's assumed ability to locate the resonances of the instruction as based in the authoritative traditions known elsewhere'.[86] Brooke provides three examples of allusions to Genesis in *Musar leMevin*. The first is found in 4Q416 2 iii line 20 - 4Q416 2 iv line 5 where phrases such as 'helpmeet of your flesh', 'from her mother He has separated her', 'she will become for you one flesh', and 'she is the flesh of your nakedness' appear.[87]

In the case of 4Q416 2 iii-iv there is little need to articulate a standard used to determine that Genesis 2.24 and 3.16 are being referred to in these lines. These lines so clearly base instruction on the creation narrative that they help to establish the significance of the tradition elsewhere in the document. One might speculate that the occurrence of Genesis 2-3 traditions here are intertwined with, or transform allusions to, Deuteronomy 13.7 and 28.54 elsewhere in this fragment (4Q416 2 ii 21). In light of the phrase 'wife of your

---

[85] BROOKE, 'Biblical Interpretation,' p. 211.
[86] BROOKE, 'Biblical Interpretation,' p. 212.
[87] BROOKE, 'Biblical Interpretation,' p. 212.

bosom' in 4Q416 iv line 5, the case may be made that 'vessel of your bosom' in 4Q416 2 ii line 21 could relate to a Genesis tradition and to (or rather than) a Deuteronomy tradition. The significance of adjudicating the occurrence of an allusion could at times alter the interpretation of the theology of the document.

Brooke's second example of wisdom as narrative exegesis is from 4Q417 1 i line 16 which contains significant phrases such as 'children of Seth/Sheth,' 'Vision of Hagu', and 'inheritance to Enosh/humanity'.[88] Brooke justifies a reading of 'Enosh' in these lines as the antediluvian figure of Enosh as opposed to 'mankind'.[89] The identification of the allusion in 4Q417 1 i may be correct and will be considered in more detail in chapter four. However, for the moment it may be noted that determining the referent of an allusion is made more difficult in the case of a damaged and partially preserved document. Brooke engages in a careful consideration of these lines and yet, in the end, the lists of criteria do not always resolve the exegetical impasse. This passage (4Q417 1 i 15-18) is among the most vigorously debated in the document. The application of principles suggested may guide us in reading allusions in *Musar leMevin*, but do not eliminate the validity of other interpretations. Perhaps a developed discussion around multiple occurrences of allusions to creation in *Musar leMevin* and other early Jewish literature will help advance an explanation of these lines.

The fifth category, *wisdom as pesher*, is almost a non-category for wisdom documents as no biblical source is ever explicitly cited and then interpreted in a pesher style in a known composition.[90] However, Brooke does suggest that the רז נהיה, which occurs in *Musar leMevin* and the *Book of Mysteries*, is similar or suggestive of a pesher interpretation. While the רז נהיה almost certainly does not refer to scripture, he sees it as a tradition like the Torah that is available to all and is used similarly to Torah in some instances. The chapters to follow will re-raise this understanding of the רז נהיה and attempt to broaden any possible relationship between the mystery and themes surrounding creation.

These categorisations by Brooke highlight more specifically the four ways that biblical sources are being used in *Musar leMevin*. Three of the categories (narrative, halakhah, and pareness) represent a usage that is at times more explicit than the category of wisdom as biblical poetry, which tends to be less explicit. The relevance of developing criteria for adjudication is most clearly seen when attempting to locate non-explicit use of tradition in the category of poetry.

---

[88] BROOKE, 'Biblical Interpretation,' p. 212-13.
[89] BROOKE, 'Biblical Interpretation,' p. 212-13.
[90] BROOKE, 'Biblical Interpretation,' p. 9.

6. Synthesis of Approaches and Criteria

Several basic observations emerge from the preceding analysis of the study of non-explicit citations. Especially helpful is Dimant's use of the expression 'free narrative'. Citing the book of Tobit as an example of this type of allusion, she has demonstrated an independent reworking of a tradition which employs a sequence of motifs that suggest Job was used as a model throughout the book. The 'referential value' occurs in the number of coincidental motifs and terms between two texts. Dimant's category of 'free narrative' is helpful for considering *Musar leMevin's* non-explicit use of traditions, especially Genesis 1-3. When one conceives of the possibility of a 'free narrative' use of Genesis 1-3 in *Musar leMevin*, criteria that focus, for instance, on lexical and syntactical overlaps are placed within a broader category. If a running allusion to Genesis 1-3 can be established in *Musar leMevin*, then the likelihood of suspected non-explicit citations may be argued with greater certainty.[91]

The contributions by Hays, Allison, Williams, Dimant, Holm-Nielsen and Kittel for developing a method and criteria for identifying the occurrence of non-explicit traditions all overlap to some extent. The following is a compiled adaptation of these criteria that are applicable to the document *Musar leMevin*, with certain nuances changed where appropriate. The intention of these criteria is not to provide a checklist for possible allusions in *Musar leMevin*, but rather these categories provide basic guidelines to be used implicitly when considering an allusion to creation. In many instances there is no way to prove the occurrence of an allusion unless, perhaps, each of the below criteria were to apply. An allusion becomes likelier when more of the criteria can be applied. However, an allusion cannot be ruled out if some of the criteria do not apply. Therefore, this list serves to measure intertextual occurrences generally rather than provide criteria that would exclude the possibility of an allusion.

Categories For Identification:

(1) *Accessibility*. The author(s) had access to the source both in terms of the practical and chronological. Understanding the significance of other sources and *Musar leMevin's* knowledge and relation to those sources has at present only begun.
(2) *Vocabulary and Syntax*. The suspect non-explicit tradition shares specific and significant vocabulary or syntactical patterns with the proposed referent.

---

[91] In commenting upon Hays' criterion of 'Recurrence' for the identification of allusions/echoes Shum writes: 'the more specific a quotation from an earlier source-writing, the more significant the evidence that it provides in determining whether the document's author consciously had knowledge of that source-writing when composing her/his work'; in Shum, *Paul's Use of Isaiah*, p. 8.

(3) *Imagery and Motifs*. The more distinctive the imagery/motif of a suspect non-explicit tradition, when similar but not precise vocabulary or syntax occur, and similarly unique imagery/motif occurs in a biblical source the likelihood increases.

(4) *Literary Context*. Proven significance of a tradition established elsewhere in a document lends credibility to less pronounced occurrences that may be employing imagery without specific vocabulary shared with the referent. This is both a criterion of recurrence and volume.

(5) *Similar Tradition(s)*. The occurrence of similar but more conclusive occurrence(s) in (an)other document(s) establishes a greater likelihood of the occurrence of a non-explicit tradition. Precedence elsewhere enhances probability here.

As these criteria show, not all the points made by others may be deemed equally relevant.[92] Several comments may be added to the list above. The author(s) of *Musar leMevin* were influenced by a wide variety of traditions that interpreted biblical traditions relating to creation. There are instances of direct lexical and syntactical agreement between the canonical Hebrew Genesis and the document. However, it is recognised that lexical agreement will not always be identical but will pick up on other traditions that use similar vocabulary and/or terms that are conjugated differently. Imagery and motifs found surrounding a considered passage may share similarities with the context of another composition, in this case an allusion may be more likely. Literary context should also consider genre. We may assume that similar language between two Hebrew sapiential compositions is more frequent than between a sapiential and non-sapiential work.

The discussion surrounding intertextual occurrences in the documents of early Judaism and nascent Christianity is most often in reference to the explicit use of biblical sources. It is helpful to distinguish between the terms 'quotation' and 'allusion' and attempt to be as specific as possible in using each of these terms. The contributions of some of the above scholars in defining 'allusion' has led to a greater precision for determining intertextual resonances. A critical evaluation and adoption of these various methodologies will be valuable when applied to the document *Musar leMevin*. Dimant's definition of the term 'allusion' is appropriate for application in the proceeding address of non-explicit citations in *Musar leMevin*. Less helpful may be an attempt to delineate between the terms 'allusion' and 'echo'. The use of these terms represents intertextual occurrences that range from explicit

---

[92] SHUM, *Paul's Use of Isaiah*, p. 10, concludes that he can only accept three of HAYS' criteria: volume, recurrence, and thematic coherence. He writes that *'availability* and … *historical plausibility*, though useful, are not always workable, and that both involve a high degree of conjecture… As for the criteria of *the history of interpretation* and *satisfaction*, our verdict is this: they are much less useful than expected, and cannot be taken as appropriate testing for the examination of alleged allusions or echoes'.

('quotation') to increasingly less explicit ('allusion' and 'echo').[93] Such a delineation in the case of *Musar leMevin* is not helpful and in the discussions that follow non-explicit citations will simply be referred to by the term 'allusion'.

Finally, any honest approach to identifying the occurrence of allusions must admit the reality of the hermeneutical event. The further away an occurrence is from a formal citation the more significant the role of the criterion of satisfaction. We may even go so far as to claim to understand what would have satisfied readers or hearers of an earlier period based on our possession of the Hebrew Bible. Hopefully, scholarly efforts are bringing us closer to the world of previous centuries, however, our thoughts are not informed in the same way or by all the same sources as 2nd c. or 3rd c. BCE readers. Therefore, it is important to recognise not only that subjectivity *would have been* an inherent part of identifying allusions in the distant past, but that it has become even more so the farther removed we are from the time of composition.

7. Conclusion

The relevance of the study of Genesis 1-3 creation traditions in *Musar leMevin* will quickly become apparent. Manuscripts 4Q416 1 and 4Q417 1 i have each been assigned to the beginning of *Musar leMevin*, given the different content of these fragments, it is thought that they represent divergent recensions of the same document. In the case of 4Q417 1 i such a hypothesis may never be substantiated. However, 4Q416 1 - 2 almost certainly represent the opening columns of 4Q416.[94] In the case of 4Q417 1 i and 4Q416 1 - 2 there are a number of explicit and possible non-explicit usages of Genesis 1-3 creation traditions. Also notable is 4Q423 which explicitly and possibly non-explicitly uses Genesis 1-3 traditions and likely stands near the end of the document.[95] Elsewhere in the document, as noted above, other identifiable uses of Genesis 1-3 occur. The importance of Genesis for *Musar leMevin* is thus not questioned, rather the extent to which the tradition was used and the degree of its influence on the document has yet to be examined in depth. The probability that the document began with creation motifs and then continued this theme through to the latter portion of the composition should raise questions regarding the role of the theme elsewhere in the document.

---

[93] For HAYS, the term 'allusion' is used of obvious intertextual references and 'echo' of subtler references; however, it should be questioned whether this delineation serves to clarify occurrences or further obfuscate the identification of non-explicit uses of traditions.

[94] *DJD XXXIV*, p. 73; TIGCHELAAR, *To Increase Learning*, pp. 191-93.

[95] *DJD XXXIV*, p. 505; TIGCHELAAR, *To Increase Learning*, p. 169.

The purpose of establishing preliminary guidelines for approaching and discussing the occurrence of non-explicit traditions elsewhere has been to establish a framework within which to determine the use of Genesis 1-3 traditions throughout *Musar leMevin*. The identification and adjudication of a non-explicit use of a Genesis tradition may hold insights into how sapiential themes were formulated throughout the document. It is already understood that cosmological and anthropological concepts owe dependence, to varying degrees, to a tradition that extends back to Genesis. By exploring some of these more certain themes and identifying possible allusions to Genesis 1-3 it is hoped a fuller picture of the theology of *Musar leMevin* will be understood.

CHAPTER 3

Identification of Allusions to Genesis Creation Accounts

1. Introduction

This chapter explores a number of fragments of *Musar leMevin* which may or may not contain an allusion to traditions related to Genesis 1-3. Once identified some might be grouped according to similar themes and motifs and expanded upon in the chapters to follow. Others might simply be noted as containing an allusion, thereby substantiating the significance of creation traditions in the document, with little more comment outside of their identification and adjudication here. In general, if it can be displayed that *Musar leMevin* contains a type of running allusion (or free-narrative) to Genesis creation traditions, or at least repeatedly turns in allusion to traditions stemming from Genesis, the overall likelihood of more contestable allusions might be made more certain.

The preceding chapter on methodology attempts to develop the conversation surrounding the identification of non-explicit uses of literary traditions for the chapters to follow. This was done in order to be transparent in the difficulties posed in arguing for an allusion as well as to suggest criteria that might aid in adjudicating the likelihood of an allusion. In this chapter the criteria adopted and developed there will be used, however, not in a formulaic manner. Some language and assumptions will be evident based upon chapter two, but the process of arguing for an allusion will not conclude with a list of criteria that match the allusion to a given passage. It will be evident, for instance, that the criterion of shared vocabulary and syntax or literary context is being used without having to note it explicitly. Finally, the chapters that follow this chapter will attempt to organise allusions in a more thematic manner, which will further serve to demonstrate allusions. While this chapter simply identifies allusions based upon the general criteria adopted in chapter two, the following chapters will examine how these allusions relate to one another and their influence on various theological themes. The issues raised in chapter one (רז נהיה, the language of 'poverty', angelology, and anthropology) may be elucidated by conceptions of creation and serve as a way forward in resolving unanswered questions.

A brief physical description of the fragments is provided as well as a transcription of relevant lines. If the use of Genesis traditions in *Musar leMevin* proves to provide any structure for the document this physical description will lay the groundwork for possible location of fragments. Placement of fragments in the reconstructions of Elgvin, Steudel and Lucassen (S/L), and Tigchelaar are provided in the introduction of each fragment. However, detailed explications of selected lines and their relationship to the document as a whole will be reserved for the following chapters.

The organisation of the discussion in this chapter follows the numerical designation and sequencing of the fragments as found in DJD 34. The reasons for this ordering are: (1) it facilitates a more objective approach that allows allusions to emerge from the fragments; and (2) serves as a resource that might be easily referred to in following chapters as opposed to a thematic grouping.

2. Presentation of Fragments

2.1 4Q415 2 i + 1 ii

Fragments 4Q415 2 i + 1 ii consist of nine lines that are preserved with the centre of the column destroyed. The margins on both the left (2 i) and right (1 ii) are preserved but neither the top nor bottom remain. These fragments are unaccounted for in the reconstructions of Elgvin, S/L and Tigchelaar.

Fragment 4Q415 2 i + 1 ii preserves several words that seem to reflect an agricultural sense[1] that may stem from a paraphrase of the Garden of Eden account in Genesis 1-3. Lines 5-6 are written in the second and third person and appear to be exhortations or warnings. Lines 8-9 describe the rebirth or regularity of the seasonal cycle. Thus the fragments maintain in content a use of imagery from nature throughout.

]ב עולם /זרע	]∘ יכה ∘∘∘[ ]ב (4
כ[יא לוא ימוש זרעכה	קודשכה לוא[(5
א[ותשיש פרי	מנחלת[(6
]∘ נדיבים	](7
לכו]ל קצים יפרח	](8
]ם והתחדש	](9

---

[1] One might consider reading 'your seed' in the sense of 'your offspring' ('children'), however, the surviving context would also indicate an agricultural usage of the term 'seed'.

4) in [ ] your [   ] . . . eternity, seed
5) your holiness not[   ] your seed will not be removed
6) from the inheritance of [   ] and rejoice in the fruit
7) [   ] nobles
8) [*at al*]*l* times it will blossom
9) [   ] and be renewed

The agricultural terms זרע and פרי appear within close proximity in Genesis
1.11, 1.12 and 1.29 and only appear together again in Leviticus 27.30. The
suggestion that this fragment reflects the use of a Genesis creation narrative
may be made not only on the basis of vocabulary from Genesis 1-3 but also
on the basis of forms in other fragments of the document that preserve more
certain allusions. Most importantly, 4Q423 1, 2 i clearly paraphrases the
Garden of Eden account and may suggest that some agricultural imagery in
Musar leMevin is used throughout with reference to an Edenic garden (see
§2.15 below).

A number of similarities occur between 4Q415 2 i + 1 ii and 1QH[a] xvi.
Column xvi of the *Hodayot* uses explicit imagery of the Garden of Eden
throughout. The word עולם frequently occurs (ll. 6, 8, 12, 14, 20) in this
extensive allusion to Eden. Two of these uses are rare phrases also found in
4Q418 81 (1QH[a] xvi 6 מטעת עולם, 8 מקור עולם; cf. 4Q418 81 1 מקור עולם, 14
למטעת עו]לם) which might possibly suggest correspondences to Eden for both
4Q415 2 i + 1 ii and 4Q418 81. The word פרי is also used several times in
1QH[a] xvi (ll. 11, 13, 20). The term פרח also occurs often in 1QH[a] xvi (ll. 6, 7,
10, 20, 30) and in one instance (l. 20) occurs within a phrase with 'Eden':
עולם לעדן כבוד פר]ח ('eternal, for the abundant garden bloss[oms'). There is
yet another possible connection between language used in the *Hodayot* and
Musar leMevin. 4Q423 1, 2 i and 1QH[a] xvi both cite the identical phrase from
Genesis 3:18 (קוץ ודרדר). Finally, apart from the *Hodayot*, the word נדיבים
occurs in 4Q416 2 iii in a context that is laden with allusions to creation.

One might also note similarities that occur between 4Q415 2 i + 1 ii and
the *Book of Watchers* 5.1-4 where it reads:

Observe how the verdant trees are covered with leaves and they bear fruit. Pay attention
concerning all things and know in what manner he fashioned them. All of them belong to him
who lives forever. His work proceeds and progresses from year to year. And all his work
prospers and obeys him, and it does not change; but everything functions in the way in which
God has ordered it.[2]

---

[2] Translation by E. Isaac in J. H. Charlesworth (eds.), *The Old Testament Pseudepigrapha, vol. 1* (New York: Doubleday, 1983) pp. 14-15. See also critical additions by M. Black, *Apocalypsis Henochi Graece* (Leiden: E. J. Brill, 1970) pp. 20-21; and M. A. Knibb, *The Ethiopic Book of Enoch: A New Edition in the Light of the Aramaic Dead Sea Fragments* (Oxford: Clarendon Press, 1978) pp. 8-10.

Like *Book of Watchers* 5.1ff., 4Q415 2 i + 1 ii appears to conceive of the regularity of nature and seasons: (1) in line 5 we read that seed will not be removed; (2) in line 8 that something (seed or fruit?) will sprout in every period or season; and (3) in line 9 that it will be 'renewed'. The opening column of *Musar leMevin*, 4Q416 1 discussed below, also reflects this theme.

Other possible hints of creation traditions occur in this fragment. First, line 6 contains the words ותשיש פרי ('rejoice in the fruit'). Negative connotations associated with eating from the tree of knowledge are not envisaged in *Musar leMevin*, but rather the ability to differentiate between good and evil has positive connotations (cf. 4Q417 1 i; 4Q423 1, 2 i). The idea that one rejoices in the fruit could be identified with a positive conception of gaining knowledge after eating the fruit.[3] Second, the occurrence of the term 'eternal' followed immediately by 'seed' (l. 4) might be associated with the phrase 'eternal planting' (4Q418 81 13) a term which could itself allude to Genesis 1-3. Third, the terms 'inheritance', 'eternal' and 'nobles' in this fragment each suggest the possibility that more than straightforward agricultural matters (alone) are being discussed. The term 'inheritance', as Murphy discusses, is used metaphorically within the document.[4] As discussed briefly in chapter one, and to be discussed in greater detail in chapter 4, the term 'noble' is not used simply for a class of the wealthy.[5]

On account of the degree to which 4Q415 2 i + 1 ii is fragmentary, it is impossible to draw any certain correlation between it and the Genesis creation narrative. Both words זרע and פרי are extremely common, both in the Hebrew Bible and other early Jewish literature, though they occur rarely in such close proximity.[6] Similarities between the *Hodayot* and this fragment are also suggestive of reading an allusion to Eden in these lines. If a compelling case

---

[3] *Musar leMevin* envisages the acquisition of wisdom and knowledge positively. The ability to distinguish between good and evil is central to wisdom (e.g. 4Q417 2 i 17-18). At least one other sapiential work (Sirach 17.7) conceived of the eating of the tree of knowledge in Eden positively. Similarly, the author(s) *Musar leMevin* interpreted wisdom bearing trees in Eden positively (4Q423 1, 2 i). Therefore, 'rejoicing in the fruit' could be joy derived from eating of the tree of the knowledge of good and evil.

[4] MURPHY, *Wealth*, pp. 173-74. *Musar leMevin* conceives of every creature having an 'inheritance' and is a regular theme in the document.

[5] On two occasions the addressee is called both a נדיב ('noble') and 'poor'; in 4Q416 2 iii 11 he is seated among the נדיבים (cf. 4Q418 177). It may be questioned whether the occurrence of the term 'noble' (5x in *Musar leMevin*), as a possible epithet for 'angelic beings', could relate indirectly to creation.

[6] In the Hebrew Bible פרי occurs approximately 200x and זרע 400x. The terms פרי and זרע occur in the same context 3x in Gen 1; elsewhere 1x in Lev 27.30; 2 Kgs 19.29; Is 37.30; Zech 8.12; Ps 21.11; and 107.37. In the DSS they do not occur together and in other early Jewish literature see 4 Ezra 4.29-30; and 8.5.

can be made for a running allusion to a Genesis 1-3 tradition in *Musar leMevin* the likelihood of this fragment resonating such a tradition increases.

2.2 4Q415 2 ii

Fragment 4Q415 2 ii is the second column of fragment 4Q415 2, and thus follows the fragmentary text just discussed. This column survives in nine lines with only the right margin intact and neither top nor bottom remaining. The text and the material it preserves are unaccounted for in the reconstructions of Elgvin, S/L and Tigchelaar.

The column below is addressed to one who is identified in the second person feminine singular. This unusual occurrence of a female addressee is highly significant and will be discussed in detail in chapter 5. Line one exhorts a woman to honour someone like a father. In lines 2 and 4 the woman addressed is exhorted not to 'remove' or 'reject' a covenant. Line 8 could be read as a good wife being praised by men. Lines 7 and 9 address the origin or birth-time, presumably, of the female addressee although nothing indicates this syntactically in line 9.

```
(1 כאב כבדי ∘[ ]∘[ ]
(2 אל תמישי בלבבך וע[ן
(3 כול היום ובחיקו בר[
(4 פן תפרעי ברית קוד]ש
(5 ואריבת לנפשך וב[ן
(6 א]ו/י[שה]7 עד לש[ן
(7 בבית מכו[רותיך ]ובבריתך ת[ן
(8 תהלה [ ]∘ 8∘ כל אנשים[
(9 [ ]ל[ ] מבית מולדים[
```

1) Like a father honour [
2) do not return/remove your heart [
3) all the day/continually, and in his bosom [
4) lest you ignore a holy covenant [
5) and one hated by your soul [
6) [ ] a w[if]e/its fo[undat]ion[9] (?) until [

---

[7] Reconstruction not represented in *DJD XXXIV*.

[8] The editors suggest possibly reconstructing בפי or על פי, *DJD XXXIV*, p.49.

[9] A rare plene spelling א[י]שה ('woman') could be reconstructed here. אישה can be read in 4Q417 1 i 9 as well. Elsewhere, אשה ('woman') occurs only once (4Q416 2 iii 20) and אשת, in construct, on two occasions (4Q416 2 iv 5, 13). אוש with the pronominal suffix -ה ('its foundation') could also be reconstructed. Another option is to read it as 'her husband', however, the 3rd fem. would not seem to fit the surrounding context of a direct address to a female. The editors comment: 'In the context, this may perhaps be אישה, ארושה, or אורשה–but why the change to the 3rd fem.?' *DJD XXXIV*, p. 49. LANGE, *Weisheit*, p. 50 reads אישה as

7) in the house of yo[ur origins] and in your covenant[

8) a praise [   ] all men[

9) from the time of birth[10] [

Several items in this column suggest the occurrence of an allusion to a creation tradition. First, lines 7 and 9 use language that might be related to beginnings or derivation in the phrases בית מכו[רותיך and בית מולדים, likely the woman's origin is conceived of in these lines. These phrases may also be considered synonymous since they are both in construct with בית. Second, in line 3 the 3rd masculine pronominal suffix occurs with the noun 'bosom' (חיקו), which is a term that occurs elsewhere in the document in the construct 'wife of your bosom' (אשת חיקכה; 4Q416 2 iv 5, 13) and 'vessel of your bosom' (כלי חיקכה; 4Q416 2 ii 21). 4Q416 2 is a large fragment preserving portions of four columns and contains a number of clear allusions to Genesis 1-3. Apart from 4Q416 2 columns and the fragment here, the term חיק does not occur in *Musar leMevin*.

Line 7. Strugnell and Harrington reconstruct the word מכו[רותיך ('your origins') in line 7. The two obvious reconstructions of 'מכו]' that they consider are מכו[ר and מכו]ן. The editors comment that a suffixed form of מכון could be possible, but dismiss the idea citing the term's usual occurrence elsewhere in a context associated with God and temple.[11] To support a reconstruction of 'origins' in line 7 they note the occasion in Ezekiel 16.3 where מכרתיך occurs alongside ומלדתיך (cf. מולד in l. 9).[12] In addition, in line 9 the term בית precedes the occurrence of the word 'origin' and likewise in line 7 the word בית occurs before the fragmentary word 'מכו]', a similarity that further supports the reconstruction מכור. The addition of the 2nd person singular feminine pronominal suffix ך- to מכור is based upon the number of spaces available for reconstruction and the same suffix in the following word בריתך.

'woman'. Reading 'woman' both here and in 4Q417 1 i 9 is appealing because of interest in the document on wives and daughters, especially in possible allusions to creation.

[10] The editors provide the second person singular 'thou' in their translation: '*from* the house where thou wert born'; בית מולדים 4Q299 1 4, 3a ii-b 13, and 5 5 in *DJD XX* is always translated 'times of birth', which also indicates origins and creation. See also Morgenstern, 'The Meaning of בית מולדים,' pp. 141-144.

[11] 4Q415 11 13 has a suffixed form of מכון (מכוניה), and is a fragment also concerned with a daughter or wife. If this is the preferred reading the translation of 'your establishment' is possible instead of 'your origins'. The editors also reconstruct בית מו]לדים in 4Q415 11 11, *DJD XXXIV*, p. 58.

[12] *DJD XXXIV*, p. 49. The word מולד is a significant term in *Musar leMevin*, occurring seven times, and is apparently something that should be considered as a point of meditation or consideration in a way similar to the רז נהיה. Not only does it occur alongside the רז נהיה (4Q416 2 iii line 9 רז נהיה דרוש מולדיו), but identical exhortations occur on every occasion except in 4Q415 2 ii that one should 'seek' it (דרוש; 4Q418 9, 9a-c line 8) or 'take' it (קח; 4Q415 11 line 11; 4Q416 2 iii line 20; 4Q417 2 i line 11; 4Q418 202 line 1).

Line 9. Lange and Tigchelaar have both emphasised similarities, and allusions shared, between *Musar leMevin* and the *Book of Mysteries*.[13] Furthermore, *Mysteries* is a sapiential work that itself alludes frequently to creation. The best preserved context for the phrase בית מולדים is in 4Q299 3 ii. Allusions to creation in the fragment are found in several lines, including the following. In lines 4-5 the description of wisdom occurs with the term ערם√, which likely is an allusion to creation (Gen 2.25-3.1, 3.5): 'wisdom is hidden except crafty wicked wisdom' (חוכמת עורמת רוע).[14] There is mention of the 'word of his maker' (דבר עושו) twice (ll. 7, 8). Lines 10-12 are concerned with the establishment of all things from before the world (מקדם עולם), as well as reference to 'plans' (מזמות) and perhaps 'establishment' ([מכון]). The final line (l. 16) of the fragment speaks of the creation of the nations (עמים כי בראם ומעשיהם). The immediate preceding and following context of each line is not known, however the fragmentary lines 11-13 leading up to the occurrence of בית מולדים speak of 'design' and 'making', they read as follows:[15]

[כול רז [ומכון] כול מחשבת עושה כול]	] (11
[ה]וא מק]דם עולם הואה[16] שמו ול]	] (12
[ות]ל מ]חשבת בית מולדים פתח ל]	] (13

11)]every mystery, and [establishment] of every design, makes every[
12) it] is from be[fore] eternity, 'He' (?) is his name and to[
13) the] design of the house of origins he opened [

Harrington and Strugnell note that the abstract מולדים is not found in the Hebrew Bible, but only in *Musar leMevin* and *Mysteries*. In post-biblical Hebrew the word can mean: 'issue', 'offspring', 'descendants', 'act of giving birth', 'being born' or 'origins'. 4Q299 5 is a small fragment that preserves portions of the final 5 lines of the same column that 4Q299 3 ii preserves. These lines are reconstructed as follows:

[	[ות כוכבים ל]זכר]ון שמ]	] (1
[	[רות רזי אור ודרכי חו]שך	] (2
[	[דין מועדי חום עם ק]ץ	] (3
[	[ומוצא לילה]	] (4
[	[בית מולדים]	] (5

---

[13] LANGE, 'In Diskussion'; TIGCHELAAR, 'Wisdom and Counter-Wisdom'.

[14] Perhaps this phrase could help explain the cryptic phrase חכמת אוט in *Musar leMevin* (4Q416 2 ii 12; 4Q418 8 13).

[15] Hebrew text is from *DJD XX*.

[16] הואה is spelled with four letters perhaps as a reference to God with a tetragram.

1)]stars for [the remembr]ance of
2)]mysteries of light and ways of dark[ness
3)]periods of heat with [
4)]the going out of night[
5)]house of origins[

These fragments taken together suggest that 4Q299 as a whole reflects on the design and order of the world based upon creation allusions.[17] If one were to reconstruct שמ[ו ('his name') at the end of 4Q299 5 1 then it would likely be a reference to creation as a memorial to its creator. This memorial, the reference in 4Q299 3 ii 12 ('"He" is his name'), and the references discussed above show several emerging themes: (1) the role of the creator; (2) the eternal design; and (3) the ordering of times (Gen 1). Creation is interwoven with ethical instruction for the addressee and good and evil are likely compared with the physical ordering of the universe (4Q299 3 ii 7-9; 4Q299 5 2). The phrase בית מולדים occurs in a column that reflects on the order of creation and proper behaviour. While it is not possible to determine with precision the best translation of the phrase it is likely that it be understood as a term closely related to creation and origins. Thus, both 4Q415 2 ii and 4Q299 suggest בית מולדים alludes to creation and in these contexts is best translated as 'house of origins' or simply 'origins'.

   4Q415 2 ii is apparently concerned with how the female addressee ought to relate to a man, who is probably her husband. In addition, her origin is likely referred to twice if the reconstruction of the final word in line 7 proposed in DJD 34 is correct. The final lines of 4Q416 2 iii and the following column 4Q416 2 iv make use of portions of Genesis 2.20-25 and, it will be argued, allude several times to that passage as well. In the latter two surviving columns of 4Q416 2 the addressee is instructed in various ways how he should relate to his wife. 4Q416 2 iii line 20 exhorts the addressee to consider her origins (קח מולדי[ה)[18] when one has taken a wife. In the lines that follow (2 iii 21-2 iv 13) frequent explicit and non-explicit uses of Genesis 2 occur, including the phrase אשת חיקכה in 4Q416 2 iv lines 5 and 13. Three similarities emerge from a comparison between 4Q415 2 ii and 4Q416 2 iii-iv: (1) interest in the origins of the female; (2) the term חיק used in a context somehow related to a female; and (3) a general concern with how a female should relate to males or males to females. Though much more could be said

---

[17] 4Q299 6 i, also probably preserving the same column as 4Q299 3 ii and 5, alludes to creation (the temple and perhaps a flood?) as well. Creation allusions in 4Q299 6 i 7 are: בגברתו ברא ('by His might He created' cf. Gen 1.1), 9 כל צאצא[יה ('everything goes forth from it'), 10 מטבורו פרש ('from its navel he separated'), 13 כי מעפר מבניתם ('for from dust is their structure' cf. Gen 2.7), 14 כול מקויהם ('all their pools' cf. Gen 1.9-10), 15 נתן ממשל ('He gave dominion' cf. Gen 1.26).

[18] Reconstruction mine.

regarding both columns and their use of a Genesis tradition, it may be concluded for now that allusions to Genesis in 4Q415 2 ii are likely.

2.3 4Q416 1

Tigchelaar provides a composite text of 4Q416 1 (overlaps 4Q418* 1, 2, 2b; 4Q418 229; and a conglomerate of small 4Q418 fragments) [19] that is significantly more extensive than DJD 34's transcription of 4Q416 1. The reconstruction below is that of Tigchelaar. Elgvin locates 4Q416 1 in column 7 while S/L, Tigchelaar and the editors of DJD 34 agree in locating 4Q416 1 in the first column of *Musar leMevin*. The location of 4Q416 1 in the first column is based upon the width of the right margin of the fragment.

The selected lines below primarily reflect cosmological concerns regarding the order of creation. The text as a whole is concerned with cosmology in relation to judgement and anthropology.

כוכבי אור[	כל רוח[	(1
ירוצו מעת עולם[	ולתכן חפצי[	(2
ואין להדמות בכושר ילכן[	מועד במועד ו[	(3
ת לממלכה[	לפי צבאם למ[שור במשורה ול	(4
	וממלכה למד[י]נה ומדינה לאיש ואיש	(5
	לפי מחסור צבאם [ומשפט כולם לו	(6
	וצבא השמים הכין ע[ן]ל	(7
	למופתיהמה ואתות מו[ן]עדיהמה	(8
	זה לזה וכל פקודתמה י[שלימו וי[ספרו]	(9
[א	להכון צדק בין טוב לרע ל[ ]ר כל משפ[ט	(15
[ל ל	י[]צר בשר הואה ומבינ[	(16
	בראתיו כי ה [	(17

1) every spirit [stars of light]
2) and to determine the matters of [they run from eternal times]
3) season upon season, and [without standing still. Properly they go,]
4) according to their host, to ke[ep in its keeping, and to   for kingdom]
5) and kingdom, for jurisdi[ction and jurisdiction, for each and every
6) according to the lacking[20] of their host. [And statute of them all to him/it

---

[19] TIGCHELAAR, *To Increase Learning*, pp. 175-76.

[20] TIGCHELAAR, *To Increase Learning*, p. 179, discusses the possibility that מסחור 'going around' should be read rather than מחסור 'poverty' or 'lacking' on the grounds of scribal error. While this would make line 6 much more comprehensible, the frequency of the word מחסור throughout *Musar leMevin*, at times with unusual nuances, may argue against his correction. If 'lacking' (מחסור) and 'poverty' (אביון, רש) are seen to describe more than the material poverty of the addressee in *Musar leMevin*, as this line indicates, the description of the host as 'lacking' may be insightful. For instance, 4Q418 55 and 69 discuss angelic beings,

7) And the host of heaven He has established ov[er   and luminaries]
8) for their omens and the signs of [their] se[asons
9) one to another. And all their appointments [they] will [complete, and they will] number [

15) to let the righteous distinguish between good and evil, to [ ] every stat[ute
16) [incl]ination of the flesh is he/it. And understand[
17) His creatures for [

A number of lexical similarities can be observed between 4Q416 1 and Genesis 1-2. This cluster of terms serves to strengthen the allusion to Genesis: רוח (Gen 1.2; 416 1 1), אור (Gen 1.3, 14-16; 416 1 1), מועד (Gen 1.14; 416 1 3), אתת (Gen 1.14; 416 1 8), ככב (Gen 1.15; 416 1 1), שמים (Gen 1.14-20; 416 1 7). In line 15 the phrase 'to let the righteous understand between good and evil' (להכון צדק בין טוב לרע) may be a reflection of the statement 'to distinguish between the light and the darkness' (ולהבדיל בין האור ובין החושך) in Genesis 1.18 (cf. *Instruction on the Two Spirits*). The phrase יצר בשר in line 16 might be related to the creation of man in Genesis 2.19-20. Lastly, in line 17 the term בראתיו occurs (cf. Gen 1.1) which concretely introduces the theme of creation in the document.

The ordered course of the heavenly bodies is described in the first nine lines of 4Q416 1 and serves as the backdrop for the motif of judgement in the following six lines. Thus *Musar leMevin* commences with a statement about cosmology based upon the orderly creation of heaven and earth followed by motifs of judgement and then exhortations for the righteous addressee to distinguish between good and evil. The luminaries' regulation or rule (משל) of the cosmos is widespread in early Jewish literature (e.g. 1QS x 1ff.; 1QM xi 8ff.; 1QH[a] ix 25-26; 1QH[a] xx 7ff.; 4Q299 5; *1 Enoch* 2-5; 81-83). The origin of luminaries as governing times and seasons can be traced back to the first verses of Genesis 1.17-18 (ולמשל ביום ובלילה ולהבדיל בין האור ובין החושך). Harrington comments upon this aspect of 4Q416 1:

It would appear that the wisdom instructions that follow in the main part were intended to help the one who is being instructed both to align himself with the correct order of the cosmos (as discerned from Genesis 1 and probably on the basis of a solar calendar) and to prepare for the divine judgment when the righteous will be vindicated and wickedness will be destroyed forever. If fragment 1 of 4Q416 is indeed the beginning of the great sapiential instruction, then it must have provided the theological perspective in which the sage's advice on various issues was to be interpreted. And that perspective was cosmic and eschatological.[21]

---

in contrast to the addressee, as pursuing truth without becoming tired. Angelic beings pursue truth and are likely to be seen as models for the addressees; however, if 'lacking' refers to the imperfect *obtainment* of wisdom (רז נהיה) the hosts here may be described as 'lacking' too. Compare the *Astronomical Book of Enoch*, which on the one hand describes the heavens as elaborately organised and ruled (*1 Enoch* 78-79) yet on the other, faltering and erring (*1 Enoch* 80).

[21] HARRINGTON, *Wisdom Texts*, p. 41.

4Q416 1 establishes sapiential instruction with an appeal to the created order and emphasises the importance of discerning the created order for purposes of ethical behaviour and justice. In terms of the significance of this opening column of the document, it suggests the importance of creation in the document as the basis for the instruction to follow.

2.4 4Q416 2 iii

Column 4Q416 2 iii consists of 21 lines (4Q416 2 i; 2 ii are 22 line columns) which are preserved in a four column fragment (4Q416 2 i, ii, iii, iv). The bottom of 4Q416 2 iii has damage points that correspond to those of 4Q416 2 i, ii while 4Q416 2 iv only preserves the text from the first 13 lines. Whereas Elgvin locates 4Q416 2 iii in columns four and five of the document (i.e. before 4Q416 1), S/L place it in column nine while Tigchelaar locates 4Q416 2 i, ii, and iv but not 4Q416 2 iii in his reconstruction table.

In column 4Q416 2 iii (cf. par. 4Q418a 16b + 17) as well as the following column 4Q416 2 iv, a number of allusions to Genesis 2.20-25 occur. While allusions are more straightforward in the last lines of 4Q416 2 iii, and first few lines of 4Q416 2 iv, an argument can be made for 4Q416 2 iii lines 15-18 having a conceptual basis in Genesis 1-3 as well. Lines 15-18 discuss the nature and likeness of man's creation. Lines 19-21 allude to Genesis 2.20-25 in order to instruct the addressee on how to relate to his wife. These lines read as follows:

15) חביט ואז תדע מה מר לאיש ומה מתוק לגבר כבוד אביכה ברישכה[22]

16) ואמכה במצעריכה כי כאב[23] לאיש כן אביהו וכאדנים לגבר כן אמו כי

17) המה כור הוריכה וכאשר המשילמה בכה ויצר על הרוח כן עובדם וכאשר

18) גלה אוזנכה ברז נהיה למען כבודכה ובן]הדר פניהמה

19) למען חייכה וארוך ימיכה *vacat* ואם רש אתה כשה[

20) בלוא חו/יק[25] *vacat* אשה לקחתה ברישכה קח מולד[ן]ה[24]

21) מרז נהיה בהתחברכה יחד התהלך עם עזר בשרכה[

---

[22] The terms 'poor' (רש) and 'head' (ראש) are frequent in 4Q416 2 iii and appear with both plene and non-plene spellings. On two occasions a *waw* is inserted to clarify that 'head' rather than 'poverty' is intended, the various readings in the column are: (l. 2) ראש; (l. 6) ברא'שכה and רישכה; (l. 11) ראש and רא'שכה; (l. 12) רש; (l. 15) רישכה; (l. 19) רש; and (l. 20) רישכה. The unusual plene spellings here may strengthen the case for reading אישה as אשה elsewhere. Here, the two occurrences of ראש could technically be taken as 'head'.

[23] This composite transcription has an important variant between manuscripts 4Q416 2 iii and 4Q418 9 17. 4Q418 reads, כאל rather than כאב.

[24] Reconstruction mine.

[25] Possible variant mine.

15) you will gaze. Then you will know what is bitter for a man and what is sweet for a man. Honour your father in your poverty,

16) and your mother in your low estate. For as God is to a man so is his own father and as אדנים are to a man so is his mother, for

17) they are the oven of your origin. As He set them in authority over you and fashioned by the spirit, so serve them. As

18) He uncovered your ear to the רז נהיה, honour them for the sake of your honour, and with [ ] venerate their presence,

19) For the sake of your life and of length of your days. *vacat*. If you are poor as[

20) without statute/bosom (?) *vacat*, you took a wife in your poverty, understand [her] origins[

21) from the רז נהיה, in your uniting together (with her). Walk together with the helper of your flesh

2 iv 1) his father and mother [

Before an examination of possible allusions to Genesis 1-3 in 4Q416 2 iii lines 15-21, the preceding context of the column may be summarised. Discussed briefly in chapter one was 4Q416 2 iii lines 2-14 which contain a number of statements about poverty. Most discussed was the phrase 'you are poor' (אתה אביון/ראש/רש) which occurs a number of times (ll. 2, 8, 11, 12, 19, 20) in the column. In lines 5-6 the addressee is exhorted not to take wealth (אל תקח הון) from someone unknown lest it adds to one's poverty, leads to death and corrupts the spirit. When one avoids taking wealth in Line 7 a positive consequence occurs, the addressee's remembrance is said to 'flower forever' and an inheritance of joy is then left to their progeny. The seeking of something outside one's inheritance, described in the lines that follow (ll. 8-9), results in confusion and the displacing of one's boundary. The focus of the addressee's pursuit should be the רז נהיה. The רז נהיה in 4Q416 2 iii line 9 is the source by which one studies (his/its?) 'origins' (מולדיו) and knows allotments. Line 11 states that God has lifted the addressee's head out of poverty (כי מראש הרים ראשכה) and made him to dwell among the נדיבים ('nobles') and to rule over a glorious inheritance. However, in the lines that follow (ll. 12-13) the addressee is reminded that he is needy and should not use poverty as an excuse for not studying and seeking knowledge. Line 14 again exhorts the addressee to study the רז נהיה in order to understand the ways of truth and roots of iniquity.

Tigchelaar suggests that the phrase אביון אתה, and similar phrases, should be read as conditionals ('if you are poor'). Indeed, in 4Q416 2 iii line 19 there is a clear occurrence of such a phrase (ואם רש אתה). Several observations might suggest that poverty and inheritance in this column are conceived of as metaphorical at times, particularly the notion of being seated among the nobles but being poor. While not the focus of the present discussion, it should be noted that references to poverty in lines 15-21 (e.g. l. 15 'honour your father in your poverty'; l. 20 'you have taken a wife in your poverty') are interwoven with an exhortation to study the רז נהיה and the מולדים (l. 9). This is especially significant in light of lines 16-18, which address the derivation of the addressee (i.e. the offspring of his parents) in a context related to poverty.

Lines 15-18. Line 15 begins with an exhortation to pursue and gain knowledge, comparing the understanding of good and evil to sweet and bitter. In the following lines 15b-16 two unusual words occur. First is the term כאב (cf. 4Q415 2 ii line 1) which in parallel fragment 4Q418 9a-9c reads with the variant כאל. Whether the term כאב ('as the Father') is read or כאל ('as God') the referent is undoubtedly to God. The term that presents a challenge to translate is אדנים, rendered by Strugnell and Harrington as 'nobles'. The editors suggest that אדנים functions as the *middah* ('מדה') of אל. Divine names are occasionally contrasted with one another (e.g. יהוה = grace/mercy and אלהים = judgement) by way of an interpretative method of juxtaposition, which they suggest is known in later Judaism as the *middoth* (for instance in *b. Pes* 70b).

In the context of 4Q416 2 iii line 16 the editors propose that these two divine names אל (= creator and sovereign) and אדנים (= merciful and loving) contrast with one another.[26] The difficulties of accepting this theory are: (1) אב is not a divine name and אל is not accepted as the better reading; (2) אדנים is not necessarily a divine name either; (3) this would be the only document I am aware of that contrasts אל with אדנים; and (4) nothing in the context of 4Q416 2 iii suggests the implied attributes Strugnell and Harrington associate with the two titles.[27] The form אדני occurs very infrequently in the Hebrew Bible and Jewish literature from the Graeco-Roman period outside of 4Q416 2 iii and its parallel in 4Q418 9a-9c. In 4Q416 2 iii the text addresses, among other topics, the idea of parentage and birth. While lines 15-16 allude to the Decalogue[28] lines 15-18 are fundamentally concerned with the origin and formation of the addressee. The parents are to be honoured because of the role they have played in his creation. The earthly mother and father's function in the formation of their offspring is likened in these lines to two other beings: a father to the Father/God and a mother to 'lords' (אדנים).

Line 17 explicitly relates honouring and venerating parents with the notion that they begot the addressee ('they are the womb that was pregnant with you'). Also in line 17 the addressee is told that he has been fashioned according to a spiritual likeness (*by* the Spirit?), although the exact sense and precise translation of this statement is difficult to determine.

---

[26] *DJD XXXIV*, p. 121.

[27] 'A man's father represents אל (God *qua* Creator, Sovereign, and Judge, and his mother (*qua* merciful, loving, and gracious) represents אדנים'; *DJD XXXIV*, p. 121.

[28] Compare the fifth commandment in Ex 20.12: כבד אביך ואת אמך; with ll. 15-16 above: כבוד אביכה ברישכה ואמכה במצעדיכה.

Line 18 returns to the רז נהיה, which is already noted as connected to מולדים in line 9. A case for an allusion to Genesis creation traditions on the basis of motifs surrounding ideas of origins has already been made and is further strengthened by this column. In speaking about birth, the nature of humanity's creation is likely being referred to in lines 15-18. This suggestion may be made on the basis of three factors: (1) other occurrences of origins in the document; (2) the indisputable allusions to Genesis that directly follow (4Q416 2 iii 21 - 4Q416 2 iv); and (3) the relationship that might exist between 4Q416 2 iii 15-18 and 4Q417 1 i 15-18.

Collins suggests 4Q417 1 i lines 15-18 allude to an interpretative tradition of Genesis 1.26 where the plural 'us' refers to angelic participation in the creation of Adam.[29] While 4Q417 1 i will be discussed in detail both here and in the next chapter, it will be proposed that 4Q416 2 iii lines 15-18 may be attributing the addressee's origins to both God and angels similar to Collins' understanding of 4Q417 1 i. Human creation may be related to both an earthly parentage and a heavenly creation, an idea perhaps expressed in 4Q416 2 iii lines 15-18. If this is the case, one may question how the term אדנים in line 16 should be understood, as a case might be made for it having connotations to angelic beings. If אדנים refers in any way to angelic beings and if Collins' theory of reading 4Q417 1 i lines 15-18 as stemming from an allusion to a tradition interpreting Genesis 1.26 is correct, then a similar allusion may be operative in 4Q416 2 iii lines 15-16 as well.

Line 20. An alternative transcription and translation of 4Q416 2 iii line 20 is possible. The editors propose reading this line as: '[without statute (חוק), thou hast taken a wife in thy poverty, take her offspring (מולד[י]ה)'. However, one might just as easily read: 'without bosom (חיק); you have taken a wife in your poverty, understand her origins (מולד[י]ה)'. The context is not adequately provided to determine which of these meanings is the more likely and the phrase 'without bosom' is indeed nonsensical. The suggestion that the second letter be read as a *yod* (חיק) rather than *waw* (חוק) is based upon: (1) the following context (4Q416 2 iv) where the phrase אשת חיקכה occurs twice; (2) the possible occurrence of חיק in the preceding context (4Q416 2 ii 21); and (3) the subject matter relates to the addressee's wife in these contexts and is also an important theme elsewhere in the document (e.g. 4Q415 2 ii; 4Q415 9; 4Q415 11).[30] The imperative קח is used in *Musar leMevin* with the רז נהיה (4Q418 77 4) as the object of the verb and could also be understood in the

---

[29] COLLINS, 'In the Likeness'.

[30] 4Q415 fragments refer relatively frequently to women. Both 4Q423 1, 2 i and 4Q416 2 ii-iv speak about women in relation to Genesis allusions. A number of similarities may be explored and terminology perhaps elucidated if read in light of creation narratives (e.g. 4Q415 11 11 ואם נפרדה מדריתכה קח מו[ן]לדיה and 4Q423 1, 2 i 5 ילדה וכל רחמי הורו[ת]). See also editors comments on 4Q423 1, 2 i 5 in *DJD XXXIV*, p. 510.

sense of 'understand' or 'grasp' rather than literally 'take'. The suggestion that the term מולד be translated as 'origin' rather than 'offspring' is made on the basis of: (1) line 9 ('by the רז נהיה study the origins (מולדיו) thereof'); (2) the discussion of origins in lines 15-19; (3) here in line 20 the term מולד is followed almost immediately by the רז נהיה; and (4) the occurrence of the term in 4Q415 2 ii (cf. 4Q299 1 4; 3 ii, 5). I would propose that 4Q416 2 iii 9 - 4Q416 2 iv fundamentally addresses issues of the origin of the addressee and his wife. The reconstruction with the 3rd person feminine pronominal suffix ה- is not without parallel in *Musar leMevin*. Significant for this reconstruction is the editors own choice to reconstruct קח מו[ןלדיה in 4Q415 11 line 11, a column concerned with issues pertaining to one's wife and/or daughter.[31]

Line 21. The most straightforward allusion to Genesis 2 occurs in the final line of 4Q416 2 iii and continues through the beginning lines of 4Q416 2 iv. Here the addressee is exhorted to unite together (התחבר) and walk with his wife or 'helper of your flesh' (עזר בשרכה). The nature of woman as man's helper is found in Genesis 2.18 (אעשה לו עזר כנגדו). A similar allusion (quotation?) occurs in 4Q*Meditation on Creation A* (4Q303) line 10: עשה לו עזר and further demonstrates the use of this tradition. Any explication of this line should be done in conjunction with 4Q416 2 iv discussed below.

2.5 4Q416 2 iv

4Q416 2 iv is the final column of a four column fragment (4Q416 2 i, ii, iii, iv). Originally, 4Q416 2 iv consisted of either 21 or 22 lines; however only 13 presently remain. The column is also preserved in fragments 4Q418 10a, b. Elgvin places 4Q416 2 iv in columns 5-6, while S/L and Tigchelaar place it at the top of column 10.

Column 4Q416 2 iv is generally concerned with advice about the relationship of a wife to her husband after leaving her parents. Here it is the husband who is addressed. Allusions to Genesis 2 appear throughout the column.

1) את אביו [ו]את אמו וד∘ב]ק באשתו והיו בשר אחד
2) אותכה המשיל בה ותש] [∘   אביה]
3) לא המשיל בה מאמה הפרידה ואליכה [תשוקתה ותהיה]
4) לך לבשר אחד בתכה לאחר יפריד ובניכה]
5) ואתה ליחד עם אשת חיקכה כי היא שאר ער]ותכה
6) ואשר ימשול בה זולתכה הסיג גבול חייהו ברוחה
7) המשילך להתהלך ברצונכה ולא להוסיף נדר ונדבה

13) אשת חיקכה וחרפ]

―――――――
[31] *DJD XXXIV*, pp. 58-59.

1) his father [and] mother and cleave [to his wife],

2) he has set you in authority over her, [her father]

3) has he not set in authority over her, from her mother he has separated her, but towards you [will be her *desire* and she will be]

4) for you one flesh, he will separate your daughter to another man and your sons [

5) and you will be a oneness with the wife of your bosom, for she is flesh of [your] nak[edness']

6) and whoever rules over her, beside you has removed the border of his life. Over her spirit

7) he has set you in authority to walk in to your good pleasure. And let her not increase vows and votive offering[

13) wife of your bosom and shame[

In 4Q416 2 iv line 1 an allusion to Genesis 2.24 occurs and on that basis the editors reconstruct the line.[32] The following two lines are concerned with the husband's authority over his wife, which is the consequence of eating from the tree of knowledge in Genesis 3.16. Separation of a wife from her mother and new devotion to her husband allude to Genesis 2.24. Line 3 clarifies and may help render a difficult to translate passage in 4Q415 11 11-13 that may also refer to the separation of a woman.[33] Line 4 is to be associated with Genesis 2.24 where the addressee's own daughter will be separated from him and joined to another man. The phrase בשר אחד ('one flesh') in line 4 occurs only in Genesis 2.24. The enigmatic phrase אשת חיקכה ('wife of your bosom') appears in both lines 5 and 13 and will be explored later in relation to the surrounding allusions to Genesis and similar language elsewhere in *Musar leMevin* (cf. 4Q418 186, 187). In line 5 the addressee is said to be made a 'unity' (ליחד) with the 'wife of his bosom' and also states that she is the 'flesh of [your nakedness]'; both these statements likely allude to Genesis 2.21-24.

Line 6 of 4Q416 2 iv begins a transition briefly to the theme of a husband's authority over his wife (so ll. 7-10); in *Musar leMevin* this authority is applied to the exhortation that the husband forbid his wife from making many vows. Strugnell and Harrington, as well as Brooke, note that lines 7-10 have their closest affinity to Numbers 30.[34] Numbers 30.15-17 detail various vows that a daughter or wife may bind that, given the circumstances, the father or husband may bear the guilt when voiding. The transitional line 6, between a

---

[32] The editors reconstruct and translate 4Q416 2 iii 21 and 4Q416 2 iv line 1 as: 'Walk together with the helpmeet of thy flesh [*According to the statute of God that a man should leave*] his father and mother And should cl[eave to his wife, So that they (. . . ?) should become one flesh]'; *DJD XXXIV*, pp. 113, 125.

[33] The editors translate 4Q415 11 11-13: (11) if *she be divided* (?) when she is pregnant for thee, Take thou *the* off[spring *of her* ...] [ואם נפרדה בהריתכה קח מן]לדיה] (12) her walking consider very diligently. If male [or female ...] (13) *her* foundations [מכונים] thou shalt not find. *By* these things test *her*[. The possible reconstruction of מן]לדיה here in 4Q416 2 iii, iv may be translated alternatively.

[34] *DJD XXXIV*, p. 129.

clear allusion to Genesis and then Numbers, makes the statement that 'who[ever] desires to rule over her, apart from you, has displaced the boundary of his life'. Genesis 3.16 and Numbers 30.17 share one basic similarity: both are concerned with the authority of the husband over his wife. Also, Genesis 2.20-25, like Numbers 30.17, is concerned with proper relations within the family between a man, on the one hand, and his wife and daughters on the other. Philo also links and discusses Numbers 30 with Genesis 2 (*Leg.* 2 63-64) as does 4Q416 2 iv. 4Q416 2 iv lines 6-9 are ultimately concerned with the father and husband's relationship to daughter and wife.

Line 13 ends after the word חרפ[ן and could be reconstructed as חרפ]תכה ('wife of your bosom and your shame'). One could speculate that חרפ]ן begins a new thought or separate clause and is not directly related to אשת חיקכה. However, given the preceding context in line 5 (אשת חיקכה כי היא שאר ער[ותכה) it is more likely the phrase 'wife of your bosom' is related to 'shame' or 'nakedness' in line 13 as well.

The columns of 4Q416 2 iii lines 15-21 - 2 iv lines 1-13 may be said to contain significant allusions to Genesis 1-3. At this stage of analysis the more obscure terms and phrases (e.g. אדנים, כלי חיקכה, אשת חיקכה) will simply be noted as possibly derived from a tradition of Genesis 1-3. However, in the case of the final line 21 of 4Q416 2 iii and first lines of 4Q416 2 iv there can be little doubt that Genesis 1-3 traditions are used. We will return to this passage for further examination in chapter four.

2.6 *4Q417 1 i*

Fragment 4Q417 1 i consists of twenty-seven lines. Both margins are visible with the left margin connecting to 4Q417 1 ii of the same fragment. Though the top and bottom of the column are very fragmentary, line 27 is clearly followed by the lower margin. Elgvin does not attempt to locate 4Q417 1 i in his reconstruction. However, S/L place this fragment within the context preserved in 4Q418 (ii). Tigchelaar locates the fragment in the third column of the document. Tigchelaar, in discussing S/L's unpublished reconstruction, correctly observes, '[S/L's] claim that 4Q417 is a shorter manuscript than, for example, 4Q416 and 4Q418, has not yet been presented with full argumentation. It appears that they suggest that 4Q417 1 was the beginning of the manuscript. That would imply that 4Q416 and 4Q417 represent different stages of redaction'.[35] Moreover, in the conclusion of his monograph, Tigchelaar concludes that S/L's 'grounds for regarding 4Q417 1 i as the first column of 4Q417 are not cogent'.[36] Regardless of this dispute, both S/L and Tigchelaar agree to locate the fragment within the first few columns of the document. The reasons provided by Tigchelaar are convincing in my opinion

---

[35] TIGCHELAAR, *To Increase Learning*, p. 167.
[36] TIGCHELAAR, *To Increase Learning*, p. 247.

and there appears to be no reason to definitively conclude that 4Q417 1 i was the first column of a manuscript of *Musar LeMevin*.

The content of 4Q417 1 i is addressed in the 2ⁿᵈ person singular. Significant motifs in this column include the רז נהיה, judgement, reward, and discernment of good and evil. Only a few of the lines of this fragment are relevant for consideration as allusions to Genesis 1-3 creation traditions. Lines 2-3, 8-9 and 15-18 read and translate as follows:

2) [ ] ۰۰۰ הבט [ו]ברזי פלא[י] אל הנוראים תשכיל ראש ۰   [

3) [ ]לו בפ۰[ ]۰۰۰ [כה ۰۰۰ והבט] ברז נהיה ומעשי קדם למה נהיה ומה נהיה]

8) עד ואז תדע בין [טו]ב ל[ר]ע כ[מעשי]הם [כי]א אל הדעות סוד אמת ברז נהיה

9) פרש את אישה³⁷ ומעשיה ۰۰۰[לכל חכ]מה ולכל] ע]רמה יצרה ממשלת מעשיה

15) כי חרות מחוקק לאל על כול ע۰[   ]   [ ] בני שות וספר זכרון כתוב לפניו

16) לשמרי דברו והואה חזון ההגוי לספר זכרון וינחילונו לאנוש עם ˢᵖ רוח כנ[י]א

17) כתבנית קדושים יצרו ועוד לוא נתן הגוי לרוח בשר כי לא ידע בין

18) [טו]ב לרע כמשפט [ר]וחו] *vacat*[*vacat* ואתה בן מבין הבט ברז נהיה ודע

2) [ ] . . . gaze, and on the mysteries of the wonders of the God of the awesome ones, you will understand the *beginning of* [38]

3) [ ] and gaze[on the רז נהיה and the deeds from before, on what was and what will be

8) of eternity. And then you will know between good and evil according to all their deeds, for the God of knowledge is the foundation/mystery of truth, by the רז נהיה

9) He made woman[39] distinct and her deeds for all wisdom and all craftiness, He fashioned her, rule over her deeds

15) because engraved is that which has been ordained by God against all the i[niquities] of the sons of perdition and a book of memorial is written before him

16) for those who keep his words, and it is the vision of Haguy for a book of memorial. He gave it as an inheritance to humanity together with a spiritual people [becau]se

---

[37] The editors transcribe אושה here (אוש as 'foundation' + ה-) and translate these two lines as: 'of eternity. Then thou shalt discern between *the* [goo]d and [evil according to their] deeds. For the God of knowledge is the *foundation* of truth And *by/on* the mystery that is to come He has *laid out its* (=truth's) *foundation*, And its deeds [He has *prepared with all wis*]dom And *with* all[c]*unning* has *He fashioned it*, And the *domain* of its *deeds* (*creatures*)'. They also consider the possibility of אישה as 'her husband' but have difficult making sense of this reading. *DJD XXXIV*, pp. 151, 154, see fn. 9.

[38] ראש] is preserved in 4Q418 43 and appears to preserve traces of a final letter, perhaps ראשיך. 4Q416 2 iii uses ראש as 'poverty' ('you shall understand your poverty').

[39] LANGE, *Weisheit*, p. 50, reads אישה and translates l. 9: 'hat er (die) Frau unterschieden, er hat gemacht […] und für sie alle, und was ist ihre Gesinnung'.

17) according to the image of the holy ones is his formation, but no more[40] does He give Haguy to a spirit of flesh because it knew not the difference between

18) good and evil according to the judgment of his spirit *vacat* and you, understanding one, gaze *vacat* on the רז נהיה and know[41]

Lines 1-2. The first two lines of 4Q417 1 i may vaguely have the created order in view. Harrington and Strugnell have interpreted the word ראש in line 2 in a chronological sense, but raise the possibility of reading 'poor' or 'poverty' as well.[42] If the rendering of ראש is 'the beginning of', then the phrase מעשי קדם[43] (literally 'deeds of before') likely refers to creation. Further, this phrase is followed by the double מה נהיה, which could be read in either the sense of: 'what has been' or 'what will be'. It may be questioned whether there is a purposeful ambiguity in the use of נהיה as depicting both past and future, co-ordinating *Urzeit* with *Endzeit*, and thus illuminating the רז נהיה.

Lines 8-9. Another possible allusion to Genesis (2.20-25) occurs in lines 8-9 of 4Q417 1 i. The editors struggle to transcribe and translate these lines. They consider the possibility that the third term of line 9 could be transcribed as אישה and translated as 'her husband'. However, they conclude that: 'since the preceding סוד can mean "foundation", it becomes at least plausible to read here too אוש "foundation", with its suffix referring to אמת'.[44] One difficulty of this reading is identifying the referent to the suffixes of the following מעשיה and יצרה. Furthermore, the description of laying truth's foundation in wisdom and fashioning it with craftiness (ערמה) as well as ruling over the deeds of truth seem implausible.

Reading אישה as 'woman' may make better sense of these lines, however, this would be the only instance in the Qumran literature where 'woman' is spelled with a *yod*. In the case that it is woman, lines 8-9 would then be concerned with the acquisition of wisdom through the role of the female in Genesis 2. The phrase פרש אישה (שׁ פרש rather than פרשׁ) at the beginning of the line refers to the separation of woman from man in Genesis 2.20-25. Line 9, taken as a reference to the division of male and female in Genesis 2,

---

[40] Another obvious translation of ועוד לוא is 'not yet', reading here 'He had *not yet* given Haguy to the spirit of flesh [Gen 2] because it did not know the difference between good and evil'. These lines could recount Genesis 2-3 as a past event in such a way that the 'spirit of flesh' is a description of humanity that has not yet eaten from the tree of knowledge. Once (some of) humanity ate of the tree, the vision of Haguy was given and humanity became 'spiritual'. The continuing distinction between two groups of people (fleshly and spiritual) would be based upon a continuing conception of Eden where only a portion of humanity partakes of wisdom.

[41] This translation will be discussed and supported in chapter 4.

[42] *DJD XXXIV*, p. 156.

[43] 4Q418 148 ii line 6 may elucidate the phrase בינה לקדמוניות שים translated by the editors, 'To understanding of the former things set [*thy mind*'.

[44] *DJD XXXIV*, p. 158.

elucidates several phrases in the surrounding lines. First, the exhortation to discern between good and evil in line 8 falls under the rubric of gaining knowledge of good and evil in Genesis 2-3. Second, the terms [חכ]מה and, especially, [ע]רמה in line 9 are a play upon the female's role in partaking of the tree of the knowledge of good and evil. The term ערום is not only used in a word play in Genesis 2.25 and 3.1 but the female in 3.10 responds to God after gaining wisdom, saying: את קלך שמעתי בגן ואירא כי עירם אנכי ואחבא ('I heard your voice in the garden and I was afraid because I am naked and I hid'). The phrase 'her deeds' (מעשיה) in line 9 is a reference to her eating of the tree of knowledge for all 'wisdom' and 'craftiness'. This is followed by a statement regarding her fashioning (יצרה) perhaps in Genesis 2. The phrase וממשלת מעשיה at the end of line 9 is an allusion to Genesis 3.16 and the consequence of eating from the tree of knowledge: והוא ימשל בך (and he will rule over her'). Recall that 4Q416 2 iv intertwines ruling over wives vows (ruling over deeds) with Genesis creation allusions.

4Q417 1 i line 9 is likely an allusion to the creation of the female from the male. In lines 8-9 we find allusions to Genesis 2-3 in: (1) gaining knowledge of good and evil; (2) 'wisdom' and 'craftiness' (nudity?); (3) the female's fashioning; and (4) the male's authority over the female. Also of importance is the occurrence of the רז נהיה as instrumental at the end of line 8. It may be questioned, particularly in 4Q417 1 i, whether this mystery is a mystery relating to Genesis 1-3.

Lange argues that the רז נהיה in 4Q417 1 i likely refers to the history and origin of humankind. The mystery in these lines is instrumental; by it God has separated the woman from man.[45] Lange writes on line 8:

Gott ist das Fundament, auf dem die der Schöpfung zugrundeliegende Wahrheit ruht. Wie dies gemeint ist, zeigen die folgenden Zeilen (1₈₋₁₀). Dort wird die Schöpfung der Frau beschrieben...[46]

Lange relates the separation of woman in this line with God's creation of categories in the document. The teacher in *Musar leMevin* is able to differentiate between good and evil on account of the pre-existent order of creation. Distinguishing between men and women here is part of a larger differentiation in the document.[47]

Lines 15-18. The text in lines 15-18 distinguishes between those who are in the form/inclination of the holy ones and a spirit of flesh. The pronominal suffix of יצרו refers to אנוש which could be understood, initially, as: (1) the antediluvian 'Enosh' the son of Seth (Gen 4.25ff.); (2) 'humanity'; or (3),

---

[45] LANGE, *Weisheit*, p. 59.
[46] LANGE, *Weisheit*, pp. 62-63.
[47] LANGE, *Weisheit*, p. 66.

more specifically, the first man Adam. The distinction between the interpretations is perhaps the difference between reading this as a historical event or as a general anthropological statement (Enosh and a spiritual people of that time, or humanity and the people of the Spirit).

Regardless of the ambiguity of אנוש, it is evident that the author understood the formation of אנוש and the עם רוח ('people of spirit') as being in the form/inclination of קדושים ('holy ones'; i.e. 'angels').[48] In contrast to the עם רוח, no meditation is given to the רוח בשר ('spirit of flesh'). The text thus appears to distinguish between two classes of human beings.

Collins has suggested that אנוש be read not simply as 'humanity' but literally the first man Adam. The creation and formation of Adam in Genesis 1.26 is alluded to in 4Q417 1 i. His reading of אנוש as a reference to Adam is based on a similar use of אנוש in 1QS iii 17-18:

$$\text{והואה ברא אנוש לממשלת תבל וישם לו שתי רוחות להתהלך בם עד מועד פקודתו}$$

He created humanity/Adam to rule the world and placed within him two spirits so that he would walk until the moment of his visitation.

Just as אנוש in 1QS iii-iv, in drawing on Genesis 1.26, refers to the human being, so *Musar leMevin* understands two types of humanity. Humanity's creation is based on a reading of dual creations found in Genesis 1 and 2: a spiritual people formed according to the pattern of the holy ones (1.26) and a spirit of flesh (ch. 2). Collins explains that, while the *Instruction on the Two Spirits* and *Musar leMevin* formulate their ideas differently the concept remains the same: humanity is dualistically divided right from the very beginning, at the time of creation.[49]

It is unlikely, continues Collins, that the antediluvian 'Enosh' is the recipient of the revelation of the book of memorial (l. 16) when there is no parallel in a number of references to him in the *Hodayot*, *Serekh haYahad* and other key texts. The book of memorial has strong apocalyptic overtones (Mal 3.16), and heavenly books are frequently mentioned in the books of *1 Enoch* (47.3; 93.1-2; 108.3), Daniel (7.10; 10.21; 12.1) and *Jubilees* (30.20-22). Collins concludes from this that the knowledge contained in the book of Hagu (l.17) derives from angels, particularly in light of references such as *1 Enoch* 93.1-2: 'Enoch began to speak from the books . . . according to that

---

[48] The term קדושים is typically used as an epithet for 'angels' in early Jewish literature (e.g. 1QS xi 8; CD xx 8; 1QM x 12, xii 1; 4Q403 1 i 40; *1 Enoch* (Ethiopic) 1.9, 12.2, 14.23, 81.5). On some occasions it is used as a reference to a holy community of humans (e.g. 1QM vi 6, xvi 1; 4Q274 1 i 6); however, some references are ambiguous (e.g. 1Q13 ii 9; 1QSb iii-iv; *Shirot 'Olat ha-Shabbat*).

[49] COLLINS, *Jewish Wisdom*, pp. 124-25.

which appeared to me in the heavenly vision, and which I know from the words of the holy angels understood from the tablets of heaven'. Collins' understanding of these lines, in summary, is that two types of humanity were created, and that the addressees are offered the opportunity to share in the knowledge of the holy ones.[50]

Drawing on T. H. Tobin's work of the creation of man in Philo,[51] Collins argues that *Musar leMevin* has in mind the creation of two Adams in the formulation of 4Q417 1 i:

Philo understands the two Adams in his own philosophical framework. The Qumran Sapiential text understands them as two types of humanity, a spiritual people in the likeness of the Holy Ones and a "spirit of flesh."[52]

However, it may be that the contribution of Philo to our interpretation of *Musar leMevin* is his preservation of an exegetical tradition of Genesis 1.26 in which humanity and angels are correlated, based in part upon the plural address 'let us' of Genesis 1.26. The notion of the creation of two types of human images in the first creation may have given rise to the division of humanity in *Musar leMevin*. On four occasions (*Op.* 72-76, *Conf.* 171-174, *Fug.* 65-70, *Mut.* 27-34) Philo refers to the role of angels in creation based upon Genesis 1.26.[53] In each case that Philo takes up the theme of the first creation in Genesis, he correlates the plurality of images with a duality of inclinations. A comparison of Philo's exegesis, in the following chapter, with that of *Musar leMevin* will aid in setting the sapiential texts in a broader exegetical context and further elucidate the angelology and anthropology of these lines. As will be explored in chapter four, further evidence of this exegetical tradition of Genesis 1.26 is also found in targumic and rabbinic texts (e.g. *Tg. Ps.-J.* 1.26, *Gen. R.* 1.26, *B. San.* 38b).

In concluding, in 4Q417 1 i lines 15-18 the author has in mind the creation of humanity (or Adam) in Genesis 1-2 according to the form/inclination of the angels in the first creation. However, it is not entirely clear in *Musar leMevin* what the implications of the angelic image are for the understanding of human nature. While these issues and opposing interpretations will be explored in detail in chapter 4, it is enough here to agree with Collins that allusions to Genesis 1-3 are at work in 4Q417 1 i lines 15-18. It may also be suggested that formation and divisions based upon line 9 and lines 15-18 are important motifs in the column. Thus, the column as whole holds significant allusions to Genesis and may be read afresh in light of Genesis allusions.

---

[50] COLLINS, *Jewish Wisdom*, pp. 123-24.

[51] T. H. TOBIN, *The Creation of Man: Philo and the History of Interpretation* (CBQMS 14; Washington D.C.: The Catholic Biblical Association, 1983).

[52] COLLINS, *Jewish Wisdom*, pp. 124-25.

[53] For an overview of the relation of assistants in Philo to Platonism see D. T. RUNIA, *Philo of Alexandria and the Timaeus of Plato* (Leiden: Brill, 1986): 242-51.

2.7 4Q418 69 ii

4Q418 69 is a fifteen line fragment preserved with the right margin intact. Neither the top nor bottom remain. Elgvin locates 4Q418 69 in column nine of his reconstruction. S/L locate the fragment in column thirteen. Tigchelaar suggests a possible placement of the fragment somewhere between 4Q417 1 and 2. Tigchelaar questions the editor's opinion[54] that 4Q418 69 (and 4Q418 55) were not written by the author of *Musar leMevin* but are likely independent compositions integrated by the author(s) at a later stage.[55] Tigchelaar concludes that 4Q418 69 ii (and 4Q418 55) 'have some features in common with the rest of *Instruction*… which may indicate that they have the same provenance as the rest of *Instruction*. However, it is not impossible that these shared features should be attributed to slight editorial reworkings of a *Vorlage*.'[56]

Lines 1-4 of 4Q418 69 addressed in the 2nd person singular contrast with the remainder of the column where the address is in the 2nd person plural (אוילי לב in ll. 4 and 8, the בחירי אמת in l. 10, and the בני שמים in ll. 12-13). At the end of line 15 the addressee is called בן מבין ('understanding one'). In the first half of the fragment the 'foolish-minded' are said to be fashioned by God though certain judgement and destruction await them. According to the latter half of the fragment the 'chosen ones' and 'sons of heaven' are expected to rise up in judgement against the wicked and are encouraged to pursue knowledge for an eternal reward. Lines 4-6 below appear to describe the creation and fashioning of the 'foolish-minded':

4) [   ] [הם[57] ובדעה כול גליהם   *vacat*   ועתה אוילי לב מה טוב ללוא

5) [   ] ומה] השקט ללוא היה ומה משפט ללוא נוסד ומה יאנחו מתים על כ]ל יומ]ם

6) [ה   אתם] [ל נוצרתם ולשחת עולם תשובתכם כי תקי]ן]∘∘   [חטאכמ]ה]

4) [ ] of them and in knowledge all their waves *vacat* and now, foolish-minded ones, what is good to one who has not

5) [been?[58] What] is quietness to one who has not been? What is judgment to a man who has not been established? What mourning will the dead make over their own death?

6) you were brought into existence [by] Go[d] but to the eternal grave you will return, for it will awaken [   ] you[r] sin

---

[54] *DJD XXXIV*, p. 14.

[55] TIGCHELAAR, *To Increase Learning*, p. 212.

[56] TIGCHELAAR, *To Increase Learning*, p. 224.

[57] TIGCHELAAR, *To Increase Learning*, p. 92, reconstructs the first two words of this line, where *DJD XXXIV* does not, as כול מימי]הם]. This supplement of the translation is based on *DJD XXXIV*.

[58] TIGCHELAAR, *To Increase Learning*, p. 92, reconstructs [ומה] נוצר ('been created, [and what]'), which further emphasises the motif of creation in these lines.

Similar to 4Q417 1 i lines 15-18, this text depicts the creation and fashioning of humanity. It appears that the question 'what is good to a man who has not been' in lines 4-5 pose a rhetorical question that may imply the cessation of wicked.[59] Neither the wicked nor righteous can be silent if they have not come into existence, judgement is meaningless for those never established, and the dead certainly do not fear or mourn death. Line 6 emphasises that the wicked were fashioned by God but, as this line and those that follow state, judgement and destruction await them. While the future of the wicked and righteous are underscored in this fragment, concepts of the future are shaped by the motif of creation. The wicked are created and fashioned by God just as the righteous (l. 6 ל מא[ן]נוצרתם[אתם)[60], which may be read in 4Q417 1 i discussed above. 4Q418 69, in describing the condemned segment of humanity (i.e. the spirit of flesh), details their creation. Those who judge them are described as seekers of truth (l. 7 דורשי אמת).[61] Fashioning and establishment in this column reflect the notion of creation, similar motifs occur elsewhere in the document and indicate a possible allusion to Genesis. Reflection on creation, as is known from other apocalypses, is the basis for formulating ideas of judgement.

2.8 4Q418 77

4Q418 77 survives in two fragments (a-b) with a parallel in 4Q416 7 at the beginning of lines 3-4.[62] The lines below are a composite text consisting of 5 lines. Neither fragments 4Q418 77 nor 4Q416 7 have visible margins on top or bottom. This fragment has not been assigned in the reconstructions of Elgvin, S/L, and Tigchelaar.

4Q418 77 is too fragmentary to characterise generally. Lines 2 and 4 use the imperative קח ('take') in relation to the generations/origin of Adam as well as to the רז נהיה. Line 4 uses the imagery of a season or period, which recurs throughout *Musar leMevin* (approx. 21 occurrences; e.g. 4Q416 1 3, 8, 14; 4Q416 3 3, 4; 4Q417 1 i 7; 4Q418 69 ii 14; 4Q418 81 13; 4Q418 286 3; 4Q423 5 5).

---

[59] The editors propose reconstructing and translating lines 4-5 as: 'what is good *to* a man who has not [*been created*? And what] is *tranquillity* to a man who has not come into activity?'; *DJD XXXIV*, p. 283. They comment on the likely reconstruction of ללא נוסד or ללא היה, DJD XXXIV, p. 285.

[60] There are approximately 3-4 letter spaces available for reconstruction. The editors do not reconstruct the Hebrew but do offer a translation of these lines as 'You were fashioned [by *the power of* G]od'. *DJD XXXIV*, p. 283.

[61] Two descriptions of two types of humanity are used in *Musar leMevin*: (1) 'spiritual' and 'fleshly'; and (2) pursuers of wisdom and neglecters of wisdom. These categories should be seen as stemming from a division of two groups of humanity in relation to creation itself and also pursuit of wisdom in an Edenic Garden.

[62] *DJD XXXIV*, p. 297.

[שמש ה] [בה]   ] (1

[רז נהיה וקח תולדות] א[דם וראה בכוש]ר   ] (2

[ופקודת מ]עשהו ואז תבין במשפט אנוש משקל]   ] (3

[מזל שפתיו לפי]רוחו וקח ברז נהיה על [מ]שקל קצים ומדת] (4

[ל] [ ] עד[ן]   ] (5

1) [   ] sun [

2) [   ] רז נהיה and grasp the *nature* of [m]an and gaze on legitimacy/being[

3) [and the care of] his [deed] and then you will discern the judgement on humanity, weighing [

4) [to the outpouring of his lips and according to] his spirit, grasp the רז נהיה upon [w]eighing the end and the grief of[

The phrase קח תולדות אדם in line 2 could be another allusion to creation in so far as it is concerned with the motif of origins or birth. It might initially be suggested that an allusion to Genesis 5.1 (זה ספר תולדת אדם ביום ברא אלהים אדם)[63] occurs in 4Q418 77; however, a few items taken together make this suggestion unlikely. First, as the editors note, the term can mean 'nature' or 'characteristics'.[64] Jacob Licht comments on the terms' broader usage in the Hebrew Bible and Tana'itic writings as: טעמה לעולם מה שנולד, התוצאות, ולא מקום-הלידה, המוצא.[65] In the Dead Sea scrolls it is similar to the term מולד. Second, the imperative 'take' (קח) has תולדות as the object which has parallels both in this fragment and elsewhere. For instance, in line 4 the addressee is exhorted to 'take' (לקח√) the רז נהיה, which should be understood literally in the sense of 'grasp' but also has the sense of 'study' or 'seek'. Moreover, the addressee is told in 4Q417 2 i line 11 to 'comprehend the origins/birth-times of salvation' (קח מולדי ישע). A variety of imperatives precede the רז נהיה in *Musar leMevin* and 'take' is just one among those. 'Understanding' (בינה) is also an object of the imperative (4Q418 177 4). As discussed above, 4Q416 2 iii line 9 could read, 'seek (דרוש) its origins' and then in line 20 'grasp/understand her origins'. Here in 4Q418 77 line 4 the רז נהיה occurs in parallel with the תולדות אדם, indicating the possibility that the two are similar in nature. Third, the term תולדות is not a frequent word in the Hebrew Bible, occurring a total of 12 times with 10 of those in Genesis (Gen 2.4, 5.1, 6.9, 10.1, 11.10, 11.28, 25.19, 36.1, 36.9, 37.2; Num 3.1; Ruth 4.18). Genesis 2.4 uses the word תולדות in the sense of 'origin' of the universe

---

[63] However, if one were to argue for the allusion it is conceivable that a book describing the nature of Adam as being in the likeness of אלהים (i.e. angels) could be read in Gen 5.1 and subsequently 4Q418 77.

[64] *DJD XXXIV*, p. 298.

[65] J. LICHT. *The Rule Scroll: A Scroll from the Wilderness of Judaea* (Jerusalem: The Bialik Institute, 1965) p. 85. תולדות has the sense of 'what is born' or the 'results/outcome' and not the 'place of birth' or 'going forth'.

or account of the creation of the world rather than the strict sense of the 'genealogy' or pedigree of a person as it is used frequently elsewhere (e.g. Gen 10.1, 25.12, 36.1; Ex 6.16; Num 1.20).[66] The *Instruction on the Two Spirits* begins (1QS iii 13) with an exhortation for the teacher to instruct the sons of light about תולדות כול בני איש ('the nature of all men'). The *Instruction on the Two Spirits* directly addresses the nature of humanity, creation and purpose. Identifying the term תולדות with the nature and origin of humanity is semantically possible and is congruent with the emphasis on beginnings in the document as a whole. The likeliest referent of the allusion is Genesis 2.4 and possibly to creation and the רז נהיה.

The occurrence of the term עדן ('Eden') in 4Q418 77 line 5 is not certain. The first two letters are clearly distinguishable in the photograph but the final *nun* is more difficult to decipher. Even if the final *nun* were to be restored, the word may well be translated as 'luxury' rather than the proper name 'Eden' (cf. Gen 2.10, 15). There is no occurrence of the word עדן elsewhere in *Musar leMevin* where a context survives (cf. 4Q418 138 3; 4Q418a 25 2).[67] Thus, though 'Eden' may occur in 4Q418 77, ultimately it remains uncertain.

2.9 4Q418 81 + 81a

The composite text 4Q418 81 + 81a consists primarily of the larger surviving fragment 4Q418 81. 4Q423 8 is a four line fragment with only seven to eight words preserved and parallels lines 2-5 of 4Q418 81. 4Q418 81 is the first column on a sheet, portions of the left and right margins remain as well as the top. The surviving column consists of 20 lines with the final 16 lines missing approximately a third of the end of each line. Both Elgvin and S/L locate 4Q418 81 in column 15 of *Musar leMevin*. Tigchelaar tentatively locates it between columns 13 (4Q418 167) and 19 (4Q418 103) and suggests that 4Q418 103 is derived from the same sheet.[68]

Column 4Q418 81 + 81a is written in both the 2nd and 3rd person, often varying between the two. The author(s) describes what God has done and concludes how the addressee should respond or be considered in light of God's action.

1) שפתיכה פתח מקור לברך קדושים אתה כמקור עולם הלל ∘[א]ז הבדילכה בכול

2) רוח בשר ואתה הבדל מכול אשר שנא והנזר מכול תעבות נפש[כי]א הוא עשה כול

3) וויורישם איש נחלתו והוא חלקכה ונחלתכה בתוך בני אדם ובנ[חלתו המשיל/כ/מה ואתה

---

[66] The LXX has a variant reading on Gen 2.4 which might be translated 'book of origins' (Αὕτη ἡ βίβλος γενέσεως). The targums contain no significant or insightful variants on Gen 2.4.

[67] The phrase 'Garden of Eden' occurs by name in 4Q504 8 line 6.

[68] TIGCHELAAR, *To Increase Learning*, p. 165.

4) בזה כבדהו בהתקדשכה לו כאשר שמכה לקדוש קודשים] לכול]תבל ובכול[א]ל[י]ם[

5) הפיל גורלכה וכבודכה הרבה מאדה וישימכה לו בכור ב]   [ל]

6) וטובתי לכה אתן ואתה להלוא לכה טובי ובאמונתי הלך תמיד]

1) He has opened your lips, a spring to bless the holy ones, you are like an eternal spring of praise [th]en He has separated/distinguished you from every
2) spirit of flesh, and you are separated/distinguished from everything that He hates, and (should) abstain from all abhorrences of the soul, [fo]r He made everyone
3) and each one will inherit their inheritance, and He is your portion and your inheritance among humanity, [and over] His [in]heritance has He set you in authority, and you
4) honour Him in this: sanctifying yourself to Him, as He has placed you as a most holy one [ ] world, and with all angels
5) He cast your lot, and multiplied your honour/glory very much, and placed you for Himself as a first-born
6) and my good things I will give to you. And you, are not my good things yours? So, in my faithfulness always walk

4Q418 81 + 81a shares a number of similarities with 4Q417 1 i lines 16-17 (cf. 1QH[a] xvi; 4Q299 3 ii; 5). First, both columns conceive of a division between the addressees and a 'spirit of flesh'. The idea of an inheritance is found in both as well. In 4Q417 1 i line 17 refers to the fashioning of humanity, while here in 4Q418 81 + 81a line 2 the 'making' (עשה) of everything is mentioned. Certainly both of the words נחלה and רוח בשר appear frequently in *Musar leMevin*, but only in these two columns are the three themes of a division from all flesh, inheritance and creation. The occurrence of an allusion to creation is most explicit in the phrase עשה כול ('He made everything'). This statement is composed with general vocabulary that does not occur verbatim in Genesis 1-3, though the verb עשה itself does occur repeatedly in acts of creation in Genesis (1.7, 11, 12, 16, 25, 26, 31; 2.2, 3, 4, 18); for example, the conclusion of chapter 1 וירא אלהים את כל אשר עשה והנה טוב מאד. In addition, the verb עשה is used twice in 4Q422 1 lines 6-7 (4Q*Paraphrase of Genesis and Exodus*) in regard to God's creative work in Genesis 1.[69]

A few more similarities may be observed between 4Q418 81 + 81a and creation in Genesis. First, lines 1-2 use the verb בדל√ ('distinguish' or 'separate'; cf. 4Q418 126 ii 8; 4Q418 221 4). These first two lines exhort the addressee to distinguish (הבדילכה) between the 'spirit of flesh' so that he might be separated (הבדל) from all that God detests. These statements, concerned with differentiation, are followed immediately at the end of line 2 and beginning of line 3 with: 'because He made everything and caused each man to inherit his own inheritance'. The Genesis 1 creation account also uses

---

[69] Line 6 reads: השמים והארץ וכול]צבאם עשה בד[('the heaven and earth and all their host He made); line 7: אש[ר עשה ורוח קודש]ו ('that He made and/by His holy spirit').

the verb בדל√ on a number of occasions. In Genesis 1.7 the text reads: 'and God made (ויעש) the firmament and He distinguished (ויבדל) between the water below the firmament and that which is above the firmament'. The verb to 'distinguish' is used in Genesis 1 on three of the six days of creation: day one (vs. 4); day two (vss. 6-7); and day four (vs. 18). The acts of creation can be summarised as the dividing, separating, and ordering of creation of each thing to its kind and season. Here in 4Q418 81 + 81a lines 1-3 the combination of the motifs of creation and separation strongly support that we have here an allusion to Genesis 1.

2.10 4Q418 126 i-ii

4Q418 126 i-ii preserves text from 16 lines. In fragment i, neither top nor bottom margins remain, but the right margin to lines 4-13 is visible. Fragment ii preserves the last portion of the final 8 lines. Neither Elgvin, S/L nor Tigchelaar assign a location to these fragments within the document in their reconstructions.

In lines 1-7 the general content is concerned with judgement of the wicked and the reward of the righteous or 'poor'. The address is composed in the third person:

1) [ ]   ל]וא ישבות אחד מכול צבאם ה[
2) או [ ]°ן באמת מיד כול אוט אנשים א[
3) [כי]בא[י]פ[ה]ת אמת ומשקל צדק תכן אל כול מ[
4) פרשם באמת הוא שמם ולחפציהם ידרש]ו
5) יסתר כול וגם לוא נהיו בלוא רצונו ומחוכ]מתו
6) משפט להשיב נקם לבעלי און ופקודת ש[
7) ולסגור בעד רשעים ולהרים ראוש דלים [
8) בכבוד עולם ושלום עד ורוח חיים להבדיל [
9) כול בני חוה ובכוח אל ורוב כבוכו עם טובו [

1) n]ot one from all their host will stop [
2) [ ] in truth from every אוט of men [
3) [for] with a true ep[ha]h and correct weight God ordered everything
4) He separated them by truth, he placed them, and for their desires they will seek[
5) everything will be hidden and also they shall not be(come) without his will and from [his] wisdom[
6) judgement, to return vengeance to the masters of iniquity and visitation of [
7) and to close up on all wicked ones and to lift up the head of the poor[70]
8) In eternal glory and peace everlasting and to separate the spirit of life [from   ]

---

[70] The idea of lifting the head of the poor is identical to 4Q416 2 iii 11 (מראש הרים ראשכה). The contrast of the wicked with the poor in line 7 further suggests that at times poverty language is a categorical description of the addressee.

9) all the children of Eve and in the strength of God and the multitude of His glory together
with his good things [   ]

The phrase בני חוה in line 9 is found neither in the Hebrew Bible nor
elsewhere in extant documents of early Judaism. Strugnell and Harrington
note that Eve is the 'orignatrix' and at times 'primogenetrix' of sin and death
in intertestamental texts (e.g. *Jub* 3.20-25; *The Life of Adam and Eve* 10-11;
and *1 Enoch* 62.7).[71] However, in non-biblical documents from the Dead Sea
Scrolls the name Eve does not occur, nor does the epithet 'sons of Eve'. The
condition of 4Q418 126 i-ii is too damaged to determine whether the phrase
בני חוה is used negatively or positively. One possibility is that the phrase was
used as a counterpart to בני אדם. However, for the task at hand any attempt to
identify the meaning of the phrase is unnecessary. Rather, it is significant that
חוה occurs only twice in the Hebrew Bible (Gen 3.20, 4.1) and is probably an
allusion to 'Eve' in Genesis.

If an allusion to Eve occurs in line 9 the preceding lines may be understood
in relationship to motifs surrounding creation in other columns. Line 3 clearly
describes God's perfect ordering. The reference to 'hosts' in line 1 could be to
angelic or heavenly hosts and line 3 to their establishment. In line 4 is another
occurrence of the theme of dividing (פרש; cf. 4Q417 1 i 8-9 above). Line 5
conveys that nothing comes into being without God's will and wisdom. The
translation offered above indicates, among other themes, an interest in
creation and judgement. Anthropological and cosmological divisions based
upon creation may be seen to be part of future judgement.

2.11 4Q418 177 (& 178)

4Q418 177 is an 8 line fragment with no surviving margins, top or bottom.
Neither Elgvin, S/L or Tigchelaar locate this fragment in their reconstructions.
The address is in the second person that reads:

שׁח[ת אבדון אשר בקצהו לוא]	(2 [
[*vacat* וכסה חרפתכה]	(3 [
[°וקח בינה האזינה ל°]	(4 [
[אתה רש ונדיבים י°]	(5 [

2) [the pi]t of Abaddon which in its boundary no[
3) [   ] and cover your shame *vacat* [
4) [   ] . . . and grasp understanding, give ear to [
5) [   ] you are poor and/but nobles [

---

[71] *DJD XXXIV*, p. 354. Several articles have been produced on the children of Eve in this
regard; most recently see GARCÍA MARTÍNEZ, 'Eve's Children in the Targumim,' in G. P.
LUTTIKHUIZEN (ed.) *Eve's Children: The Biblical Stories Retold and Interpreted in Jewish
and Christian Traditions* (Leiden: Brill, 2003) pp. 27-46.

The case for 4Q418 177 alluding to Genesis 1-3 should be made in conjunction with the content of 4Q418 178 below. Strugnell and Harrington suggest that these two fragments could have originally been proximate to one another.[72] Both fragments have the obscure phrase כסה חרפתכה, which is not a construction found in the Hebrew Bible; however, חרפתכה occurs in a cluster of allusions to Genesis in 4Q416 2 iv (l. 13). Neither of the words כסה or חרפה occur in Genesis 1-3 but it may be speculated that it alludes to ערם (or ערוה in 4Q416 2 iv) in Genesis 2-3. Perhaps the state of Adam and/or Eve's nudity after partaking from the tree of knowledge is understood shamefully. Acquisition of wisdom in Eden is thought of positively in 4Q423 1, 2 i, however, might there be 'shameful' consequences or possible negative consequences? *Jubilees* 3.21-31 applies similar language in the Garden of Eden narrative where Adam and Eve are said to 'cover their shame' after eating the forbidden fruit. Other traditions may be discovered that support a connection here to Genesis creation.

4Q418 177 line 2 mentions the relatively rare word אבדון. Among the six occurrences of אבדון in the Hebrew Bible (Job 26.6, 28.22, 31.10; Ps 88.12, Prov 15.11, 27.20) Job 26.6 (ערום שאול נגדו ואין כסות לאבדון) combines terms that appear here (and 4Q418 178), in Genesis, 4Q416 2 iv and 4Q418 177. It may be allusions to Genesis and Job combine to provide instruction about women. Observe the following similarities:

4Q418 177 & 178	4Q416 2 iii-iv	Genesis 2-3	Job 26.6
אבדון			אבדון
(2x) כסה חרפתכה	אשת חיקכה חרפ[ת]כה		כסות
רש ונדיבים	ראש... נדיבים		
עזור	עזר בשרכה	(כנגדו) עזר	
	ער[ו]ה (?) ער[ו]ם	ערום	(נגדו) ערום

The book of *Jubilees* depicts Adam and Eve as being naked and uncovered just as Abaddon and Sheol are in the Job passage. The term חרפה could relate to 'shame' or 'nudity' and, vis-à-vis 4Q416 2 iii-iv, an allusion to Genesis 2.25-3.1 and perhaps Job 26.6. Perhaps the language of 'naked' Abaddon in Job 26.6 is picked up and used to describe 'shame' in Genesis as preserved in *Jubilees* (3.27-31). It may be that these lines use an allusion to uncovered *Sheol* and naked *Abaddon* as being in some way analogous to 'shame' in Eden and/or in connection with one's wife. While the connection between Job 26 and Genesis 2-3 in 4Q418 177 is not certain, similarities occur between it and 4Q416 2, *Jubilees* and Genesis 2-3. Unfortunately, the context is too fragmentary to allow for any definitive conclusion.

---

[72] *DJD XXXIV*, p. 403.

2.12 4Q418 178

4Q418 178 survives in 5 lines with only lines 2-4 containing legible words. This fragment preserves latter portions of the same column as 4Q418 177. None of the margins of this fragment are extant. Elgvin, S/L and Tigchelaar do not locate 4Q418 178.

4Q418 178 line 4 has been reconstructed by Strugnell and Harrington to read כס]ה חרפתכה. As just discussed the exact phrase only occurs here and in 4Q418 177. The reconstruction כס]ה is based on its occurrence in 4Q418 177 and the surviving *heh* which precedes חרפתכה here. This fragment is written in the 2nd person masculine singular address. The fragment reads:

ב]ביתכה תעזור *vacat* [	(2 [
תמ]צא בית מכונים [	(3 [
כס]ה חרפתכה]	(4 [

2) [in] your house she will help *vacat* [
3) [she will f]ind a house, dwelling [
4) [cove]r your shame[

The exhortation to cover one's shame is found in a context that is likely concerned with the role of a female. In line 2 a woman is described as a helper (עזר). The statement in line 3 'find your house prepared/established' envisages the female helper playing a prominent role in the preparation of the addressee's dwelling place. A female described as a helper would likely be an allusion to Genesis 2.18: 'I will make for him a helper corresponding to him' (אעשה לו עזר כנגדו). Recall 4Q416 2 iii line 21 (cf. 4Q418a 16b + 17 3) and the clear allusion to Genesis 2: התהלך עם עזר בשרכה. This allusion is more convincing when coupled with the occurrence of כסה חרפתכה here and in 4Q418 177. Taken together, 4Q418 177 and 178 appear to contain a running allusion (free-narrative, re-written or paraphrase) to Genesis 2-3.

2.13 4Q418 206

4Q418 206 is a five line fragment with the left margin intact but neither top nor bottom survive. Smaller fragments, such as 4Q418 206, are nearly impossible to locate when no overlaps with larger fragments exist. Thus, Elgvin, S/L and Tigchelaar have not attempted to locate it. Line 3 is addressed in the second person. These fragmentary lines read:

קור] [מל]ך [	(2 [
מם חיה ועוף כיא]	(3 [
מל]וכה ומלכה ממשל	(4 [
הל ואתה יגעתה]	(5 [וממשל

2) [   ] . . . [   ]reigns
3) [   ] animal and bird for
4) [king]dom and realm, dominion
5) [and dominion   ] and you have become weary

The proximity of the words חיה and עוף in line 3 followed by ממשל in lines 4 and 5 are suggestive of the role given to man to rule over creation in Genesis 1.26-28. The phrase חיה ועוף occurs verbatim in Genesis 1.20. The word ממשל in line 4 is used in reference to a husband's rule over his wife in Genesis 3.16, while the word וירדו is used in Genesis 1.28 in relation to creatures being in submission to humanity. Both 4Q422 1 line 9 (4Q*Paraphrase of Genesis and Exodus*) and 4Q504 8 line 6 (4Q*Words of the Luminaries*[a]) are fragments that recount creation in Genesis 1-3 and substitute the verb משל for רדה in their paraphrase of the Hebrew Bible. The term משל is common in *Musar leMevin* (approx. 23 times)[73] and is used in a variety of ways. Most common is the notion of husband ruling over his wife (e.g. 4Q415 9 8; 4Q416 iii 21-iv). The addressee is also said to have been placed in authority over a glorious inheritance (4Q416 2 iii 12) and elsewhere in authority over Adam's/God's inheritance (4Q418 81 + 81a 3). At one point it is used in the context of ruling over creation (4Q423 1, 2 i). 4Q418 206 provides no context within which to view these similarities in vocabulary. Based upon the certain context of ruling or having authority in 4Q423 1, 2 i, and the probability of a similar context here, the occurrence of 'authority' in close relation to the terms חיה and עוף may indicate an allusion to creation. Similar to the notion of 'distinguishing', which could be traced back to creation, 'ruling' also seems to be a motif that could stem from the first chapters of Genesis.

2.14 4Q418a 16b + 17

Fragment 4Q418a 17 consists of 5 lines with approximately a 10 character width. Elgvin, S/L and Tigchelaar do not attempt to locate this fragment. Lines 2-3 read:

רו]חכה בעל מכון]∘	] (2
] ה עם עזר ב]שרכה	] (3

---

[73] Not including parallel occurrence these are: 415 9 8; 416 2 i 19; 416 2 iii 12, 17; 416 2 iv 2, 3, 6, 7; 417 2 i 13; 418 47 1; 418 81 + 81a 3, 9, 15; 418 228 2; 418 259 2; 418a 18 4; 423 1, 2 i; and 423 5 3. The editors comment: 'among the Qumran texts, המשיל is almost totally confined to 4QInstruction and very characteristic of it...4QInstruction uses המשיל with regard to the relation between parent and child (4Q416 2 iii 17), husband and wife (4Q416 2 iv 2, 6, 7), as well as in a symbolic meaning (4Q418 81 3, 9, 15; 4Q416 2 iii 12)'; *DJD XXXIV*, p. 509.

2) your spirit, master of the established (one/place?) [
3) [   ] with the helper of [your flesh

Strugnell and Harrington note the similarities between 4Q418a 17 and 4Q416 2 iii line 21.[74] The reconstruction of בשרכה is plausible but not certain. If one can confidently reconstruct this phrase as 'helper of your flesh' it would have similarities with 4Q418 178 and likely refer to women in an allusion to Genesis 2.18.

2.15 4Q423 1, 2 i

Elgvin, the editor of 4Q423 in DJD 34, notes that there is no continuous text which supports the association of fragments 1 and 2. It is, however, the shape of the fragments that warrants that they be placed together.[75] The left margin of fragment 2 and the top margin of both fragments are extant. Elgvin places 4Q423 1, 2 i in column 22 of his reconstruction, S/L do not locate it, while Tigchelaar assigns it to column 20. Tigchelaar is confident that 'most or all fragments [of 4Q423] belong to one of the final sections of the composition'.[76] The agreement between Elgvin and Tigchelaar in assigning 4Q423 1, 2 i among the final columns of the document are convincing.

4Q423 1, 2 i lines 1-2 are written in the 2nd and 3rd person, while lines 3-4 and 6-8 are in the 2nd person, and line 5 is given in the 3rd person. This column is among the clearest of all materials examined thus far in alluding to and paraphrasing (or re-writing) Genesis 1-3.[77]

(1) [ ] [ ]וכל פרי תנובה וכל עץ נעים נחמד להשכיל הלוא גן נ]עים
(2) [ ]הוא ונחמד]ל[ה]שכיל מ]וא[דה ובו המשילכה לעבדו ולשמרו vac גן נא]ות
(3) [ ] האדמה] קוץ ודרדר תצמיח לכה וכוחה לא תתן לכה
(4) [ ] במועלכה vacat [ ]
(5) [ ] vacat]ילדה וכל רחמי הור]ת [ל]ל[ה ש]]תה כל אוטכה
(6) [ ]בכל חפציכה כי כל תצמיח]לכה [ם תמיד לא
(7) [ ]ובמטע]]בם ה [ ] מו]אס]הרע יודע הטוב

---

[74] *DJD XXXIV*, p. 490.

[75] *DJD XXXIV*, p. 508.

[76] TIGCHELAAR, *To Increase Learning*, p. 169; elsewhere he explains his rationale: 'Since the preserved 4Q423 fragments do not overlap with 4Q416, 4Q417, or 4Q415, one may surmise that they all originated from a section of the scroll not covered by those of other manuscripts, and that they all should be placed not too far from 4Q418 103', p. 165. TIGCHELAARS's putative column 4Q418a 4 (column 19 out of a total of 23) overlaps with 4Q418 103 ii.

[77] TIGCHELAAR, 'Eden and Paradise: The Garden Motif in Some Early Jewish Texts (1 Enoch and other texts found at Qumran),' in G. P. LUTTIKHUIZEN (ed.), *Paradise Interpreted: Representations of Biblical Paradise in Judaism and Christianity* (Leiden: Brill, 1999) pp. 37-62; he compares the Genesis Eden narratives of *1 Enoch*, *Jubilees*, 4Q303-305, 4Q422, 4Q405 and 4Q423 1, 2 i.

ב]ין דרכו ודרך   ] (8

1) [   ] and every fruit of produce and every pleasant tree, desirable to make wise, is it not a lovely garden

2) [and desirable]to make wise? He made you to rule over it to labour in it and guard it *vacat* an [enjoya]ble g[arden]

3) [the earth] thorns and thistles it will sprout for you, and its strength it will not deliver to you, [

4) [   ] in your unfaithfulness

5) [   ] her child, and all the mercy of her that is pregna[nt   ]you [...]ed all your secrets

6) [   ] in everything of your delights, for everything it will sprout forth [for you   ] not always

7) [   ] and in a planting[   ]them [rejecting]the evil and knowing the good,

8) [be]tween his way and the way [of

The table below demonstrates the lexical and conceptual parallels between 4Q423 1, 2 i and Genesis 1-3:

4Q416 1, 2 i	Genesis 1-3
(1) וכל פרי תנובה וכל עץ נעים <u>נחמד</u> <u>להשכיל</u> הלוא גן נ[עים	(2.9) ויצמח יהוה אלהים מן האדמה כל <u>עץ נחמד</u> למראה וטוב למאכל ועץ החיים בתוך הגן ועץ הדעת טוב ורע (3.6) כי טוב העץ למאכל וכי תאוה הוא לעינים <u>ונחמד העץ להשכיל</u>
(2) הוא ונחמד ל[ו]ה[שכ]יל מ[ו]א[]דה ובו המשילכה לעבדו ולשמרו ג]ן נא]ו]ת	(1.28) <u>ורדו</u> בדגת הים ובעוף השמים ובכל חיה הרמשת על הארץ (2.15) ויקח יהוה אלהים את האדם וינחהו בגן עדן <u>לעבדה ולשמרה</u> (and 2.9; 3.6)
(3) האדמה] <u>קוץ ודרדר תצמיח</u> לכה וכוחה לא תתן לכה	(3.18) <u>וקוץ ודרדר תצמיח</u> לך ואכלת את עשב השדה
(4) במועלכה	--
(5) <u>ילדה</u> וכל רחמי הור[]ת []תה כל אוטכה	(3.16?) אל האשה אמר הרבה ארבה עצבונך והרנך בעצב <u>תלדי</u> בנים ואל אישך תשוקתך והוא ימשל בך
(6) בכל חפציכה כי כל <u>תצמיח</u>]לכה [ם תמיד לא	(2.9) ויצמח (3.18) <u>תצמיח</u>
(7) ובמטע] [בם ה] [<u>הרע יודע</u> <u>הטוב</u>	(3.5?) כי ידע אלהים כי ביום אכלכם ממנו ונפקחו עיניכם והייתם כאלהים <u>ידעי</u> <u>טוב ורע</u>
(8) ב]ין דרכו ודרך	--

In line 1 an allusion to Genesis 3.6 occurs with reference to 2.9. Genesis 2.9 describes the tree of knowledge as 'desirable' (נחמד) in appearance, which is expanded upon in 4Q423 1, 2 i with the description 'lovely' (נעים). The text in 4Q423 1, 2 i line 1 alludes directly to Genesis 3.6 where the tree is described as desirable (נחמד) to make one wise. A significant difference exists between this line here and Genesis. In Genesis (2.9) it is only the tree in the centre of the garden that makes one wise while here in *Musar leMevin* it is the produce of every tree (כל עץ) that is desirable for making one wise.

Line 2 repeats the content of line 1 with the statement that the trees are 'desirable to make wise'. The phrase בו המשילכה ('He set you in dominion *over it*') in line 2 is of particular interest while Adam in Genesis 2.15-16 is made to rest (נוח) in the entire garden and care for it, but is not specifically given dominion over the tree of knowledge. Genesis 1.28 exhorts Adam to rule over creation, but not necessarily the entire garden as we find in the narrative of the following chapter. Outside of Genesis 1.28 the motif of dominion only explicitly occurs in 3.16 where male is given dominion over female. 4Q423 1, 2 i line 2 stands in contrast to Genesis 2.16-17 where Adam is warned off from the tree of knowledge; however, both have a command 'to work' (לעבדה/ה) and 'to keep' (לשמרה/ה) the garden.[78]

Elgvin finds an allusion to Genesis 2.15-16 in the word המשיל. He states that the term 'describes God placing man as steward over creation' (cf. Ps 8.7; Dan 11.39).[79] However, the general sense of stewardship over creation found in Genesis is somewhat different than the emphasis on dominion over trees of knowledge here. In 4Q*Paraphrase of Genesis and Exodus* (4Q422) a tradition is preserved with this precise distinction: המשילו לאכול פרי [ ] לבלתי אכול מעץ הדעת ('he gave him dominion to eat the fruit of…except for eating from the tree of knowledge').[80] 4Q*Words of the Luminaries* (4Q504 8 6) simply states that Adam was made to rule in the Garden of Eden: בגן עדן אשר נטעתה המשלתה אותו ('in the Garden of Eden which you planted you made him rule'). It can be observed that in the first two lines of 4Q423 1, 2 i two significant interpretations of Genesis 2-3 occur. First, all trees in the Garden bear wisdom. Second, dominion over these knowledge-bearing trees

---

[78] The editors comment on the change of suffixes: 'while the suffixes referring to גן in Gen 2:15 are feminine, this text changes them to masculine, the usual gender for this word'; *DJD XXXIV*, p. 509.

[79] *DJD XXXIV*, p. 509.

[80] The editors cite several texts that refer to humanity's dominion over the earth, however, these either allude generally to the dominion of Gen 1.28 or not specifically to dominion over the tree of knowledge: 1QS iii 17-18; 4Q381 1 6-8; 4Q301 3 6; 4Q504 8 6. Note also that *Jub* 2.14 emphasises human dominion over the earth based upon Gen 1.28. TIGCHELAAR, 'Eden and Paradise,' p. 55, writes that it is not 'clear in what sense or with what purpose the Gen narrative [of 4Q423 1, 2 i] was being paraphrased. In view of some instructions in 4Q*Instruction* to farmers, one may consider the possibility that Eden and the paradise narrative is a metaphor for the earth (האדמה) in general, or the farmer's own land in particular, with, in the lost part between lines 2-3, the protasis of a conditional sentence'. See comments on 4Q423 5 below (§ 3.2.16).

has been granted. The combination of these factors suggests that an interpretation of the Garden of Eden account is known where, in contrast to some traditions, partaking from the tree of knowledge is positively conceived.[81]

In line 3 the phrase describing the curse on man in Genesis 3.18 re-occurs: קוץ ודרדר תצמיח ('thorns and thistles it will sprout'). The curse is combined with an allusion to the curse on Cain in Genesis 4:12 'it will not give its strength to you' (כי תעבד את האדמה לא תסף תת כחה לך).[82] Here in 4Q423 1, 2 i a paraphrase of Genesis 2-3 that uses the imagery of 'thorns and thistles' clearly should not be understood as an interpretation of a curse for eating of the tree(s) of knowledge. Rather, since knowing the difference between good and evil is positively viewed (e.g. 4Q417 1 i 17-18) language of the curse must describe something other than a punishment for disobedience. One possibility is that curse language describes the difficulty of pursuing wisdom. The inherent struggle of faithfully pursuing and obtaining knowledge is reflected throughout the document (cf. The Parable of the Sower in Mk 4.1-20). After all, *Musar leMevin* is deeply concerned with the division of humanity, a comparison between humanity and angelic beings, and reward based upon merit. Linking Genesis 3.18 with 4.6-7, therefore, may be motivated by a portrayal of the pursuit of wisdom.

In line 4 survives only one word and while one may guess how 'in your unfaithfulness' (במועלכה) could relate to the Genesis narrative, there is simply not enough context to come to a judgement. Line 5 is generally concerned with a woman's bearing of children (?) and might be related to the curse on woman in Genesis 3.16. In line 6 the term 'it will sprout' (תצמיח) occurs which clearly continues with imagery from a planted garden.

Elgvin in DJD 34 considers line 7 to mark a change of subject from the garden to the elect end-time community. The term מטעה ('planting') occurs in the phrase מטעת עולם ('eternal planting') in 4Q418 81 line 14 as a term for the community. Elgvin comments on the transition of subject stating that 'the

---

[81] Sirach 17.7 is not the only sapiential tradition that preserves a positive view of gaining knowledge of good and evil; see also 1QS iv 26; 4Q300 3 2 (*Book of Mysteries*); and below discussion on 4Q303 8-9 (*Meditation on Creation A*); and 4Q305 2 2 (*Meditation on Creation C*).

[82] J. DOCHHORN, '»Sie Wird Dir Nicht«,' pp. 354-355 observes the combination of Gen 3.17-18, 4.12; 4Q423 1, 2 i and *Apoc Mos* 24.1-2; p. 363 he concludes: 'Daß hinter Apc Mos 24, 4Q423 Fragment 2 und Gen 3,17 eine alte kombinatorische Lektüre von Gen 3,17-19 und Gen 4,11-12 steht, legt eine Parallele nahe, welche die Verfluchung Evas und gleichfalls die Kain-Erzählung betrifft. In der Rede Gottes an Kain (4,6-7) begegnet ein Passus...der deutlich an Gen 3,16...anklingt. Wahrscheinlich ist irgenwann im Laufe der Textüberlieferung dafür gesorgt worden, daß beide Texte an dieser Stelle einander so stark ähneln, wohl mit dem Ziel, einen Querverweis zu schaffen.' Gen 3.16 and Gen 4.7 may be alluded to in 4Q416 2 iv 3 and refer to the curse in both chapters of Genesis, see comments on 4Q416 2 iv 3 in chapter 5.

community is thus described with a term fitting the "garden theme" of this section'.[83] He argues that both מטעה (CD i 7; *1 Enoch* 84.6; 93.5, 10) and מטעת עולם (1QS xi 8; 1QH[a] xiv 15, xvi 6) occur elsewhere in Qumran literature as designations for the end-time community. Among these occurrences of 'planting' as a description for the community, 1QH[a] xvi 6 alone sets it within a garden context. Here in 4Q423 1, 2 i, even though an epithet for the community may occur, it is not convincing that it is being used to refer to an end-time community.[84] There is no compelling reason to view a transition of subject from an allusion to Genesis creation in the latter lines of the fragment.

The final words (הרע יודע הטוב[) of line 7, as well as language of planting, should be understood as alluding to or paraphrasing Genesis. Furthermore, although there are occurrences of similar language in other early Jewish literature, caution should be taken in drawing lines of influence, based upon vocabulary, that infer similar theology. Elgvin suggests the reconstruction of מואס ה[רע יודע הטוב ('rejecting the bad and knowing the good') for 4Q423 1, 2 i line 7, basing it on Isaiah 7.15-16 (מאוס ברע בחור בטוב). Since *Musar leMevin* is concerned with knowing the difference between good and evil one could expect something in line 7 closer to: '*understanding* evil and knowing good'.

4Q*Meditation on Creation*[a-b] (4Q303-304)[85] also preserves a paraphrase of Genesis 1-3 and is useful as a source of comparison and contrast with 4Q423 1, 2 i because of its positive conception of gaining the knowledge of good and evil. The text of 4Q305 below preserves a fragmentary statement that this knowledge was given to Adam:

1) ויברא בו חיות]
2) נתן לא]דם דע]ת
3) ורע לדעת]

1) and He created in it life [
2) He gave to Adam knowled[ge
3) and evil to know[

Beginning with line 1, this fragment describes God as the creator of life. In line 2 God is said to have given to Adam knowledge. *Contra* the Genesis

---

[83] *DJD XXXIV*, p. 511.

[84] On the metaphorical language of 'planting' see TILLER, 'The "Eternal Planting",' p. 312-35; J. LICHT, 'The Plant Eternal and the People of Divine Deliverance,' in C. RABIN and Y. YADIN (eds.), *Essays on the Dead Sea Scrolls in Memory of E. L. Sukenik* (Jerusalem: Hekhal ha-Sefer, 1961): 1-27; D. FLUSSER, 'He has Planted it as Eternal Life in our Midst,' in *Tarbiz* 58 (1988-89): 147-53.

[85] See *DJD XX*, pp. 153-58.

account, 4Q305 may well preserve a tradition wherein God is depicted as having been an active provider of knowledge.

Fragment in 4Q303, like 4Q305, supports a positive conception of the gaining of the knowledge of good and evil. Another significant aspect of this fragment is the references to Adam's created partner:

8) [ ]ר ושכל טוב ורע ל[
9) [ ]לוקח ממנה אדם כיא[
10) [ ]עשה לו עזר כ[
11) [ ]לו לאשה כיא ממנו[

8) [ ]and understand good and evil for[
9) [ ]^Adam taking from her because[
10) [ ]He made for him a help[
11) [ ]for him for a wife because from him[

This paraphrase shares significant lexical overlaps with Genesis. However, it is conspicuous that the events of Genesis are given here in reverse order. Whereas the account of the woman's creation precedes the eating of the tree of knowledge in Genesis 2, here in 4Q303 the retelling of Adam accepting (the fruit?) from Eve comes before the description of woman's creation. If it is the fruit that man takes in 4Q403 line 9, and woman is described as a 'helper' in the following line 10, the woman's act of giving from the fruit of the tree would be seen as positive (thus a 'helper'). Furthermore, in 4Q303 line 9 Adam takes (something?) from her (ממנה) and the woman could be taken from him (ממנו). It could be speculated that this is a play on the idea that woman was taken from man and man takes from woman.[86]

The possession of the knowledge of good and evil is positive in *Musar leMevin* and, therefore, the woman's portrayal as the bearer of fruit is an unlikely focus of a possible negative depiction of her. This is a significant divergence from other early Jewish literature where the opposite motif is frequently taken up (e.g. 1 Tim 2.14; Sir 25.24; 4 Macc 18.6-8; *Apoc. Mos.* 29.9, 32.2). The determination of the interpretation of woman in the Garden of Eden, whether she bears guilt or responsibility for her role in introducing disobedience into the world, has importance for understanding views of woman throughout the document. This is especially the case since a cluster of allusions to Genesis 1-3 regarding women occur in *Musar leMevin*.

---

[86] One might also compare *4QParaphrase of of Genesis and Exodus* (4Q422) and 4Q*Words of the Luminaries* (4Q504). See E. G. CHAZON, 'The Creation and Fall of Adam in the Dead Sea Scrolls,' in J. FRISHMAN and L. VAN ROMPAY (eds.), *The Book of Genesis in Jewish and Oriental Christian Interpretation: A Collection of Essays* (Leuven: Peeters, 1997) pp. 13-24.

Goff and Fletcher-Louis both discuss 4Q417 1 i lines 15-18 and the knowledge of good and evil in relation to 4Q423 1, 2 i. Goff writes:

4QInstruction is devoted to an addressee with an elect status. He has access to higher wisdom through revelation [4Q417 1 i] and is proclaimed to be among the lot of the angels. He has been granted authority over the Garden of Eden (4Q423 1 2), an assertion that presents his elect status as a restoration of the relationship God *originally* enjoyed with Adam.[87]

Fletcher-Louis also understands the purpose of wisdom in *Musar leMevin* is to restore the primal order that he sees attested elsewhere in the Dead Sea Scrolls. Fletcher-Louis argues that humanity was originally created angelmorphic and 4Q417 1 i is an expression that attempts to rediscover the 'prelapsarian order' of creation and is 'Essene realised eschatology as the reflex of protology'.[88] Goff in his commentary on 4Q417 1 i lines 15-18 writes:

One can speculate that the "fleshly spirit" once enjoyed the vision of Hagu, like the "spiritual people" and that they were originally a single group. In this reading the vision was taken away from the "fleshly spirit" when it failed to distinguish between good and evil. This is an interpretive possibility. But it is unlikely, given that 4QInstruction displays no awareness of a fall of humankind rooted in Adam's sin. In my translation above עוד is understood as "moreover." This emphasizes the separation of two groups without implying that the "fleshly spirit" ever had the vision of Hagu.[89]

While Goff one the one hand does not view a fall of humanity in 4Q417 1 i, on the other, his reading of 4Q423 1, 2 i clearly envisages a fall and *restoration* in the Eden story. *Contra* Goff, reading 'no more' in 4Q417 1 i does not necessitate reading a fall of humanity rooted in Adam's sin. Neither 4Q423 1, 2 i nor 4Q417 1 i conceive of a fall of humanity. Eden should be seen as a metaphor for the condition of the addressees.[90] On this basis we might view other agricultural imagery, especially in 4Q423 fragments, as continuing the metaphor of an Edenic Garden and the condition of the addressees.

In the following chapters many of the themes that have been raised concerning 4Q423 1, 2 i will be returned to. The division of humanity in 4Q417 1 i and how humanity relates to the Eden like garden of 4Q423 1, 2 i

---

[87] GOFF, *The Worldly*, p. 219. Italics mine.

[88] FLETCHER-LOUIS, *All the Glory of Adam*, pp. 116-17.

[89] GOFF, *The Worldly*, p. 99. Italics mine.

[90] GOFF, *The Worldly*, p. 103, comments: 'Eden can be a metaphor for maintaining the lifestyle advocated by 4QInstruction and can also signify the addressee's failure to do so. Eden is used as a metaphor for the human condition. Both the right path and the wrong path are represented by Eden.' Similarly, it is likely that the motif of poverty and lacking also are part of a metaphor for the human condition of the addressees.

will be discussed. Line 5 raises issue about women and this fragment will be placed alongside other allusions to women and creation as well as other passages that deal with issues pertaining to women generally.

2.16 4Q423 5

4Q423 5 is an 11 line fragment with neither top, bottom nor right margin. The left margin is barely distinguishable at the end of lines 6-7. The first line, designated by the editor as line 1a, does not appear to have been part of the original composition. Lines 5-6 are the most fully preserved portions of the fragment and show a damage point near the centre of line 6. The address is in the third person. This fragment is not located by Elgvin and S/L. Tigchelaar, as noted above, locates all 4Q423 fragments to the final columns of the document.

3) [הו]א פלג [נ]חלת כל מושלים ויצר כל[מעש]ה בידו והוא פעולת

4) [מעשיהמה ידע וישפו]ט כולם באמת יפקוד לאבות ובנים[לגרי]ם עם כל אזרחים ידבר

5) [אם אתה א]יש אדמה פקוד מועדי הקיץ ואסוף תבואתכה בעתה ותקופת

6) [קציר למועדו ה]תבונן בכל תבואתכה ובעבודתכה השכ[י]ל בדעת ה[טוב עם הרע

3) [H]e divided the inheritance of all rulers and formed every [dee]d by His hand and the product of

4) [their deeds He knew, and He will judg]e all of them in truth and He will punish fathers and sons,[visitors]s along with every native, He will speak

5) [if you are a f]armer, observe the appointed times of the season and gather your produce in time, and the season

6) [of harvest in its appointed time. C]onsider all your produce, and in your labour be wi[se in the knowledge of] good and evil

4Q423 5 line 1, which is among the lines that precede the text above, begins with a phrase not found in precisely this form in the Hebrew Bible: משפט קורח (cf. Num 16; 4Q491 1-3). Lines 1-2 mention that 'he opened your ears', presumably to the רז נהיה, followed by a fragmentary reference to a 'leader of your people'. Line 3 is concerned with the inheritance of rulers (נחלת כל מושלים) and the fashioning of deeds (יצר כל מעשה), both motifs that recur throughout *Musar leMevin* (e.g. 4Q416 2 ii 18; 2 iii 10-11; 4Q417 1 i 24; 4Q418 81 3, 11, 20). The inheritance of rulers in line 3 could conceivably be related to other notions of ruling in *Musar leMevin* (Genesis 1.28?) and especially 4Q423 1, 2 i line 2 where the addressee is regarded as a ruler over a garden. Both 4Q417 1 i lines 17 (כתבנית קדושים יצרו) and 4Q416 2 iii line 17 (המשילמה בכה ויצר על הרוח) address issues of formation and perhaps of creation, and it may be that 4Q423 5 line 3 has connotations of creation (ויצר כל[מעש]ה בידו) as well.

Lines 5-6 contain a number of agricultural terms and motifs. Line 5 opens with the phrase אדמה איש ('man of the earth' or 'farmer') which Elgvin understands as an allusion to Noah (Gen 9.20).[91] Both lines exhort the reader to observe the regular cycle of nature (cf. 4Q416 1 1-9) in order to discover a knowledge of good and evil. The term איש אדמה may not allude to Noah at all, but rather to the addressee who metaphorically cultivates wisdom as a farmer within an Edenic garden. This fragment should be understood in light of 4Q423 1, 2 i. Agricultural motifs in *Musar leMevin* may be both metaphorical and at times convey straightforward advice to a farmer.[92] The additional context that includes knowledge of good and evil suggests that more than straightforward agricultural advice is meant. It is somewhat uncharacteristic in agricultural advice to emphasise meditation on crops or seasons for understanding good and evil; however, it fits well with the order of the world based upon creation discussed in fragments above. It also makes sense within the context of a general meditation on the created order and the garden of 4Q423 1, 2 i and acquisition of wisdom defined as knowledge of good and evil. Though Genesis 1-3 never uses the phrase אדמה איש, Adam is clearly cast as a worker of the earth in Genesis 2.15-16.

3. Conclusions

As has been demonstrated above, creation traditions derived from Genesis are numerous in *Musar LeMevin*. We can hypothesise with relative certainty that allusions to creation both introduce and conclude the document (4Q423 fragments). Fragment 4Q416 1 can be confidently located in the first column of the document.[93] The introduction of this sapiential instruction presents themes of cosmology and eschatological judgement and in line 15 exhorts the addressee to understand the difference between good and evil. The cosmological theme that luminaries order seasons clearly alludes to Genesis 1. An exhortation to distinguish between good and evil occurs at times in the document and is a theme that is broadly related to gaining wisdom in Genesis 2-3. Fragment 4Q417 1 i is likely located in a column shortly after 4Q416 1.

4Q417 1 i lines 15-18 may conceive of the fashioning of humanity in the likeness of the 'holy ones' (Gen 1.26-27) and, if so, then proceeds to ground an understanding between good and evil on this view. Accordingly, 4Q417 1 i

---

[91] *DJD XXXIV*, p. 521; ELGVIN also finds a reference to Noah in 4Q423 1-2 (=4Q418 201 1) that further substantiates this claim. The suggestion that the name 'Noah' occurs in *Musar leMevin* has not gained popular support.

[92] ELGVIN, 'The Reconstruction,' p. 580, summarises the contents of 4Q423 1-2 as 'The conditions of the farmer in light of the Eden story'.

[93] If one follows S/L it might be (?) that manuscript 4Q417 existed in a different redaction and 4Q417 1 i was the first column.

lines 17-18 describe the acquisition of knowledge of good and evil in terms of 'people of spirit' and 'spirit of flesh'. 4Q416 2 iii lines 15-18 describe the origin of the addressee as directly related to parents but in a complex with perhaps greater depth than simple earthly parentage – an analogy occurs with God and the rare term 'Lords' (אדנים).

4Q418 81 states that God 'has made everyone' but has separated the righteous from 'flesh' as well as given them bounty and goodness. 4Q418 69 refers to the 'fashioning' of the wicked and concludes that even though the wicked were created by God, certain judgement and destruction await them. As Elgvin and Tigchelaar have demonstrated, it can be reasonably assumed that fragments 4Q423 1, 2 i and 5 are located somewhere near the end of the composition along with the other 4Q423 fragments. Again, 4Q423 1, 2 i addresses the acquisition of the knowledge of good and evil in a paraphrase of Genesis 1-2. 4Q423 5 makes reference to 'fashioning' and the addressee is exhorted in both these fragments to know the difference between good and evil. This cluster of references to knowing good and evil appears to be linked to a running allusion to Genesis 1-3 traditions. From the beginning of *Musar leMevin* onward these themes re-occur and play a prominent role in the formation of the document's theology.

Fragment 4Q415 2 ii appears to refer to the origin of woman. Fragment 4Q416 2 iii makes similar statements, describing woman as 'flesh of your nakedness' and 'wife of your bosom'. While the fragment consists of only a few damaged lines, 4Q418a 16b + 17 likely has the phrase 'helpmeet of your flesh' which is presumably a reference to one's wife. The context of fragments 4Q418 177 and 178 are poorly preserved but might allude to woman in Genesis as well. Finally, 4Q418 126 i-ii uses the phrase 'sons of Eve', though the connotations of this reference are indiscernible. Not only do these fragments display a number of allusions to Genesis 1-3 but a heightened interest on women in *Musar leMevin*.

Fragment 4Q415 2 i + 1 ii may allude to Genesis 1-3 in the words 'fruit' and 'seed'. Fragment 4Q418 206 uses the terms 'beasts' and 'birds' as well as 'dominion' which suggests a possible reference to Genesis. The use of agricultural imagery and the concept of cultivation occur throughout the document as seen in 4Q423 1, 2 i and 4Q423 5 above. Furthermore, 4Q418 81 bounty and goodness given to the righteous may relate to this theme. Agricultural motifs occur throughout *Musar leMevin* and could be used metaphorically at times for the addressee's role as a keeper of the garden.

The identification of allusions to Genesis in *Musar leMevin*, though questionable in some cases, establishes the significance of creation in the document. The allusions proposed above will be explored in chapters 4 and 5 thematically throughout the document as well as placed within a history of reception context along side other literature from early Judaism. These

chapters will attempt to locate clusters of allusions and relate them to the
issues identified in chapter one.

CHAPTER 4

Angelology and Anthropology

1. Introduction

In chapter one angelology was identified as one of the remaining issues yet to be extensively considered in *Musar leMevin*. In chapter three (§3.2.6) column 4Q417 1 i has been shown to contain an allusion to Genesis 1.26, in which clear reference is being made to the involvement of angelic beings in creation. Elsewhere in the document terms used as designations for angelic beings occur as well (e.g. 4Q418 55, 69 and 81). The focus of this chapter will be on a re-examination of 4Q417 1 i as an allusion to creation and the significance of the column for angelology throughout the document. In addition, other allusions to angelic beings may be identified within the context of multiple allusions to creation. Motifs of creation as found in 4Q417 1 i may be explored throughout the document and either elucidate or reveal similar themes elsewhere. 4Q417 1 i lines 15-18 also have implications for anthropology. The creation of humanity and the reflection of the addressees on Genesis creation narratives will also be further investigated.

2. 4Q417 1 i lines 15-18

A number of very different translations and interpretations for 4Q417 1 i lines 15-18 exist among researchers on *Musar leMevin*. A critical review of scholarly interpretations of these lines will be provided here. This will serve not only to demonstrate the significance of these lines for defining angel/human relations in *Musar leMevin*, but also to identify where difficulties in reading these lines lie.

4Q417 1 i presents a number of interpretive difficulties not least of which is simply transcribing the lines. Collins points out, among the more contentious terms to interpret are: אנוש, תבנית, קדושים, and יצרו.[1] However, in order to make sense of these lines several more words should be added. Furthermore, among the various attempts to translate 4Q417 1 i lines 15-18 no

---

[1] COLLINS, 'In the Likeness,' pp. 609ff.

translation has been able to find total agreement with other scholars on
account of their state of preservation, numerous contentious terms and
relationship to surrounding theology in the document. The column as a whole
is replete with words that challenge translators and thus cannot be summarised
easily. Like most fragments of *Musar leMevin*, the damaged state of many
lines hinders our understanding of the column. The present inquiry will be
limited to lines 15-18 alone.

2.1 Armin Lange

Lange, one of the first to write on the document *Musar leMevin*, was one of
the earliest to offer a translation of 4Q417 1 i lines 15-18. The Hebrew lines
below are taken from DJD 34 and are followed by Lange's translation.

15) כי חרות מחוקק לאל על כול ע∘∘] [∘∘]² בני שות וספר זכרון כתוב לפניו

16) לשמרי דברו והואה חזון ההגוי⁴ לספר זכרון וינחילונו³ לאנוש עם ᵖᵖ רוח
[כי]א

17) כתבנית קדושים יצרו ועוד לוא נתן הגוי לרוח בשר כי לא ידע בין

18) [טו]ב לרע כמשפט [ר]וחו] *vacat* ואתה בן מבין הבט
vacat ברז נהיה ודע⁵

(15) denn Eingemeißeltes wurde eingehauen von Gott um all der F[revel] der Söhne Seths
willen, und das Buch der Erinnerung wurde vor ihm geschrieben (16) für die, die auf sein
Wort achten, und die Vision der Erklärung ist das Buch der Erinnerung. Und er hat es Enosch
gemeinsam mit dem Volk des Geistes zum Erbteil gegeben, [den]n (17) gemäß der Gestalt
der Heiligen ist seine [Ge]sinnung. Doch die Erklärung wurde nicht dem Geist des Fleisches
gegeben, denn er vermag nicht, zwischen (18) Gut und Böse zu unterscheiden gemäß dem
Gesetz seines Geistes. *vacat* ⁶

In discussing the phrase כיא כתבנית קדושים יצרו, he suggests an alternative
reading to that given by Wacholder/Abegg.⁷ Wacholder/Abegg, similar to

---

² ELGVIN, 'Wisdom with and Without,' p. 25, reconstructs עולת here.

³ HARRINGTON and STRUGNELL comment: 'Materially, the reading of the first hand was
וינחילה; the second hand has deleted the top of the *he* and converted its left stroke to a *nun*,
ligating to a *waw*. The residual right stroke of the *he* has an odd shape for a *waw*, but our
reading (i.e. manu¹ᵃ וינחילה and manu²ᵃ וינחילונו) seems inescapable.' *DJD XXXIV*, p. 163.
ELGVIN, 'Wisdom with and Without' p. 25 reads וינחילה; so too GARCÍA MARTÍNEZ and
TIGCHELAAR, p. 858.

⁴ ELGVIN reads הגי.

⁵ The Hebrew text here is taken from *DJD XXXIV* and is not part of LANGE'S presentation.
A number of translations of these lines will be discussed below and the Hebrew is provided
here for reference purposes.

⁶ LANGE, *Weisheit*, p. 53.

⁷ They translate: 'And he (Seth?) bequeathed it to Enosh with the people of the spirit.
Because he created it as a sacred blueprint (*tabnith*). But Haguy had not as yet been entrusted
to the spirit of flesh since it (spirit of flesh) had as yet not known the distinction between

Elgvin (§4.2.2 below), want to relate תבנית to the ספר זכרון and translate 'because he created it as a sacred blueprint'. This reading is based upon occurrences of the term תבנית that connote 'blueprint' in several passages of the Hebrew Bible and *Shirot 'Olat ha-Shabbat* (e.g. Ex 25.9, 40; 2 Kgs 16.10; 4Q403 1 i 43ff.). Lange rejects this reading and raises several arguments against it. First, the phrase 'because he created it as a holy blueprint' does not explain why the 'Vision der Erklärung' was given to Enosh and a 'spiritual people'. Second, it would be very surprising in the context that the verb יצר should denote the creation of this heavenly book, especially when the preceding context uses the verbs כתב, חרת and חקק. Lange prefers to relate the term קדושים as a reference to heavenly angelic beings, as is the case in *Shirot 'Olat ha-Shabbat* (e.g. 4Q403 1 i 24, 31). The term יצר should be understood as a noun rather than a verb with the 3rd person masculine suffix -ו. This suffix refers to 'Enosh' and serves as a reference to his character. Turning to *Shirot 'Olat ha-Shabbat*, Lange prefers to read the term תבנית as 'die Gestalt' or 'das Wesen' of the קדושים (cf. 4Q403 1 ii 3; 11Q*ShirSabb* ix 4). According to Lange's interpretation, Enosh is the only human being who was given the 'Vision der Erklärung' for the very reason that his character corresponds with the 'people of spirit'.

Lange understands the phrase עם רוח as referring to heavenly angelic beings or 'Engelvolk'.[8] He explains the significance and function of both אנוש and the עם רוח as counterpoints to the רוח בשר in 4Q417 1 i.[9] He refers to occurrences of the phrase רוח בשר in the *Hodayot* (1QH^a iv 37; v 30) where, according to the *opinio communis*, it denotes the spirit of a human being. In the *Hodayot*, the terms 'flesh' and 'spirit' are not used in the Pauline sense of

---

good and evil.' in B. Z. WACHHOLDER and M. G. ABEGG, *A Preliminary Edition of the Unpublished Dead Sea Scrolls. The Hebrew and Aramaic Texts from Cave Four*, Fascicle 2 (Washington: Biblical Archaeology Society, 1992): xiii. In this translation, one sense is that humanity was once designated as a 'spirit of flesh' and had not yet become spiritual. COULOT, 'L'image de Dieu,' pp. 173 offers a translation and brief description of these lines as well.

[8] LANGE, *Weisheit*, p. 86.

[9] J. FREY, 'Flesh and Spirit,' pp. 378-85 addresses classic parallels of בשר in the DSS. In the first category are usages where בשר is defined by complements עול and אשמה (1QM iv 4; 1QS ix 9). Next are occurrences of בשר that denote the notion of sin without complement. 1QH^a v 30-36 contains the phrase רוח בשר, which in this instance is incapable of grasping God's deeds, counsel or appreciate His glory (the phrase occurs in context with the phrases מבנה עפר, ילוד אשה, and רוח נעוה). Later in the same psalm this 'spirit of flesh' is contrasted with another 'spirit' that provides insight. Two other *Hodayot* passages taken up by Frey are 1QH^a vii 34ff. and 1QH^a xii 30ff. In relation to the latter he writes, 'only through the "spirit" created by God can "flesh" grasp the power of God... the praise of God's salvific acts is strengthened by the corresponding confession of human incapability'. 1QS ix 26-xi 22 also receive attention by FREY. Important to note is the expression in these passages of בשר as a term representing sinful humanity while the community member confesses to sharing in this lot as well (e.g. 1QS ix 9ff.; 1QH^a xii 30ff.). In the *Hodayot* specifically, those praying are flesh and sinners and yet simultaneously participate in revelation and salvation.

two cosmic powers. Rather, in 1QHᵃ v 30 the infinitive להבין is used to describe the purpose of the 'spirit of flesh' and points to the fact that 'spirit of flesh' refers to a type of human ability to understand and gain some sort of insight. The phrase occurs elsewhere in *Musar leMevin* (4Q416 1 12; 4Q418 81 1ff.) and is used as a negative designation for a social group or segment of humanity who are ungodly. In these two contexts the use of the phrase is much closer to the contrast of 'spirit' and 'flesh' in Paul rather than the *Hodayot*.

Lange argues it is very unlikely that the term אנוש in 4Q417 1 i is the noun designating all humanity, *contra* Elgvin below. Since for him אנוש does not refer to the 'spirit of flesh', who are a segment of ungodly humanity, it is difficult to understand the term as a reference to all humankind. The reasonable option that remains for Lange is that it is a reference to the proper name 'Enosh' the son of Seth (Gen 4.26). He finds confirmation for this reading in the comment that the ספר זכרון was written due to the outrage of the sons of Seth, a motif found in rabbinic traditions.[10] Lange also finds grounds for reading the name of the antediluvian 'Enosh' in the positive portrayal of his person in Genesis 4.26 and *Jubilees* 4.12. Lange asserts that a myth set during the time of Seth's sons, in which the fall of the angels and the beginning of the outrage occurs, is the backdrop that 4Q417 1 i should be read against. According to this myth, Enosh together with the 'people of spirit' are portrayed as the only righteous ones who inherit the ספר זכרון as a result of these wicked events.[11]

The phrase עם רוח is known only from 4Q417 1 i and, according to Lange, could designate either a group of humanity positively qualified or a people of heavenly spirits ('ein Volk himmlischer Geister'). The latter suggestion is supported by a few arguments. First, since the 'Vision der Erklärung' was given to Enosh alone, the only individual selected among all humanity on account of his character, this would clearly correspond with the angelic beings (קדושים). Furthermore, angelic beings are frequently called רוחות and רוחים in texts from Qumran, this is especially the case in *Shirot 'Olat ha-Shabbat*. In 4Q400 it is emphasised that God created heavenly tablets in the presence of different angelic beings for all spiritual creatures (4Q400 1 i 4-6). In light of this, the phrase עם רוח in 4Q417 1 i most likely refers to a heavenly spiritual people. According to Lange, it may be understood that the 'Vision der Erklärung' was revealed to the antediluvian 'Enosh' together with a 'Volk himmlischer Geister'. Lange then concludes:

---

[10] LANGE does not cite any specific rabbinic passages, but notes S. D. FRAADE, *Enosh and his Generation: Pre-Israelite Hero and History in Postbiblical Interpretation* (SBLMS 30; Chico: Scholars Press, 1984).

[11] LANGE, *Weisheit*, pp. 87-88.

Enosch und das Volk der Geister stehen dem Geist des Fleisches gegenüber, Weisheit der Torheit, Wahrheit dem Frevel etc. Erkenntnis ist nur wenigen Auserwählten, die sich würdig erweisen, möglich (I 11.16-18) – eine schroffe Abkehr von der in der Weisheit für jedermann angenommenen Erkenntnismöglichkeit.[12]

Musar leMevin, he explains, presents a pre-existing order of existence and a creation that is comprised of a dualistic understanding of the world. Unlike the wisdom of the Hebrew Bible, true knowledge and understanding are not available to everyone, but rather only a few chosen people have access to wisdom through exclusive revelation. Whether this is a type of dualism that exists as a fact of creation or behaviour is not discussed by Lange. This issue will be raised in relation to these lines below.

2.2 Torleif Elgvin

In an article concerned primarily with relating *Musar leMevin* to Enochic traditions and the Essenes, Elgvin translates and comments on 4Q417 1 i.[13] His translation is as follows:[14]

... for the engraved is decreed by God for all the iniquity(?) of the sons of perdition. And the Book of Memory was written before Him for those who keep His word. It is the Vision of Hagi and a Book of Memory. He gave it as inheritance to man with a spiritual people, for He fashioned it as a model for the holy ones. He had not before given Hagi to the spirit of flesh, for he could not discern between [goo]d and evil with the judgment of his [sp]irit. And you, a disciple of a man of understanding, gaze on the mystery to come, learn ...

Elgvin understands חזון ההגוי to be a heavenly book rather than the 'Vision of Hagu' and identifies it with the Book of Memory (ספר זכרון). He further argues that the phrase חרות מחוקק refers to the engraving of the Law of Moses, and appeals to the use of the phrase חוק חרות in 1QS x 8. Therefore, there are two books: (1) the Law of Moses; and (2) the heavenly Book of Hagi also referred to as the Book of Memory (cf. 4 Ez 14.44ff.; Dan 12). The earthly book and the heavenly book are contrasted: the Mosaic Torah was given to the people of Israel to reveal their iniquity, while the heavenly book was revealed only to the elect. According to Elgvin, the עם רוח in line 16 are considered to be the 'elect' and should be equated with the קדושים in line 17 and not to angels. The word תבנית at the beginning of line 17 is translated as 'image' or 'model' and refers to God's fashioning (יצרו) of the Book of Hagi as a model for the elect rather than the fashioning of the 'spiritual people' as Lange interprets. Elgvin reads the phrase בני שות as a reference to the evil

---

[12] LANGE, *Weisheit*, p. 89.

[13] ELGVIN, 'The Mystery to Come,' pp. 139-47.

[14] The enumeration in the following discussion is taken from *DJD XXXIV* rather than ELGVIN's original.

generations of both past and present (i.e. Balaam's Oracle in Num 24.17) rather than to 'the sons of Seth' (Gen 4.26). He understands the word אנוש in line 16 as 'man' or 'mankind' ('humanity') as is most often the case in the Dead Sea Scrolls. Elgvin notes that the term אנוש occurs in three other places in *Musar leMevin* (4Q416 4 11-12; 4Q418 55 11; 77 3) and always has the meaning: 'man' or 'humanity'.

It is difficult to understand Elgvin's interpretation of the phrase וינחילה אנוש, which he states 'refers to God's bequeathing the Hagi and eschatological salvation to the elect community'. If the term אנוש were understood as a reference to humanity generally, then its use as a reference to the 'elect community' makes little sense. Elgvin defends his translation of אנוש as 'humankind' by referring to 1QS xi 5-6 where 'the secrets of God are revealed to the elect, but withhold [*sic*] from אנוש'. *Contra* Elgvin, it appears that 1QS xi 5-6 uses the term אנוש in a way that would actually prohibit the use of the word as a reference to the elect community.[15] In 4Q417 1 i אנוש is associated with a 'spiritual people' whereas in 1QS they are opposed to the elect and identified with the 'assembly of flesh' (מסוד בשר). While Elgvin may be correct in translating the term אנוש as 'humanity', it seems unlikely that as such it can also be a term that refers to the elect. One cannot disagree with Elgvin's conclusion that the term אנוש is used most often of 'humanity' in the Qumran literature. However, Elgvin does not adequately resolve the dilemma of 'humanity' and a 'spiritual people' occurring in conjunction with one another in the context of 4Q417 1 i lines 15-18.

Elgvin is alone in suggesting that אנוש should be read as 'humanity'. This reading is consistent with the interpretation of בני שות as a reference to Balaam's Oracle rather than to the 'Sons of Seth'. Lange and others justify reading אנוש, in part, as the antediluvian figure 'Enosh' based upon reading 'Sons of Seth', unconvincingly, in the preceding line. While a good case may be made for reading אנוש as 'humanity' generally, Elgvin fails to resolve the issue of the existence of some sort of dualism between 'spiritual people' on the one hand, and 'humanity' and the 'spirit of flesh' on the other. Furthermore, his translation, as others, renders the phrase ועוד לוא נתן הגוי לרוח בשר as 'He had not before given Hagi to the spirit of flesh'. Clearly, one viable reading of ועוד לוא is as 'and not yet', however, 'and not before' is a peculiar rendering of the phrase. I would suggest that 'and no more' is a better reading and would allow Elgvin's interpretation of אנוש as

---

[15] 1QS xi 4-7: 'For the truth of God is the rock of my steps and His might the support of my right hand. From the spring of his justice is my judgement and from the wonderful mystery is the light in my heart. My eyes have observed what always is, wisdom that has been hidden from mankind, knowledge and prudent understanding (hidden) from the sons of man, fount of justice and well of strength and spring of glory (hidden) from the assembly of flesh.' GARCÍA MARTÍNEZ and TIGCHELAAR, p. 97.

'humanity' to make sense. However, the division between a 'people of spirit' and 'spirit of flesh' in this context would still need to be resolved.

2.3 George J. Brooke

Brooke comments on 4Q417 1 i as well and suggests that the preceding context (l. 15) where 'Seth' is mentioned justifies the reading of אנוש as the antediluvian 'Enosh' and 'not... a general reference to mankind'.[16] Brooke argues that familiarity with the biblical narrative (i.e. Enosh the son of Seth) displays how the author(s) of 4Q417 1 i incorporate an allusion to the antediluvian Enosh. Brooke regards Enosh in these lines as significant because he is the father of spiritual knowledge and possesses an item of eschatological and prophetic importance (i.e. the book of Hagu).[17] Brooke seems to suggest that the phrase בני שית/שות alludes to both Genesis 4.26 (and 'Seth') and Numbers 24.17 (not 'Seth'), the only place in the Hebrew Bible where the phrase is found.[18] The phrase בני שות found in Numbers 24.17 appears elsewhere in Qumran literature (4Q175 13, 1QM xi 6, CD vii 21) and in every reference it refers to opponents of God.[19] Brooke writes:

'Enosh was son of Seth. At one stroke the wisdom writer incorporates both an item which has an eschatological or prophetic ring to it, as well as an allusion to the significance of Enosh as the father of some specialist spiritual knowledge (prayer).'[20]

Brooke's interpretation of the allusion is primarily to Genesis 4. However, Brooke is not concise in defining or adjudicating whether the 'sons of Seth' is an allusion strictly to Genesis 4 or to Numbers (as well?). The identification of the 'sons of Seth' with Numbers 24.17, as Brooke notes, calls into question a reading of 'Enosh' as the antediluvian figure.[21]

---

[16] BROOKE, 'Biblical Interpretation,' p. 213.

[17] BROOKE, 'Biblical Interpretation,' p. 213.

[18] Gen 4.26ff. spells the name of the antediluvian figure as שת. The oracle in Num 24.17 addresses the beating down of כל בני שת, perhaps sons of 'strife,' 'pride,' or a place name on account of being parallel with Moab.

[19] BROOKE notes these passages where 'sons of Seth' is derived from Num 24.17, p. 213, fn. 38; see also *DJD XXXIV*, p. 163.

[20] BROOKE, 'Biblical Interpretation,' p. 213.

[21] The antediluvian 'Seth' is consistently portrayed positively in Second Temple literature (e.g. *Jubilees*, *Apocalypse of Moses*, Philo). See A. F. J. KLIJN, *Seth in Jewish, Christian and Gnostic Literature* (SNT 46; Leiden: Brill, 1977): 1-36. It could perhaps be argued that the negative portrayal of 'Seth' in the context of 4Q417 1 i is due to a positive correlation of humanity and angels in Gen 1.26 and the absence of this correlation in reference to Seth in Gen 5.3.

2.4 *John J. Collins*

Collins, discussed in relation to 4Q417 1 i lines 15-18 in chapter 3, argues that while the term אנוש is frequently used as a designation for human beings, this particular rendering in 4Q417 1 i is problematic. Collins argues that since אנוש' is associated with a "spiritual people" but is not identified with them and is also distinguished from the "spirit of flesh"... the word, then, cannot be taken to refer simply to humanity in general'.[22] Whether this summary of the issue truly negates the possibility that the term אנוש might be used to refer to 'humanity' will be revisited below. Collins is also opposed to reading the term אנוש as 'Enosh' the son of Seth. Several factors cause him to call this rendering into question. The primary argument for reading 'Enosh' is based upon the preceding occurrence of the name 'Seth'. However, the patriarch's name usually occurs as שת, whereas in 4Q417 1 i it should be pointed as 'Sheth' (שות). As such, it would clearly be a reference to Balaam's Oracle (Num 24.17) as discussed in relation to Brooke (cf. Elgvin). Even if the issue of spelling could be resolved, Collins finds several other difficulties with reading the name of the patriarch Enosh here. Collins understands אנוש and the 'spiritual people' as constituting a righteous remnant.[23] He also notes that there is no known parallel for the interpretation where Enosh is set over against the sons of Seth. Also without parallel is the notion that Enosh is given a book. Rather than read the term simply as 'humanity' or 'Enosh', Collins finds a third way that אנוש might be understood:

'In the *Instruction on the Two Spirits* we read והואה ברא אנוש לממשלת תבל, "He (God) created אנוש to rule the world." In this case the reference is not to the son of Seth, but to Adam, the original human being created by God.'[24]

Collins' third way for interpreting אנוש is to read the word as the first man 'Adam'.[25] However, if the author(s) of 4Q417 1 i truly had in mind an allusion to the creation of two types of Adam, he would likely have not used such an ambiguous term. *Contra* Collins, the *Instruction on the Two Spirits'* use of the term אנוש is not so much an allusion to the first man Adam ruling over creation, but rather purposefully uses the term to indicate 'humanity' ruling over creation.[26]

---

[22] COLLINS, 'In the Likeness,' p. 610.

[23] LANGE, in reading אנוש as 'Enosh', views iniquity as beginning with the generation of Enosh, contrary to the idea of אנוש and the 'spiritual people' forming a righteous remnant.

[24] COLLINS, 'In the Likeness,' p. 612.

[25] *Musar leMevin* is not adverse to using the term אדם, it occurs seven times in the document (4Q418 55 11, 77 2, 81 3, 81 16, 251 1; 4Q423 8 2, 13 4).

[26] See J. BARR, 'Adam: Single Man, or All Humanity?' in J. MAGNESS and S. GITIN, Hesed Ve-Emet: Studies in Honour of Ernest S. Frerichs (Scholars Press: Atlanta, 1998) pp. 3ff.

Collins presents a case for the term תבנית being used in the sense of 'image' or 'likeness'. In the Hebrew Bible the term תבנית is used both with the sense of a 'blueprint for a construction' (cf. Ex 25.9, 40) and for 'figure' or 'image'. In the occurrences of the term as 'image' or 'figure' Collins cites several references (Deut 4.16-18, Is 44.13, Ez 8.3, and 10.8). In Ezekiel the term תבנית is used as a variant at times for the word דמות. The word also occurs in a number of places in *Shirot 'Olat ha-Shabbat* (4Q403 1 ii 3; 4Q405 20 ii 8; 11QShirShabb v-vi 2) that demonstrate a clear usage as 'image' or 'likeness'.

Collins agrees with Lange in reading קדושים as angelic beings. He notes that while there is the well-known reference in Psalm 34.10 to Israel as 'holy ones' and that there are also a few ambiguous passages in the Dead Sea Scrolls, the majority of references clearly have in mind heavenly beings in the use of the term קדושים. In the cases where the reference is ambiguous it is due to sectarians enjoying some sort of fellowship with angels (e.g. 1QM x 10). There is no place where the term קדושים refers to human beings unambiguously in the Dead Sea Scrolls.

Collins gives attention to how the term יצרו in 4Q417 1 i should be read. Regardless whether one renders the word as a noun or verb, 'if God fashioned אנוש in the likeness of the Holy Ones (reading *yasaro*) then his inclination (reading *yisro*) is in their likeness too'.[27] The term יצר is used in Genesis 2 (וייצר) in the description of the formation of man and, Collins points out, the two *yods* in *Genesis Rabbah* 14.3 are the basis for instigating a portrayal of humanity as having two inclinations.[28] *Genesis Rabbah* 14.3 also cites Genesis 1.26-27 for the purpose of describing the formation of man as being in the likeness of the angels. The affinity between Adam and the angels is based upon creation in Genesis 1 and Adam is understood to be formed of both celestial and terrestrial elements. Similar to *Genesis Rabbah*, 4Q417 1 i can be understood as a paraphrase of Genesis 1.26. The term אלהים can be used to refer to angels (e.g. 4Q400 1 ii 7; 2 2; 11QMelchizedek ii 10) and so the phrase that אדם was made בצלם אלהים could be read as the first man

---

[27] COLLINS, 'In the Likeness,' p. 614.

[28] 'There were two formations [one partaking of the nature] of the celestial beings, [the other] of the earthly creatures… He created him with four attributes of the higher beings [i.e. the angels] and four of the lower creatures [i.e. the beasts].… R. Tifdai said in R. Aha's name: The celestial beings were created in the image and likeness [of God] and do not procreate, while the terrestrial creatures procreate but not created in [His] image and likeness. Said the Holy One, blessed be He: "Behold, I will create him [man] in [My] image and likeness; [thus he will partake] of the [character of the] celestial beings, while he will procreate [as is his nature] of the terrestrial beings." R. Tifdai [also] said in R. Aha's name: The Lord reasoned: "If I create him of the celestial elements he will live [for ever] and not die; while if I create him of the terrestrial elements, he will die and not live. Therefore I will create him of the upper and lower elements, if he sins he will die, and if he dies he will live.' H. FREEDMAN and M. SIMON (New York: Soncino, 1983).

Adam's formation in the likeness of angels. Collins cites other passages in the midrashim where Adam is said to be created in the likeness of angels rather than God (*Gen. R.* 21.5; *Ex. R.* 30.16). In support of reading 4Q417 1 i as Adam being fashioned in the likeness of the angels and the recipient of a book, Collins finds a parallel in *The Letter Sent to Adam by God* where Adam receives a revelatory writing from God.

Collins suggests that since in 4Q417 1 i אנוש is formed in the likeness of the holy ones without the qualification of a celestial and terrestrial element, like *Genesis Rabbah*, not all humanity shares the likeness. Only Adam and the 'people of spirit' share the likeness of the angels. 4Q417 1 i contrasts two kinds of human beings: the 'people of spirit' and the 'spirit of flesh'. Unlike *Serekh haYahad*, where God created אנוש to rule the world and appointed two spirits in which to walk, in 4Q417 1 i אנוש does not walk in both spirits but is strictly associated with the 'people of spirit'. The statement לאנוש עם ‎[כי]א רוח ‎כתבנית קדושים יצרו represents an interpretation of Genesis 1.26-27 and the phrase בצלם אלהים, whereas the 'spirit of flesh', those who do not discern between good and evil, represents an interpretation of the second creation in Genesis 2. This failure to discern between good and evil by the 'spirit of flesh' assumes a tradition according to which the tree of knowledge was not prohibited, but in fact humanity was encouraged to partake of it. Furthermore, as noted previously, Sirach 17.7 retells Genesis 1-3 and similarly conceives of Adam receiving the knowledge of good and evil from God at the beginning of creation.

Collins argues that in 4Q417 1 i 'the one who fails to distinguish between good and evil is not the same human being who was created in the likeness of the Holy Ones.'[29] 4Q417 1 i, however, does not need to be read as excluding all humanity from creation in the likeness of the holy ones as Collins suggests. It is important to readdress creation in these lines, especially within the framework that Collins' proposes. While Collins represents one tradition of interpreting Genesis 1.26-27, the phrase 'in our image and our likeness' has a broader interpretive history than so far detailed.

In both Philo and 4Q417 1 i the two accounts of the creation of Adam in Genesis are used to portray two distinct types of humanity. While Philo and these Qumran documents conceive of two Adams each within their own philosophical framework, they share the same biblical text and possible elements of the same interpretative tradition. According to Tobin the two creation accounts in Genesis 1-2 are understood by Philo as depicting the creation of a heavenly man who is part of the intelligible world and an earthly man who is part of the sensible world.[30] This duality is something that is different than that which is found in the *Instruction on the Two Spirits* (1QS

---

[29] COLLINS, 'In the Likeness,' pp. 616-17.
[30] TOBIN, *The Creation of Man*, p. 108.

iii-iv). 1QS does not allude to Genesis 1.26-27 but reflects a dualism of Zoroastrian character: light and darkness. *Musar leMevin*, argues Collins, in its own way conceives of the creation of Adam and a 'spiritual people' in the likeness of the angels in the first creation and a 'spirit of flesh' in the second creation. Since *Musar leMevin* positively conceives of the first creation and a correlation with the angels for a segment of humanity, and since these are set against the 'spirit of flesh', there is no room in Collins' interpretation for the term אנוש as a reference to 'humanity' generally.

In a more recent article Collins compares Wisdom of Solomon with *Musar leMevin* and makes several important observations which are relevant for the present discussion of 4Q417 1 i.[31] Collins set forth the same interpretation here, namely, that 4Q417 1 i conceives of two types of humanity with their origin in two types of creation. However, Collins offers a fresh observation on the text, which is: in both Wisdom of Solomon and *Musar leMevin all humanity possesses immortality*. In comparing these two compositions, Collins argues they share the view 'that it was the intention of the creator that humanity should be immortal,' and 'this view was grounded in the understanding of Gen 1:27, which says that Adam was created in the image of God.'[32] In *Musar leMevin* this likeness is related to the angels while in Wisdom of Solomon to the eternality of God, but in both documents the likeness entails immortality. The creation image of Genesis 1.27 is contrasted with the creature of earth or flesh in Genesis 2.

Musar leMevin, argues Collins, relates the distinction between the two types of people as based upon both creation and behaviour. *Musar leMevin* does not associate flesh with corruption and mortality, but rather represents 'the weakness of unaided human nature, and sometimes it is regarded as sinful'. In 4Q417 1 i, however, those regarded as the 'spirit of flesh' are just as immortal as the 'people of spirit' since they survive for punishment in the hereafter. Collins maintains that the term אנוש, meaning the first man Adam, along with the 'spiritual people' should be understood as sharing the likeness of the holy ones. Collins, though raising an important observation, does not adequately resolve the basis upon which *Musar leMevin* conceives of all humanity as possessing immortality. Does all humanity possess immortality based upon the same creation or not?

If all humanity generally is immortal as Collins suggests, this would seemingly be founded upon creation in Genesis 1.26-27, and the term אנוש should be rendered as 'humanity'. According to Collins, two creations are at play in 4Q417 1 i lines 15-18. Are we to assume that those of the second creation, that is a segment of humanity derived from earth, were not a part of the first creation and yet are portrayed as immortal? The distinction between

---

[31] COLLINS, 'The Mysteries of God,' pp. 287-306.
[32] COLLINS, 'The Mysteries of God,' p. 303.

the two peoples ('people of spirit' and 'spirit of flesh') could be based solely upon behaviour and not the dualistic creation conceived of by Collins. In addition, issues of divine revelation and the mystery may also have a significant influence on the division of 'spirit' and 'flesh' and the origin of 'humanity' in this column. Collins' observation that *Musar leMevin* conceives of both groups as immortal may actually serve to delineate more precisely who is meant by the term אנוש.

2.5 Matthew J. Goff

Matthew Goff, a student of Collins, is one of the most recent contributors to the discussion on *Musar leMevin*.[33] His translation of 4Q417 1 i is as follows:

because engraved is that which has been ordained by God against all the in[iquities of] the sons of Sheth. The book of remembrance is written before him for those who keep his word – that is, the vision of Hagu for the book of remembrance. He bequeathed it to אנוש together with a spiritual people, be[cau]se he fashioned him according to the likeness of the holy ones. Moreover, he did not give Hagu to the fleshly spirit because it did not distinguish between [go]od and evil according to the judgment of its [spi]rit.[34]

In agreement with Elgvin and Collins, Goff states that the phrase בני שות should not be understood as referring to the patriarch Seth. Tracing traditions of Seth throughout the literature of the period, he concludes that nowhere is the patriarch Seth depicted in negative terms. Instead, Seth is portrayed positively as one who possesses the image of God and served as a foil to Cain. Relating the appearance of the phrase בני שות in other documents from Qumran, primarily the *Damascus Document* (vii 21-viii 1), Goff concludes that the likely reference is to Numbers 24.17. In the *Damascus Document* and *Musar leMevin* the phrase בני שות 'refers to the wicked whose punishment is determined but not yet fully realized'.[35] The phrase בני שות is related to the 'fleshly spirit' who also await future judgement (cf. 4Q416 1 12; 4Q416 2 ii 2-3; 4Q418 69 ii 8), and both should be understood as terms used of the wicked.

In regard to the interpretation of the term אנוש in 4Q417 1 i, Goff follows Collins. Since special revelation has been given to אנוש, he finds the translation of the term as 'humanity' in general difficult. However, Goff also translates the phrase ועוד לוא נתן[36] as 'moreover, he did not give' rather than

---

[33] GOFF, *The Worldly*, pp. 83-115.

[34] GOFF, *The Worldly*, p. 84.

[35] GOFF, *The Worldly*, pp. 92.

[36] The translation of עוד לוא as 'moreover' is obscure; the two clear options are 'not yet' or 'no more'. 'Not yet' for ועוד לוא would imply a future time of giving revelation to the 'spirit of flesh', an interpretation that is difficult to reconcile in the context. COULOT, 'L'image de Dieu,' p. 173 translates similarly to GOFF: 'et de plus'.

the expected 'and no more does he give', negating a reference that the 'spirit of flesh' at one time may have possessed revelation. While Goff does not detail his own misgivings with the rendering of the term as the antediluvian figure 'Enosh', he is clearly not inclined to understand the word as such. Goff sees in 4Q417 1 i an explanation of human behaviour and the creation of a 'spiritual people' in the likeness of the holy ones and the 'fleshly spirit' that is not. The word אנוש should be understood in line with its use with 1QS iii 17-18 where the first man Adam is referred to. Genesis 1-3 is used as the basis for a dualistic anthropology. The 'god-like Adam' in the first creation is juxtaposed to the earthly Adam in the second creation. This 'god-like Adam' corresponds to the 'spiritual people' while the earthly Adam corresponds to the 'fleshly spirit'. The phrase בצלם אלהים of Genesis 1.27 is used in 4Q417 1 i lines 15-18 as exegetical support of the view that some people were created in a way that is more like angels than others.[37]

Goff's translation of the phrase ועוד לוא נתן הגוי לרוח בשר in line 17 as 'moreover, he did not give Hagu to the fleshly spirit', along with most other translations of this phrase, is problematic. While it is clear that the 'spiritual people' are aligned with the holy ones and receive heavenly wisdom, Goff makes the assertion that the 'fleshly spirit' never received 'Hagu'.[38] This is dependent on both the certainty that אנוש should not be rendered as 'humanity' as well as a translation of ועוד לוא as 'moreover' rather than 'and no more'. Goff states that the distinguishing feature between the 'spiritual people' and the 'fleshly spirit' is access to divine revelation – recall Collins' suggestion that the distinguishing characteristic between the two is behaviour and creation. Goff's distinguishing characteristic of 'access to divine revelation' itself is dependant upon the certainty that אנוש should not be read as 'humanity' as well as the unlikely translation of ועוד לוא as 'moreover' in line 17.

Goff states that reading the term אנוש as 'Adam… points towards the theme of the knowledge of good and evil'.[39] Wisdom is the acquisition of the knowledge of good and evil and in Genesis 1-3 Adam attempts to possess such knowledge. However, if the phrase כתבנית קדושים truly is an adaptation of בצלם אלהים in Genesis 1.27 with angelic connotations, than the knowledge of good and evil is more than a simple knowledge of right and wrong, it entails a divine status (cf. Gen 3.5; 3.22). Goff notes that the translator of Genesis 3.5 in the LXX understands that the knowledge of good and evil would make Adam like divine beings (καὶ ἔσεσθε ὡς θεοὶ γινώσκοντες καλὸν καὶ πονηρόν). אנוש, then, along with the 'spiritual people' are given

---

[37] GOFF, *The Worldly*, pp. 97-98.
[38] GOFF, *The Worldly*, p. 99-100.
[39] GOFF, *The Worldly*, pp. 100-4.

revealed knowledge through the 'vision of Hagu' which is angelic and heavenly in nature.[40]

If Collins is correct in observing that behaviour is the distinguishing characteristic between 'spirit' and 'flesh' and that judgement will be meted out to the 'spirit of flesh', then it may stand to reason that *Musar leMevin* conceives of all humanity as having possessed the knowledge of good and evil at one time. Furthermore, whether Goff or Collins, a dualistic anthropology based upon creation is not completely convincing and other interpretive options may be available.

2.6 Harrington and Strugnell

The editors' translation of 4Q417 1 i lines 15-18 reflects the vagueness of these lines. Harrington and Strugnell allow humanity to be a possible recipient of Haguy. Furthermore, they suggest that 'man' is fashioned according to the likeness of the holy ones. The spirit of flesh no longer has meditation because they apparently did not know the difference between good and evil. They translate:

> For engraved *is* that which is ordained by God *against* all the *ini[quities of]* the children of שׁוּת, *And* written in His presence is a book of memorial of those who keep His word. And that *is* the appearance/*vision of the meditation* on a book of memorial. And *He*/שׁוּ(?) *gave* it as an inheritance to *Man/Enosh Together with* a spiritual people. F[o]r according to the likeness of the Holy Ones *is his* (man's) fashioning. *But* no more *has* meditation been given to *a* (?) fleshly spirit, For *it* (sc. flesh) knew/knows not the difference between good and evil according the judgement of *its* [sp]irit. *vacat* And thou, O understanding child, gaze on the mystery that is to come, and know[41]

Commenting upon line 17 and the phrase כתבנית קדושים יצרו, the editors remark that either God fashioned 'Enosh' or 'humanity' according to the likeness of the holy ones or according to the likeness of the holy ones is his יצר (i.e. 'inclination' or 'formation'). In determining whether 'Enosh' or 'mankind' (or 'Adam') are in view here, the editors write:

> 'It is still uncertain whether אנוש refers to mankind or to Enosh the son of Seth... The reader... would be completely unprepared for a reference to the individual Enosh in such an

---

[40] The angelic likeness of אלהים ('angels') in Gen 1.27 and angelic likeness Gen 3.5 (on the day you eat from it [the tree of the knowledge of good and evil] your eyes will be opened and you will be like אלהים knowing good and evil') may be alternatively understood if all humanity is created in the likeness of angels in Gen 1.27. 4Q417 1 i line 17 is concerned with the knowledge of good evil and all humanity may be created in the likeness of the angels; however, in light of 4Q423 1, 2 i partaking of the trees (= seeking knowledge) may be an interpretation of Gen 3.5. Partaking of the trees in the garden may distinguish between the groups of humanity.

[41] *DJD XXXIV*, p. 155.

ethico-theological context or even in a narrative about a celestial court and judgement scene...While אנוש 'mankind' is frequent in Qumran literature and in 4Q415 ff., 'Enosh' is not (unless when mentioned in a patriarchal context, e.g. if justified here by a preceding 'Seth'. Both names, Seth and Enosh, occur in the chain of succession of wisdom teachers (Sir 49:16), but in general proper names are exceedingly rare in 4Q415 ff.'[42]

The editors also succinctly summarise what is at stake in interpreting the term as 'Enosh' or 'humanity'. If 'Enosh' is the one who is referred to then this is an occurrence of a historical narrative statement about 'a transaction with Enosh in primordial times'.[43] An interpretation as 'humanity' would be a general anthropological statement. Implications of these lines on anthropology in *Musar leMevin* could be significant. The term יצרו could also be a statement of anthropology generally, stating a truth about the present as much as the past. Whether the statement in line 17 is of a historical nature or a general anthropological statement concerning a group of the righteous (i.e. either 'Enosh' and the עם רוח or 'humanity' and the עם רוח), they are collectively contrasted with the 'spirit of flesh' who are a group of evil humanity. If it is a general anthropological statement, when contrasted with the 'spirit of flesh', there would be support for taking the preceding suffix of יצרו as a reference to אנוש as 'humanity'. A historical statement that 'God bequeathed to him... for He formed him, etc.' could be a reference to either 'Enosh' or 'humanity'.

Another particularly important comment by Strugnell and Harrington has to do with their translation of the phrase ועוד לוא in line 17 as 'and no more'. The editors state in the commentary, 'the sense is probably not "not yet...", but rather "and no more, after being given to Enosh/mankind, was (the power of) meditation given to the רוח בשר"'.[44] The rendering of this phrase will have a crucial role to play in interpreting these lines.

2.7 Summary and Translation of 4Q417 1 i lines 15-18

From the outset, disputed terms with special importance for understanding human/angel relations in *Musar leMevin* were identified by Collins as: אנוש, תבנית, קדושים, and יצרו. Following the evaluation of the contributions by Elgvin, Lange, Brooke, Collins, Goff and the editors of DJD 34, it can be observed that little consensus exists in translating 4Q417 1 i lines 15-18. In addition to Collins disputed terms should be added: בני שות וינחילה and ועוד לוא. Based upon the evaluation of these words above, the following translation is proposed:

---

[42] *DJD XXXIV*, p. 164.
[43] *DJD XXXIV*, p. 163.
[44] *DJD XXXIV*, p. 166.

…(15) because engraved is that which has been ordained by God against all the i[niquities] of the sons of perdition and a book of memorial is written before him (16) for those who keep his words, and it is a Vision of Haguy for a book of memorial. He gave it as an inheritance to humanity together with a spiritual people [becau]se (17) according to the image of the holy ones is its (humanity's) formation, but no more does He give Haguy to a spirit of flesh because it knew not the difference between (18) good and evil according to the judgment of his spirit *vacat* and you understanding one gaze *vacat* on the רז נהיה and know…

The most contentious item in the above translation is no doubt the rendering of אנוש as 'humanity'. 4Q417 1 i lines 15-18 depict the creation of all humanity in the image of the angels as well as recipients of special revelation (Haguy). Collins' suggestion that this creative likeness is based upon a tradition of reading Genesis 1.27 and 'Enosh' should be identified with 'Adam', necessitate further discussion. However, several things may be said about the dispute over rendering אנוש as 'humanity' or 'Enosh'. The editors make two observations that argue against the interpretation 'Enosh': (1) אנוש is almost always used of 'humanity' in early Jewish literature;[45] and (2) proper names in *Musar leMevin* are exceedingly rare.[46] The one exception which would permit rendering אנוש as 'Enosh' in line 16 would be the identification of the phrase בני שות with Genesis 4.26 (בני שת). However, the editors write that 'the engraved decree would almost certainly be a heavenly text condemning the 'sons of Seth'.[47] Clearly, the phrase 'sons of Seth' derived from Numbers 24.17 (בני שות) is relatively frequent in Qumran literature. The negative context in which this phrase is found in 4Q417 1 i, similar occurrences elsewhere, and the positive portrayal of Seth in other traditions leads to the conclusion that the phrase connotes 'sons of perdition' rather than 'sons of Seth'.[48] Therefore, the most reasonable translation of אנוש in line 16 is 'humanity'.

A contextual problem exists in the translations of Lange, Collins and Goff that prevents an interpretation of אנוש as 'humanity'; and thus, a general anthropological statement. How is one to understand the creation of all humanity in the likeness of קדושים when a clear distinction between two peoples is presented? One solution may be that the division between the עם רוח and humanity is a delineation between a dualism at the present time that was not part of primordial creation. Both the original state of creation without a division and the present reality of two types of humanity are woven

---

[45] In the case of the *Instruction on the Two Spirits* (1QS iii 17-18) the interpretation of 'Adam' in these lines, i.e. the author(s) use of אנוש as opposed to אדם, demonstrates in my opinion an interpretation of 'Adam' as 'humanity'. Therefore, the *Instruction on the Two Spirits* supports the rendering of the term אנוש as 'humanity' rather than *vice versa*.

[46] *DJD XXXIV*, p.164.

[47] *DJD XXXIV*, p. 162.

[48] This translation of the phrase with a different epithet, though highly interpretive, avoids ambiguity.

together in 4Q417 1 i lines 15-18. The designation 'fleshly spirit' is given to those who 'knew not the difference between good and evil' (l. 17) and for whom revelation is *no longer* available. Thus, the author(s) can say of the 'spirit of flesh' in line 18: 'according to the judgement of his spirit'. For this reason all humanity in *Musar leMevin*, whether those of the 'elect' or those who are among the 'fleshly spirit' are, as Collins details, immortal. The creation of all humanity in the image of קדושים and the bequeathing of divine revelation to them were followed by a subsequent failure of a segment of humanity to know and adhere to a pursuit of wisdom. The condemnation of this group of humanity follows their failure to seek wisdom, the result of which was the loss of access to revelation for these people and their designation as the 'spirit of flesh'. All humanity is immortal and prone to judgement because they were originally created with the ability to know good and evil through revelation.

The straightforward translation of ועוד לוא as 'and no more' confuses the interpretations of Lange, Collins and Goff. If the 'spirit of flesh' no longer has possession of divine revelation the obvious conclusion is that they once possessed it. If they once possessed it then the portrayal of two creations, such as Collins and Goff propose, needs to be reconsidered. Therefore, translations of the phrase as 'He had not before given' and 'moreover' have been preferred to 'and no more'.

The phrase ועוד לוא occurs seven times in the Hebrew Bible (Gen 17.5; Deut 18.16; 2 Sam 7.10; Is 47.8; Jer 23.4; Job 24.20; 1 Chron 17.9) and is clearly used in the sense of either 'no more' or 'not yet'.[49] The phrase should

---

[49] GOFF, *The Worldly*, p. 99, comments on the possibility of the translation 'no more': 'One can read the expression ועוד in 4Q417 1 i 17 as "but no more." This would suggest that at a certain point God stopped giving the vision of Hagu to this spirit: "But no more (ועוד) did he give Hagu to the fleshly spirit." One can speculate that the "fleshly spirit" once enjoyed the vision of Hagu, like the "spiritual people," and that they were originally a single group. In this reading the vision was taken away from the "fleshly spirit" when it failed to distinguish good from evil. This is an interpretive possibility. But it is unlikely, given that 4QInstruction displays no awareness of a fall of humankind rooted in Adam's sin'. Collins, 'The Mysteries of God', p. 302, likewise comments: '…but no more has Hagu been given to the spirit of flesh. This would mean that the Vision of Hagu was initially given to Adam, but withdrawn when he failed to distinguish between good and evil. In this case, however, we might wonder why Adam failed to distinguish between good and evil in the first case, since he had been endowed with the vision of Hagu as his inheritance. It is not clear to me, however, that 4QInstruction envisions a Fall, or a sin of Adam, at all'. Clearly, both GOFF and COLLINS interpretations are limited by their rendering of the term אנוש strictly as the first man 'Adam'. Furthermore, a traditional Fall is clearly not conceived of in *Musar leMevin*. The pursuit of wisdom, hidden or otherwise, is portrayed as an arduous task in the document and the ultimate good. 'Fall' language refers to the disobedience of Adam and Eve for partaking from the forbidden tree of knowledge.

be translated in 4Q417 1 i as 'no more' as well, indicating that at one time all humanity had access to wisdom and Haguy.[50]

The concept of primordial possession and present ability to fail in understanding good and evil fits with the concept of the fatigable human pursuit of wisdom elsewhere in the document. Moreover, an urgency exists in the document for the addressee to seek wisdom, most often found in the revelation of the רז נהיה, with angelic beings as a type of exemplary model.[51] Exhortations to know good and evil, pursue knowledge and not go astray align themselves more closely to a dualism based upon behaviour and revelation rather than creation. Motifs and imagery from the creation of two types of humankind in Genesis 1-2 in *Musar leMevin* need, then, to be understood as reflecting something other than the creations of two peoples (i.e. a created dualism). The angelic (spiritual) fashioning of Genesis 1 and earthly creation of Genesis 2 may serve as categories to which portions of humanity relate to as opposed to the creation of two types of humanity. One should not read a Fall here, but rather a loss of access to Haguy for a segment of humanity who gave in to their earthly nature (e.g. laziness) and thus now stand condemned.

2.8 Philo, Genesis 1.26 and 4Q417 1 i lines 15-18

Philo is an important point of departure for Collins in his portrayal of the dualism in 4Q417 1 i, therefore further exploration of Philo's compositions may prove fruitful. The contribution of Philo to our interpretation of *Musar leMevin* is his preservation of an exegetical tradition of Genesis 1.26 in which humanity and angels are correlated. While Collins is concerned with the creation of two types of man (Gen 1 and 2), *vis-à-vis* Tobin's research on two creations in Philo, the contribution of Philo extends beyond this dualism.[52] Humanity is dualistically divided in Philo on the basis of Genesis 1.26 and not only Genesis 1 and 2. On four occasions Philo addresses the role of angels in

---

[50] See also 4Q417 2 i line 23 'and you can no longer trust' (ולוא תאמין עוד).

[51] This comes as little surprise as the superiority of the angels is something to which the community aspires in *Shirot 'Olat ha-Shabbat* (4Q400-406).

[52] FREY, 'Flesh and Spirit,' pp. 375-77, addresses the terms σάρξ and πνεῦμα in Philo in relation to Qumran sapiential texts and notes the following: 'But even if it is true that there are numerous examples for the negative view on human corporality, there is no clear evidence for the dualistic antithesis of σάρξ and πνεῦμα;' he also notes in comments upon *De gigantibus* 29ff. that 'in contrast to the Hebrew text, Philo applies the term πνεῦμα not to the Divine breath and the gift of life but to the spirit of pure insight...which is hindered by the fleshly nature of the human being...in this passage, flesh is even called "the chief cause of ignorance"...like σῶμα, the term σάρξ denotes the material and bodily life which burdens the soul and prevents it from its ascent to the divine sphere'; and 'in contrast to Paul, σάρξ is considered neither to be the reason or occasion for sin... even where Philo describes the flesh with personal images, he always withdraws them immediately and avoids any kind of mythic dualism'.

creation based upon Genesis 1.26. In every instance that Philo addresses the exegesis of the first creation in Genesis, he uses the plurality of images 'let us' to introduce a duality of inclinations and creators distinct from the perceived creation accounts of Genesis 1 and 2. A comparison of Philo's exegesis with that of *Musar leMevin* will aid in setting the sapiential texts in a broader exegetical context. More specifically, Philo's exegesis of Genesis 1.26 displays that a division between the 'spiritual people' and the 'spirit of flesh' may be understood within a tradition where all humanity shared in the first creation rather than the dual creation of two peoples exclusive from one another.

The first explicit reference to Genesis 1.26 is in *de Opificio mundi*. Philo raises the exegetical question in regard to the reason for ascribing the creation of humanity to several (πλέιοσιν) creators (72) and relates that the heavenly bodies, or angelic beings, are the second image of creation in Genesis 1.26. Before the creative process begins God is said to be without counsellor to help (23). The heavenly bodies who share the creative images with God on the sixth day of creation are said to be created on the fourth day. In this account, Philo describes the first days of creation and angelic beings are created who later serve God as counsellors for the creation of humanity.

Philo explains God's reliance on other participants in the creation of humanity for the ultimate purpose of assigning blame for the existence of evil to subordinates (72-76). This is a repetitive theme in Philo. Philo's explanation and reasoning concerning the origins of human wickedness is revealed in his description of creation. In existence, Philo discusses, are plants and animals which are absent of mind and reason and are therefore not partakers in virtue nor vice. Mind and reason are the dwelling place of virtue and vice and are by nature constructed for their dwelling. The heavenly bodies are living creatures; each is a mind unto itself, which participates in virtue only, not in vice.

The minds of the heavenly beings are free from the temptation of any evil. Philo describes humanity (ἄνθρωπος) who is of mixed nature: vice and virtue. This explanation emphasises that the existence of evil or vice does not have its origin with God, for it is written 'let *us* make'. Subordinates to God are responsible for attributes that are contrary to God's goodness. Consistently, however, Philo's description of creation presents two types of creatures (animal life and heavenly bodies) which possess no vice. Philo's purpose is to use the passage of Genesis 1.26 within an exegetical tradition that supports his theology rather than to develop an explanation of the biblical narrative as a whole.[53]

---

[53] See P. Borgen, *Philo of Alexandria: An Exegete for His Time* (SNT 86; Leiden: Brill, 1997) p. 62 on Philo's rewriting of the Bible concludes: 'The rewriting can elaborate on the form of blessings and curses, and can have the form of a chain of biblical cases which serves

An examination of Philo's preservation of an exegetical tradition at this point raises an important observation. The attribution of vice to those who share in the process of creation is not simply a duality in human nature that can be explained as a division between what is heavenly and what is fleshly (i.e. the creation narratives in Gen 1-2).[54] Philo is producing a duality in the nature of the soul of man before the second creation in Genesis 2.7. It is necessary to distinguish between the two because Philo often emphasises the duality of spirit and flesh in creation (e.g. *Quaestiones et Solutiones in Genesin*), but the duality of forms produced from Genesis 1.26 is distinct from this division.

Another instance in which Genesis 1.26 is given explicit attention by Philo occurs in *de Confusione linguarum*. In the context that precedes an explanation of Genesis 11.7 and a subsequent quotation from Genesis 1.26 (171), Philo emphasises the omnipotence of God before explaining that God has around him numberless Potencies (δυνάμεις). The Potencies are described somewhat elusively as participating in the creation of the material world (172) and are further described as having their fairest parts in the sun, moon and sky (173). In the sky, bodiless beings that scripture call angels (ἄγγελοι) are a constituent of these heavenly powers (174).[55] Philo emphasises that God was not in need of others at creation but nevertheless includes angels in creation as servants who bear the responsibility for human vice.

Following the introduction of angels into the act of creation, Philo provides an explanation of the nature of humanity and angels (176-178). The categories of creation are again as they were previously (*Op*.72-77; see also *Gig*.): (1) reasoning and mortal beings; (2) reasoning and immortal beings; and (3) unreasoning and mortal beings. The first category describes the nature of humanity while the second category is applied to bodiless souls in the sky. The second category, based on the previous description (174), refers to the angels. The angels are free of a body and immune from evil while humanity is aware of good and evil. The third category is assumedly the remainder of created beings.

---

the purpose of argumentation in support of a thesis (*Virt.* 198-210) or which provides documentation of a certain theme which leads to a concluding exhortation (*Leg. all.* 3 77-106).'

[54] See also *Instruction on the Two Spirits* (1QS iii 18ff.): '[He] placed within him [humanity] two spirits so that he would walk with them until the moment of his visitation: they are the spirits of truth and deceit. From the spring of light stem the generations of truth, and from the source of darkness the generations of deceit.'

[55] Philo portrays stars as living beings in *Gig*.8, *Plant*.12, and *Somn*. 1 135. Angels are thought of as stars in *1 Enoch* 43.1-4; and stars as bad angels in 86.1-6; and 90.20-27; Job 38.7; Matt 2.9-11; Rev 9.1, 12.4; and *T. Sol.* 20.14-17.

As in *de Opificio mundi* (72-77) the beings that are recipients of the address in Genesis 1.26 are themselves free from evil but are included in creation to explain the origins of human vice. However, in the introduction of Genesis 1.26 in this context (179), further details are provided in regard to who specifically is addressed and what their role is in the creation. The recipients of address are the angels to whom God delegated the fashioning of reason in the soul of humanity. The two parts of humanity are a portion that is good while the other is free to choose (179). The portion of the soul that God is responsible for is the involuntary and good portion, while the angels are responsible for the voluntary portion (179).

In the following, Philo elaborates on a judgement theme, which develops parallel to the duality thus far presented. The judgement of the wicked is assigned to God's subordinates (180), which Philo supports by a partial quotation of Genesis 48.16: '…the God who nourishes me from my youth; the angel who saves me from all evils'. This passage (181) is elsewhere repeated by Philo in conjunction with Genesis 1.26 (*Fug.* 66) and is likely indicative of its importance for Philo's exegetical tradition or a tradition behind Philo. Philo uses the reference to make the statement that God is the nourishing one (ὁ τρέφων) and the angels' role is to divert any implication of evil from God (ὁ ῥυόμενός με ἐκ πάντων τῶν κακῶν). Along with taking part in the creation of humanity, all things considered evil including punishment, are assigned to angels. In the context of exacting vengeance from the humans who created the tower of Babel (Gen 11.7), God calls upon the angels to be judges. Philo makes it clear that in a scenario where salvation is needed it is God's role to nourish or to save (81-82).

A reference to Genesis 1.26 also occurs in *de Fuga et inventione*. In this passage there is a larger discussion on unintentional homicide where Philo introduces ministers of punishment (65-67). Similar to the context in *de Confusione linguarum*, Philo quotes Genesis 48.15 in reference to the angels' role as agents of punishment. The angels again divert from God any responsibility for evil, sin or human vice (ὅσα ἐκ φυγῆς ἁμαρτημάτων περιγίνεται θεράποντι θεοῦ). Here, Philo's exegesis of Genesis 1.26 is brief but specific (68-70). God is consulting with powers (δυνάμεσιν) which he has permitted to fashion the mortal portion of the human soul (69). God formed the sovereign portion of the soul while his subjects (ὑπηκόων) formed the subjected (ὑπήκοον) portion. The primary reason the angels are necessary in creation is because the human soul is vulnerable to both good and evil (70). Consistently, Philo attributes the responsibility of the creation of freewill and potential human vice to the angels.[56]

---

[56] *De Fuga et Inventione* 68ff. reads: '[Moses] described man alone as having been fashioned with the co-operation of others. His words are: "God said, let us make man after our image" (Gen. i. 26), "let us make" indicating more than one. So the Father of all things is

The final occurrence of Genesis 1.26 is in *de Mutatione nominum*. This reference is similar to what has been observed previously, but is followed by a uniquely stated duality. Preceding the quotation of Genesis 1:26 God's self-sufficiency is emphasised (27-30). As expected, Philo stresses again that God had no involvement in creating the wickedness of the soul. There is more than one creator involved in the formation of the human soul and the wickedness of that portion is due to the angels' role in creation.

Almost immediately following this passage Philo explains the implication of the Genesis passage (32-34). Since God is the maker of what is good alone, those composed of the good voluntarily relieve themselves of external concerns and whatever is valued by flesh. The ones who discipline themselves serve the soul and in the end become bodiless minds. The duality of the images in Genesis 1.26 here helps provide an opportunity for the division of humanity into categories of spirit and flesh. The first creation of Genesis 1 and the division of some to the category of 'spiritual' and others as 'fleshly' may be constructed on the *identification* of the individual with one or the other.[57]

The correlation of humanity and angels in 4Q417 1 i 16-17 is based upon humanity (אנוש) and a spiritual people being fashioned in the form of the holy ones. In Philo both God and angels, on the basis of Genesis 1.26, create humanity. Philo consistently uses an exegetical tradition of the plurality of images to assign the existence of free will and human vice to God's subordinates or other powers. The motifs of the 'spiritual people' and the 'spirit of flesh' in 4Q417 1 i may be based upon two types of creation (Gen 1-2), but the role of angels in the creation of Genesis 1.26 could be understood as playing a crucial role in the perception of humanity as having two potential parts as well. Collins' suggestion that the two creations are the basis upon which humanity is divided, some are created as spiritual being and others as fleshly beings,[58] is only one division within Philo's exegetical tradition. Humanity is also created by two creators and has both a spiritual and fleshly (virtue and vice) aspect that comes from angelic participation in the first creation.

---

holding parley with His powers, whom he allowed to fashion the mortal portion of our soul…. Therefore God deemed it necessary to assign the creation of evil things to other makers, reserving that of good things to Himself alone.' Translation by F. H. COLSON (LCL) p. 47.

[57] *De Mutatione nominum* 33 reads: 'Fine lusty and athletic are those who use the body as a menace to the soul. Pale, wasted and withered, so to speak, are the children of discipline. They have made over the bodily muscles to serve the powers of the soul and in fact are resolved into a singular form that of a soul, and become unbodied minds.' Translation by F. H. COLSON. GOFF, *The Worldly*, p. 124 observes: 'In both Paul and 4Qinstruction an individual can act either "fleshly" or "spiritually".'

[58] COLLINS, *Jewish Wisdom*, p. 124.

Musar leMevin and Philo, on these occasions, correlate angels and humans on the basis of the role of angels in the first creation. In the four passages reviewed above Philo preserves a tradition of Genesis 1.26 wherein humanity is created and formed by God and angels. In one passage (*Mut.* 32-34) Philo's use of the Genesis passage serves not only his purposes of assigning the existence of vice to angels, but also implies a division of humanity into 'soul' and 'flesh'. The correlation with angels and the division of humanity appear in both *Musar leMevin* and Philo. 4Q417 1 i appears to conceive of both a fashioning of humanity in the likeness of angels as well as a division between spirit and flesh. This being the case, both a division of humanity on the basis of dual creators and humanity's relation to these images (Gen 1.26) in addition to two creation accounts (Gen 1-2) may be at play in *Musar leMevin*.

Philo's reason for correlating humanity with the angels is to explain the material side of anthropology. The angels are not negative themselves but are responsible for the less virtuous and earthly qualities of humankind. *Musar leMevin* uses the correlation for positive purposes of exhortation. But, one may ask, could *Musar leMevin* also use the correlation between angelic beings and humanity to explain the existence of the 'spirit of flesh'? This remains a possibility, but would not be similar to what is found in Philo. The angels in *Musar leMevin*, as discussed in detail below, appear to be venerated by the community and are portrayed as ideal models to be followed. The image of the holy ones in 4Q417 1 i serves to identify and exalt the ones who share their likeness as elect ones. The image in the first creation in 4Q417 1 i is used to enhance those who share the image not explain the origins of the fleshly nature that some of humanity are identified with. However, the creation of all humanity in 4Q417 1 i in the likeness of angels does not mean they are automatically 'spiritual'. Spiritual identification is derived from an angelic likeness, but one must continue to seek this through Haguy and the רז נהיה (thus *Musar leMevin's* persistent exhortations). In the case of *Musar leMevin*, identification with angels is seen to be positive and perhaps potentially 'spiritual'. An explanation of a 'fleshly' inclination in 4Q417 1 i must be found elsewhere and is perhaps related to capitulating to the slothful nature of all humans (see 4Q418 55; 69).

Musar leMevin and Philo share a correlation of humanity and angelic beings, and this correlation is derived in both from Genesis 1.26. However, in what way has this plural address been dealt with by other authors? More specifically, is there a coherent thread discernible among Jewish exegetes or has each author more or less represented their own point of view? Several late traditions preserve similar interpretations of Genesis 1.26, but the implications on anthropology and angelology are not entirely clear. In reviewing these traditions *Musar leMevin* may be more closely situated in its history of interpretation.

2.9 Targums on Genesis 1.26 and 4Q417 1 i lines 15-18

The Aramaic targum of Pseudo-Jonathan preserves a very clear interpretation which includes angels as playing a part in creation (Gen 1.26).[59]

ואמר אלקים למלאכייא דמשמשין קומוי דאיתבריין ביום תניין לבריית עלמא
נעבד אדם בציולמנא כדייוקננא וישלטון בנוני ימא ובעופא דבאויר שמייא ובבעירא
ובכל ריחשא דרחיש עילוי ארעא

God said to the angels ministering before him, being created on the second day of the creation of the world, 'let us make man in our image and our likeness and they will rule the fish in the sea, the birds in the air of the sky, and the cattle and over every creeping thing that creeps upon the earth.'

The angels here are said to have been created on the second day of creation, though in the targum they are not explicitly mentioned on the second day of creation. As noted previously, Philo clearly portrayed the angels as part of the created order as well, though he believed that their creation was on the fourth day (*Op.* 23ff.). Nothing is known about the creation of angels in *Musar leMevin*, so little can be said on this point. The only observation that can be made is that Pseudo-Jonathan correlated humans and angels on the basis of Genesis 1.26.

2.10 Rabbinic Literature on Genesis 1.26 and 4Q417 1 i lines 15-18

Rabbinic literature on occasion conceives of the angels as the recipients of God's address in Genesis 1.26 as well. According to *B. Sanhedrin* 38b the angels are created beings whom God consults in creation. Two hosts of angels, sequentially, appear before God and are consulted about the creation of humanity. Angelic beings, speaking with words of scripture, ask, 'what is man that you are mindful of him and the son of man that you visit him'. God takes offence at this challenge to his authority and destroys them. A third host of angels is consulted about the creation of humanity and they reply 'the whole world is yours so whatever you wish to do there, do it'.

---

[59] BROOKE addresses the use of targums in relation to earlier traditions, specifically Qumran material, in *Exegesis at Qumran*, pp. 25-36. BROOKE concludes: '…it seems evident that throughout the targumic material available for study there can be located very specific uses of particular exegetical methods for rendering the Hebrew text more intelligible according to a particular tradition of that text's interpretation, and that these exegeses belong in many instances to pretannaitic times. Furthermore, the targumic use of such exegetical principles shows that they belong not only in Alexandria, as Philo's work has shown, but also in Palestine. The use of the Bible at Qumran confirms the pervasiveness of these principles in Judaism and the Hellenistic era.' J. BOWKER, *The Targums and Rabbinic Literature: An Introduction to Jewish Interpretations of Scripture* (Cambridge: Cambridge University Press, 1969) pp. 106-9; discusses targumic and rabbinic traditions on Gen 1.26.

Genesis Rabbah 1.26 presents four explanations of the plural address. First, R. Joshua b. Levi suggests that counsel was taken with the works of heaven and earth. R. Samuel b. Nahman says that the works of each day were consulted. R. Ammi says that God consulted his own heart. Finally, R. Hanina proposes that *the ministering angels were consulted.* As the midrash continues, the angels express their concern that wickedness will spring from humanity. Ultimately God creates humans and declares them to be good. Note that *Genesis Rabbah* addresses the issue of the nature of humanity and God's role in creation even if the outcome greatly differs from the account of Philo.

2.11 Genesis 1.26 Traditions and Conclusions on 4Q417 1 i lines 15-18

The primary purpose of consulting these sources is to observe a continuation of an exegetical tradition and the ease with which this plural address lends itself as a reference to angels. The 'spiritual people' are not the only ones formed in the likeness of the holy ones; but rather, the subject of the pronominal suffix of יצרו in line 17 refers to all humanity (i.e. אנוש in l. 16). This 'fashioning' (יצר), rather than 'inclination', of all humanity should be conceived of as being in the likeness of the holy ones who are angelic beings. However, the imagery of two creations in Genesis 1-2, spiritual and fleshly humanity, is still at work in 4Q417 1 i. Unlike Philo, in *Musar leMevin* the angelic role in the formation of humanity should be viewed as positive rather than as a possible loophole by which God might be excused from participation in the creation of human vice. Whereas for Philo the origin of human evil (negative attributes of humanity) is found with angels, *Musar leMevin* emphasises the 'fleshly spirit' as the culprit. *Musar leMevin* finds fault with those of the flesh because they do not know the difference between good and evil. The spirit of flesh, who were not called so from creation, once had access to such knowledge and it was later removed from them. This would suggest that the correlation of humanity with angels, even though positive, does not guarantee a positive identification with the 'spiritual people'.

Unlike the traditional Christian interpretation (e.g. Rom 5.12-14; 1 Cor 15.45ff.) of Genesis 1-3 that conceives of a temptation, disobedience and subsequent Fall of humanity, *Musar leMevin* values the possession of the knowledge of good and evil as the greatest good. It is not necessary to read 4Q417 1 i lines 15-18 dualistically as a 'spiritual people' created in the likeness of the holy ones and a 'fleshly spirit' that is not. Instead, *Musar leMevin* states that 'no more has meditation been given to a fleshly spirit, for flesh knew not the difference between good and evil according to the judgement of its [sp]irit '. All humanity should be understood as having been formed in the likeness of the holy ones. Therefore, all humanity had (has?) the ability to gain possession of the knowledge of good and evil and identify with the spirit (Gen 1) or identify with the creation of flesh (Gen 2). Indeed, Philo finds a flesh and spirit dichotomy in Genesis 1.26 in angelic participation in creation (*Mut.* 33). More precisely, the distinction or division of humanity here could be based upon pursuit and acquisition of the knowledge of good and evil (cf. 4Q418 221 5). The absence of this knowledge and failure to identify and seek a spiritual identity with the holy ones are what divides the two types of humanity and allows the designations 'spiritual' and 'fleshly'. This failure led to special revelation being taken away from a segment of humanity who once had it but did not pursue it.

3. Angelic Reference in 4Q416 2 iii

Fragment 4Q416 2 iii may, like 4Q417 1 i, be based upon conceptions of dual creators that ultimately derive from an interpretative tradition of Genesis 1.26. This suggestion has not been ventured among scholars thus far. 4Q416 2 iii lines 15-18 reads:

15) תביט ואז תדע מה מר לאיש ומה מתוק לגבר כבוד אביכה ברישכה
16) ואמכה במצעריכה כי כאל לאיש כן אביהו וכאדנים לגבר כן אמו כי
17) המה כור הוריכה וכאשר המשילמה בכה ויצר על הרוח כן עובדם וכאשר
18) גלה אוזנכה ברז נהיה כבדם למען כבודכה ובן]הדר פניהמה

15) you will gaze. Then you will know what is bitter for a man and what is sweet for a man. Honour your father in your poverty,
16) and your mother in your *low estate* (lit. 'littleness'). For as God is to a man so is his own father and as *angels* (אדנים) are to a man so is his mother, for
17) they are the oven of your origin (lit. 'parentage'). As/when/while He has set them in authority over you and (He) *fashioned*/formed *upon* (על) the spirit so serve them. As/when/while
18) He uncovered your ear to the רז נהיה, honour them for the sake of your own honour And *with* [   ] *venerate* their presence,

Column 4Q416 2 iii is best understood against the backdrop of Genesis 1.26 and 4Q417 1 i lines 15-18. As discussed in detail above, the formation of humanity in *Musar leMevin* enters into a tradition of Genesis 1.26 where the plural 'us' refers to angels (קדושים = אלהים) participating with God in creation. In 4Q416 2 iii line 15b-16 an exhortation occurs to honour one's father and mother. Immediately following, the conjunction כי ('for') introduces the simile that 'as the Father is to a man so is his father and as the אדנים (literally 'lords') are to a man thus a mother'. It is possible that these lines conceive of both God and the angels (אדנים) playing a role in the creation of humanity. This creative reality, or ontological fact for the author(s), serves as the basis upon which the exhortation to honour one's parents is founded. Since both had a role in humanity's creation, they should both be honoured: mother and father along with heavenly counterparts, God and angels. 4Q416 2 iii lines 16ff. appear to maintain a deliberate ambiguity at points in regard to referent; the creators or parents could be either the earthly or heavenly.[60] Line 17 states that 'they are the oven of your origin' which could, conceivably, refer to either pair as well. Similarly, the notion that 'they have been placed in authority over you' could refer to either. The phrase 'fashioned you *according to their spirit, so serve them*' in the latter half of line 17 is reminiscent of 4Q417 1 i lines 15-18 according to which humanity is fashioned in the pattern of the holy ones. The idea of 'serving them' followed in line 18 with the statement 'he exposed your ears to the רז נהיה' is also in keeping with the results of creation described in 4Q417 1 i, as well as a general veneration (הדר; also 'serve them'; l. 17) of angels elsewhere in *Musar leMevin*.

3.1 Translating the Term אדנים

The suggestion that 4Q416 2 iii lines 15-21 base wisdom upon conceptions from Genesis 1.26 is hindered by the identification of the term אדנים. What is clear is that parents are honoured because they played a role in creation just as אב and אדנים are an ultimate source of origin. Also clear is the general significance of Genesis 1-3 in this fragment. Line 20 makes the statement that the addressee has taken a wife and progresses to address issues regarding offspring of that union. The beginning of line 21 mentions once again the רז נהיה followed by an allusion to Genesis 2.20-25 in the phrase that the wife taken is the 'helpmeet of your flesh' (cf. 4Q418a 16b + 17) and then 'according to the statute of God that a man should leave his father and mother' (4Q416 2 iv 1). Though the exact phrase 'helpmeet of your flesh' does not occur in Genesis 1-3, there can be little doubt that an allusion to these chapters is at work.[61] Although the ending of 4Q416 2 iii is fragmentary, it appears that it continues to base ethical instruction upon cosmological conceptions derived from a Genesis creation tradition. The significance of Genesis traditions serves to complement the suggestion that the text has dual workers of creation in view.

The use of the fifth commandment of the Decalogue (Ex 20.12) in 4Q416 2 iii lines 15-18 is apparent. In addition to this allusion, there is also a probable

---

[60] Terminology and motifs in *Musar leMevin* are multivalent in places. An apocalyptic worldview in the document creates a purposeful ambiguity at points between imagery that could be read as either this-worldly or heavenly. Recognition of the occurrence of tensive-symbols and steno-symbols in *Musar leMevin* may hold valuable insights and fresh perspectives on the theology of the document.

[61] 4Q303 10 (*Meditation on Creation A*) follows the Hebrew Bible in עשה לו עזר.

allusion to Malachi 1.6 as well. It may be questioned whether the occurrence of the term אדנים in 4Q416 2 iii (and parallel MS 4Q418 9a-9c) alludes directly to any passage of the Hebrew Bible. If an allusion does occur here, it is possible that the author(s) has in mind Malachi 1.6, which has several significant similarities with 4Q416 2 iii lines 15-16 that are readily apparent:

בֵּן יְכַבֵּד אָב וְעֶבֶד אֲדֹנָיו וְאִם־אָב אָנִי אַיֵּה כְבוֹדִי וְאִם־אֲדוֹנִים
אָנִי אַיֵּה מוֹרָאִי אָמַר יְהוָה צְבָאוֹת לָכֶם

A son honours a father and a servant his master. If I am a father where is my honour? And if I am lord(s) where is my respect? says the LORD of hosts to you.

Conjecture that a link exists between 4Q416 2 iii and Malachi would help create an important connection with a targum. The tradition of linking Exodus 20.12 and Malachi 1.6 is preserved in *Targum Pseudo-Jonathan* on Malachi 1.6 and is further evidence of a broader tradition where the two passages were combined, as may be the case in 4Q416 2 iii:

הא על ברא אמיר ליקרא ית אבא ועבדא למדחל מן קדם
אנא אן דאתון דחלין מן קדמי אמר יוי צבאות רבוניה
ואם כאב אנא אן דאתון מיקרין קדמי ואם כרבון

Behold concerning the son it has been said that he is to show honour to the father, and the servant that he should show fear from before his lord and if I am like a father how are you showing respect before me? And if I am like a lord (sing.) how are you fearing from before me? Says the Lord of hosts.[62]

The targum begins by introducing a reference to the fifth commandment of the Decalogue in the phrase 'it has been said', establishing a tradition of the linking of Exodus 20.12 and Malachi 1.6. For the most part the translation follows the Hebrew Bible closely, and only changes the plural אדונים to the singular Aramaic אתון. The plural reading of 'lords' is rather difficult and the change in the targum to the singular form of the word is not an unexpected correction. The non-explicit use of Exodus 20.12 and Malachi 1.6 in 4Q416 2 iii evidently chooses to preserve the difficult plural form (אדנים) in a conflation of the two passages. A deliberate preservation of the plural form may indicate the intent of the author(s) to denote more than simply 'lord'.

In the Hebrew Bible Malachi 1.1 begins with the traditional phrase 'and the word of the Lord came to Israel by the hand of...' followed by the name of the prophet, 'Malachi' (מלאכי). The Septuagint translates מלאכי as ἀγγέλου αὐτοῦ, which indicates one interpretation of the proper name

---

[62] Translation mine.

'Malachi'. Moreover, it indicates that the Hebrew could have been read as 'my messenger/angel' and the Greek, clearly, 'his messenger/angel'. 4Q417 1 i line 16 likely alludes to Malachi 3.16 and suggests that Malachi may indeed be the focus of an allusion in 4Q416 2 iii.

The term 'lords' (אדנים/אדונים) occasionally occurs elsewhere in the Hebrew Bible (5x); however, with an orthographic variance from Malachi (אדנים). For the most part the term occurs in a context that exalts the God of Israel (אדני אדנים) over all other gods (e.g. Deut 10.17; Is 26.13; Ps 136.3). On two occasions the term might be better understood in the sense of earthly masters (1 Kgs 22.17, par. 2 Chron 18.16; Is 19.4).

The term אדנים occurs only once in the Dead Sea Scrolls; however, it occurs a number of times in *Hekhalot* literature. Some of these occurrences may hold significant contributions for translating the term in 4Q416 2 iii line 16. Due to the paucity of occurrences of the term אדנים in the literature of the period, the significance of its use in these passages as a likely reference to angels is significant. First, 1Q*Book of Noah* (1Q19 2) line 5 uses the term אדנים in a context that is concerned with proper names and designations for angelic beings:

קדש[י הש]מים   (1

לאמר גלו מש[פטנו לפ]ני עליון   (2

[ולא תחתך]   (3

מיכאל ואוריאל רפ[א]ל וגבריאל [(4

אדון] אדונים וגב]ור גבורים   (5

1) [Holy One]s of hea[ven
2) [saying, reveal] our [ca]se before [the Most High
3) [ ] and not under you [
4) [Michael, Uriel, Rapha]el and Gabriel [
5) [Lord] of lords and Migh[ty One of mighty ones[63]

Assuming that Barthélemy and Milik's reconstruction of 1Q*Book of Noah* is accurate, line five indicates God's dominion over angels. Though fragmentary, line 1 mentions the 'Holy Ones of heaven', which is a clear reference to angelic beings.[64] Line 4 refers to the archangels by name, which establishes the context for the use of the term אדנים in line 5. The phrase גבור גבורים as a reference to angels may be seen in the use of the term גבורים as

---

[63] Hebrew text taken from *DJD I*.

[64] 1Q19*bis* is popularly identified as 1Q*Book of Noah* but may be a fragment from *1 Enoch*. 4QEn[b] ar iii (=*1 Enoch* 8.2-9.4; 4Q202 iii) shares a number of similarities to 1Q19 including the names of archangels, however, the term אדונים does not occur here. See K. BEYER, *Die aramäischen Texte vom Toten Meer* (Göttingen: Vandenhoeck & Ruprecht, 1994) pp. 124-27.

an angelic epithet in *Shirot 'Olat ha-Shabbat* (4Q402 1 4, 4Q403 1 i 21).
1Q*Book of Noah* line 5 clearly uses the term אדונים as a designation for
angelic beings.

Among the three occurrences of the term אדונים in *Hekhalot* literature two
occurrences can clearly be demonstrated as containing angelic connotations. It
may be justifiably questioned how medieval manuscripts serve as a witness to
a 1st century CE document.[65] The use of Aramaic targums, rabbinic literature
and, more recently, *Hekhalot* literature is notoriously difficult to use as a
witness for earlier compositions. Perhaps the *Hekhalot* sources only display
the ease with which the seldom used form of this term lent itself as a reference
to angels. The first occurrence is in א34 588§ (N8128):

תפילה שנייה תתקדש יהוה אלהי ישראל שמים וארץ אדון אדונים אדיר אדירים
כרובים רוכב כרובים אל צבאות וממשלתי על צבאות אל משרתים

(In) a second prayer: you will be sanctified Lord God of Israel of heaven and earth, Lord of
lords and Glorious One of glorious ones, cherubim riding cherubim, God of hosts and ruler
over hosts, God of ministers.[66]

Here, the term occurs in a list of angelic epithets: glorious ones, cherubim,
hosts and ministers. While the Hebrew Bible uses the term משרתים to refer to
the priests who serve in the temple (e.g. Ez 44.11), the term is used in post-
biblical texts with angelic connotations (cf. 4Q286 3 2; 4Q287 2 9-12; 4Q400
1 i 4-7; 4Q405 23 i 3-6; 4Q511 35 4). The use of the term אדונים in a list of
angelic epithets displays the second occurrence of the term as a designation
for angels.

The second important occurrence of the term in *Hekhalot* literature is in
ב13 277§ (N8128). Metatron, the angel of Israel, is the subject of these lines:

---

[65] J. R. DAVILA concludes briefly on the origins of *Hekhalot* literature: 'There is a greater
degree of consensus about the authorship and life situation of the *Hekhalot* literature. It is
generally agreed that the movement has its roots in *Amoraic* (and perhaps even *Tannaitic*)
Palestine, but that important and perhaps crucial developments also occurred in Amoraic and
Geonic Babylon, and that (apart from the [Cairo] Geniza fragments) the surviving *Hekhalot*
texts have also undergone a lengthy period of transmission and redaction in the hands of
European Jewish communities'; in *Descenders to the Chariot: The People behind the
Hekhalot Literature* (JSJS 70; Leiden: Brill, 2001) p. 22. See also G. G. SCHOLEM, *Major
Trends in Jewish Mysticism* (3rd ed; New York: Schocken, 1954); M. D. SWARTZ, *Mystical
Prayer in Ancient Judaism: An Analysis of Ma'aseh Merkavah* (Tübingen: Mohr Siebeck,
1992); P. SCHÄFER, *The Hidden and Manifest God: Some Major Themes in Early Jewish
Mysticism* (Albany: State University of New York Press, 1992); D. J. HALPERIN, *The Faces
of the Chariot: Early Jewish Responses to Ezekiel's Vision* (Tübingen: Mohr Siebeck, 1988).

[66] Hebrew text taken from P. SCHÄFER, *Synopse zur Hekhalot-Literatur* (Tübingen: Mohr
Siebeck, 1981) p. 224.

Metatron whose name is called by eight names: Marguel is his name; Giutiel is his name; Ziutiel is his name; Izihiel is his name; Huiel is his name; Miuel is his name; Sagsagiel is his name; Magar(?)yadi(?) is his name. Within love, those that love him, in the heights calling him, in the camps Metatron, servants of the LORD, slow to anger, abundant in mercy, blessed are you LORD, wise of mysteries (הרזים), Lord of Lords (אדון אדונים) and the secrets (הסתרים), amen, amen.[67]

The majority of the occurrences (approx. 17x) of the term אדונים in *Hekhalot* literature are in the construct 'lord of lords' and usually set among similar constructs such as 'king of kings' and 'God of gods' (e.g. א33 O1 253§; ב12 N 262§). In the pericope above; however, the preceding context describes aspects of the revered Metatron and the phrase 'lord of lords' occurs within an angelic context.

These three texts demonstrate that on the few occasions where the term אדונים occurs it is used as a reference for angelic beings. These sources demonstrate that the use of the term אדונים in 4Q416 2 iii line 16 as 'angels' is not only a possible translation but a likely rendering. It should also be noted that Greek traditions (cf. 1 Cor 8.5) may preserve occurrences of the terms κύριος and κύριοι as epithets for angels as well.[68]

The combination of several factors from the context of *Musar leMevin* leads to an even higher probability that 4Q416 2 iii line 16 uses the term אדונים to refer to angels in the act of creation. First, 4Q417 1 i lines 15-18 most probably conceive of humanity being formed in the likeness of the holy ones. Second, 4Q416 2 iii line 17 states that both father and mother as well as God and lords are the 'oven of your origin', establishing a context and language not ordinarily associated strictly with earthly parentage. Third, the enigmatic

---

[67] Translation mine.

[68] M. WERNER, in his seminal work *Die Entstehung des christlichen Dogmas* (Tübingen: Katzmann-Verlag KG, 1941) pp. 307-12, provides six reasons he thinks that the term κύριοι was used in early Judaism and nascent Christianity for angels: (1) the term κύριος is not a transference of the LXX name for God to Christ since there is not one occurrence of the term used for God by Paul; (2) 4 Ezra uses the term κύριος for angels repeatedly and calls himself 'servant' as does Paul in relation to Christ; (3) the Christian apocalyptic works *Shepherd of Hermas*, *Ascension of Isaiah*, and *Apocalypse of Zepheniah* preserve a use of the term κύριος as a designation for angels; (4) Acts 10.3ff. describes Cornelius addressing the angel as κύριε and in Acts 9.5 Paul addresses the heavenly appearance of Jesus as κύριε (cf. the use of the term κυριότητος in Eph 1.21; Col 1.16; Jude 8; 2 Pet 2.10) indicating that the term in the NT is used for a class of angels; (5) the term κύριοι in 1 Cor 8.5, where Paul speaks of many lords and Christ as the one lord, serves as a link between early Jewish and primitive Christian teaching about the Christ and apocalyptic doctrine of angels; (6) and *1 Enoch* 41.10 describes the anointed among the hosts of angels and the 'angels of lordship (κυριότητος)'. WERNER's case for the use of the term 'lords' as a designation for angels stemming from early Judaism is made through relatively late Greek sources. The above discussion on the use of the term אדונים serves to strengthen his hypothesis. See the response to WERNER by W. MICHAELIS, *Zur Engelchristologie im Urchristentum. Abbau der Konstruktion Martin Werners* (GBTh 1; Basel: Majer, 1942). See also my 'Reconsidering an Aspect' article.

phrase ויצר על הרוח כן עובדם in 4Q416 2 iii line 17 is reminiscent of 4Q417 1
i line 17 and is concerned with formation beyond human parentage.[69] Fourth,
4Q416 2 iii line 18 exhorts the addressee to 'venerate their presence', which, I
will argue below, is congruent with concepts of angel veneration elsewhere in
the document.

3.2 Interpreting the Term נדיבים

The use of the term אדנים as a reference to angels in 4Q416 2 iii may have an
important influence on the unusual use of the term נדיבים, typically translated
as 'nobles' or 'princes', that occurs in 4Q416 2 iii line 11 as well as one other
fragment of *Musar leMevin* (4Q418 177 5).[70] The use the term נדיבים demands
further investigation if we are to understand this column. Though the term is
not used of angelic beings elsewhere in the Hebrew literature of the period,
reading the term as an angelic epithet makes the best sense of this column.
The pertinent lines are as follows:

9) גבולכה ואם[]]ישיבכה לכבודכה התהלך וברז [נ]היה דרוש מולדיו ואז תדע
10) נחלתו ובצדק תתהלך כי יגיה אל ת[אר]הו בכל דרכיכה למכבדיכה תן הדר
11) ושמו הלל תמיד כי מראש הרים רא'שכה ועם נדיבים הושיבכה ובנחלת
12) כבוד המשילכה רצונו שחר תמיד *vacat* אביון אתה אל תאמר רש אני ול[וא]
13) אדרוש דעת בכל מוסר הבא שכמכה ובכל] •[צרוף לבכה וברוב בינה
14) מחשבותיכה רז נהיה דרוש והתבונן בכל דרכי אמת וכל שורשי עולה

9) your boundary, and if [ ] he restore you to your glory walk in it and by the רז נהיה seek its
origins and then you will know

10) its inheritance, in righteousness you will walk for God will lighten its a[ppearance] in all
your ways, to the one honouring you, give veneration,

11) and his name praise always, because out of poverty he lifted your head and with angels
(נדיבים) he has seated you and over a glorious inheritance

12) he placed you in authority; always strive after his good *vacat* you are needy, do not say 'I
am poor and will n[ot]

13) seek knowledge, bring your shoulder under all instruction and in all [ ] prove your heart
and in the abundance of understanding

14) your thoughts, seek the רז נהיה and understand all ways of truth and all roots of iniquity

In 4Q416 2 iii lines 11-12 it is said of the addressee that he has been: (1) lifted
from poverty; (2) seated among the נדיבים; and (3) placed in authority over a

---

[69] COULOT, 'L'image de Dieu,' pp. 178-81 focuses on imagery of God as 'father' and the
addressee as 'son' in *Musar leMevin*.

[70] The editors comment on the term נדיבים stating that it is a term 'frequent in 4Q415ff.',
DJD XXXIV, p. 118. The term occurs five times in *Musar leMevin* and two of those
occurrences are in 4Q416 2 iii and parallel manuscript 4Q418 9, 9a-c. The other occurrence is
in 4Q418 177, discussed here, and the remaining two survive isolated in fragmentary lines
(4Q415 2 i + 1 ii; 4Q418 149).

glorious heritage. In addition, line 10 contains the term הדר ('glorify', 'honour', 'venerate'), which occurs in line 18 of this column. In line 12 continuing through lines 13-14 the addressee is told that he is needy, but should: (1) not use poverty as an excuse for not seeking knowledge; (2) study the רז נהיה; and (3) know the difference between truth and the roots of iniquity. Similarly, in 4Q418 177 line 5 the fragmentary line reads, 'you are poor but (-ו, and?) princes (נדיבים)' and is followed in line 7a with the line, 'know his mysteries (רזיו)'.[71] Both fragments indicate an unusual use of the concept of nobility and poverty.

4Q416 2 iii lines 11ff. state that the addressee has been removed from poverty and shares a place with the nobles and yet remains in an impoverished state in the following lines. 4Q418 177 line 5 is not preserved well enough to know if it contains the somewhat paradoxical concept of poverty that occurs here in 4Q416 2 iii. How can a state of economic poverty and a place among wealthy 'nobles' (cf. 1 Sam 2.8) co-exist? A number of conceivable options are available to reconcile the two. In the case of 4Q416 2 iii lines 11-14 an option is that the addressee's poverty denotes something other than, or in addition to, economic deficiency.[72] Another option may be that *Musar leMevin* conceives of the addressee as sharing an inheritance with the angels even though in this world he is materially poor. These two options are not mutually exclusive. The addressee could be seated among the 'angels' and his poverty is a deficiency (i.e. human frailty or weakness) in his ability to pursue the רז נהיה and the knowledge of good and evil. If this were the case, the repeated reminder that the addressee is poor/lacking would be anthropological and make these lines more comprehensible.[73]

If 4Q416 2 iii lines 11-12 state that the addressee has been seated among angelic beings, lifted from poverty, and has authority over an inheritance, but is closely followed with a statement of present poverty and potential failure (ll. 13-14) then lines 11-12 speak a reality not yet fully realised. The suggestion that lines 16ff. ultimately address issues of ontology would then function as an expansion on the relation of humanity to angelic beings and the proper response to it. These lines will be revisited below.

---

[71] 4Q415 6 line 2 reads אביון אתה ומלכנים. Cf. 416 2 ii; 1 Sam 2.8; Tg. Ps-Jn. On 1 Sam 2.

[72] COLLINS, *Jewish Wisdom*, p. 118-19, is right in stating that, 'this poverty is not at all an ideal' but one should be reticent in suggesting that, 'the text has material poverty in mind' exclusively. MURPHY, TIGCHELAAR, WRIGHT and GOFF conclude that material poverty is being discussed in this column as well. See also GOFF, *The Worldly*, p. 209.

[73] 4Q417 1 i 2 could be reconstructed and read as 'understand you[r] poverty' (תשכיל ראשנ[ך]); the editors comment: 'ראש could be the object of תשכיל (which is dubious) or of another verb in a new asyndetic sentence. Could ראש mean "poor" or "poverty"? Or is it preferable to take it as an object...?" *DJD XXXIV*, p. 156. If one were to read 'understand your poverty' and understood it as anthropological, the implication may be to be diligent.

4. Indefatigable Angelic Models

Musar leMevin depicts everything in creation as having an inheritance. This includes angelic beings. As discussed briefly in chapter 3, 4Q416 1 line 6 contains the fragmentary statement 'according to the lacking of their host'. Furthermore, angels seek understanding similarly to the addressees of *Musar leMevin* only without becoming weary. Angels in this document are portrayed in a way that may at times be without direct parallel in other early Jewish literature. They too share in a heavenly economy[74], seek wisdom and are described as 'lacking'. In all of this, however, they are conceived of as positive, but perhaps not perfect, role models for humanity to follow.

4.1 4Q418 55

Fragment 4Q418 55 lines 8-12 may assist in comprehending the complexities of 4Q416 2 iii line 11 and the nature of the addressees as well as the relationship between angels and humans generally.[75] These lines are among the most significant for understanding the relationship between angels and the addressees. The bottom margin follows line 12.

8) [היד]עתם אם לא שמעתמה כיא מלאכי קודש][ל]ו[ן] בשמים

9) [אמת]וירדפו אחר כול שורשי בינה וישקדו על

10) [ול]פי דעתם יכבדו איש מרעהו ולפי שכלו ירבה הדרו

11) [°[ ]הכאנוש הם כי יעצל ובן אדם כי ידמה הלוא

12) [עד והם אחזת עולם ינחלו הלוא ראיתם

8) have] you [not kn]own, have you not heard that the holy angels in heaven to [him]
9) [   ] truth, and they will seek after all the roots of understanding and will be watchful over

---

[74] STUCKENBRUCK, '"Angels" and "God",' p. 65 fn. 60, comments on FLETCHER-LOUIS' assertion that 'nothing connects the notion of "inheritance" to angels' in *Musar leMevin*, he writes: 'A fragmentary text in the first song of the *Shirot 'Olat ha-Shabbat* (4Q400 frg. 1 col. i, lines 10-13) refers to the 'princes' (line 12), apparently a class of angelic beings. If the pronominal suffixes in the phrases "in their territories and in their inheritance" refer to them, there is indeed evidence – and among the Dead Sea documents – that links inheritance to a (privileged) class of angels. See further 11Q13 col. ii, line 5, in which "the inheritance of Melchizedek" is referred to twice....'

[75] TIGCHELAAR, *To Increase Learning*, p. 224, questions whether 4Q418 55 and 4Q418 69 ii should be considered to have the same provenance as the rest of *Musar leMevin*, he concludes that the shared vocabulary (e.g. אל הדעות, אמת, נחל) between these columns and the rest of the document 'should be attributed to slight editorial reworkings of a *Vorlage*'. I am not convinced that the content or language of these columns warrants the conclusion that they were not a part of the original composition. However, even if they do have a different provenance one should not assume that the theology of these fragments was not adopted by the author(s) of *Musar leMevin*. See GOFF, *The Worldly*, p. 175.

10) [Ac]cording to their knowledge they will honour a man more than his neighbour, and according to one's insight one's veneration will be multiplied
11) [   ] are they like humanity? For [humanity] it is idle, and are they like a son of man? For he perishes, will not
12) [everlas]ting, and they will inherit an eternal possession, have you not seen

Fragment 4Q418 55 lines 8-9 compare heavenly angels who sanctify God with human beings who seek after the roots of understanding. The task of humanity is to seek understanding with the incentive (l. 10) of personal adoration or honour in the obtainment of knowledge. The task of performing truth and seeking knowledge undertaken by humanity varies with each individual as is indicated by degrees of recompense (l. 10). Beginning with line 11 the angels are juxtaposed with humanity. Humans (אנוש) are dissimilar to angels in that they are idle or slothful. A person (בן אדם) is unlike an angel because s/he is mortal. Line 12 speaks of an eternal possession that 'they' (הם), most likely the angels from line 8, will inherit.[76] Reading line 12 as a reference to angels inheriting an eternal possession is suggested by two factors: (1) line 11 uses הם as a reference to angels in distinction to humanity; and (2) line 12 contains the third person plural address הם and switches to a second person plural address (ראיתם) directed toward the readers/hearers.

4Q418 55 lines 10-11 establish that the addressee is to pursue knowledge and yet is deficient and mortal in efforts to do so. Conversely, the angels are indefatigable and as such are portrayed as inheriting an eternal possession. 4Q416 2 iii lines 11ff. portray the addressee as seeking knowledge by the רז נהיה, seated among angels, lifted from poverty and yet hindered in the pursuit of knowledge by their deficiency. It appears that 4Q416 2 iii lines 11ff. conceive of the addressee as, on the one hand, being given a special situation (i.e. given the רז נהיה and being placed among nobles) while on the other hand, subject to human conditions that potentially hinder a pursuit of knowledge.[77]

4.2 4Q418 69

In 4Q418 69 the wicked are created and fashioned by God just as the righteous (l. 6 מא[ל]אתם נוצרתם). 4Q418 69 also describes the condemned segment of humanity (i.e. the spirit of flesh) and details their creation. Those

---

[76] FLETCHER-LOUIS, *All the Glory*, p. 119, discusses 4Q418 69 ii but not 4Q418 55. Here he asks: 'where else in QL or contemporary Jewish traditions do angels have an 'inheritance'? This is the privilege of the human elect, not angels'. The editors' view is that angels are recipients of an inheritance in the document, *DJD XXXIV*, pp. 290-91. Whether or not evidence can be found in other early Jewish literature is not relevant, the contexts of 4Q418 55 and 69 ii strongly suggest that angels are in view. See fn. 74 above.

[77] *Shirot 'Olat ha-Shabbat* may similarly conceive of human deficiency in regard to worship and praise, 'what is the offering of our mortal tongue (compared) with the knowledge of angels?' (4Q400 2 7).

who judge them are described as seekers of truth (l. 7 דורשי אמת). Fashioning and establishment in this column reflect the notion of creation, similar motifs occur elsewhere. 4Q418 69 lines 10-15 are concerned that the addressees weary in pursuit of knowledge and works of truth. These lines read:

10) [שוקד]ים[   ] [משח] [ואתם בחירי אמת ורודפין vacat   [(10

11) בכול מ]   [על כול דעה איכה תאמרו יגענו בבינה ושקדנו לרדוף דעת[   ] [(11

12) [   ] ולא עיף בכול {נ} שני עולם הלוא באמת ישעשע לעד ודעה [(12
תשרתנו וב]ני[

13) שמים אשר חיים עולם נחלתם האמור יאמרו יגענו בפעלות אמת ויעפ]נו [(13

14) בכול קצים הלוא באור עולם יתהל]כו   כ]בוד ורוב הדר אתם [(14

15) ברקיע י]   [בסוד אילים כול [   ] vacat ואתה בן [(15

10) *vacat* and you, chosen ones of truth and pursuers of [ ] [ ] watchful
11) over all knowledge, how can you say: we are weary of understanding and we were watchful to pursue knowledge [   ] in all [
12) and does not tire in all the years of eternity, is not pleasure taken in truth forever, and knowledge [ ] serve him, and the s[ons of
13) heaven, whose lot is eternal life, will they say: we are weary in the deeds of truth and [we] are tired
14) at all times, will [they] not walk in eternal light [g]lory and abundant adoration, you [
15) in the firmament [   ] in the council of angelic beings is all [ ]. *vacat* and you, son of [understanding]

The addressees here are called בחירי אמת and are said to pursue truth and keep vigil over knowledge. The implication of the question in line 11 regarding how the addressees can say they are tired of pursuing knowledge is that weariness threatens their vigilance. In lines 11-12 the editors reconstruct the phrase '*For [the Understanding One tires not] at all ti[mes]*'.[78]

In the editors' reconstruction 'the Understanding One' (God?) is portrayed as a perfect model who delights in truth and whom truth serves. The reconstruction of a term for a single individual in line 11 is likely on account of the 3rd person masculine suffix of תשרתנו ('serve him') in line 12. The end of line 12 through line 14 address the nature of the 'sons of heaven'. The editors of DJD 34 note that the phrase בני שמים, 'is usually a non-metaphorical epithet for a group of heavenly beings, …not a metaphorical title for a group of human "sons of God" whose lives are assimilated to those of the angels'.[79] The editors cite several references (1QS iv 22, xi 8; 1QH[a] iii 22; 4Q181 1 2) that use the phrase as a non-metaphorical epithet[80] while several other

---

[78] *DJD XXXIV*, p. 283.

[79] *DJD XXXIV*, p. 290.

[80] See for instance 1QS iv 21-22, 'He will sprinkle over him the spirit of truth. . .in order to instruct the upright ones with knowledge of the Most High, and to make understand the wisdom of the sons of heaven to those of perfect behaviour. For those God has chosen for an

occurrences are available (1QH^a xi 21, xxvi 11; 1Q19 2 1; 4Q427 7 ii 18; *1 Enoch* 101.1; 2 Macc 7.34).[81] The occurrence of the phrase בני שמים in 4Q418 69 lines 12-13 should be read as a class of angels.[82] Both 4Q418 55 and 69 clearly envisage angelic beings as having an inheritance just as each creature in the document. 4Q418 69 line 13 poses the identical question of the sons of heaven, regarding growing weary in pursuit of knowledge, as is asked of the addressee in 4Q418 55 line 11. However, line 11 introduces the question with 'how can you say' as opposed to line 13 'will they say' preceded by 'whose lot is eternal life', which sets the sons of heaven and the addressees in stark contrast with one another. The exhortation of lines 10-15 appears to encourage the addressee to continue in vigilant pursuit of truth and knowledge based upon the models of God and the angels.

In light of the nature of humanity and the angels as portrayed in 4Q418 55 and 69, fragment 4Q416 2 iii lines 11ff. should be understood as referring to the addressees' relation to angels as well. Reading the term נדיבים[83] as the addressees being seated with the angels clarifies how, at the same time, the reference to removal from poverty (l. 11) might be reconciled with an insistence on present poverty and deficiency as an excuse for not studying (ll. 12-13). Moreover, the insistence of the addressee's poverty likely reflects on anthropology especially as he contemplates the angels' pursuit of understanding.

In 4Q418 55 and 69 the addressees are doers of truth and chosen ones of truth who do not pursue knowledge perfectly. In contrast, the angelic model is invoked in both fragments as an example of exemplary pursuers of knowledge. 4Q416 2 iii lines 9-10 could be read as an exhortation that the

---

everlasting covenant'; 1QS xi 7-8, 'to those whom God has selected he has given them as everlasting possession; and he has given them an inheritance in the lot of the holy ones. He unites their assembly to the sons of the heavens in order (to form) the council of the Community.' However, less clear is 4Q181 1 ii 2, 'According to the powerful deeds of God and in line with their evil, according to {the foundation of their impurity} their impurity, he delivered the sons of the he[avens] and the earth to a wicked community until its end'.

[81] 1QH^a xi 21-23 read, 'the depraved spirit you have purified from great offence so that he can take a place with the host of the holy ones, and can enter in communion with the congregation of the sons of heaven. You cast eternal destiny for man with the spirits of knowledge'.

[82] The editors write: 'to understand "sons of heaven whose lot is eternal life' as the angels seems inescapable; that it should be another description of a human and sectarian, group, the elect etc., though theoretically possible, is ruled out by the fact that the text has moved from being an address in the 2nd plural to being a question in the 3rd plural; and nothing points to the presence here of a distinct (3rd person) human group nor to the likelihood that the בחירי אמת (line 10) were an angelified group of humans'; *DJD XXXIV*, p. 290.

[83] *Shirot 'Olat ha-Shabbat* uses infrequent terms as designations for angels and the term נדיבים may have a parallel with the term נשיאים (4Q400 1 ii 14, 3 ii 2, 4Q401 1 i 1, 10, 21, 4Q405 13 2-5, 7). 4Q416 2 ii 9-14 likely allude to 1 Sam 2:8, Tg. Ps-Jn. gives 2:8 an eschatological and angelic setting. Cf. Ps 113; Tob 11.2 and 4Q491c lines 5 and 11.

addressee study the origins/birth-times (מולדיו) of his/its inheritance by the
רז נהיה in order to know 'what is *allotted* to it'. The end of line 11 and
beginning of line 12 state that the addressee has been placed in authority over
a glorious inheritance. Line 17 states that one's mother and father as well as
God and angels are the 'oven of your origin' and have been placed in
authority over the addressee. If lines 15-18 are read as a reference to the role
of dual creators in the formation of humanity, then the exhortation of line 9 to
study one's origin probably has this union in mind. Being seated among the
angels relates to the nature of the addressee's formation in the lines that
follow.

Therefore, angelic beings participated with God in the creation of
humanity. While they are exemplary models to be followed they are not
necessarily perfect in all respects, they themselves may be understood to be
poor (4Q416 1, לפי מחסור צבאם) and not yet have come into possession of
their inheritance.[84] Angelic beings are not only models for the addressees but
the focus of admiration for their creative role in humanity's formation. The
addressees see themselves as having a place among the angels, however, this
has not become reality for them in the present.

5. Reconstruction and Identification of 4Q418 81

4Q418 81 has attracted nearly as much scholarly attention as 4Q417 1 i and is
another column that is highly significant for understanding the relationship
between humans and angels in *Musar leMevin*. Among the various issues
raised on this column are the authorship, addressees, identity of the 'holy
ones', and reconstruction of various lines. The text and translation presented
are those of Tigchelaar:[85]

1) שפתיכה פתח מקור לברך קדושים אתה כמקור עולם הלל [ ] מא[ז הבדילכה מכול
2) רוח בשר ואתה הבדל מכול אשר שנא והנזר מכול תעבות נפש[ן כי]א הוא עשה כול
3) ויורישם איש נחלתו והוא חלקכה ונחלתכה בתוך בני אדם [ובנ]חלתו המשילכה ואתה
4) בזה כבדהו בהתקדשכה לו כאשר שמכה לקדוש קודשים[לכול]תבל ובכול
[מ[ל]אכליו[86]

---

[84] The possible portrayal of angels as imperfect in 4Q416 1 would have an impact on the
nature of humanity in the formation of God and angels. Even though the 'people of spirit' and
angels are positively portrayed, they are lacking. This deficiency, if it is to be seen as part of
the nature of humankind, could be seen as the result of angelic participation in creation.

[85] TIGCHELAAR, *To Increase Learning*, p. 94 and pp. 230-231. In addition to *DJD XXXIV*
and there commentary on these lines, TIGCHELAAR'S commentary is very useful for
reconstructing and translating this column.

[86] *DJD XXXIV*, pp. 300-1, the editors reconstruct the final word of line 4: [מ]ל[י]כ[א]
('angels').

5) הפיל גורלכה וכבודכה הרבה מואדה וישימכה לו בכור ב]   [ל]

6) וטובתי לכה אתן ואתה ל הלוא לכה טובו ובאמונתו הלך תמיד]

7) מעשיכה ואתה דרוש משפטיו מיד כול יריבכה בכול מו°]

8) אהבהו ובחסד {עולם} וברחמים על כול שומרי דברו וקנאתו]

9) ואתה שכל פ]תח לכה ובאוצרו המשילכה ואיפת אמת פ'קו]ה

10) אתכה המה ובידכה להשיב אף מאנשי רצון ולפקוד על]

11) עמכה בטרם תקח נחלתכה מידו כבד קדושיו ובט]רם

12) פתח [ ]   קד]ושים[87] וכול הנקרא לשמו קודש]°

13) עם כול ק]   []ו[88] פארתו למטעת עו]לם

14) [ ]°ה תב]ל] בו יתהלכו כול נוחלי ארץ כי בשמ]ים

1) (of) your lips He has opened a spring, to bless the holy ones. And you, as (with) an eternal spring praise [*His name*. Long ag]o, He separated you from every

2) spirit of flesh. And you, keep yourself apart from everything He hates, and keep aloof from all what is detestable. [Fo]r He has made everyone,

3) and has given every man his own inheritance. And He is your portion and your inheritance amongst the children of mankind. [And over] His inheritance He has given you authority. And you,

4) honour Him by this: by consecrating yourself to Him, in accordance to the fact that He has appointed you to be a most holy one [of all] the world. And among all [His a]n[gels]

5) He has cast your lot. And he has exceedingly multiplied your glory. And He has appointed you for Himself as a first-born son among [   ] [

6) And my goodness I will give to you. And you, is not His goodness for you, and in faithfulness to Him walk continuously [

7) your works. And you, seek His judgements from every adversary of yours in all [

8) love him. And with {eternal} kindness and mercy towards all those who keep his word, and in zeal for him [

9) And you, He has [op]ened insight for you, and He has given you authority over its treasure; and a true measure is entrusted [

10) are with you. And it is in your hand to turn away anger from the men of good pleasure, and to appoint over [

11) your people. Before you receive your inheritance from His hand, honour His holy ones, and befo[re

---

[87] *DJD XXXIV* the editors reconstruct these first words of line 12 - שיר[] כול קדושים פתח. The photographs do not entirely substantiate either reading, which appear to read - [ ]פתח[שים[ק] כול /ור°; another possible reconstruction may be: פתח ור]שים[דו]ק כול מק]ור and rendered as 'he opened a spring for all holy ones'; see ELGVIN, 'Wisdom With and Without,' p. 26. STUCKENBRUCK, '"Angels" and "God",' p. 63, fn. 50 comments: 'Reading this text all depends on whether the tiny fragment containing these words has been correctly joined with fragment 81 (cf. Harrington and Strugnell, DJD 34, p. 308 to lines 11-12; see photo on Plate XVIII). If this placement may be granted, several considerations favour מקור over בשור[ן ?] as a restoration: (1) the ligature atop the left vertical stroke of a letter following the lacunae is more consistent with a ק than with ש; (2) *contra* Strugnell and Harrington, the lacunae on line 12 and the varying shape of the tail of ק in the manuscript make it possible to restore קור[ם; and (3) a ש would require the foregoing space after פתח to be wider than spaces between any of the other words in the column.'

[88] *DJD XXXIV*, pp. 300-1, the editors reconstruct two words here: קצים הדרו.

12) open [ho]ly ones. And everyone who is called by His name, holy [
13) with all [ ] his beauty for the eter[nal] plantation [
14) [ ] wor[ld]. In it will walk all who inherit the earth, for in hea[ven

Several items about the recipient(s)[89] of address may be ascertained from the column: (1) line 1 places him in a venerative position to the 'holy ones'; (2) lines 1-2 describe the addressee as separated from 'all flesh' at a point in the past as opposed to a separate creation; (3) all humanity has an inheritance and 'He', presumably God, is his inheritance among the children of humankind; (4) in line 3 the addressee has authority over God's inheritance; (5) in line 4 he is instructed to consecrate himself on account of his most holy status in the world and his position among the angels; (6) line 5 speaks of his manifold glory and appointment as first-born son; (7) line 9 indicates that insight has been revealed, authority over a treasure entrusted and true measure given to him; (8) he has a role turning wrath from 'men of good pleasure'; (9) line 11 indicates that his inheritance is not yet fully realised or realised in a continuing sense; and (10) lines 11-12 repeat the motif of venerating 'holy ones'.

A number of scholars have written on 4Q418 81 offering their own interpretive suggestions. However, none of these contributions has attempted to analyse 4Q418 81 and angelology within the document as a whole. Fletcher-Louis offers the most comprehensive discussion on angelology, but he does not take into account 4Q418 55 or angelic references in 4Q416 2 iii. A review of scholarship on 4Q418 81 followed by a brief discussion of angel veneration in early Jewish literature will precede a synthesis of this column in the larger framework of angelology and anthropology in the document.

5.1 Armin Lange

Lange has suggested that 4Q418 81 'should be interpreted as describing the election of either Aaron or Aaronite priests'.[90] The beginning point for this claim is the nearly explicit quotation of Numbers 18.20 in line 3, these texts may be compared:

והוא חלקכה ונחלתכה בתוך בני אדם (4Q418 81 3)

אֲנִי חֶלְקְךָ וְנַחֲלָתְךָ בְּתוֹךְ בְּנֵי יִשְׂרָאֵל (Num 18.20)

In the context of Numbers 18.20 Aaron is, of course, the recipient of the inheritance and the allusion here in 4Q418 81 is, for Lange, indicative that the

---

[89] While the address is in the singular ואתה it could well be understood in a collective sense.

[90] LANGE, 'Determination of Fate by the Oracle of the Lot' in D. K. FALK *et al.* (eds.), *Sapiential, Liturgical and Poetical Texts from Qumran* (Leiden: Brill, 1999) p. 40.

identity of the addressee is the same. Lange finds confirmation that the addressee in *Musar leMevin* is an Aaronic priest in the following arguments: (1) line 4 speaks of God placing an elected one 'at the holiest of holy things' (לקדוש קדושים); (2) line 1 speaks of praising God at an 'eternal well' which he states is an allusion to the motif of the priestly praise of God in the temple;[91] (3) line 2 exhorts the addressee to keep separate from all that God hates and uses the term נזר, which is often used in post-exilic literature with priestly connotations; and (4) the addressee in line 7 is instructed to דרוש משפטיו, which is a phrase that Lange suggests denotes a specific priestly function.[92] The conclusion reached is that 4Q418 81 should be interpreted as describing the election of Aaronic priests by way of the 'oracle of the lot' (l. 5), which is a metaphor for the instrument used by God to determine the fate of human beings.[93]

A few questions and observations may be raised in regard to Lange's analysis of 4Q418 81. The previous discussion in chapter 2 on the use of citations and allusions of biblical traditions raised the question whether it is reasonable to assume that an allusion bears the context of the biblical source. The allusion to Numbers 18.20 in 4Q418 81 line 5 does not necessarily carry the Aaronic priestly meaning or content from Numbers. Observations of intertextuality, especially in a document such as the *Hodayot*, display that allusions and citations are used rather freely. As this is the case, the four points of confirmation produced by Lange need careful consideration.

First, the placement of the addressee לקדוש קדושים, depending on how one translates the phrase, may fit with the conception that they preserve the true and faithful priesthood. Second, Lange considers the use of מקור in line 1 as an allusion to the motif of priestly praise of God in the Temple. The term מקור occurs in the Dead Sea Scrolls about 20 times, mostly in the *Hodayot*, and does not demand connotations of priestly praise in the temple, though at times it does (1QH[a] iv 21; ix 22; x 18; xiv 17; xvi 4, 8; xix 19; xx 25, 29; xxiii 10, 12, 13; 1QS x 12; xi 3, 6; 1QSb i 3, 6; 4Q504 frags. 1-2 v 2; 4Q511 frags. 52, 54-55, 57-59 2; 63 iii 1).[94] While the term may be used with priestly

---

[91] LANGE, 'Determination of Fate,' points to evidence from the Hebrew Bible (Ez 47.1ff.; Pss 36.10, 46.5, 65.10) as well as the work of B. EGO, 'Der Strom der Tora – Zur Rezeption eines tempeltheologischen Motivs in frühjüdischer Zeit,' in B. EGO *et al.* (eds.), *Gemeinde ohne Tempel – Community without Temple* (WUNT2 118; Tübingen: Mohr Siebeck, 1999) pp. 205-14; EGO discusses the use of well imagery in Ben Sira as depicting the teaching of Torah.

[92] LANGE, 'Determination of Fate,' pp. 40-41.

[93] LANGE, 'Determination of Fate,' p. 48.

[94] Many of these occurrences have intriguing similarities for *Musar leMevin*: 1QS xi 6 speaks of מקור צדקה, מקוה גבורה and עין כבוד; 1QSb i 3 invokes a blessing upon the faithful and invites God to open a מקור עולם which does not dry up; 4Q511 52, 54-55, 57-59 2 states that God is a מקור הטהור for Adam and his offspring; 4Q511 63 iii 1 has the author extolling God's justice and having placed upon his lips a מקור תהלה; 1QH[a] iv 21 (cf. 1QH[a] ix 21-22; xx

connotations in the Hebrew Bible or Ben Sira, there is little to substantiate the claim that this term necessarily indicates temple imagery in 4Q418 81. The most striking parallel to the language of 4Q418 81 is found in 1QS xi 3 where both the terms מקור and רז נהיה occur. Here, the author compares himself with the 'benders of the law' and states that in contrast God has opened a source of insight for him (i.e. the author) that enables him to know the רז נהיה:

2) ...כיא אני לאל משפטי ובידו תום דרכי עם ישור לבבי

3) ובצדקותו ימח פשעי כיא ממקור דאתו פתח אורי ונפלאותיו הביטה עיני ואורת לבבי רז

4) נהיה...

2) ...For me, to God are my judgements and in his hand is the perfection of my way with uprightness of heart
3) with His justice he shall erase my iniquities, for from a spring of knowledge He has opened my light and His wonders my eyes have viewed, and the light of my heart the רז
4) נהיה....

Column xi of 1QS is missing in one manuscript of *Serekh haYahad* (4Q259) and is most probably an addition to the document. The author(s) claims in this column (ll. 5-6) that his eyes have gazed upon wisdom (תושיה) that has been hidden from the rest of humanity (נסתרה מאנ׳ש). At the end of line 6 this wisdom is described as a מקור צדקה. In the lines to follow the establishment of a righteous and elect community is portrayed with language found in 4Q418 81 ('everlasting plantation', 'in the lot of the holy ones'). However, the writer does not locate himself in this community, but rather laments his unfaithful state and iniquitousness and hopes on God's mercies. 1QS xi expresses an individual who has access to the רז נהיה, which is likened to a 'spring (מקור) of righteousness', but falls miserably short of righteousness. There is no indication of a priestly identity in this column. 1QS xi reflects many motifs that occur in *Musar leMevin* and may further elucidate similar but divergent theologies. Significantly, 1QS xi uses both the רז נהיה and מקור צדקה as terms for concealed wisdom.

The term נזר is not a highly frequent word in the Dead Sea Scrolls and is found nowhere in the Hebrew Bible in parallel with the term נבדל, as it is in

---

25) describes one born of woman as a structure of dust and water a מקור נדה with a depraved spirit; 1QH[a] x 18 (cf. 1QH[a] xx 29) has God placing on the heart of an understanding one a מקור דעת; 1QH[a] xiv 17-18 (cf. 1QH[a] xxvi 4, 8) have the elect with the holy ones and as an everlasting plantation watered by the streams of Eden and a spring of light that will be למקור עולם.

4Q418 81 line 2.[95] However, the term נבדל does occur in parallel with נזר in *Damascus Document* vi lines 14-15 where we read:

14) ...ישמרו לעשות כפרוש התורה לקץ הרשע ולהבדל
15) מבני השחת להנזר מהון הרשעה הטמא בנדר ובחרם

14) they should watch to do according to the details of the Torah, for the time of wickedness and to *distinguish*
15) between the sons of the pit and to abstain from the defiling wealth of the wicked in vow and in *consecration*

In the *Damascus Document* the terms are not used with a priestly sense; rather, they are used in a context of general admonition. The term נזר does not necessarily denote priestly behaviour and there is no reason to demand such a connotation in 4Q418 81. Finally, Lange suggests that the phrase דרוש משפטיו is definitely a priestly task. In the Hebrew Bible this is certainly not the case: the phrase generally has the sense of exacting justice (cf. Is 1.17; 16.5). In 1QS vi 7-8 both the phrases דרוש בתורה and לדרוש משפט occur, in this context there is an assembly of men together with a priest who seek to understand the regulations. However, the context in 4Q418 81 does not equate משפט with תורה; but rather, the term could be understood in the sense of 'judgements' that will be exacted against God's adversaries. In conclusion, Lange's arguments that identify the addressee of 4Q418 81 as an Aaronic priest do not necessarily compel one to conclude that the addressee should indeed be understood as a priestly figure.

5.2 Torleif Elgvin

Elgvin identifies the addressee of 4Q418 81 as a member of the end-time community. He writes that the column is 'a meaningful entity only if the addressed individual is seen' as part of the end-time group.[96] Terms for the elect are found in the phrases אנשי רצון as well as the מטעת עולם (cf. 1QH[a] xvi). These terms indicate that the author of *Musar leMevin* understood his 'circle(s) as the nucleus of the community of the end-time, that will exist forever'.[97] Specifically, the imagery of the 'planting' is connected with conceptions of an end-time inheritance of the land. The elect in 4Q418 81 are exhorted to praise the holy ones who are the angels (ll. 1, 4, 11). The fellowship between the elect community and angels exists amidst images such

---

[95] LANGE, 'Determination of Fate,' suggests translations of the term as 'to dedicate, devote, consecrate oneself'. TIGCHELAAR, *To Increase Learning*, p. 232, writes: 'Lange's suggestion that √נזר is used because of its priestly connotations argues, in my opinion, the wrong way around.'
[96] ELGVIN, 'Wisdom With and Without,' p. 26.
[97] ELGVIN, 'Wisdom With and Without,' p. 27.

as 'garden', 'planting', 'sprout' and 'fountain', all of which are used in exilic and post-exilic texts in connection to Eden and the temple. As such, Elgvin believes that the circles behind *Musar leMevin* understood themselves as a spiritual temple. The phrase פתח מקור for him, *apropos* Zechariah 13.1 and selected lines from the *Hodayot*, clearly has temple connotations. Therefore, the addressees, according to Elgvin, are the elect end-time community estranged or separated from faithless Israel.[98] Elgvin understands the elect as a group who were estranged from and opposed to the Aaronic Jerusalem cult,[99] and the priesthood is 'reinterpreted as a promise to the elect individual'.[100]

One final comment on Elgvin's interpretation may be directed at his translation of the phrase לקדוש קדושים. Elgvin takes the term לקדוש as an infinitive and renders the entire phrase as 'to sanctify the holy ones'. He also notes that if 'holy of holies' was the intended reference the spelling would have been קודש קדושים.[101] However, as Tigchelaar recognises, the term לקדוש as an infinitive cannot mean 'to sanctify' but could possibly be translated as 'to become holy'.[102]

5.3 Harrington and Strugnell

The editors of DJD 34, in their extensive notes on 4Q418 81, comment upon several aspects of the column. First, they maintain that the phrase פתח מקור[103] in line 1 is related to blessing the holy ones, which is significant for line 12 where the word פתח appears and is followed by a gap of approximately three letter spaces, followed by the word קדושים. The sense of the metaphor in line 1 is to 'open up a spring for the utterance of words'.[104] The editors reconstruct פתח []שיר in line 12 whereas Tigchelaar leaves the space blank. They note the possibility that the word [מק]ור could be reconstructed in line 12 which would be a complementary reconstruction to the preceding line.[105] The primary

---

[98] ELGVIN, 'Wisdom and Apocalypticism,' p. 244.

[99] FREY, 'Flesh and Spirit,' p. 387, notes that, 'there are no indications linking it [*Musar leMevin*] to a specific religious community, let alone a community separated from the Temple...'; see also LANGE, 'In Diskussion,' p. 131.

[100] ELGVIN, 'The Mystery to Come,' p. 121.

[101] ELGVIN, 'An Analysis of 4QInstruction,' p. 136.

[102] TIGCHELAAR, *To Increase Learning*, p. 233. The infinitive לקדוש does not occur in the Hebrew Bible only the *piel* infinitive construct לְקַדֵּשׁ (Ex 29.1, 29.33; Jer 17.27; Ez 46.20; Neh 13.22; 2 Chron 29.17), the singular masculine noun לְקֹדֶשׁ (Ex 31.11; 1 Kgs 6.16, 7.50; 2 Chron 4.22) and on one occasion the masculine singular adjective לִקְדוֹשׁ (Is 58.13).

[103] The editors note that these two words appear in relation to one another elsewhere in the DSS (e.g. 1QS xi 3; 1QH^a ii 18, viii 21, x 31, xi 19, xviii 10).

[104] *DJD XXXIV*, p. 303.

[105] Judging from the photographs it is my opinion that the two surviving letters of the second word are *waw* and *resh* rather than *yod* and *resh* (compare the *yod* of the following word קדושים or the *yod* of מקור in line 1). See fn. 83 above.

difficulty for the editors in reconstructing the term [מק]ור[ו] here is the absence
of any traces of the tail of a *qof*. Careful analysis of the photograph reveals
significant damage to the letter *qof* and on this basis would be difficult to
reconstruct confidently. Regardless of how the second word of line 12 is
reconstructed it is the opinion of the editors that glorification of angels is
present in these lines.[106]

The reconstruction of 4Q418 81 line 4 is also significant with regard to
anthropology and angelology. The editors reconstruct here:

לקדוש קדושים] לכול [תבל ובכול] א[ל]י[ם]

('among all the angels', continuing in line 5 'has He cast thy lot') whereas
Tigchelaar reconstructs the final word of line 4 as [מ]ל[אכי]ו. The editors
question whether the addressee is being appointed as 'someone holy (or as a
sanctuary)[107] for all the world'. They also raise the possibility that lines 4-5
could refer to the special lot of Aaronic Priests, but wonder if it is not more
likely in a sapiential context that 'they treated of the priestly or quasi-priestly
station of the maven in the administration'.[108] The editors can offer no
definitive statement regarding the priestly status of the addressee and are
reluctant to identify him as such.

Harrington and Strugnell identify and comment on references to the
addressee as קדוש קדושים and בכור, as well as the use of the phrases אנשי רצון
(l. 10) and מטעת עולם (l. 13) – all of which are important for understanding the
recipient(s) of address in 4Q418 81. They state that identifying the *maven* as a
first-born is 'a little surprising' and as a 'holy of holies' as 'not impossible'.
The editors make no comments on their translation of קדוש קדושים as 'Holy of
Holies' but offhandedly suggest that this refers to a sanctuary. With regard to
the occurrence of the phrase אנשי רצון in line 10, they suggest that it is a
'theological description of the authors own group' and may not be a 'sectarian
self-characterization (cf. the Lucan passage and the parallel in the Aramaic
4Q*Visions of Amram*ᶜ ar (4Q545) 9 18; cf. also מטעת עולם in l. 13, which need
not have been one either)'.[109] The phrase 'eternal planting' is found elsewhere
in the Dead Sea Scrolls (1QS viii 5, xi 8; 1QHᵃ vi 15, viii 6) and is often
understood as a reference to a strictly sectarian group.[110] However, the editors
consider that the phrase 'need not presuppose a dualistic or specifically
sectarian theology' since the motif occurs in the Hebrew Bible. In conclusion,

---

[106] *DJD XXXIV*, p. 308.

[107] TIGCHELAAR, *To Increase Learning*, p. 233, comments on the phrase לקדוש קדושים:
'The translation 'holy of holies' should perhaps be avoided, since it may suggest that the
addressee is appointed as a sanctuary.'

[108] *DJD XXXIV*, p. 305.

[109] *DJD XXXIV*, p. 305.

[110] See especially TILLER, 'The "Eternal Planting",' pp. 312-35.

the editors express some surprise at the descriptions used of the addressee and view the phrases אנשי רצון and מטעת עולם as references to the author's community, which is not sectarian. According to DJD 34, the address of the column has in mind both an exalted addressee and a community that is subjugated to him.

5.4 Eibert J. C. Tigchelaar

Tigchelaar's reconstruction and translation of 4Q418 81, as noted above, differs at several points from that of others. In addition to the transcription and translation above, several other comments are beneficial for understanding this column. Tigchelaar explains the promise to Aaron in the allusion to Numbers 18.20 and the identification of the phrases רוח בשר and בני אדם in lines 1-3 as follows:

> The phrase 'he has separated you from every spirit of flesh', may be interpreted in the light of line 3 והוא חלקכה ונחלתכה בתוך בני אדם which quotes the promise to Aaron in Num 18.20. In Num 8.14 and 16.9 the same verb הבדיל is used with regard to the Levites, where it is said that they have been separated from the midst of the Israelites, or the congregation of Israel. Deut 10.8-9 combines these concepts: בעת ההוא הבדיל יהוה את שבט הלוי, 'at that time the Lord set apart the tribe of Israel' for several cultic tasks, followed in verse 9 by על כן לא היה ללוי חלק ונחלה עם אחיו יהוה הוא נחלתו. Just as בני אדם in line 3 replaces the biblical בני ישראל, so רוח בשר replaces בני ישראל or עדת ישראל in this phrase. In other words, רוח בשר and בני אדם seem to be synonymous in this fragment.[111]

The allusion to Numbers 18.20, in my observation, would appear to depict the addressee as being separated from the 'spirit of flesh' and serves the purpose not to communicate a priestly division but to distinguish him from a portion of humanity. There is no reason to conclude that the allusion here, which is not a verbatim quotation, is meant to remind the reader or hearer of the earlier text's (Num 18.20) context. The significance the allusion to Numbers 18.20 is thought to have in the lines that follow may not be warranted. Furthermore, how is one to understand רוח בשר and בני אדם as synonymous in these lines when in one line the addressee has been separated from them (ll. 1-2 'long ago, He separated you from the רוח בשר') and in the next he is among them (l. 3 'amongst (בתוך) the children of בני אדם')? Tigchelaar's identification and interpretation of these lines in light of Numbers are difficult.

The column as a whole contains very little priestly language (e.g. purity language like נדה, טהרה, טמאה).[112] The possible explanation that Tigchelaar provides for the absence of such language is his hypothesis of differing addressees. He concludes that most of the references to a possible priestly

---

[111] TIGCHELAAR, To *Increase Learning*, p. 232.

[112] Other sapiential literature such as Ben Sira or *Mysteries* have a greater occurrence of this priestly terminology.

addressee are 'obscure and broken'. Nevertheless, he argues that evidence for a priestly addressee may be found in the following two observations: (1) columns 4Q418 81 and 4Q415 1 ii-2 i contain about half of all words related to the root קדש in the document; and (2) the addressee enjoys an elevated status such as when he is told to consecrate himself, is described as 'most holy', and blesses the holy ones. This elevated figure functions as an intermediary between the 'children of mankind or the men of good pleasure, and the holy ones'.[113]

The ultimate conclusion reached by Tigchelaar is similar to that of the editors: the column addresses both an exalted figure and a class of humanity of a lesser status. The interpretation of the 'holy ones' as angels and the interpretation of the intermediary role of an elevated addressee is convincing. However, the equating of the רוח בשר with the בני אדם on the basis of Numbers 18.20 and Deuteronomy 10.8-9 is less persuasive. The phrase בני אדם is more likely a term for all of humanity and רוח בשר a designation for a category of wicked humanity.[114]

5.5 Crispin Fletcher-Louis

Fletcher-Louis has written briefly on 4Q418 81. He understands the addressee in this column to have a 'transcendent ontology' and points to his separation from the spirit of flesh and his status as first-born. Much of Fletcher-Louis' attention is focused upon lines 1, 11, and 12 where, as we have seen, angels (קדושים) are the recipients of blessing, glorification and perhaps song. Fletcher-Louis questions whether there is sufficient evidence to read these lines as concerned with angel (i.e. the term קדושים should not be interpreted as 'angels', but 'holy ones') veneration or worship and states that 'unequivocal and extensive support in the primary texts has been difficult to find'. Rather than interpret these lines as a veneration of angels, he argues that '*the individual here described is a priest who is set apart from the laity, who are the "holy ones", whom he is called to bless and glorify*'.[115]

---

[113] TIGCHELAAR, *To Increase Learning*, p. 236.

[114] 1QS xi 6-7 describe wisdom as hidden from the assembly of flesh who are equated with the בני אדם. The author identifies himself with the בני אדם in 1QS xi and is not an exalted or holy figure.

[115] FLETCHER-LOUIS, *All the Glory*, p. 178. STUCKENBRUCK, '"Angels" and "God",' p. 64, comments: '[Fletcher-Louis] is right, of course, that the mere use of the terms "bless" and "glorify" do not in themselves indicate that the text is concerned with angels....More important, however, is the wording of the passage itself. The beginning of line 1 refers to the opening of the addressee's lips; the opening of lips is activity whose subject is likely to be God. In the Hebrew Bible [Pss 51.15; 59.12; 63.3; 71.23; 119.171] and the Dead Sea documents [1QS x 6; 1QH^a ix 27-31; 4Q511 63+64 iii 1-2] the opening of lips (or even use of lips – when the language of blessing and praise occurs – is restricted to instances that refer to praise of God, that is, not to a blessing of the human community'.

Fletcher-Louis' argument for the identification of the addressee as priestly is made by appealing to Lange's discussion. Fletcher-Louis emphasises the strong priestly connotations of the term נזר, understanding it in the sense of 'sanctification' and relating it to the blessing of Levi in *Jubilees* 31.14.[116] Another criterion is the occurrence of the phrase 'holy of holies' in line 4 which is congruent with ways in which the priesthood within the Qumran community are established as a 'holy of holies over against the laity who are the holy ones'.[117] However, Fletcher-Louis takes for granted that the phrase לקדוש קדושים should be translated as 'holy of holies', a translation discussed in relation to Elgvin. He further understands the reference to 'holy of holies' as part of a cultic cosmology where the priest is set apart and functions as a sacred centre of the whole cosmos, so that he and the rest of God's people embody the 'true Adam'.

Fletcher-Louis finds a distinction between the righteous in general and the position of the addressee specifically in lines 3-4: '*each* [the righteous ones] man has his inheritance, and God is *yours* [singular 'your' which refers to the exalted individual]'.[118] He argues, 'in this case the addressee is a priest who, like the high priest in 1QSb iv 28, is set apart "for the holy of holies" and given the divine privilege assigned to Aaron by the biblical text'. Fletcher-Louis also finds priestly language in line 4 where he glorifies God, כבדהו (cf. Sirach 50; 1QSb iv; *Aristeas* 99). In line 10 the phrase להשיב אף מאנשי רצון is related to the same activity of the priest Phineas who turns away God's wrath from the righteous and is thus further evidence of priestly language in 4Q418 81. Other evidence that the turning away of God's wrath is strictly a priestly vocation is found in an assortment of other texts (1 Macc 3.3-9; Wis. Sol. 18.15-16; *Joseph and Aseneth* 22). Another priestly vocation is found by Fletcher-Louis in line 9 where the addressee has been given authority over a treasure, an authority of such magnitude that it is only conceivable that it is given to a priest.[119]

Fletcher-Louis' case that the addressee in 4Q418 81 is to be identified as a priest is based upon two primary reasons. First, he depends strongly on Lange's conclusions. Second, he emphasises the phrase קדוש קדושים as 'holy of holies'. While it may be that there is a likelihood that the identity of the addressee is priestly, the arguments presented by Lange are not without their limitations and should not be understood as definitively pointing to a priestly addressee.[120] The translation of לקדוש קדושים as 'holy of holies' is not

---

[116] See discussion above where LANGE'S use of this term is used to identify the addressee as priestly.

[117] FLETCHER-LOUIS, *All the Glory*, p. 179.

[118] FLETCHER-LOUIS finds a shared theology in 1QS viii-ix; 4*QMMT* and 4Q511 35.

[119] FLETCHER-LOUIS, *All the Glory*, pp. 182-83.

[120] STUCKENBRUCK '"Angels" and "God",' p. 64 interacts with FLETCHER-LOUIS on this point: 'The possibility that that one addressed is a priest cannot be discounted, as it is hard to

straightforward, it would have to be a plene spelling for the expected
לְקֹדֶשׁ הַקֳּדָשִׁים. Tigchelaar's translation of the phrase as 'a most holy one'
seems the more probable and would limit notions of temple cosmology in the
column.

Fletcher-Louis' idea that the task of turning away God's wrath is strictly a
priestly vocation has merit. However, that the turning away of wrath is limited
to a priest in *Musar leMevin*, rather than any one among the elect who are not
necessarily priests, is too strict. The claim that the act of honouring God
(כבדהו) is inflexibly a priestly vocation is only convincing if it can be
demonstrated that the entire document is addressed to priests, which is highly
unlikely. The concept of glorifying God is common throughout *Musar
leMevin* (e.g. 4Q416 2 ii 18; 4Q416 2 iii 10, 15, 18; 4Q417 1 i 13; 4Q417 20
5; 4Q418 9 12; 4Q418 69 ii 14) and is scant evidence for the addressees'
identity. Finally, the addressee's charge over a treasure would seem to have
little significance for identifying the priestly status of the figure. Throughout
the document the addressees are portrayed as possessing the רז נהיה and אוט
(?) which could be related directly or indirectly to the treasure in line 10.

Fletcher-Louis makes his argument for treating the blessing and
glorification of the 'holy ones' in lines 1, 11 and 12 as a witness to the
theology of divine priesthood. His primary argument for reading these lines as
a witness of angel veneration is the sheer lack of evidence in the Judaisms of
the period.[121] Fletcher-Louis finds in *Jubilees* 31.15 an 'angelmorphic
priesthood separated from all flesh [who] is to "bless all the seed of the
beloved"'. 4Q418 81 lines 1, 11 and 12 should, he suggests, be understood
within this context. Other corroborative evidence is found in 1 Maccabees 3.3
where Judas Maccabee 'enlarged the glory' of his people. Sirach 44-50 is also
cited: Simon the high priest brings glory to Israel and 'encomiastic "praise of
the fathers"'.[122] In conclusion, Fletcher-Louis is convinced that 4Q418 81 is
addressed to a priestly individual who is separated from the laity ('holy ones')
and whom the addressees are to bless and glorify. While an exalted individual
may be in view over against an elect community, the identification of the
'holy ones' as a reference to the community is not sustainable. Traces of
angelmorphology are not apparent in the document.

Fletcher-Louis' assertion that there is a general lack of evidence in the
literature of early Judaism for angel veneration provides an opportunity to
explore this topic briefly before concluding on 4Q418 81. *Contra* Fletcher-

---

construe the phrase "he has placed you as a holy of holies" otherwise (line 4). However, to
distinguish between the "understanding one" (addressed elsewhere in the document) and a
priestly figure (who is addressed here) is misleading.'

[121] FLETCHER-LOUIS, *All the Glory*, p. 186, cites 11Q*Berakhot* 1 ii lines 5-6 as one of the
only references to priestly blessing of angels: ברוכים כול מלאכי קודש.

[122] FLETCHER-LOUIS, *All the Glory*, pp.186-87.

Louis, the occurrence of the phrase קדושים in lines 1, 11 and 12 is certainly a reference to angels rather than to the community or laity. In the preceding discussion on 4Q417 1 i the referent of this term was similarly debated. Collins discusses that there is no unambiguous reference to Israel as 'holy ones' in the Dead Sea Scrolls, and even in the Hebrew Bible there is only one ambiguous occurrence (Ps 34.10). There is no reason why Collins' identification should not be accepted as normative.[123] Moreover, *Musar leMevin* is interested in angelic beings throughout and uses multiple designations for them including 'holy ones'.

5.6 Loren T. Stuckenbruck

Occurrences of angel veneration in documents from early Judaism are discussed by Stuckenbruck in relation to 4Q418 81. An analysis of his discussion, both as it is directly related to this column and early Jewish works more broadly, will assist in understanding the relationship between the addressees and angelic beings. There is a general consensus among scholars that the addressee of 4Q418 81 enjoys an exalted status and may also be a priestly figure. In addition to this figure are: (1) the 'men of good pleasure' (l. 10) and 'eternal planting' (l. 13); and (2) the 'holy ones' (ll. 1, 11, 12). Before attempting to address further the identity and relation of each of these to the other, we turn briefly to issues of angelic blessing, praise and veneration as discussed by Stuckenbruck.

It is beyond the range of the present inquiry to review extensively a history of scholarship on the topic of exalted notions of angels as related to early Christology. However, it is from scholarship on Christology and angelology that most research on angel cults, angel worship, 'angelmorphism' and related themes has stemmed.[124] Stuckenbruck has demonstrated that in a number of texts 'angels could be made objects of veneration as beings aligned with and subordinate to God'.[125] No attempt will be made here to provide an overview of human participation in angelic functions in early Judaism; rather, a brief synopsis of texts that preserve expressions of angel veneration, as set forth by Stuckenbruck, will be reviewed.

While Stuckenbruck's monograph is concerned with angel veneration as it relates to Christology in the Apocalypse of John, a more recent article summarises aspects of his original work and includes a section on 4Q418 81. In both works he distinguishes between positive and negative evidence for

---

[123] See COLLINS, *Daniel*, pp. 313-17. See also STUCKENBRUCK'S comments further below.

[124] STUCKENBRUCK, notes in his monograph that 'it is conspicuous that relatively little is said which seems to have a direct bearing on the problem of human veneration of angels', *Angel Veneration* p. 150. While the general topic of angelology in the DSS scrolls has been addressed, there remain few secondary sources that specifically deal with the veneration of angels. See chapter one for a bibliography on angelology as related to Christology.

[125] STUCKENBRUCK, *Angel Veneration*, p. 269.

angel veneration (i.e. 'polemical texts' and 'non-polemical sources').[126] While the first division primarily explores Rabbinic literature and the New Testament, the second division analyses Qumran documents and other early Jewish works. For the sake of brevity, the latter sub-section will be the focus of attention here.

The two documents from Qumran that Stuckenbruck explores in relation to angel veneration are *Shirot 'Olat ha-Shabbat* and 11Q*Berakhot* (=*Sefer haMilhamah*).[127] The first column that Stuckenbruck analyses is 4Q400 2 and the last line of connecting fragment 4Q401 14 i line 6.[128] The occurrence of angel veneration in this column was first suggested by Anna Maria Schwemer.[129] The following reconstruction is that of DJD 11 while the translation and divisions are those of Stuckenbruck:

4Q401 14 i

6)]לראשי ממשלות [   ]שמי מלכות כבודכה

4Q400 2

1) להלל כבודכה פלא באלי דעת ותשבוחות מלכותכה בקדושי ק[דושים

2) המה נכבדים בכול מחני אלוהים ונוראים למוסדי אנשים פ[לא

3) מאלוהים <י>ם< ואנשים יספרו הוד מלכותו כדעתם ורוממו]

4) שמי מלכותו ובכול מרומי רום תהלי פלא לפי כול[

5) כבוד מלך אלוהים יספרו במעוני עומדם *vacat* ו[

6) מה נתחשב [ב]ם וכוהנתנו מה במעוניהם וק[ודשנו

7) קודש[י]הם [מה] תרומת לשון עפרנו בדעת אל[י]ם

---

[126] In relation to polemical sources, STUCKENBRUCK summarises: '...we have reviewed evidence for a refusal tradition which functioned rhetorically in a narrative setting to prevent a seer from worshiping an angelic figure. In addition, it was suggested that this and some rabbinic traditions may be understood as a critique which presumes a common traditional heritage among authors and readers or between tradents and opponents. Nevertheless, no single instance of the kind of outright worship forbidden in the refusals turns up in early Jewish literature. It remains possible, if not likely, that some authors made use of polemical traditions in order to paint a dark picture of milder tendencies to venerate angels or to protect against potential misunderstanding of something within their own or similar writings. The question explored below is whether there is anything in early Jewish texts... which explains the use of the polemic in its various forms'; *Angel Veneration*, p. 164. STUCKENBRUCK, '"Angels" and "God",' p. 47-52, provides a brief review of polemical sources.

[127] Since STUCKENBRUCK'S monograph was published it has been suggested that 11Q*Berakhot* overlaps with 4Q285 and is thus a part of the *War Scroll*. See M. ABEGG, 'Messianic Hope and 4Q285: A Reassessment,' in *JBL* 113 (1994): 81-91. See also STUCKENBRUCK '"Angels" and "God",' pp. 57-62.

[128] *DJD XI*, p. 207.

[129] STUCKENBRUCK, *Angel Veneration*, p. 157; A. M. SCHWEMER, 'Gott als König in den Sabbatliedern' in *Königsherrschaft Gottes und himmlischer Kult im Judentum, Urchristentum und in der Hellenistischen Welt* (eds.), M. HENGEL and A. M. SCHWEMER (WUNT2 55; Tübingen: Mohr Siebeck, 1991) pp. 81-2 and 99-100.

[ל]נ[ר]נתנו נרוממה לאלוהי דעת] (8

ק]ודש ובינתו מכול ידע]¹³⁰ᵃ (9

(6) to the chief of the realms [   ] the heavens of Your gl[or]ious kingdom

(1) to praise Your glory,

      a wonderful thing among the *elim* of knowledge

and (to praise) the praiseworthiness of Your kingdom,

        (a wonderful thing) among the most holy ones.¹³¹

(2) They are honoured among all the camps of the *elohim*

  and revered by human councils,

    a [wonder] (3) (greater) than the *elohim* and human beings

      alike,

for they recount the splendour of His Kingdom

  according to their knowledge

and they exalt [His ... in all]

  (4) the heavens of His Kingdom,

and in all the exalted heights wonderful psalms

  according to all [their insight ...]

       (5) the glory of the King of the *elohim* they recount

  in the dwellings of their (assigned) position. *vacat*

An[d ...,]

      (6) how can we be reckoned [among] them,

and our priesthood,

  how (can it be reckoned) among their dwellings?

and [our] ho[liness,

  how can it compare with] (7) the[ir] ho[li]ness?

[And what] is the offering of our tongue of dust

  (in comparison) with the knowledge of the *elim/elohim*?

     (8) ...] our resounding,

let us exalt the God of knowledge [...

(9) ... ho[liness,

and his understanding is beyond all who [have eternal]

  knowledge.

The phrase 'chiefs of the realms' that occurs in 4Q401 14 i line 6 is 'the subject of הלל...[and] seems to be an elite group of angels probably equivalent to the נשיאים ('princes') mentioned in other *Shirot*.¹³² The role of the 'chiefs of the realm' is to praise God, which in 4Q400 2 1 is a wonderful thing among the אלים and קדושים. In the line following, the ראשים are 'characterized by two passive participial forms in predicate position; they are "glorified" and "revered"'. These lines go beyond applying attributes to angels found elsewhere; the syntax suggests that both angels and humans consider the 'chiefs of the realms' to be superior. Stuckenbruck suggests that the reason these chief angels are venerated is on account that 'they recount the

---

¹³⁰ *DJD XI*, p. 187.

¹³¹ *DJD XI* translates, 'among the holiest of h[oly ones'.

¹³² STUCKENBRUCK, *Angel Veneration*, p. 158.

splendor of His kingdom according to their knowledge'. These beings possess
a superior understanding and their attainment of knowledge and the quality of
their worship are something to which the addressees aspire. In general, the
community does not regard itself comparable in their priesthood, sanctity or
knowledge to these angels. Despite the deficiency of the community, they are
nonetheless allowed to participate in the heavenly cult. The acknowledgement
by both angels and humans of the 'chiefs of the realms' superiority, and the
glorification and reverence given them, is venerative.[133] The reason for such
veneration is similar to that of *Musar leMevin*: *the angels represent a superior
model and possess superior knowledge.*

The next column from *Shirot 'Olat ha-Shabbat* that contains a significant
occurrence of angels as objects of veneration is 4Q403 1 i lines 31b-33a. The
beginning of line 31 contains a reference to 'praiseworthy chiefs'
(ראשי תושבחות), similar to the above column. The end of line 32 and beginning
of line 33 contain the phrase בה תשבחות כול אלוהים, which Stuckenbruck
suggests be translated as 'in it/through it is the praiseworthiness of all *elohim*'.
Following the suggestion of Schwemer, he sees this as a reference to the
'praiseworthiness' of angels by the addressees rather than God's rule being
made manifest or brought to expression through the angels' praises. An
alternative reading to the praiseworthiness of the angels, he argues, does not
properly account for the parallelism between the word הדר in the preceding
phrase (כי בהדר תשבחות כבוד מלכותו); 'for in/through praiseworthy majesty is
the glory of His rule') and תשבחות here.[134] Understanding these lines as angels
being praiseworthy would seem to be the best interpretation.[135] Schwemer and
Stuckenbruck's reading of this column demonstrates the second occurrence of
angel veneration in *Shirot 'Olat ha-Shabbat*.

11Q*Berakhot* (=*Sefer haMilhamah*) contains an occurrence of the blessing
of angels. Here, God's holy angels are 'the final predicate of a brief four-fold
blessing to be recited by a (high-)priestly figure (וברוכים כול מלאכי קודשו)'. In
the three blessings that precede the blessing of angels it would appear first
that the community is blessed, then God's holy name, while the third
predicate is lost due to fragmentation. While the blessedness of the
community is dependant upon the name of God in the first blessing, the fourth
blessing of the angels functions as a form of praise. Predicate blessings of
humans and God are frequent in the Hebrew Bible, Dead Sea Scrolls, and
other early Jewish literature, while the blessing of angels is scarce (cf. Gen
48.15-16; Tob 11.14). Here the praiseworthiness of the angels is due to their

---

[133] STUCKENBRUCK, *Angel Veneration*, pp. 158-60.

[134] STUCKENBRUCK, *Angel Veneration*, pp. 160-61.

[135] FLETCHER-LOUIS, *Luke-Acts*, does not agree with STUCKENBRUCK'S findings on angel
veneration, see esp. 4Q400 2 and Pseudo-Philo (LAB 13.6) pp. 5-6; and Tobit p. 38 fn. 20.

role as protectors and ones whose presence, similar to God's presence, is conceived of as guaranteeing the 'community's well-being'.[136]

While Stuckenbruck explores a number of texts from early Jewish literature (e.g. *Ps-Philo* 13.6; *1 En* 9.1-11; 15.2; 40.6, 9; 47.1-2; 99.3; 104.1; *T. Levi* 3.5-7; 5.5-6; *T. Dan* 6.2) the doxology in Tobit 11.14-15 deserves special mention.[137] Following the recension of Tobit in Codex Sinaiticus, a four-fold doxology in the 3rd person preserves the blessing of angels twice:

(14) Blessed [be] God, and blessed [be] his great name, and blessed [be] all his holy angels; may his great name be upon us, and blessed [be] all the angels unto all ages, (15) for he has afflicted me, but now I see my son Tobias!

Stuckenbruck argues that Codex Sinaiticus preserves an earlier recension than either Codices Alexandrinus or Vaticanus.[138] These latter two codices contain shorter blessings with only one blessing of angels and are more fully integrated into the story (2nd person). These codices contain a form that renders praise to angels less excessively than Sinaiticus. Elsewhere, Codex Sinaiticus contains loftier evaluations of angels by Tobit (cf. 8.15; 12.12-15) than Alexandrinus or Vaticanus. At the same time, the recension of Sinaiticus is careful to place the praise of angels alongside God, ensuring an 'essentially monotheistic outlook'. Alexandrinus and Vaticanus appear to be later recensions which continued to transmit the text with intensified concern in this regard.[139] Tobit 11.14-15 of Codex Sinaiticus preserves Tobit's response to the restoration of his sight and safe return of his son in the blessing of both God and His holy angels. The evidence from Tobit would indicate that angels were on occasion recipients of blessing from human beings in some early Jewish literature.

Stuckenbruck demonstrates on a number of occasions that angels in documents from Qumran and other early Jewish literature were the object of varying degrees of veneration as beings subordinate to God. *Musar leMevin*, specifically 4Q418 81, is closely aligned to the sort of pattern we find in *Shirot 'Olat ha-Shabbat*. Based upon both internal (4Q416 2 iii; 4Q417 1 i; 4Q418 55; 4Q418 69; 4Q418 81) and external evidence (esp. *Shirot 'Olat ha-Shabbat*) it is reasonable that *Musar leMevin* conceives of the relationship between the addressees and the angels (קדושים) as venerative.

---

[136] STUCKENBRUCK, *Angel Veneration*, pp. 162-63.

[137] STUCKENBRUCK, '"Angels" and "God",' pp. 52ff. focuses on the 'worship' of angels in: *T. Levi* 5.5-6; *Joseph and Aseneth* 15.11-12x; Tob 11.14; 11Q14 1 ii 2-6; *Shirot 'Olat ha-Shabbat*; *Musar leMevin* (4Q418 81 1-15).

[138] For another discussion on these recensions see J. A. FITZMYER, *Tobit* (Berlin: Walter de Gruyter, 2003) pp. 279-80.

[139] STUCKENBRUCK, *Angel Veneration*, pp.165-67.

In 4Q418 81 much of Stuckenbruck's attention is drawn to the language of lines 1, 11, and 12. He notes that the language of opening one's lips, which occurs in line 1 (שפתיכה פתח מקור לברך קדושים), is an activity in the Hebrew Bible and Dead Sea scrolls used to refer to praising God. The language of line one is directed heavenward and in this case is to angels. Lines 11-12 then would follow line 1 and resume the thought. The addressee is to honour the holy ones and, perhaps, open a fountain *to* the holy ones (פתח[ ]מ[קור כול קדושים).[140] Stuckenbruck makes an important distinction in the possible sense of line 12. If his reconstruction is correct and one should read fountain as opposed to song here, is the sense to open a fountain *of* all God's holy ones or *for* all God's holy ones? Stuckenbruck comments:

> ...if the fountain is to be opened *for* "all his holy ones", then we may consider whether this watering metaphor extends to the "plantation". In this way, the fountain (perhaps referring to the instruction given to the addressee) would be that which feeds or waters the eternal plantation (i.e. the human community of "holy ones" called by God's name). In this case, the "holy ones" to be honoured could be readily identified as the righteous congregation of the elect. If the fountain, however, is *of* the holy ones, then it becomes more difficult to identify them straightforwardly with the plantation that follows.'[141]

Stuckenbruck suggests that the latter interpretation of line 12 would signify that the elect community, also called the 'eternal plantation', is allowed to 'receive or participate in the fountain which belongs to the angels'.[142] This latter interpretation makes sense not only of this column, but 4Q418 55 and 69 as well. Stuckenbruck agrees that 4Q418 55 and 69 compare humanity with angels whose activities are exemplary and views 4Q418 81 as preserving further evidence for angel veneration. If מקור could be identified with concealed wisdom, as it is in 1QS xi, the sense here would be to open up angelic wisdom. In conclusion, Stuckenbruck emphasises that the special position given to the addressee in this column is due to the activity of God rather than venerative activities towards the holy ones (cf. 4Q418 81 2).

5.7 Summary of 4Q418 81

4Q418 81 appears to be addressed to an exalted figure(s) who stands between the superior and exemplary holy ones ('angels') and a faithful community ('men of good pleasure'; 'eternal plantation'). The addressee of the column could be a priestly figure, though this claim has been set forth with greater

---

[140] STUCKENBRUCK, '"Angels" and "God",' p. 65 cautions that 'it is preferable to attempt an interpretation that adheres more strictly to the economy of words as they appear in line 12.' There is not enough space in the damage point of line 12 to allow for more than a few letter word to be reconstructed which disallows a form of שפה as in line 1 (שפתיכה).

[141] STUCKENBRUCK, '"Angels" and "God",' p. 65.

[142] STUCKENBRUCK, '"Angels" and "God",' p. 65.

certainty than the textual evidence may merit. Line 17 of 4Q418 81 exhorts the addressee: 'from each of thy teachers get ever more instruction'. From whom is the exalted addressee to learn? Is the addressee to gain instruction from a superior human teacher or do the holy ones fulfil this role? Perhaps the relationships between various figures within the column are not to be understood in a strictly static hierarchical sense. We may conceive that there are, comparatively, multiple exalted figures within the community just as there are multiple 'mavens'. In line 10 where the role of the addressee has it in his hands to 'turn away wrath from the men of good pleasure', this may be the result of pursuing learning excellently. Superior learning may serve to exalt a member of the elect who needs not be *de facto* a priest.

It may be questioned whether line 10 truly warrants a division between an exalted priestly figure and the 'laity' of the community. An understanding of these lines as fixedly defined, priestly verses laity, is not warranted by the evidence available. If the addressees of the document generally have in common access to the רז נהיה and pursue and achieve knowledge to differing degrees (4Q418 55 10: 'Ac]cording to their knowledge they will honour a man more than his neighbour, and according to one's insight is his honour'), then such a clear division may not be applicable. While the relationship between addressee(s) and 'men of good pleasure' in 4Q418 81 could have expression in terms of an exalted figure and laity, such distinctions may be too strict. Rather, it may be best to conceive of 4Q418 81 as addressed to an elect community whose members have attained varying degrees of sanctity and who all hold the holy ones in esteem as superior models who should be emulated and revered.

If one reads 4Q417 1 i lines 15-18 as a description of all humanity created in the likeness of God and the angels, and a segment losing revelation later called 'spirit of flesh', some aspects of 4Q418 81 come into sharper focus. The column begins with a statement that the addressee has been separated from the spirit of flesh (ll. 1-2). The addressee is described as an 'eternal spring', 'most holy one' (or 'holy of holies' ?) and 'first-born'. A distinction is made in line 3 that the addressee has a different inheritance (God) than others sons of Adam. The lot of the addressee is with the angels (ll. 4-5) who possess and seek knowledge. The identity of the addressee, discussed in relation to 4Q417 1 i as spiritual, is based upon behaviour and seeking knowledge. Metaphorically, the addressee dwells within an Edenic garden (4Q423 1, 2 i) and partakes of its many wisdom bearing trees. If the addressee's community is called an 'eternal planting' in line 13, it may relate to the imagery of being part of the faithful among humanity who continue to partake of the trees of knowledge in the garden. Therefore, motifs of creation and the garden converge in 4Q418 81 that distinguish the addressee from the spirit of flesh and relate him to the holy ones.

6. Conclusions

The focus of this chapter has been to explore conceptions of angelology and anthropology in *Musar leMevin*. The first text to be examined was 4Q417 1 i lines 15-18 where it was suggested that the author(s) drew upon an exegetical tradition of Genesis 1.26-27. *Musar leMevin*, it is argued, conceives of dual creators (i.e. God and angels) who fashioned all of humanity after their likeness. Bequeathed to all humanity was a divine revelation, which was rejected (or they failed to acquire it) by a portion of humanity called the 'spirit of flesh'. The association of human beings with knowledge (רז נהיה) and the understanding of good and evil serves to divide humanity into two basic categories: the עם רוח and רוח בשר. The continuing task of pursuing both knowledge and holiness appears to be laborious for the addressees as is expressed in other columns of the document (esp. 4Q416 2 iii; 4Q418 55 and 69 ii).

4Q416 2 iii lines 15-18 are presented as more explicitly reflecting the notion of dual creators of humanity. In these lines it has been suggested that an analogy exists between mother and father as well as God and angels as creative partners. Both pairs are said to be set in authority over the addressee (l. 17) and the רז נהיה revealed to them. The addressee, in response to creation, is exhorted to both honour them (father/mother; God/angels) and venerate (הדר) their presence (l. 18).

In the preceding lines 9-14 of 4Q416 2 iii are unusual occurrences of the motif of the addressee's poverty and his relationship to angels (נדיבים). The addressee is said to be both lifted from poverty, given a glorious heritage and yet still subject to poverty (cf. 4Q418 81 9 where the addressee has been set over a 'treasure'). The addressee is exhorted to study and not use poverty as an excuse for neglecting this pursuit. While poverty in *Musar leMevin* is frequently thought to be related to economic hardship, in the context of 4Q416 2 iii lines 9-14 conceptions of poverty are at times multivalent in the sense of 'to lack' anthropologically. The addressees here should be understood as having a place among the angels in a manner that is not yet fully realised. This reading is substantiated when understood in light of 4Q418 55 and 69 where the fatigable and mortal deficiency of the addressees is stated with greater clarity.

If the addressee is economically poor it does not follow that he need reminding (cf. 4Q416 2 iii 2, 8, 12), whereas if this motif wavers between connotations of worldly poverty and anthropological lacking, sense can be made of the author's insistence. This sense of poverty may share similarities with Matthew 5.3 ('blessed are the poor in spirit'; cf. Mk 6.20) and 1QM xiv 7 (עניי רוח).[143]

4Q418 55 depicts humanity as slothful in contrast to the angels who are unlike human beings. Humanity is said to pursue the 'roots of understanding' (l. 9) and each will receive his recompense according to their attainment of knowledge (l. 10). 4Q418 55 presents the deficiencies of humanity in relation to angelic beings as well as various degrees of obtaining understanding within the community. 4Q419 69 similarly expresses humanity as wearying in their pursuit of knowledge. Line 11 asks of the addressees, 'how can you say, "we are tired of understanding, and/though we have been vigilant in pursuing knowledge?" For [the understanding One tires not] at all t[imes]'.[144] These two columns express an important anthropological understanding in the document: *one of humanity's greatest tasks is the pursuit of understanding while confronted with deficiencies such as weariness and insufficiency.*

One may observe the following from 4Q417 1 i and 4Q416 2 iii. The creation of humanity is in the likeness of both God and angels. The addressees are continuing recipients of revealed mysteries and are distinguished from a portion of humanity who does not receive revelation any longer. 4Q418 55 and 69 are seen to express the frailty of humanity and their inferior ability to understand knowledge and mysteries compared to angels who are superior models for the addressees to follow. Therefore, the addressees are called upon to honour and venerate both God and angels. It is little surprise, then, that in 4Q418 81 the holy ones are set alongside God as recipients of blessing (l. 1). In light of 4Q417 1 i lines 15-18 we might better understand 4Q418 81 lines 1b-2a which read: 'long ago, He (God) separated you from every spirit of flesh'.

Musar leMevin conceives of humanity as originating from dual creators. The failure of a portion of humanity to pursue and adhere to revealed knowledge of good and evil serves to separate humanity into two groups. Those who pursue knowledge and are of the division of the 'people of spirit' conceive of angels as playing a pivotal role in their existence. The angels in the document are worthy of blessing as subordinates to God. The addressees are related to angels in creation, they look to angels as an example and will share with the angels ('seated among the nobles') in the future (or ideally in the present time). Repeated exhortations to seek the רז נהיה are based upon human nature while, simultaneously, the example of the spirit of flesh are held up as a warning. There should be no doubt, therefore, that venerative

---

[143] J. DUPONT, 'Les πτωχοὶ τῷ πνεύματι de Matthieu 5,3 et les 'nwy rwh de Qumrân,' in J. Blinzler, O. Kuss, F. Mussner (eds.) Neutestamentliche Aufsätze: Festschrift für Prof. Josef Schmid (Regensburg: Pustet, 1963) pp. 53-64.

[144] As reconstructed by the editors, *DJD XXXIV*, p. 267.

attitudes are explicitly expressed in *Musar leMevin*. These attitudes are deeply rooted in the nature of humans. Reflection on anthropology is intertwined with cosmology and angelology, all of which are framed on interpretations of Genesis creation traditions.

CHAPTER 5

Women, Wives and Daughters

1. Introduction

Several allusions to Genesis 1-3 occur in *Musar leMevin* that refer to women. In addition to this cluster of allusions the document contains instruction both to a woman (4Q415 2 ii) and about wives and daughters on several occasions. In the case of the former, the occurrence of a 2nd person feminine singular address is rare in sapiential literature and unique among hagiographic works from early Judaism.[1] This cluster of allusions and address in the feminine singular suggest not only the importance of women in *Musar leMevin*, but also raise questions about views on women and the basis for instruction to them. The characterisation of women in *Musar leMevin* and the extent to which this is based upon Genesis creation traditions will be the subject of this chapter.

More explicit allusions to Genesis 1-3 establish the significance of this tradition for the document. Also, *Musar leMevin* contains a number of references to women that are either not attested outside of the document or only occur singularly elsewhere. The language and context of these allusions are at times related to other motifs and interpretations of Genesis 1-3 that merit broader investigation both within and outside the document. Conceptions of women, her origin (or birth-time), relation to her husband and family based upon allusions to Genesis creation traditions are a few such motifs. Discussions of females outside of halakhic concerns and the role of women in relation to the 'Essene monastic' community are rare in Dead Sea Scroll scholarship and presently no comprehensive treatment has yet been produced on the female in *Musar leMevin*.[2]

---

[1] This address raises important questions about literacy and females. For instance one could ask: does this address suggest that the document was read aloud or, conversely, that women regularly read *Musar leMevin*? The following discussion may make this question clearer.

[2] Issues raised in regard to females in documents from Qumran are primarily *halakhic* or their relationship to the 'Essene monastic' community; see for instance: WRIGHT, 'Wisdom and Women at Qumran,' in *DSD* 11 (2004): 263-288; S. W. CRAWFORD, 'Not According to Rule: Women, the Dead Sea Scrolls and Qumran,' in S. M. PAUL, R. A. KRAFT, L. H. SCHIFFMAN and W. W. FIELDS (eds.), *Bible, Septuagint and the Dead Sea Scrolls in Honor of*

Allusions to creation in *Musar leMevin* are used to frame cosmology and anthropology. The order of the cosmos and creation of humanity are the basis upon which ethical instruction may be construed. However, it is not only moral behaviour that is framed on the basis of creation, but the addressees' relationship to others within the created order. Thus, human relations to angelic beings are based upon the role of angels at creation. It would not be surprising, therefore, if the relationship between men and women, already seen to be explicated in contexts that use Genesis 2-3, contemplate creation more than previously observed. Genesis details the creation of the first woman and explains her role and relationship to her parents and husband. The creation of humanity in *Musar leMevin* reflects on Genesis 1.26 and the plural address 'let *us* make man' to explain anthropology and angelology. Similarly, passages in Genesis that relate to women may interpret the creation of the first woman to provide instruction to husbands and fathers about the proper role and behaviour of women.

Creation orders the cosmos, which includes each created being, and the addressee relates to each character on the basis of understanding this structure. One might speculate that exhortations to understand the רז נהיה are related to understanding creation and categories so that one might live according to them.[3] One aspect of the mystery of creation may be the participation of angels in human formation knowable by grasping

---

Emmanuel Tov (VTSup 94; Leiden: Brill, 2003) pp. 127-50; J. R. DAVILA, 'A Wedding Ceremony? (4Q502,' in *Liturgical Works* (Grand Rapids: Eerdmans, 2000) pp. 181-201; L. H. SCHIFFMAN, 'Laws Pertaining to Women in the Temple Scroll,' in *The Dead Sea Scrolls After Forty Years* (Leiden: Brill, 1998) pp. 210-28; E. M. SCHULLER, 'Women in the Dead Sea Scrolls,' in M. O. WISE, N. GOLB, J. J. COLLINS and D. G. PARDEE (eds.), *Methods of Investigation of the Dead Sea Scrolls and the Khirbet Qumran Site: Present Realities and Future Prospects* (New York: New York Academy of Sciences, 1994) pp. 115-31; L. H. SCHIFFMAN, 'Women in the Scrolls,' in *Reclaiming the Dead Sea Scrolls* (Philadelphia: The Jewish Publication Society, 1994) pp. 127-44; H. K. HARRINGTON, *The Purity Systems of Qumran and the Rabbis* (SBLDS 143; Atlanta: Scholars Press, 1993); J. M. BAUMGARTEN, '4Q502, Marriage or Golden Age Ritual?' in *JJS* 34 (1983): 125-35; M. BLACK, *The Scrolls and Christian Origins: Studies in the Jewish Background of the New Testament* (BJS 48; Chico: Scholars Press, 1961); J. M. BAUMGARTEN, 'On the Testimony of Women in 1QSa' in *JBL* 76 (1957): 266-69.

[3] WRIGHT, 'Wisdom and Women,' p. 258 is primarily interested with the role of women in *Musar leMevin* and what it may tell us, if anything, about women and the 'Sectarian Community'. He concludes that '4QInstruction, as a part of the practical nature of its advice to the maven, has a lot to say about women. The specifics of what it says about mothers, wives and daughters, however, are less crucial than the fact that this wisdom text is preserved in eight copies at Qumran.' Further on, p. 259, he writes: '4QInstruction's place in the community's literary holdings, however, most likely did not depend on its practical advice about money, women and other mundane matters, but on the importance and centrality of the רז נהיה, "the mystery that is to come".' WRIGHT gives the רז נהיה a strictly eschatological focus and does not seek to understand this mystery in relationship to instruction in the document as a whole.

interpretations of creation in the Genesis narrative. After all, this formation has implications that affect all humanity and inform the addressees about themselves and others. Another aspect of the mystery may be observations on the creation and origin of the female as derived from Genesis 1-3. The separation of woman from man as accounted in Genesis may be part of *Musar leMevin's* interest on divisions and distinguishing between good and evil.

2. Allusions to Genesis 1-3 and the Creation of Women

In this section 4Q416 2 ii-iv; 4Q417 1 i lines 8-12; and 4Q415 2 ii will be the focus of attention. The primary concern will be to identify the use of allusions to the first woman in Genesis and possible language to her 'birth-times' or 'origins'. Consideration will be given to the occurrence of the exhortation to 'cover your shame' in the context of a running allusion to Genesis 2-3. Two fragments from 4Q415 (4Q415 9; 11), which are concerned with instruction to women but may not contain allusions to Genesis, will be considered at the end of the chapter. Language and motifs related to women in *Musar leMevin* will emerge from this initial analysis and be addressed in sections to follow. Subsections below are concerned with the phrase 'all the sons of Eve' and the dominion of the male over the female.

2.1 4Q416 2 ii-iv

The most explicit allusions to Genesis 1-3 occur in the final lines of 4Q416 2 iii and continue on into 4Q416 2 iv. These allusions occur only a few lines after the previously discussed reference to אדנים (4Q416 2 iii 15-18) which has been argued to be an allusion to the fashioning of humanity in the likeness of God and angelic beings. These lines of 4Q416 2 iii-iv read as follows:

20) בלוא חוק *vacat* אשה לקחתה ברישכה קח מולדי[ן]ה[^4]

21) מרז נהיה בהתחברכה יחד התהלך עם עזר בשרכה]

1) את אביו [ו]את אמו וד∘ב[ן] ק באשתו והיו לבשר אחד]

2) אותכה המשיל בה ותש[ן]5[°] אביה[

3) לא המשיל בה מאמה הפרידה ואליכה [תשוקתה ותהיה]

4) לך לבשר אחד בתכה לאחר יפריד ובניכה] [

5) ואתה ליחד עם אשת חיקכה כי היא שאר ער[ותכה] [

6) ואשר ימשול בה זולתכה הסיג גבול חייהו ב[רוחה] [

---

[^4]: Reconstruction mine.

[^5]: *DJD XXXIV*, p. 127 considers the reconstruction of תשוקתה in both lines 2 and 3. The editors are against reconstructing the word in line 2 because it would be 'unduly repetitive'. A number of clauses with a 2nd masculine or 3rd feminine verb that begin with a ש would fit here.

7) המשילך להתהלך ברצונכה ולא להוסיף נדר ונדב]ה   [

8) השב רוחכה לרצונכה וכל שבועת אסרה לנדר נד]ר   [

9) הפר על מוצא פיכה וברצונכה הניא]ה מב]ל]י עשות מוצא[

10) שפתיכה סלח לה]ן]למענכה אל תרב]ה חרפתכה[6   [

11) כבודכה בנחלתכה]∘∘∘   [

12) בנחלתכה פן] vacat   [

13) אשת חיקכה וחרפ]ן]תכה[7   [

20) without statute. *vacat* A wife you took in your poverty, comprehend [her] origins[

21) from the רז נהיה, in your being joined together walk with the helper of your flesh,[

1) his father and mother and clin[g to his wife and they will be one flesh]

2) He has set you in authority over her and [her father]

3) He has not set in authority over her, from her mother He has separated her and [she will yearn[8]] for you [and she will be]

4) to you one flesh, your daughter for another he will separate and your sons[

5) and you together with the wife of your bosom, because she is the body[9] of [your] naked[ness   ]

6) and whoever rules over her apart from you has misplaced the boundary line of his life, over [her spirit]

7) He has given you dominion for her to walk in your good pleasure and not to add to vows and offer[ings

8) return your spirit to your good will and every oath binding her to vow a vow

9) is annulled by what comes forth from your mouth and in your good will prevent[her from n]o[t making an utterance of]

10) your lips, He forgives her[ ]for your sake, and do not multipl[y your shame

11) your honour and your inheritance [

12) in your inheritance lest *vacat* [

13) wife of your bosom and [your] shame

In addition to the allusions in these lines two other possible allusions to Genesis occur in fragment 4Q416 2. First, the final line 21 of 4Q416 2 ii reads פן תבוז חייכה וגם אל תקל כלי חיקכה ('lest you despise your life and also dishonour the vessel of your bosom'). Second, Harrington and Strugnell suggest a possible supplement of 4Q416 2 ii line 3 with the phrase תמשול בה ('you will have dominion over her').[10] Taken together these three columns (4Q416 2 ii-iv) hold substantial and significant allusions to woman in Genesis 2-3.

---

[6] Reconstruction mine. Cf. 4Q416 2 ii 16 פן תכשל חרפתכה תרבה.

[7] Reconstruction mine.

[8] Although there is not total agreement on how one should read תשוקה in Gen 3.16, here the interpretation as sexual 'longing' or 'yearning' is clear from following lines 4 and 5 (cf. 1QS xi 22; 6Q18 ii 4). See also the LXX on Gen 3.16 (ἀποστροφή).

[9] שאר can mean 'sustenance', 'body', 'flesh' or 'intimacy'. Cf. Yeb 90[b] where the word is used for a wife (שארו זו אשתו).

[10] *DJD XXXIV*, p. 95.

Line 20. It is relatively straightforward to identify the referent of some of the allusions in 4Q416 2 iii-iv. The instruction concerning relations between the male addressee and his wife begins in line 20 following a discussion about parentage. Just as the addressee was exhorted to honour his father and mother in his poverty (likened to אל and אדנים) in line 15 of this column, so here too marital relations begin with a reminder that he is impoverished. The editors suggest reading the final words of line 21 קח מולדי as 'take [her] offspring' which I have reconstructed and translated as 'understand [her] origins'. They note that the term מולדים is not found in Biblical Hebrew but that it is frequent elsewhere in the document (4Q415 2 ii 9; 4Q415 11 11; 4Q416 2 iii 9; 4Q417 2 i 11; 4Q418 9 8; 4Q418 202 1).[11] As discussed in chapter 3 the term also occurs in 4Q*Mysteries* in construct with בית (4Q299 1 4; 4Q299 3a ii-b 13; 4Q299 5 5).[12] מולד also occurs in 4Q*Horoscope* (4Q186 2 i 4) where the physical character of a person is said to reflect the spiritual character of a person, both of which are 'from conception' (ממולדו). The translation 'origins' or 'birth-times' in *Musar leMevin*, it will be argued in this chapter, is the best rendering based upon the occurrence of the phrase throughout the document (esp. 4Q416 2 iii 9; 4Q417 2 i 11) especially in contexts related to creation allusions such as the preceding context where the topic of origins is addressed (l. 17; 'they [parent's] are the oven of your origin').

Line 21. In line 21 the phrase 'walk together with the helper of your flesh' (cf. 4Q418a 16b + 17 line 3) occurs, which is an allusion to Genesis 2.20-25. In Genesis 2.20, the female's creation is preceded with the phrase 'and for Adam a helper (עזר) was not found as his partner' (see also 2.18: ויאמר יהוה אלהים לא-טוב היות האדם לבדו אעשה לו עזר כנגדו). Following (2.23) this statement, the female is described by Adam as 'flesh of my flesh' (בשר מבשרי).[13] Significantly, nowhere else in the Hebrew Bible is the term עזר used to refer to a woman as is clearly the case here.[14]

---

[11] The term is quite frequent in the document and should not be understood as 'offspring'; see: 4Q415 11 11 ואם נפרדה בהריתכה קח מו[ן]לדיה 'understand [her] origins'; 4Q416 2 iii 9 דרוש מולדיו 'seek its origins'; 4Q417 2 i 11 הבט ברז נהיה וקח מולדי ישע 'gaze on the mystery of existence and take the birth-times of salvation'; 4Q418 202 1 קח מולדי['comprehend the origins of…'. The same imperatives 'take' and 'seek' are used of מולדים and it is found in parallel with the רז נהיה on one occasion.

[12] See MORGENSTERN, 'The Meaning of בית מולדים,' and *DJD XX* on 4Q299.

[13] While the exact wording of Gen 2.23 does not occur elsewhere similar language is used to describe a relation in 2 Sam 19.13 (עצמי ובשרי).

[14] Almost without fail the term 'helper' is used in reference to God in the Hebrew Bible while in the DSS the term is not used frequently or elsewhere of woman. The Greek traditions of Sirach and Tobit do refer to the woman as helper with the same word as is used in LXX Gen 2.18-20 (βοηθόν). Sirach 36.24 reads 'he who acquires a wife gets his best possession a helper (βοηθόν) fit for him and a pillar of support'. Tobit 8.6-7 (BA) reads 'You made Adam and for him You made Eve his wife as a helper (βοηθόν) and support. From the two of them the human race has sprung. You said, "it is not good that the man should be alone *let us* make

Chapter 5

Line 1. 4Q416 2 iv line 1 uses Genesis 2.24 with verbatim vocabulary. In line 1, the 3rd person masculine pronominal suffix ‏ו‎- (‏אביו‎) of Genesis 2.24 (‏את אביו ואת אמו ודבק באשתו‎) is not altered although both the preceding and following lines are addressed in the 2nd person masculine singular ‏כה‎- (cf. Gen 2.23-24 and l. 21 ‏בשרכה‎ and l. 2 ‏אותכה‎).[15] The use of the 3rd masculine singular suffix in line 1, as opposed to the 2nd person masculine address, indicates that this is a direct quotation rather than allusion.

Lines 2ff. 4Q416 2 iv line 2 expresses the dominion of the male over the female (‏המשיל בה‎) which is understood as congruent with one of the consequences the woman receives in Genesis 3.16 (‏ימשל בך‎) for her disobedience in partaking from the tree of knowledge. 4Q416 2 iv lines 3-4 are to be identified with Genesis 2-3 even though lexical parallels are not as strong. If the phrase ‏תשוקתה‎ ('her desire') is a reliable reconstruction in the latter part of line 3, then the allusion would be to Genesis 3.16 ('her desire will be for her husband').[16] 4Q416 2 iv line 4 contains the phrase ‏לך בשר אחד‎. The phrase 'one flesh' occurs in the Hebrew Bible only in Genesis 2.24 (‏לבשר אחד‎) and in the Dead Sea Scrolls there is no occurrence outside of *Musar leMevin*. Given the surrounding context there can be little doubt that the phrase 'one flesh' in line 4 is an allusion to Genesis 2.24.

Lines 8ff. 4Q416 2 iv lines 8-10 have been broadly noted as alluding to Numbers 30.6-9 and the husband's right to annul the vows of his wife.[17] While this allusion should not be questioned due to the strong lexical and conceptual links, little has been said in regard to its association to surrounding Genesis allusions. In this same fragment, 4Q416 2 ii line 16, the phrase 'lest…you greatly increase [‏תרבה‎] your shame' occurs. The verb √‏רבה‎ occurs eight times in *Musar leMevin* manuscripts and the 2nd person masculine singular imperfect form ‏תרבה‎ only twice, always with an extant object (cf. par. 4Q417 2 ii+23 21). A plausible reconstruction at the end of line 10 might be 'do not multipl[y your shame]'. One may question whether the allusion to Numbers 30 in these lines, in the context of a running allusion to Genesis,

---

a helper for him like himself"'. This tradition of a plural address 'let us make' occurs in LXX Gen 2.18 while in MT 2.18 the verb is singular ‏אעשה‎ ('I will make').

[15] 4Q416 2 ii lines 3-4 contain some difficult pronominal suffixes to interpret, perhaps these lines contain a quotation and can be resolved on this basis.

[16] The term ‏תשוקה‎ occurs only three times in the Hebrew Bible (Gen 3.16, 4.7; Cant 7.11). An allusion to Gen 3.16 in 4Q416 2 iv is more likely here, but the curse in 4.7 and 3.16 are likely at play in *Musar leMevin*. Compare (3.16b) 'and for your husband will your desire be and he will rule over you' and (4.7b) 'sin is lurking at the door its desire is for you, but you must rule over it (‏ואליך תשוקתו ואתה תמשל בו‎)'. Gen 4.12 is used in 4Q423 1, 2 i 3 with Gen 3.17-18. Might one construe a connection between 'ruling over sin' (Gen 4.7) with the motif of 'ruling over' one's wife? If this is correct, it would add to DOCHHORN, 'Sie Wird Dir Nicht,' p. 363 observations on 4Q423 1, 2 i and the *Apocalypse of Moses* (24.1-2) and a link between the curses in Gen 3 and 4.

[17] *DJD XXXIV*, p. 129; see also BROOKE, 'Biblical Interpretation,' pp. 201-22.

might add insight into the occurrence of 'shame' in this column and elsewhere in the document. Shame may somehow be related to the wife as derived from Numbers 30 and Genesis 1-3.

In 4Q416 2 iv lines 5 and 13 the phrase אשת חיקכה ('wife of your bosom'; cf. parallel frags. 4Q418 10a, b line 7) merits special attention. A likely related phrase, כלי חיקכה (4Q416 2 ii line 21), will also be explored in relation to Genesis 2-3 below. Another line that will be looked at in connection to these two phrases is 4Q415 2 ii line 3. This line, which occurs in a fragment addressed to a female as mentioned previously, has an occurrence of the phrase ובחיקו ('in his bosom'). How is this phrase to be understood and could it too be related to conceptions from Genesis 2-3? 4Q417 1 i lines 8-9 will also serve to elucidate the phrase.

The phrase אשת חיקך is not unknown in the Hebrew Bible or Dead Sea Scrolls although it is rare. [18] In the Hebrew Bible it occurs only in Deuteronomy 13.7 and 28.54 (אשת חיקו) in a list of familial titles and exhortations for Israelites not to worship idols or false gods.[19] The *Temple Scroll* (11Q19 liv 20) is the only other document among the Dead Sea Scrolls other than *Musar leMevin* that uses the epithet 'wife of your bosom'. In the *Temple Scroll* the occurrence is undoubtedly reliant upon Deuteronomy 13.7.[20] If *Musar leMevin* does not derive the phrase from Deuteronomy or the *Temple Scroll* then other possible connotations of this epithet might be suggested. Sirach 9.1 uses the epithet as well stating 'do not be jealous of the wife of your bosom (γυναῖκα τοῦ κόλπου σου)' which is similar to the Septuagint's rendering of Deuteronomy 13.7 (ἡ γυνὴ ἡ ἐν κόλπῳ).[21]

While the phrase 'wife of your bosom' in the contexts of Deuteronomy and the *Temple Scroll* appear to be simply an idiomatic expression for a man's wife, two observations might be made. First, the epithet is infrequent and is not well attested in the Hebrew from the period, but is used on at least two occasions in *Musar leMevin* independently from Deuteronomy.[22] Second, the idiom taken quite literally is descriptive of the origin of the female in Genesis 2.20-25 (vs. 21; ויקח אחת מצלעתיו) and may have been selected by the author

---

[18] The editors of *DJD XXXIV*, p. 128, initially consider the possibility of reading אשת חוקכה ('your lawful wife') but decide against this reading in light of the phrase כלי חיקכה. The closest parallels to אשת חיקך in the Hebrew Bible occur only in: (1) Gen 16.5 (בית אדניך ואת נשי אדניך בחיקך ואתנה לך את); and (2) 2 Sam 12.8 (אנכי נתתי שפחתי בחיקך).

[19] The targums on Deut translate the phrase in a variety of ways: *Onqelos* 'the wife of your covenant'; *Ps.-Jn.* 'the wife who sleeps on your bosom' while *Neofiti* preserves the original 'wife of your bosom'.

[20] See Y. YADIN, *The Temple Scroll*, vol. 2 (Jerusalem: Israel Exploration Society, 1983) p. 246. The dependence of *Temple Scroll* liv 20 on Deut 13 is readily apparent.

[21] This portion of Sirach is not extant in Hebrew.

[22] To the best of my knowledge the phrase 'wife of your bosom' occurs nowhere else in the literature of the period, including both targums, *Hekhalot* literature and Rabbinic literature, outside of these references.

on this account (i.e. it was already in use as a reference for a 'wife' and could be adapted for the author's concern for the creation of woman). It has been argued in chapter 4 that *Musar leMevin* instructs the addressee on the basis of his origin. The creation of the female in the use of this epithet could be used to raise issues of her derivation to provide ethical instruction both *to* her and *in regard to* her.

The creation of the female, according to Genesis 2.20-25, contrary to the present natural order in which women alone bear life, portrays man bearing the first human being: woman. Here Adam gives birth to the first woman by way of a creative act of God in the garden. Genesis 2.23 uses the narrative to explain the Hebrew term used of the female: 'she will be called woman (אשה) for from man (איש) was she taken'.[23] *Targum Pseudo-Jonathan* (cf. *Neofiti*) on Genesis 2.23 place these words on the lips of Adam: 'this time, but never again will woman be created from man as this one has been created from me'.[24] Likewise, the author of 1 Timothy 2.13 implicitly takes up the idea that Eve came from Adam: 'for Adam was formed first and then Eve'. The first woman, fashioned from one of Adam's ribs, is literally a creation from the breast (צלעה)[25] of man. Paul, in 1 Corinthians 11.7-12, also speaks of the creation of woman stating explicitly that 'indeed man was not made from woman but woman from man'. The narrative of Genesis 2.20-25 is intricately woven and both separates a helper for man and then reunites man with his helper (והיו לבשר אחד).[26]

4Q416 2 iv line 5, in addition to allusions in the preceding lines, is also dependent on Genesis 2.20-25 traditions: 'you will be a unity with the wife of your bosom because she is the body of your nakedness'. The final word of line 5 has been reconstructed based on the context. The fragment itself reads 'שאר ער[ן' with approximately four letter spaces available for reconstruction. The choice to reconstruct שאר ער[וה here is based upon the occurrence of the phrase בשר ערוה in Exodus 28.42.[27] However, with the general appeal to Genesis 2.20-25, another possibility is the reconstruction שאר ער[ומכה. Not

---

[23] Reading the ה- of אשה as a directive *heh* is a further grammatical indication of the origin of woman.

[24] See also Philo (*QG* 1 27); and Plato's *Symposium* (189-191) where some interesting points of comparison occur.

[25] The LXX translates πλευρά; cf. 4 Mac 18.7 and the mother's testimony after the martyrdom of her seven sons (vss. 6-10): 'The mother of seven sons expressed also these principles to her children: "I was a pure virgin and did not go outside my father's house: but I guarded the rib (πλευρά) from which woman was made." No seducer corrupted me on a desert plain, nor did the destroyer, the deceitful serpent, defile the purity of my virginity. In the time of my maturity I remained with my husband…while he was with you he taught you the law and prophets. He read to you about Abel slain by Cain…'

[26] 1 Cor 11.12 states the reversal of order as 'for just as the woman is from the man, so also the man is through the woman'.

[27] *DJD XXXIV*, p. 128; see also TIGCHELAAR, *To Increase Learning*, p. 48.

only would this fit with the description of Adam and his wife as naked
(עֲרוּמִּים) in Genesis 2.25, but also with the play on the depiction of the serpent
in the following verse (3.1; עָרוּם). This word is also attested elsewhere in the
document (4Q417 1 i 9) unlike the term עֶרְוָה.[28] While the two terms carry
distinct meanings, they share a general definition of 'naked'.[29] This singular
occurrence of the phrase that one's wife is 'flesh of your [husband's]
nakedness' preceded almost immediately by the description of the unity of
man and woman in the same line has its closest affinity with Genesis 2.24-25
('for this reason a man will leave his father and mother and cling to his wife,
and *they will be one flesh*, and the two of them were *naked*, Adam and his
wife, and were not ashamed').

The final line 13 of 4Q416 2 iv may be valuable for deciphering line 5.
Here the phrase אשת חיקכה is immediately followed by the term חרפה
('shame' or 'reproach'). If the term חרפה in line 13 should be understood as
synonymously parallel to a corresponding term in line 5, then might ערוה/הערום
be related to it? In line 13 a context is not preserved that aids in understanding
the term 'shame'. However, in a sub-section below the phrase 'cover your
shame' (כסה חרפתכה; cf. 4Q418 177; 178) in *Musar leMevin* will be explored
as it relates to women and Genesis 2-3. The significance of 4Q416 2 iv line 13
for the moment is the proximity of the term 'shame' and the epithet 'wife of
your bosom'. Although the phrase 'cover your shame' in other fragments of
Musar leMevin might be displayed as relating to women, line 13 provides the
most significant link between 'shame' and the female.

If the phrase 'wife of your bosom' in 4Q416 2 iv is rightly to be associated
with Genesis 2.20-25 what significance, if any, does this have for an
interpretation of the epithet כלי חיקכה in 4Q416 2 ii line 21? Both Strugnell
and Elgvin consider this phrase as a background for 1 Thessalonians 4.4 and
the phrase σκεῦος κτᾶσθαι.[30] More recently, Menahem Kister has argued that
the phrase כלי חיקכה should not be read at all, but rather בלי חוקכה.[31] If the
phrase כלי חיקכה is to be read, how helpful is 1 Thessalonians for
understanding the phrase in *Musar leMevin*? 1 Thessalonians contains only
the term 'vessel' and *Musar leMevin* the epithet 'vessel of your bosom' – the
supplement of חיקכה is significant. Certainly 4Q416 2 ii states 'do not
dishonour' in contrast to the positive exhortation to 'honour' in 1

---

[28] The term occurs in 4Q417 1i line 9 'He has prepared with all wisdom and with all
cunning [ערמה] has He fashioned it'; and 4Q423 22 line 2]וְהוֹן[עָרְמָה['craftiness/nudity (?)
and riches'. 4Q417 1 i line 9 could be a play on Gen 2-3.

[29] עָרוּם can mean either 'naked' or 'crafty/cunning' while עֶרְוָה can mean 'nudity', 'shame'
or 'pudenda'. A reconstruction of עֶרְוָה here would relate one's wife with 'shame' elsewhere
in the column.

[30] ELGVIN, 'To Master his Own Vessel'. See also J. E. SMITH, 'Another Look at 4Q416 2
ii.21'.

[31] M. KISTER, 'A Qumranic Parallel'.

Thessalonians; however, the extent to which the interpretation the one has on the other should not be exaggerated.[32]

2.1.1 Menahem Kister on 4Q416 2 ii line 21

Kister has suggested that 4Q416 2 ii line 21 should be read בלי חוקכה (or בלו חוקכה), meaning 'without your prescribed portion'.[33] Kister prefers this to the reading proposed by the editors of DJD 34, כלי חיקכה, 'the "vessel" (or "wife") of thy bosom'.[34] In regard to the phrase 'vessel of your bosom' Kister writes that it 'appears (almost certainly) not to be the correct reading of the text'.[35] This conclusion is based upon a twofold argument: (1) the first letter of the phrase 'looks more like *bet* than *kaf* especially in 4Q417 2 ii 25; and (2) 'this reading makes better sense in the context'.[36] In both regards Kister's conclusion may be challenged.

Based upon palaeography one cannot determine whether בלי חוקכה or כלי חיקכה should be read. First, the term בלי/כלי in 4Q416 2 ii line 21 itself is far too damaged to conclude whether *bet* or *kaf* is the better reading. However, 4Q417 2 ii line 25, a parallel manuscript, preserves the top one third of the three letters of the word. On the basis of the top third of these letters Kister states that 'the traces of the *bet* are clear in 4Q417'.[37] The 'traces' of which he writes can only be assumed to be either the left downward stroke (pronounced tick) that begins the letter or the right tick.

The editors note in their discussion on the palaeography of 4Q417: 'In the *bet*, the tick of the right upper shoulder is maintained... in the medial *kaf*, one can observe how the descender is in fact a separate stroke, though sometimes the tick at the upper right shoulder is flattened'.[38] The upper right tick of *bets* and *kafs* do not distinguish them from each other; nor does the beginning left

---

[32] The exhortation to 'not dishonour' in *Musar leMevin* is likely related to negative qualities attributed to the woman in the following column 4Q416 2 iv ('wife of your bosom and shame['). MURPHY, *Wealth*, p. 189; observing this exhortation states: 'in the context of living within one's means, dishonoring one's wife might mean depleting her dowry, which functioned as her chief asset if divorced or widowed. This suggestion is borne out by the subsequent advice against taking from goods which one holds in deposit. Legally, the dowry functioned as a deposit, from which the husband enjoyed the right of usufruct but only while married to his wife.' MURPHY, in reading this column as traditional sapiential material, does not consider this unusual epithet or question why the author would employ it.

[33] KISTER, 'A Qumranic Parallel,' pp. 365-71. See also my 'Reconstructing,' pp. 205-11. Cf. 4Q416 2 iii 20 בלוא חיק/חוק.

[34] *DJD XXXIV*, p. 93.

[35] KISTER, 'A Qumranic Parallel,' p. 366.

[36] KISTER, 'A Qumranic Parallel,' p. 366.

[37] KISTER, 'A Qumranic Parallel,' p. 366, fn. 9 expresses his gratitude to E. QIMRON for confirming his reading and checking it with the original in the Israel Museum. The photographs are clear, however, not enough of the fragments themselves appear to survive in order to decipher between *bet* and *kaf*.

[38] *DJD XXXIV*, p. 144-45.

stroke. The left tick of *bets* and *kafs* in 4Q417 are often identical. One characteristic that may help distinguish *bets* and *kafs* in this manuscript is the length of the top horizontal left to right stroke. Typically, this stroke of a *bet* is longer while that of a *kaf* is slightly shorter. Based upon the photograph provided in DJD 34 it would appear that the top stroke here is shorter than other *bets* preserved in the same column and, therefore, actually a *kaf*. However, this by no means proves which letter it originally was. In this early Herodian hand a *kaf* may only really be distinguished from a *bet* according to the depth of the letter. The bottom two-thirds of the word בל/כלי is not extant in 4Q417 2 ii 25. *Contra* Kister, it is impossible to conclude on the basis of palaeography that בלי rather than כלי should be read in 4Q416 2 ii line 21.

Furthermore, Kister's proposal that חוקכה ('prescribed portion') be read rather than חיקכה ('your bosom') should be questioned as well. First, *yods* and *waws* are indistinguishable in this hand. Second, the editors comment that 'it is unlikely that the same scribe would read כלי חוקכה in col. ii and אשת חיקכה in col. iv'.[39] There is no clear occurrence of חוק in *Musar leMevin*, however, the term חיק is used on three occasions. First, in the twice occurring phrase אשת חיקכה in 4Q416 2 iv lines 5 and 13. Second, it occurs in 4Q415 2 ii line 3.

This observation returns us to Kister's second criterion, that is: his reading makes better sense. Kister interprets the phrase as part of instruction regarding poverty and living within one's means.[40] While poverty, particularly the term מחסור, is abnormally frequent in *Musar leMevin*, so too are references to women both in this fragment and elsewhere in the document. Both poverty and women are equally important themes in the document, particularly in 4Q416 2 ii-iv. Below, I will argue that the phrase כלי חיקכה fits best within a cluster of references to the female and allusions to Genesis creation traditions. Following the editors, the phrase כלי חיקכה and אשת חיקכה should be read in light of one another.

---

[39] *DJD XXXIV*, p. 108.

[40] KISTER, 'A Qumranic Parallel,' pp. 366-67, translates פן תבוז לחייכה וגם אל תקל בלו חוקכה as: 'lest you be unmindful of your life. And do not be disgraced by (living) not according to your prescribed portions'. In the remainder of the article KISTER argues that the wisdom of this line parallels other worldly wisdom that encourages the addressee to live beneath one's means (e.g. 4Q416 2 iii 8-9: if you are poor, do not aspire to anything but your portion, and do not harmed by it, lest you decrease your boundary). In a personal correspondence, D. SCHWARTZ has commented that KISTER'S translation of line 21 is unnatural: (1) the verbs תבוז and תקל should be read as parallels so if the first is "do not scorn" the second should not be passive; and (2) correspondingly, just as תבוז is followed by ל, and refers to scorning something else, so too תקל is normally followed by ב and refers to scorning something else. KISTER'S reading requires the second verb be vocalized תִּקַּל and then ב taken to refer to the medium through which one is scorned.

2.1.2 Elgvin on 4Q416 2 ii line 21

Elgvin, in his discussion of the phrase כלי חיקכה, is opposed to reading the term כלי as either 'wife', 'vessel' or 'body' and argues that in 4Q416 2 ii it is a euphemism for the 'male member' (i.e. 'phallus').[41] Speaking of Essene modesty, Elgvin details the prohibition against uncovering one's member (יד) in 1QS vii lines 12-14 as well as Josephus' description of Essene decency while defecating (*Bellum* 8 148). Elgvin has no difficulty with viewing both the terms יד ('phallus') and כלי חיקכה as synonymous in the Qumran literature. To support his reading of the phrase as the 'male member', Elgvin refers to 1 Thessalonians 4.4 where he concludes that there also the term σκεῦος is used of the 'male member'. The argumentation used by Elgvin, that 1 Thessalonians 4.4, in light of 1 Samuel 21.6, supports the reading 'male member' in 4Q416 2 ii and *vice versa*, is unconvincing in my opinion.[42] Even though 1 Samuel 21.6 uses the term כלי as he suggests, as a euphemism for 'phallus', the term itself is well attested in Hebrew literature but only in 1 Samuel is it used in this sense. Also, 4Q416 2 ii line 21 uses the term כלי in construct with חיקכה, neither 1 Samuel or 1 Thessalonians uses the term as such.

2.1.3 Harrington and Strugnell on 4Q416 2 ii line 21

Harrington and Strugnell are also not persuaded by Elgvin's argumentation that the term should be rendered as the 'male member'.[43] As discussed briefly above, they translate 4Q416 2 ii line 21 as 'do not treat with dishonour the "vessel" (or "wife") of thy bosom', thus favouring a translation of כלי as 'woman' as opposed to 'body' or 'phallus'. One of the relevant objections for translating the Greek term σκεῦος (כלי) as 'woman' in 1 Thessalonians 4.4, in relation to 4Q416 2 ii, is the assertion that there is no evidence for the term's usage as such elsewhere. However, those who have advocated a reading of 1

---

[41] These three translation options are the only ones that either ELGVIN or the editors consider for the term כלי. According to ELGVIN there exists no occurrence of the term כלי with the meaning 'wife' in the Hebrew literature of the period whereas the term is used in the sense of 'male organ' in 1 Sam 21.6. Worth noting is that 1 Sam 21.6 is the only occasion where the term is so used among 522 occurrences in the Hebrew Bible and approximately 30 occurrences in the DSS. ELGVIN states 'the phrasing of the term כלי חיקה for the male organ was probably influenced by the expression אשת חיקך/חיקו "the wife of your/his bosom", Deut 13.7, 28.54 (28.56 has the parallel איש חיקה "the man of her bosom") and the use of כלי "vessel" in 1 Sam 21.6.' ELGVIN does not elaborate upon this theory and I find the relationship as explained here lacking. See ELGVIN, 'To Master His Own Vessel,' pp. 607-8.

[42] Nor has this interpretation been convincing to many others. J. WHITTON, 'A Neglected Meaning of *skeuos* in 1 Thessalonians 4.:4,' in *NTS* 28 (1982): 142-43 argues for the rendering of the term as a euphemism for the male member.

[43] *DJD XXXIV*, p. 109.

Thessalonians 4.4 as a reference to 'woman' cite a few Rabbinic texts as evidence.[44]

The first is found in *b. Meg.* 12b (par. *Esther R.* 1.11) and reads 'Ahasveros said to them "the vessel [כלי] which I use is neither Median nor Persian but Chaldean, do you want to see her?" they answered "only if we can see her naked"'. The second occurrence is in *b. Baba Mezia* 84b (parallels *Pesiqta* 94 b; y. *Shab.* 10.6; *Qoh. R.* 11.2) where the widow of Rabbi Eleazar b. Simeon replies to Judah the Prince's request for marriage with the statement 'should the vessel [כלי] which was used by a holy man be used by a secular man?'

While both texts understand the term כלי as carrying significant overtones of a wife as a sexual object there can be no doubt that the term is indeed used for 'wife' or 'woman'. Harrington and Strugnell comment upon this sense of the term stating, 'when כלי…occurs in literary texts like frg. 2 ii 21, whether it refer to a lawful wife or contemptuously (?) to a concubine, …the original metaphorical reference to sexual organs and sexual partnership, which developed independently in many languages fades, and the metonymous sense "woman" is no longer felt to need justification'.[45]

Although Elgvin views such uses of the term כלי as connoting the female pudenda and thus verification of an earlier use as a reference for the male organ, the editors note this tendency in the document to use metonyms. Also significant is the use of the term רחם ('womb') and בטן ('womb') as references simply to 'woman' in *Musar leMevin* (e.g. 4Q415 9 2) even though they can also be technical terms for the pudenda.[46] In general, the view of the editors is that 4Q416 2 ii line 21 is directing the fifth commandment of the Decalogue, to honour one's father and mother (cf. 4Q416 2 iii), to the addressee's wife (כלי חיקכה).[47]

As demonstrated above, 4Q416 2 iv contains several allusions to Genesis 2-3. The phrase אשת חיקכה occurs in a fragmentary context in conjunction with terms for shame or nudity (ערוה or ערום in l. 5 and חרפה l. 13). The

---

[44] In support of rendering the term σκεῦος as 'wife' in 1 Thess. 4.4 see O. L. YARBROUGH, *Not Like the Gentiles: Marriage Rules in the Letters of Paul* (SBLDS 80; Atlanta: Scholars, 1985) p. 7; R. F. COLLINS, ' "This is the Will of God: Your Sanctification" (1 Thess 4:3),' in *LTP* 39 (1983): 27-53; F. F. BRUCE, *1 & 2 Thessalonians* (WBC; Waco: Word Books, 1982): 83-84; C. MAURER, 's.v. σκεῦος,' in *TDNT* 8 (1971): 365-67.

[45] *DJD XXXIV*, p. 109. Predating the DJD volume, STRUGNELL published the article, 'More on Wives and Marriage in the Dead Sea Scrolls: (4Q416 2 ii 21 [cf. 1 Thess 4:4] and 4QMMT § B),' in *RevQ* 17 (1996): 538-40.

[46] The phrase להורות במנכה occurs in 4Q415 9 line 2 and the editors comment that the word בטן may mean 'wife' (cf. Job 3.10; 19.17) though they are uncertain about the precise form of הרה here. The term בטן occurs elsewhere in *Musar leMevin* as: 4Q423 3 ראשית פרי במנכה 'first-born of your womb' likely meaning 'your wife's first-born'; and 4Q423 3a בפרי במנו 'the fruit of his womb' meaning 'his wife's offspring'.

[47] STRUGNELL, 'More on Wives,' p. 539.

epithet כלי חיקכה is not attested in the Hebrew literature and suggestions for interpreting the phrase have been largely dependent upon the use of the term כלי or σκεῦος, not in a construct state, used elsewhere. Though the phrase will undoubtedly remain somewhat cryptic due to the fragmentary nature of the document and to the lack of external parallels, the discussion below will attempt to shed further light on the phrase in several ways. First, a few more comments might be made regarding the rendering of the term 'vessel' elsewhere in the New Testament – a case, for example, could be made for reading the term as 'body'. Second, the phrase may be synonymous, or closely related to, the epithet אשת חיקכה and an allusion to Genesis 2. 4Q417 1 i lines 8-12, it will be suggested, address issues pertaining to the female's origin or birth-time. Finally, 4Q415 2 ii contains an occurrence of the term בחיקו in a fragment that is addressed to a female and might be helpful for understanding epithets in 4Q416 2 ii-iv.

2.1.4 1 Peter 3.7

1 Peter 3.7 is a passage that neither Strugnell and Harrington nor Elgvin note in their discussion of the phrase כלי חיקכה. While 1 Thessalonians 4.4 is the closest parallel in the New Testament, 1 Peter 3.7 clearly uses the term σκεῦος in relation to one's wife but not necessarily as a term for 'wife', such a use in this context would clearly be redundant. Furthermore, like 1 Thessalonians the occurrence of the term in 1 Peter also associates the concept of honour with wives:

Οἱ ἄνδρες ὁμοίως, συνοικοῦντες κατὰ γνῶσιν ὡς ἀσθενεστέρῳ σκεύει τῷ γυναικείῳ, ἀ πονέμοντες τιμὴν ὡς καὶ συγκληρονόμοις χάριτος ζωῆς εἰς τὸ μὴ ἐγκόπτεσθαι τὰς π ροσευχς ὑμῶν.

Likewise husbands, live with your wives in an understanding way as with a weaker vessel, since she is a woman and grant her honour as a fellow heir of the grace of life, so that your prayers may not be hindered.

The majority of exegetes and commentators on 1 Peter 3.7 understand the term σκεῦος here in terms of 'body'.[48] References in the New Testament that elucidate a flexible and at times similar use of the term are: (1) 2 Timothy 2.20-25 where σκεῦος is used in the sense of 'a *member* in a great house'; (2) Romans 9.21-23 where it is used to describe *elements* of humanity; and (3) most significantly 2 Corinthians 4.7 where it is simply a metaphor for the fleshly *body*. The term כלי and equivalent Greek term σκεῦος occur elsewhere

---

[48] See for instance J. H. ELLIOT, *1 Peter* (New York: Doubleday, 2000); P. J. ACHTEMEIER, *1 Peter* (Minneapolis: Fortress Press, 1996); J. R. MICHAELS, *1 Peter* (Waco: Word Books, 1988); J. N. D. KELLY, *The Epistle of Peter and of Jude* (New York: Harper & Row, 1969).

and are indicative of a broader knowledge of 'vessel' as 'body' terminology (e.g. Philo *Migr. Abr.* 193; *De. somn.* 1 26; *T. Naph.* 8.6; *Barn.* 7.3; 11.9. 21.8; *Herm. Man.* 5.1.2). The term σκεῦος as 'body' in 1 Peter 3.7 implies the weakness of the female form physically.[49] This is a notion that is also mentioned by Philo (*Ebr.* 55). 1 Peter 3.7 uses the term 'vessel' in the sense of 'body', but here, as seen above, it refers to the wife. Of course there are also several who read the term σκεῦος in 1 Thessalonians 4.4 as 'body' as well.[50] On the one hand, if the term כלי in 4Q416 2 ii is best understood as 'body', the majority opinion that 1 Peter 3.7 uses the term 'vessel' for 'body' is strengthened. On the other hand, those who interpret σκεῦος in 1 Peter 3.7 as 'body' lend support for rendering כלי as 'body' in *Musar leMevin*.

2.2 4Q417 1 i lines 8-12

Reconstructing and translating 4Q417 1 i lines 8-12 are particularly challenging due to their state of preservation. The difficulty of making sense of line 9 in DJD 34, for instance, is apparent from the commentary offered by Harrington and Strugnell. They suggest the following rendering of lines 8-9:

8) עד ואז תדע בין [טו]ב ל[רע כ]מעשי[הם]כיא אל הדעות סוד אמת ברז נהיה

9) פרש את או/ישה[51] ומעשיה ∘∘∘[לכל חכ]מה ולכל[ע]רמה יצרה וממשלת מעשיה

8) of eternity. Then thou shalt discern between *the* [goo]d and [evil according to their] deeds. For the God of knowledge is the *foundation* of truth And *by/on* the mystery that is to come
9) He has *laid out* its (= truth's) *foundation*, *And its* deeds [He has *prepared with all* wis]dom And *with* all [c]unning *has He fashioned it*, And the *domain* of its *deeds* (creatures)

Lines 8-9 were discussed in chapter 3 (§3.2.6). I suggested there, similar to Lange[52], that much more sense can be made of these lines if the formation of the female is in view. In addition, lines 15-18 have already been demonstrated as referring to the creation and formation of humanity. I propose that lines 8-9 have in view the separation of the female from the male and her formation. Rather than reading אושה ('foundation') a rare plene form of 'woman' (אישה) should be read.[53] Furthermore, better sense can be made of the term פרש if it is

---

[49] Biologically speaking muscles account for approximately 23% of the female body weight while for males it is nearly 40%. Such natural observations were clearly reflected upon in theological discussions.

[50] LÜHRMANN, 'The Beginning of the Church at Thessalonica', in D. L. BALCH, E. FERGUSON, and W. A. MEEKS (eds.), *Greeks, Romans and Christians: Essays in Honor of Abraham J. Malherbe* (Minneapolis: Fortress Press, 1990) pp. 237-49; M. McGEHEE, 'A Rejoinder to Two Recent Studies Dealing with 1 Thess 4.4,' in *CBQ* 51 (1989): 82-89.

[51] Reconstruction mine.

[52] LANGE, *Weisheit*, p. 50.

[53] There are a number of defective spellings in 4Q415ff.

read as פרש ('separated') rather than פרש ('laid').[54] I propose the following translation of lines 8-9:

8) of eternity. And then you will know *the difference* between good and evil according to their deeds, for the God of knowledge is the foundation/mystery of truth, in/by the רז נהיה
9) He separated woman[55] and her deeds for [all wis]dom and all [cra]ftiness, He fashioned her, rule over her deeds

In lines 10-12 that follow, the column may be further demonstrated to be addressing issues of formation and creation than previously discussed in regard to lines 15-18 in chapter 4:

10) לכ[ו]ל∘∘∘למה[56] וכול[א[ת כ[ו]ל∘∘בא∘פרש למ[ו]ב]ינתם לכול מ[ן עשי]ה להתהלך

11) ב[י]צר [מבינתם ויפרש לא∘[ ] ∘∘ [ ]]ריה ובכושר מבינות נוד[עו נס[תרי

12) מחשבתו...

10) for all [*her secrets*] and everything [ ] [ ] He separated for their understanding, all her deeds/creation, to walk
11) in the likeness of their understanding, and He separated for m[an (?)   ] and in the fitting understanding which was made known in the secrets of
12) his design....

4Q417 1 i lines 8-12 may be read as a description not only of the separation of the female, but separations in creation generally. In line 9 the dominion of the addressee over (her) deeds could be expressed. This is a motif likely derived from Genesis 3.16 ('he will rule over you') and found also in 4Q416 2 iii line 2 ('He has set you in authority over her'). The רז נהיה (l. 8) could be understood as instrumental; it appears to be a mystery that reveals, in part, the order and nature of creation and thus divisions. A local understanding of ב- could be taken as knowing about woman's separation in the (i.e. from the)

---

[54] See *DJD XXXIV*, p. 154 'פרש. Both here and in line 10, this verb can be reconstructed in the light of its clear occurrence in line 11; in each case, however, the context does not help to establish the correctness of the supplement or to define the sense of the verb and phrase. In line 9 one has an uncertain את אושה as object, and ∘∘ בא∘ [פ]רש למ[ו]ב]ינתם לכול מן] in line 10. Other 3rd fem. sing. suffixes occur in the surrounding text (מעשיה and יצרה). Since אישה 'her husband' would be surprising and unexpected as an object, and since the preceding סוד can mean 'foundation', it becomes at least plausible to read here too אוש 'foundation' with its suffix referring to אמה (cf. also probably the suffixes in מעשיה and יצרה). But what meaning of פרש would be possible? Is it perhaps parallel to a verbal יָצְרָה? In order to say 'lay a foundation', one might perhaps use פרש 'spread, lay out a foundation...'

[55] Or 'He made woman distinct'.

[56] *DJD XXXIV*, p. 159 the editors suggest a variety of possible reconstructions of this poorly preserved word: לכל חכ[מה] ('all wisdom'); לכל ער[מה] ('all craftiness'); and לכל תעל[מה] ('every secret'). I have followed the editors hypothetical reading of לכל תעל[מה], the photographs appear to preserve the upper traces of a *lamed*.

mystery. The terms 'wisdom' and 'craftiness' in line 9 may be allusions to the gaining of knowledge (cf. 1. 8) in Genesis 2-3 and the description of the serpent as 'crafty' in Genesis 3.1. The phrase 'his design' in line 12 is followed by the beginning of a new colon.

4Q417 1 i is likely to be located in the first few columns of the document. As such, this description of the separation of the female and command to rule over her deeds most likely preceded the phrases אשת חיקכה and כלי חיקכה discussed above. 4Q416 2 iv is concerned with the annulment of a wife's vows, which is one example of ruling over her deeds. However, the idea that a husband is to rule over the deeds of his wife may take place in a garden metaphor.

2.3 4Q415 2 ii

4Q415 2 ii is another column that may elucidate the phrases אשת חיקכה and כלי חיקכה. Here in line 3 the phrase בחיקו occurs. 4Q415 2 ii is the only other place outside of 4Q416 2 ii and iv where the term חיק occurs in *Musar leMevin*.[57] This fragment was discussed in chapter 3 in relationship to language of origins and the reconstruction and translation of line 6 as 'woman'. These lines have been reproduced below:

1) כאב כבדי[
2) אל תמישי בלבבך וע[ן
3) כול היום ובחיקו בר[א][58]
4) פן תפרעי ברית קוד[ש
5) ואויבת לנפשך וב[ן
6) א[י]שה[59] עד לש[ן
7) בבית מכו[רותיך]ובבריתך ת[ן
8) תהלה [ ] י כ'ל אנשים[
9) [ ][ל]מבית מולדים[

1) like a father honour[
2) do not remove your heart[
3) the whole day and in his bosom[*He created*
4) lest you ignore a holy covenant[
5) and one hated by your soul and in[
6) a w[i]fe until[
7) in the house of yo[ur origins] and in your covenant[
8) a praise [   ] all men[
9) [   ]from the time of birth[

---

[57] The term does not occur frequently in Qumran literature.
[58] Reconstruction mine.
[59] Reconstruction mine.

Lines 1, 3 and 4 all use the 2nd person feminine singular address. As the editors note, there is nothing to suggest hypostatised wisdom in this fragment; but rather, this is a rare occurrence of a sapiential address to a female, perhaps a wife or daughter.[60] The fragment begins in line 1 with a command for the female to honour someone 'like a father'.[61] Previously discussed is the occurrence of an allusion to the fifth commandment of the Decalogue in 4Q416 2 iii lines 16-18 (cf. 4Q416 2 ii 21).[62] The editors suggest that the woman's father-in-law could be in view here, though they raise it only as a possibility. Perhaps a more likely figure whom the woman is exhorted to honour is her own husband.[63] This suggestion not only makes sense in light of the present discussion, but is also a tradition that Philo preserves in relation to the female in Genesis 2. In *Quaestiones et Solutiones in Genesin* (1 27) Philo queries why the woman is formed from a rib of Adam and not from the earth as were other creatures (Gen 2.21):

'why was not woman, like the other animals and man, also formed from earth, instead of the side of man? First, because woman is not equal in honour with man. Second, because she is not equal in age, but younger... Third, he wished that man should take care of woman as of a very necessary part of him; but woman, in return, should serve him as a whole. Fourth, he counsels man figuratively to take care of woman as of a daughter, *and woman to honour man as a father*. And this is proper; for woman changes her habitation from her family to her husband.'[64]

Philo preserves here an exegetical tradition in which the female's creation is linked explicitly to honouring her husband like a father. The fifth commandment of the Decalogue and the rule of men over women from Genesis 3.16 are seen to be joined in *Musar leMevin*. The emphasis of the dominion of the man over the woman from Genesis 3.16 is a motif already

---

[60] *DJD XXXIV*, p. 48.

[61] The phrase כאב is similar to the occurrence in *Jub* 1.25-26 ('like a father') and is one of the few instances of this simile in early Jewish literature (cf. 4Q416 2 iii lines 15-16).

[62] It is conceivable that the addressee of 4Q415 2 ii is called upon to honour God like a father in keeping with the concept expressed in 4Q416 2 iii line 16 'for as God is to a man so his own father', however this seems unlikely here since the phrase is 'like your father'. 4Q418 86 line 1, a five line fragment with less than ten intact words, has the phrase וכאב על ב[נ]ו[ת] 'as a father over daughters'. See also 4Q416 2 ii lines 15-16 'and then you will become for him/her (?) as a father'. Another unusual reference to a father may occur in 4Q418 168 3 'תש[וקת אבן' which the editors consider may be reconstructed as 'desire of a father for[' or 'yearning of the po[or man'; see *DJD XXXIV*, p. 391.

[63] E. M. SCHULLER, 'Women: Daily Life,' in *Encyclopedia of the Dead Sea Scrolls*, p. 983 comments briefly on 4Q415 2 ii that 'what is most distinctive is that in one place [in *Musar leMevin*] a woman is addressed directly, though the advice given to her appears to be rather conventional'. While instruction to women is often conventional, the basis for ethical instruction for women in the document appears to be noteworthy.

[64] Translation by R. MARCUS (LCL), p. 16; italics mine.

encountered elsewhere in the document (4Q416 2 iv line 7; 4Q417 1 i 8-9; cf. 4Q418 228; 4Q418a 18). If the suggestion that the female addressee is being called upon here to honour her husband like her father, then the following lines may be related to the already observed emphasis in the document on woman's creation as derived from her husband.

The latter surviving portion of 4Q415 2 ii line 3 states that 'in his bosom' which is followed immediately by 'ברׄ]'. The editors suggest a possible reconstruction of these letters as בר[ׄית in the sense of 'marriage covenant' (cf. Prov 2.17; Mal 2.14) and read the *waw* and *yod* of the preceding word as בחוקׄי ('in the statutes of') rather than as בחיקו. However, they comment that 'this reading then would give us a conceivable but banal phrase, but a reading בחיקו…would also be more congruous with the context…there would be no obvious supplement, however, for the בר/בד at the end of the line that would continue the thought of בחיקו…'.[65] Given the language of origins in lines 7 (מכו]רותיך)[66] and 9 (בית מולדים), as well as the previous suggestion that אשת חיקכה is a phrase that literally bespeaks the origin of woman in Genesis 2, an alternative reconstruction might be set forth. The term בחיקו might be supplemented with בר]א 'He created *you*' (perhaps בר]אך 'your creation' or בר]אשיתך 'your beginning').[67]

Two motifs would then emerge from 4Q415 2 ii. The first is the origin and creation of woman (ll. 1, 2, 7 and 9). The second is the woman's 'covenant' (ברית; ll. 4 and 7) which could be understood as 'marriage'. The covenant may be an allusion to Genesis 2.23 which provides the basis for ethical instruction about marriage. While the fragmentary context does not allow us to understand how these themes are interwoven, one might speculate that the creation of woman from man is the basis upon which familial codes and marital relations are founded. This would come as no surprise in light of 1 Corinthians 11.2-16 and Ephesians 5.21-33 where similar motifs are founded upon a Genesis 2 tradition.

In column 4Q416 2 iii line 20 is an occurrence of this same motif, ']without bosom *vacat* A wife you have taken in your poverty, understand her origins'. A context does not survive in which to understand how the phrase 'without bosom' could be understood. Reading חיק rather than חוק does not further the present inquiry; however, given the language of 'birth-times' and the term's occurrence elsewhere in this column, 'bosom' is a more likely

---

[65] *DJD XXXIV*, p. 48.

[66] The editors comment upon this reconstruction: 'in light of the following references to marriage (if ובבריתך should thus be interpreted also here) and birth (line 9), one may also suggest tentatively בית מכורותיך "the house of thy origins" … or "thy fixed place". מכורותיך is rare; but see Ez 21:35; 29:14; and especially 16:3, where מכרתיך is parallel to מלדתיך.

[67] 4Q418 119 is a five line fragment with only six extant words, line 3 reads מצולה נולדת ('depths she was born'). Is there any way this phrase might be construed as a reference to woman's origin?

rendering. Regardless, in the case of the phrase 'understand her origins', such a translation is easily justified in the use of the imperative קח used with the רז נהיה (e.g. 4Q418 77 4) and the term מולד used of origins in the previously discussed occurrences. Furthermore, in 4Q416 2 iii line 9, only some lines before, the term מולד is coupled with the רז נהיה and exhorts the addressee to seek its origins. It would seem then, that 4Q416 2 iii first conceives of the addressee's origins as coming from God and angels (4Q416 2 iii 15-18) and then proceeds to discuss the origins of the female in the lines that follow (4Q416 2 iii 20 – 4Q416 2 iv). 4Q416 2 iii line 20 introduces a succession of allusions, in which we find the twice occurring phrase 'wife of your bosom', with an exhortation to 'understand her origins'.

In conclusion, the occurrences of the word חיק in *Musar leMevin* always appear in relation to the female. 4Q415 2 ii uses the expression בחיקו in a fragment which is addressed to a woman and is concerned with her birth-times. Despite the fragmentary state of the column, it may be deduced that the feminine singular address of 4Q415 2 ii exhorts the female addressee to honour her husband on account of both of their place in the created ordered. In *Musar leMevin*, the female is derived from the male, separated from him, and on this basis wives are to honour husbands and they are to rule over their wives.[68]

2.4 Synthesis of References to the Origin/Separation of the Female

It may be concluded, therefore, that the term כלי in 4Q416 2 ii line 21 is best understood as 'body' and the term חיקכה as 'your bosom'. The phrase could be translated simply as 'wife of your bosom'. However, the epithet is not used simply as 'wife', but rather as a phrase used to signify one's wife as derived from man.[69] She is, literally, the vessel taken from the male addressee's side. The phrase אשת חיקכה, which occurs in a context with multiple allusions to Genesis 2-3 two columns later, may be seen as a synonymous epithet. The phrase would have been known from Deuteronomy and perhaps the *Temple Scroll*, but the author(s) of *Musar leMevin* likely used the existing epithet for one's wife with the same nuance as 'vessel of your bosom' as opposed to, for example, 'the wife who sleeps at your bosom'.

The metaphorical description of the female as 'wife/body of your bosom' is congruous with one sense of Ephesians 5.28 that 'husbands should love their wives as their own bodies'. This concept is founded upon Genesis 2.20-

---

[68] *Musar leMevin* instructs the addressee to honour his mother and father (4Q416 2 iii 15-16), similarly wives are to honour their husbands (4Q415 2 ii); therefore, an exhortation for a husband not to dishonour his wife (4Q416 2 ii 20) is very much in keeping with the teaching of the document.

[69] Perhaps in one possible sense of Eph 5.28 that 'husbands should love their wives as their own bodies'.

25 only a few verses later (see Eph 5.31 where an explicit citation of Gen 2.24 occurs). Since the woman in Genesis is literally 'flesh of my flesh and bone of my bones', Ephesians 5.29 is able to state that 'no man ever hated his own flesh (ἑαυτοῦ σάρκα)'. It is not necessarily only that the two become one flesh, but that they also are one flesh on account of the female's derivation. Here, the epithet 'wife/vessel of your bosom' is coined on the basis of the imagery of the creation of woman in Genesis 2.

In *Musar leMevin* the phrases 'vessel of your bosom' and 'wife of your bosom', as expressions of the birth of woman, are found in columns with multiple allusions to Genesis 1-3 traditions (4Q416 2 ii-iv). In addition, 4Q417 1 i lines 8-12, a column which addresses the creation of humanity, explicitly states that 'the God of knowledge...separated woman [*from man*]'. 4Q415 2 ii bases its instruction to the female on notions of honouring one's husband because of her birth-times. It has also been observed that similar motifs are taken up in the New Testament, Philo and later Targums. Taken together, these columns express a particular conception of females. Woman originated from man and women are exhorted to relate to men on the basis of that creation. Likewise, men are to relate to women, whether wives, women or daughters, in light of the order of creation. Women are to hounour their husbands 'like a father' not only because dominion passes from father to husband; but also the Genesis narrative presents the first man as the parent of woman.

2.5 Male Dominion Over the Female

In addition to 4Q417 1 i line 9, two, perhaps three, other fragments not yet discussed contain the motif of the dominion of the male over the female. The first is 4Q415 9 lines 7-8 where we read ממשל זכר את נ]קבה...רוחה המשל בה ('dominion of the male over the female...her spirit make you (m.) to rule over'). This fragment contains two other references to woman: line 2 states 'to instruct (להורות) your womb (wife, בטנכה)'; and line 11 the word 'נ]קבה[‎'. 4Q415 9 appears to allude to Genesis 3.16. This fragment will be considered at greater length near the end of this chapter (§5.2).

The second possible occurrence of this motif is in 4Q418 228, a four line fragment with only seven extant words. The editors suggest a possible translation of המשילה as 'He has [not (?)] set her in authority'.[70] This fragment is too small to discern with complete certainty what the precise meaning is; it may be suggested, however, that it is a statement of the female's subjugation to the male framed within a rhetorical statement.

---

[70] The term המשיל is abnormally frequent in *Musar leMevin* when compared to other Qumran documents and may be descriptive of other relations other than husband and wife, perhaps parents and children as well (cf. 4Q416 2 iii 17). 4Q423 1, 2 i line 2 describes the addressee as being placed in dominion over the Garden of Eden. See also 4Q418 206.

The third occurrence is in 4Q418a 18 line 4, another small fragment that survives in only three lines with less than 7 extant words. Line 4 reads המ[שילכה להתה]לך which is translated in DJD 34 as: 'over her has he set] *thee* in authority so that *she* should wal[k'. The concept of the male ruling over the female has its most likely origin in Genesis 3.16 and each of these fragments may allude to male dominion over the female (cf. 4Q417 1 i 9).

Already briefly discussed in relation to 4Q416 2 iii line 21 was the phrase עזר בשרכה. This phrase also occurs in 4Q418a 16b + 17 line 3, a fragment that survives in only five lines with less than eight intact words. These two occurrences may indicate that the phrase 'helper of your flesh' was another epithet used for 'wife' which was derived from Genesis 2.20-25. Without parallel in the Hebrew Bible or Dead Sea Scrolls, an allusion to Genesis, based upon lexical similarities (בשר; עזר) and in the context of 4Q416 2 iii-iv, is probable.[71] One might also question whether there are any similarities between the phrases 'wife of your bosom' and 'helper of your flesh' if both are to be taken as references to women or epithets for wives.

2.6 4Q423 1, 2 i and 1Q26 1

The fragmentary text of 4Q423 1, 2 i was discussed in chapter three. This well known fragment re-writes portions of the story of Eden and alludes to Genesis 4 as well. Lines 1-2 speak not of one tree of the knowledge of good and evil but of 'every fruit' of 'every tree' which is 'desirable to make wise' (נחמד להשכיל; Gen 2.9; 3.6). The whole garden provides wisdom and the addressee dwells within this garden. Line 2 recounts how the addressee (2nd person masculine singular address כה-) is set in authority over the garden to work and keep it. Line 3 alludes to Genesis 3.18 and the result of eating from the tree of the knowledge of good and evil and the curse on man (קוץ ודרדר תצמיח לכה).[72]

Only the word במועלכה ('in your transgression/unfaithfulness') is preserved in line 4 and this is followed by a *vacat*. It may be descriptive of a curse, but this does not imply a fall of Adam or humanity. Line 5 reads ']her child, and all the compassion of her that is pregna[nt'.[73] The editors mention the possibility that 'this line could paraphrase the curse of the woman, Gen 3:16, referring to pregnancy and giving birth as well as the woman's relation to her husband'.[74] Line 7 reads 'rejecting] the bad and knowing the good' and

---

[71] There is an occurrence of the term עזר used for a man in *Musar leMevin*, 4Q417 2 i 7 reads 'do not count a man of iniquity as a helper'.

[72] Both 1QH[a] xvi 25 and Heb 6.8 allude to Gen 3.18 with the phrase 'thorns and thistles'.

[73] Birth, male dominion over the female, the obstacle of poverty, and tending crops are all recurring themes in *Musar leMevin* and indicate challenges of gaining understanding within a metaphor of living within an Edenic garden that has wisdom bearing trees.

[74] *DJD XXXIV*, p. 510.

could refer to partaking of the tree of the knowledge of good and evil as described in Genesis 2.9 and 3.22 (הן האדם היה כאחד ממנו לדעת טוב ורע).[75] Line 5 is a likely allusion to the female in Genesis 3.16.

1Q26 1 (parallel 4Q423 4) is a relatively small fragment preserved in only nine surviving lines, all without either full right or left margins. The most complete are lines 5-7, two of which have been reproduced in full here. The first line contains only the phrase ברז נהיה, line 2 the term תבואתכה ('your harvest'), line 3 is indecipherable and in line 4 the phrase רז נהיה occurs again in the statement 'He has revealed your ear to the רז נהיה'. Here, a possible allusion to woman and an Eden tradition may occur:

5) [ ] [ ] לכה השמר לכה למה תכבדכה ממנו [
6) [ ] ונארותה בכול תבואתכה ונ[כל]מתה בכול מעשיכה [

5)] for you, watch out for yourself, lest she honour you more than him [
6)] and are accursed in all your produce and you be ash[amed] in all your deeds [[76]]

The context that follows is difficult to evaluate. Line 7 begins with legal terminology (ריב, מ[שפט]) and is followed by what the editors reconstruct as 'and He said to him, "I am [thy] por[tion and thy inheritance] (?)"'. However, lines 7b-8a have been extensively reconstructed and do not provide a straightforward context in which to understand lines 5-6. Line 5 appears to refer to the female honouring her husband (cf. Philo *QG* 1 27; 4Q415 2 ii) more than God while line 6 describes the curse of Adam and the resulting shame in Genesis 3. Although line 6 shares no precise lexical similarities with Genesis 3 the themes themselves are familiar: (1) a cursed earth; and (2) shame (see §4 below). If line 5 is a description of one's wife, then something may be learnt about honouring one's husband in relation to God. The exhortation found in line 5 could be derived from a reminiscence of Eve bearing some type of guilt for her actions in the garden. While the woman's act of gaining wisdom itself could be construed as positive, perhaps *Musar leMevin* conceives of women negatively in light of the story of Eden. The author(s), on the one hand, view acquisition of wisdom as entirely good; however, on the other hand, may not credit the first woman for her role in acquiring it. Instead, perhaps certain themes related to Eve in Genesis 2-3

---

[75] One of the few other Qumran texts that paraphrase the Eden story and the tree of knowledge is 4Q422 1 9-11 't]ree, He gave him dominion to eat the frui[t...with the exception of eating from the tree of kn[owledge...he rose up against him and they forgot'.

[76] See *DJD XXXIV*, pp. 536-37 for justification of translation and reconstruction by STRUGNELL and HARRINGTON. ELGVIN, *DJD XXXIV*, p. 516-17, in the same volume translates 4Q423 4 lines 1-2 almost identically '...to you. Tak]e care [lest] she honour you more than Him and[...and you be cursed in a]ll [your] crops [and put] to shame in all your deeds...'.

were focused upon (e.g. her relationship to her father and husband and childbirth). Line 6 could describe the consequences that befall man if he fails to heed the wisdom of line 5. The combination of instruction about women and agricultural imagery suggest that 1Q26 1 should be understood in light of an Eden tradition.

2.7 Summary

The identification of these allusions to Genesis 2-3 reveals that *Musar leMevin* apparently conceives of women as subjugated to man based upon her creation and 'curse'. The derivation of the female in creation and allusions to Genesis 2 in the document function both to describe and exhort husbands and wives how to relate to one another. The woman could be exhorted to relate to her husband 'like her father' both because of perceptions of him as her originatrix as well as the dominion of her literal father passing on to her husband. In general, conceptions of the origin of woman, the uniting of the woman to her husband, and results of partaking from the tree of knowledge are all themes that are related to women in *Musar leMevin*.

3. Women and Angels

Column 4Q416 2 iii lines 15-18, discussed in chapter four, have the occurrence of an analogy between two sets of creator figures (God/earthly father and angels/earthly mothers). Since angels are likened here to women ('mother'), there may be implications for women based upon a relationship between them and angelic beings. Later Aramaic targumic traditions portray woman as related to the angels at times in Genesis 2-3. The preservation of a tradition that likens women with angels based upon an interpretation of the Garden of Eden may at times be at play in *Musar leMevin*.

Targum Pseudo-Jonathan's translation and interpretation of the first three chapters of Genesis portray ministering angels as assisting God in the creation of humanity. *Pseudo-Jonathan* on Genesis 1.26 reads, 'God said to the angels who minister before him, who were created on the second day of the creation of the world, "let us make man in our image, in our likeness"'. Another variation from the Hebrew Bible in the targum is the response of the serpent to the woman after she describes God's prohibition of eating from the tree of knowledge: 'and [the serpent said] to the woman, "you will not die. But every craftsman hates his fellow craftsman. For it is manifest before the Lord that on the day on which you eat of it you will surely *be like* the great *angels*, who are able to distinguish good from evil' (3.4-5). In this targum Eve is likened to both a creator figure and an angelic being. Maher cites *Genesis Rabbah* 19.4

in relation to the statement of 'fellow craftsman'.[77] In *Genesis Rabbah*, God is depicted as eating of the tree of knowledge before creating the world and forbids Adam and his wife from partaking of the tree lest they create other worlds. In both texts (*Gen. R.* 19.4; *Ps.-Jn.* 3.4) the phrase 'fellow craftsman' is used. The interpretation of the term אלהים in the Hebrew Bible and commonly in early Jewish literature is as angels and is used in *Pseudo-Jonathan* to avoid a direct statement that the woman could become like 'God'. This interpretation of Genesis, that the woman would become or is likened to angels, shares two obvious similarities with 4Q416 2 iii 15-18.

Adam too is at times a creator figure and likened to God. *Pseudo-Jonathan* on Genesis 3.22 expands upon the Hebrew Bible stating that, 'the Lord God said to the angels who minister before him, "behold, Adam was alone on the earth *as I am alone in the heavens* on high…"'. In *Targum Pseudo-Jonathan* is an analogy between God and Adam as well as angels and Eve. In *Pseudo-Jonathan* 3.22 the analogy between God and Adam is clear, though rendered as a simile. However, the use of the phrase 'fellow craftsman' in 3.4 is also suggestive of such an analogy. *Pseudo-Jonathan* could reflect notions of humanity having creative power analogous to God and the angels. Furthermore, the statement that woman will become like the 'great angels' stands in contrast to the analogy between God and Adam (3.22).

Targum Neofiti preserves several similar interpretations. The serpent responds to the woman in the garden saying: 'on the day you eat of it your eyes will be opened, and you will be *like the angels* before the Lord' (3.5). *Targum Neofiti* also adds the statement that 'the Lord God said, "Behold, the first Adam whom I have created is alone in the world *as I am alone* in the heavens on high"'. The analogy between God and Adam continues in the following sentence: 'numerous nations are to arise from him'. McNamara suggests that the phrase 'from him' corresponds to 'of us' or 'from us' (ממנו, i.e. become like one of us') and reflects a successful attempt to avoid an inherent anthropomorphism.[78] *Pseudo-Jonathan* and *Neofiti* thus appear to preserve a tradition wherein the first man and woman are likened to both God and angels. Genesis 1-3 are interpreted variously by the targums and *Musar leMevin*, however, both draw upon similar analogies. The targums enable us to see the ease with which such an analogy may be derived from the Eden account. Constructing a broader picture of women in *Musar leMevin* should bear in mind the possibility that this interpretation may be at work elsewhere in the document.

---

[77] M. MAHER, *Targum Pseudo-Jonathan: Genesis*, (Edinburgh: T&T Clark Ltd, 1992) p. 25 fn. 4.

[78] M. MCNAMARA, *Targum Neofiti 1: Genesis* (Edinburgh: T&T Clark Ltd, 1992) p. 63 fn. 23.

Mothers are conceived of as fellow creators along with their husbands and are likened to their heavenly counterparts. The analogy between women and angels may derive not only from an interpretation to Genesis 1.26, but also 3.4-6 where the woman is told that if she eats from the tree of knowledge she will become like an angel (אלהים). An analogy of men with God and women with angels places the woman as a secondary creator, thus subjugating her further.

4. 'Cover Your Shame'

In 4Q416 2 iv lines 5 and 13 are occurrences of an epithet for wife in conjunction with terms for 'shame' and 'nudity' (אשת חיקכה וחרפ]תכה; אשת חיקכה כי היא שאר ער]ומכה/ער]ותכה). The connection in 4Q416 2 iv between a term for woman and the concept of shame within a fragment with numerous allusions to Genesis 2-3 suggests that 'shame' might be related to an Eden account both in this column and elsewhere in the document. If the concept is to be related to Eden accounts, does it bear the idea of nudity (ערום) or are there other conceptions of 'shame' at play in the document? Since wisdom is highly esteemed in *Musar leMevin,* shame might be related to the addressee's failure to gain wisdom. Another possibility is a 'shame' related to properly/improperly relating to one's wife and the created order. In order to ascertain more clearly the relationship of 'shame' here to Garden of Eden accounts, an examination of various occurrences of the term is necessary. The use of the word 'shame' elsewhere in the Dead Sea Scrolls and early Jewish literature will also aid in delineating conceptions thereof in *Musar leMevin.* The term חרפה occurs in *Musar leMevin* (approx. 8x) considerably more than any one of the other documents among the Dead Sea Scrolls (approx. 9x total).[79] The relative frequency of occurrences and broad distribution suggests its significance in the document. A brief survey of notions of shame in Eden accounts and the term's usage elsewhere will precede a treatment of it as it is used in *Musar leMevin.*

4.1 Occurrences of 'Shame' in Other Early Jewish Literature

In the conclusion of *Targum Pseudo-Jonathan* to Genesis 2, a variant from the Hebrew Bible occurs: 'the two of them were *wise,* Adam and his wife, but they did not remain in their glory' (2.25). Whereas in the Hebrew Bible it

---

[79] חרפה occurs in *Musar leMevin* in 4Q416 2 ii 3 (par. 4Q417 2 ii + 23 5); 4Q416 2 ii 16 (par. 4Q418 8 2); 4Q416 2 iv 13; 4Q417 2 i 23, 26; 4Q418 177 3; 4Q418 178 4; 4Q418ª 19 4 – 8x. In the Qumran library in 1Q34 3 i 3 (*Liturgical Prayers;* par. 4Q508 1); 1QHª x 9; x 33-34; 4Q200 1 i 3 (Tobit); 4Q200 1 ii 1; 4Q501 5 (*Apocryphal Lamentations B*); 4Q481ᵉ 3 (*Narrative H*); 4Q525 14 ii 8 (*Beatitudes*); 4Q525 15 7 - 9.

states: 'the two of them were *naked*, Adam and his wife, and they were not ashamed'. The Hebrew ערם√ can mean 'crafty', 'wise' or 'naked' and is used to describe the nudity of Adam and his wife in chapter two while in the line that follows the craftiness of the serpent. In *Pseudo-Jonathan* Adam and his wife are said to be 'wise' while in the first verse of chapter 3 the serpent is said to be 'evil'. After eating from the tree of knowledge *Pseudo-Jonathan* reads, 'the eyes of both of them were enlightened and they knew that they were naked…and they saw their shame' (3.7). The description of their nudity as 'shame' is an addition to the Hebrew Bible and occurs in *Targum Neofiti* as well. The final verse of *Neofiti* on Genesis 2 (2.25) translates, 'both of them were naked, Adam and his wife, and as yet they did not know what shame was'.

The tradition of the description of Adam and Eve's nudity as 'shame' in *Pseudo-Jonathan* (3.6; 3.10) and *Neofiti* (2.25) is also preserved in the book of *Jubilees*. In *Jubilees* nudity is described as 'shame' and may reflect a prohibition against gentile nudity in the gymnasium.[80] In *Jubilees* 1.9, in an address by God to Moses, it is predicted that, 'they [Israelites] will forget all of my commandments… and they will walk after their defilement and shame'. However, the motif of nudity is not elaborated on outside of this reference in 1.9 and the subsequent description of the fall in chapter 3. In fact in *Jubilees*, before the Garden of Eden account, Adam is said to be naked but that he 'neither knew it nor was he ashamed' (3.16). When the female partakes of the forbidden fruit the immediate result is that she first 'covered her shame' (3.20), and when Adam likewise eats, 'he covered his shame' (3.22). The next reference to 'shame' and nudity occurs in 3.30 where Adam is described as the only one among the beasts and cattle allowed to 'cover his shame'. The following verse concludes on the matter and states: 'Therefore, it is commanded in the heavenly tablets to all who will know the judgement of the Law that they should cover their shame and they should not be uncovered as the gentiles are uncovered' (3.31). *Musar leMevin*, like *Jubilees*, uses the

---

[80] G. VERMES, 'Genesis 1-3 in Post-Biblical Hebrew and Aramaic Literature before the Mishnah,' in *JJS* 43 (1992): 222 writes: 'A third brief but topical inference in Jub. 3:30-31 concerns the clothing of Adam and Eve by God (Gen. 3.21): the pre-existant Torah engraved on heavenly tablets enjoins that the Jews must always cover themselves unlike the Gentiles. This is an unmistaken protest against the nakedness of athletes in the gymnasium, introduced by Jewish Hellenists according to 1 Mac. 1:13ff.'. See also J. C. VANDERKAM, *The Book of Jubilees* (Sheffield: Sheffield University Press, 2001) pp. 23-27; J. van RUITEN, 'The Garden of Eden and Jubilees 3.1-31,' in *Bijdragen: Tijdschrift voor Filosofie en Theologie* 57 (1996a): 305-17; J. C. ENDRES, *Biblical Interpretation in the Book of Jubilees* (Washington D. C.: Catholic Biblical Association of America, 1987), M. ALBANI, J. FREY and A. LANGE (eds.), *Studies in the Book of Jubilees* (TSAJ 65; Tübingen: J. C. B. Mohr Siebeck, 1977); R. H. CHARLES, *The Book of Jubilees or the Little Genesis* (London: A & C Black, 1972). For a discussion on the female in Jubilees see B. HALPERN-AMARU, 'The First Woman, Wives, and Mothers in Jubilees,' in *JBL* 113 (1994): 609-26.

phrase to 'cover shame' (4Q416 iv; 4Q418 177 3; 178 4) in a context related to Genesis creation traditions. In addition to this the motif of a heavenly tablet or book also occurs in *Musar leMevin* (4Q417 1 i) similar to *Jubilees* (3.31). *Jubilees* contains the closest parallel from the literature of early Judaism to the phrase 'cover your shame' in *Musar leMevin*.

A similar expression to *Jubilees* occurs on the lips of Eve in the *Apocalypse of Moses* 20:4. In this apocalypse the serpent is said to be a *vessel* (16.5) of the devil. The serpent, as an instrument of the devil, deceives Eve and we read from her perspective (20.1-5):

In that hour my eyes were opened and I knew immediately that I was bare of righteousness with which I had been clothed and I wept and said to him [the serpent], 'why have you done this to me, you have deprived me of the glory in which I was clothed?' I also wept about the oath I had sworn. He descended from the tree and vanished. I began to seek in my nakedness for leaves to hide my shame [αἰσχυνην], but I did not find any for as soon as I had eaten the leaves showered down from all the trees round about except for the fig tree. From this tree, which I had eaten from, I took leaves and made a covering for myself.

In the Septuagint the term ערוה is often translated by the term αἰσχυνην (Is 20.4; 47.3; Ezek 16.36, 38; 22.10; 23.10, 18, 29). Here again the notion of nakedness, shame and covering are closely linked.[81]

In addition to the *Apocalypse of Moses*, the association of shame and nakedness also occurs in the Apocalypse of John on two occasions. The first is in 3.18: 'the shame [αἰσχυνην] of your nakedness'. The second is in 16.15: 'blessed is he who is awake, keeping his clothing that he may not go naked and be ashamed [αἰσχυνην]'. Though there is no clear connection in John's apocalypse to nakedness and shame with Adam and Eve, the association of nudity with 'shame' is significant.

The Book of Watchers in *1 Enoch* also preserves a brief paraphrase and interpretation of the Garden of Eden account. In the *Book of Watchers* (32) Enoch views the garden of righteousness (Eden) within which there is a tree described as 'the tree of wisdom, of which one eats and knows great wisdom'. Enoch describes the tree's beautiful appearance and the angel Raphael says (32.6):

'This very thing is the tree of wisdom from which your old father and aged mother, they who are your precursors, ate and came to know wisdom; and (consequently) their eyes were opened and they realized that they were naked and (so) they were expelled from the garden.'[82]

---

[81] See also DOCHHORN, '»Sie Wird Dir Nicht«' on the link between 4Q423 1, 2 i and the *Apocalypse of Moses* 24.1-2.

[82] Translation by E. ISAACS.

A few observations may be made from this passage. First, the tree of wisdom is not described in terms of good and evil (Gen 2.9) but is positively conceived as able to make one wise (Gen 3.6). Second, Eve is not portrayed as the transgressor and no specific fault is focused upon her. Finally, a sequence of cause and affect is described: Adam and Eve (1) eat of the fruit of the tree of wisdom and as a result their eyes are opened; (2) when their eyes are opened they see their nudity; and then (3) their nudity leads to their expulsion from the garden. The realisation of their nudity is emphasised over any act of disobedience or deception; certainly their eyes being opened to their nudity here is significant as it is the direct cause, though not the ultimate one, for being expelled.[83]

Three occurrences of the term חרפה in non-biblical documents may also have some bearing on the use of the term in *Musar leMevin*. 1Q*Liturgical Prayers* (1Q34) survives in only a few fragments and is a relatively short document with less than twenty intact lines. The document begins with thanksgiving to God for gathering together His exiles and having mercy upon His people. God's actions are likened with natural provision such as rainfall and produce of the earth. The order of nature, the greater light of day and perhaps lesser light of night, establish a more general order that is applicable to understanding the nature of humanity. The document clearly distinguishes between two groups of people: the wicked and the just. The just will experience redemption while the wicked will be destroyed. At one point (3 ii 2) some are said to have 'dominion over the whole world' (וממשלתם בכל תבל; cf. Gen 1.26-27), while the seed of man (אדם) has not understood his inheritance and does not know God. In the final surviving lines of the document the author praises God for renewing His covenant with the elect in the 'vision of glory' (מראת כבוד). This is done by the words of His 'holy spirit'. In addition, a 'faithful shepherd' is said to have been established for them. 1Q34 3 i lines 1-2 read:

(2 [ ] בגורל צדיק ולרשים גורל
(3 [ ] בעצמותם חרפה לכל בשר וצדיקים]

2) [ ] in the lot of the righteous and lot of the wicked
3) [ ] in their bones a shame for all flesh and the righteous ones [

What do bones have to do with 'shame'? Though the term עצם occurs in the *Hodayot* in a number of descriptions of the suffering of the author (1QH[a] xiii

---

[83] Sirach is also concerned with shame and mentions it on 15 occasions (4.21; 5.14; 6.1; 15.4; 20.22, 23, 26; 24.22; 26.8, 25; 29.14; 41.16; 42.1, 11, 14). However, none of these occurrences are directly related to creation. Sirach 42.14 relates shame to the woman: 'better is the wickedness of a man than a woman who does good; it is a woman who brings shame and disgrace'.

6-7; xiii 35; xv 4; xvi 30; xix 21), it is a very infrequent term among other
non-biblical documents found at Qumran (11QT li 4-5). In *Miqsat Ma'aseh
ha-Torah* (4Q394) 8 i lines 11-12 (par. 4Q397) a prohibition occurs against
those who are not to enter the assembly and take a wife, with the sentence
'take wives to become one bone' (ונשים לוקחים להיותם עצם אחת). In *Miqsat
Ma'aseh ha-Torah* the concept of 'one bone' would seemingly allude to
Genesis 2.23 and the concept that Adam's partner is עצם מעצמי ('bone of my
bone').[84] Flesh and bone are related in this line to shame, however, it is not
clear how they are to be associated.

Another occurrence of the term חרפה is in the so-called *Apocryphal
Lamentation B* (4Q501) line 5. *Apocryphal Lamentation B* is a short column
with only nine surviving lines. The lamentation begins with a plea not to give
the inheritance of the community to foreigners and to remember the covenant
made with them. The author appears to envisage his community in line 4 as
suffering persecution at the hands of the 'wretched ones of your people' who
are called liars. Lines 4-6b read:

4) [כפופים ואין זו]קף[85] סבבונו חילכיא עמכה בלשון שקרמה ויופכו

5) [על   כ]ה ופארתכה לילוד אשה הביטה וראה חרפת בני

6) [עמכה כיא נכמר] עורנו...

4) [for all those bowed down there is no rais]ing up, wretched ones of your [God's] people
have surrounded us with their lying tongue and they turned away
5) [   ] your (God's) bough to one born of woman, gaze and see the shame
of the sons
6) of [your (God's) people for our skin is burning...

In the following lines 7-9 the author(s) calls upon God to avenge Himself
against His enemies and concludes with a depiction of the adversary as acting
violently against the poor and needy (עני ואביון). The referent of the
pronominal suffix (כה-) in lines 4-6 is God. Though the missing portion of the
beginning of line 5 is nearly impossible to ascertain, the context suggests that
some of those who are considered to be part of God's people have gone astray
and turned from God's 'bough' (פארה; cf. Ez 31.8-13) after 'one born of
woman'. In line 6 some who are considered a part of God's people are

---

[84] See *DJD X*.

[85] 4Q501 is a fragment that survives without any right margin while the margins of both
the left as well as top and bottom are visible. The only surviving letters at the beginning of
line 4 are 'קף-' and *DJD VII*, p. 80, comments 'la restitution כפופים ואין זוקף est inspirée de
Ps 145[14] 146[8]'. It is difficult to say with any certainty the precise number of letter spaces that
originally existed in the column and BAILLET'S reconstruction is only an educated guess. The
final word of line 4, ויופכו, is the best source for searching for possible reconstructions, but it
will not be from the Hebrew Bible or other DSS since the term in this form, as far as I am
aware, does not occur.

described as shameful. The author responds to the shameful activities by expressing indignation towards them as well as a state of burning skin (cf. Lam 5.10 עורנו כתנור נכמרו; cf. 5.1 where the term חרפה occurs). While an allusion to Lamentations 5 is possible, it is also possible that Genesis 2-3 are at play here.

The term 'bough' (פארה) has possible links to the Garden of Eden. In Ezekiel 31.8-13 the nations of the earth are describe as trees in an Edenic garden. Both the word bough and a term for 'shame' occur in this chapter.[86] The word פארה occurs in only three passages in the Hebrew Bible (Is 10.33; Ez 17.6; 31.8-13) and in Ezekiel 31.8-13 is used repeatedly. This word does not occur elsewhere in the Qumran literature and 4Q501 line 5 may allude to Ezekiel. Metaphorically Assyria is described as a cedar in Lebanon, other 'trees' (nations) are said to be nothing compared with its branches (פארה). In verse 9 its branches are said to be the envy of all the trees of *Eden* in God's garden. In verse 12 foreigners (זרים; cf. 4Q501 1) cut the tree down and its boughs (פארה) lie broken and then in verse 13 wild animals dwell in it's boughs (פארה).[87]

Finally, a fragment of the *Hosea Pesher* (4Q166) associates 'shame' and hunger with divine judgement. 4Q166 i lines 12-13 read:

12) פשרו אשר הכם ברעב ובערום להיות לקלו[ן]

13) וחרפה לעיני הגואים אשר נשענו עליהם והמה

12) its interpretation: He has struck them with famine and with nakedness, to be a shameful nakedness
13) and a shame before the eyes of the nations whom they relied upon, and they

While no allusion to creation occurs in this pesher there are similarities with the Apocalypse of John. Nudity and 'shame', sometimes in a context related to nudity after partaking of the tree of knowledge, were often associated in early Jewish literature.

Targums Pseudo-Jonathan, Neophiti, Jubilees and the *Apocalypse of Moses* each introduce the idea of shame explicitly in their presentations of Genesis 2-3. 'Shame' in these contexts is directly associated with eating from the tree of knowledge and resulting realisation of nudity. In addition to this, both the *Liturgical Prayer* and *Apocryphal Lamentation B* lend some credence that the concept of 'shame' occur in allusions to Eden. In light of these sources and the occurrence of 'wife of your bosom' and 'shame' in

---

[86] See also G. J. BROOKE, '4Q500 1 And the Use of Scripture in the Parable of the Vineyard,' in *DSD* 2 (1995): 268-94, where Brooke discusses the imagery of fragment 4Q500 in relation to Eden.

[87] TIGCHELAAR, 'Eden and Paradise,' p. 37, writes: 'In a different manner [than Ez 28.12-19] the trees of the Garden of Eden enter the scene in Ezek 31'.

4Q416 2 iv perhaps some sense might be made of two small fragments discussed in chapter 3 (§3.2.11; 4Q418 177 and 178).

4.2 Occurrences of 'Shame' in Musar leMevin

4Q418 177 and 178 both have occurrences of the phrase כסה חרפתכה ('cover your shame'). In the preliminary identification of these fragments with a Genesis 1-3 tradition, a possible allusion in 4Q418 177 lines 2-3 to Job 26.6 in the phrase ערום שאול נגדו ואין כסות לאבדון ('naked is Sheol and there is no covering for Abaddon') was suggested. Job 26.6 shares two important lexical correspondences with this fragment: כסות and אבדון. The phrase 'cover your shame' in line 3 has conceptual links with Job 26.6 by way of Genesis 2-3 in the term ערום and *vice versa*.[88] Therefore, it may be possible to understand conceptions of shame as related directly to the preceding line 2 and the term 'Abaddon'. 4Q418 177 reads as follows:

שח]ת ואבדון אשר בקצהו לוא[	]	(2
] *vacat* וכסה חרפתכה[	]	(3
]∘ וקח בינה האזינה ל[∘	]	(4
]∘ אתה רש ונדיבים י[	]	(5
]הלכו כול צ[	]	(6
]אתה דע רזיו כ[	]	(7a
ה השמר מאו]ד[	]	(7
]אוטכה[	]	(8

2) [the pi]t and Abaddon which in its border no[
3)]and cover your shame *vacat* [
4)]and grasp understanding, give ear to [
5)]your are poor but nobles [
6)] all walk [
7a)] know (you) his mysteries [
7)] keep very much [
8)] your אוט [

Due to their fragmentary state, the vocabulary that occurs in the surviving lines contribute little to an understanding of the phrase 'cover your shame' in line 3. Line 4 appears to be an exhortation to understand and give ear to the רז נהיה.[89] Line 5 states that the addressees are poor and are somehow discussed in relation to nobles (angels?), a statement similar to what was

---

[88] In theory a form of Hillel's seven middoth may be at play between the Genesis and Job passages. The second middah (גזירה שוה) is an inference or linking of passages based upon either analogous terms or identical roots.

[89] Commands to 'give ear' and 'understand' in *Musar leMevin* almost always occur in relation to the רז נהיה.

discussed in chapter 4 in relation to 4Q416 2 iii. Line 7a repeats the theme of understanding or knowing mysteries. Line 8 mentions the אוש of the addressee (כה-)[90] However, the mysteries in line 7a are likely God's mysteries ('His mysteries').

In 4Q418 127 Harrington and Strugnell reconstruct the word 'Sheol'. In addition to the possible occurrence of Sheol is the term 'cover'. This fragment is 6 lines long, neither left or right margin survive and line 1 is the first line of the column following the upper margin. The first three lines are as follows:

[שאול[91]] [מקורכה ומחסורכה לוא תמצא ודאבה נפשכה מכול טוב למותן] [(1
[ה[יכס וקברת בפתחיה תבוא כי נפשכה ואותה היום כול [צפה[92]] (2
[ת[מון נגד רשף ולחומי שן למאכל והייתה [תכה[93]] [∘∘ג[ן] (3

1) [ ] from your spring, and from your lacking you will not find[94], and your soul is weary from all good things, for death[Sheol]
2) [ ]views the whole day and your soul desires that you come into its opening and buried he/it (Sheol?) will cov[er]
3) [ ] your body, and you will be food of teeth and devoured by flames[95] in the presence of dea[th

In line 4 it is predicted that seekers of pleasure will oppress the addressee. Line 5 describes God as the creator and allocator of all the pleasures of אוש. Line 6 is concerned with justice and times of judgement. Line 1 may portray those who are unable to fill their lacking and are tired from doing good. Line 2 then would depict this same person as one whose soul desires death. The end of line two is not clear but could be interpreted as the addressee covering something or death/Sheol covering something. If Sheol can be reconstructed in line 1, 4Q418 177 may be related to Job 26.6 with greater certainty.

---

[90] It is preferable not to translate אוש in order to reflect the level of uncertainty surrounding the word. *DJD XXXIV*, p. 31-32 (§3.4.a) observe that אוש occurs only in *Musar leMevin* (15x) and 4Q424 1 6 (אש). 4Q424 provides the fullest context and may use the word as 'secret', however, even here it is far from certain. For instance, GARCÍA MARTÍNEZ and TIGCHELAAR translate it as 'affair (?)', p. 889. Little is known about the precise meaning of the word in *Musar leMevin*. CLINES suggests 'storehouse' in D. J. A. CLINES (ed.), *Dictionary of Classical Hebrew, vol. 1* (Sheffield: Sheffield Academic Press, 1995) p. 150. However, 'storehouse' does not make sense in some contexts in *Musar leMevin*.

[91] *DJD XXXIV*, p. 359 comment: 'Somewhere in the lacuna there must have stood a feminine antecedent of the suffix in פתחיה, and this will have been almost certainly the order of שאול...'.

[92] *DJD XXXIV*, p. 357 reconstruct וכ]תה.

[93] Reconstruction mine.

[94] Cf. 4Q415 11 13 'her *foundations* you will not find'.

[95] See also 4Q416 2 iii line 4 where imagery of one's body suffering scorching and burning occurs.

4Q418 178, which preserves the same column as fragment 177, also has the phrase כסה חרפתכה. Additionally, 4Q418 178 contains several terms that associate it with other occurrences of woman in *Musar leMevin*:

] (2	ב[ביתכה תעזור *vacat*]	
] (3	תמ]צא בית מכונים[	
] (4	כס]ה חרפתכה[	

2) [in] your house she will help *vacat* [
3) [she will] find a house, established [
4) [co]ver your shame [

The editors suggest that 4Q418 178 be likened to 4Q415 11, a fragment they understand as relating to the addressee's marrying off of his daughter.[96] 4Q415 11 is a fragment that pertains to women, wives and daughters and shall be discussed in detail below. While understanding 4Q418 178 in light of 4Q415 11 may be helpful, relating this fragment to some of the previously discussed allusions to woman in Genesis 2-3 may also prove insightful. Each of these three lines may be related to women in Genesis traditions elsewhere in the document. Line 2 describes the role of the woman as helping in the addressee's house. Furthermore, the woman as man's 'helper' is a theme already encountered (cf. 4Q416 2 iii 21; 4Q418a 16b + 17 3). Concerning line 3, the editors comment that the words בית and מכונים are associated in 4Q415 11 line 12 and are also the object of the verb מצא. They comment that this 'phrase in 4Q415 11 12 also stood in a passage about marriage and the bride's leaving her father's *potestas* for that of her husband, with whom she will establish a permanent dwelling place'.[97] If this is indeed the sense of 4Q418 178 line 3, the likelihood of this terminology having a basis in Genesis 2.20-25 increases. 4Q415 11 too may be understood as formulating instruction in light of allusions to Genesis 2-3.

4Q418 178 line 4 and the exhortation to 'cover your shame' might be identified as having occurred in a context concerned with instruction about women. The identification of 'cover your shame' in *Musar leMevin* could be related to 'shame' as observed in the targumic Eden traditions, 'cover your shame' in *Jubilees*, and Eve's shame in the *Apocalypse of Moses*. If the covering of shame in *Musar leMevin* is related to women and an allusion to Eden, 4Q418 177-178 may elucidate the phrase. The possible association of the phrase with Job 26.6 would suggest that straightforward nudity is not the sense of 'shame', but rather death and destruction. However, before

---

[96] *DJD XXXIV*, p. 403.
[97] *DJD XXXIV*, p. 404.

attempting to infer a coherent viewpoint from this analysis, the remaining occurrences of the term חרפה need to be considered.

The term חרפה occurs twice in 4Q416 2 ii (see parallels: 4Q417 2 ii + 23; 4Q418 8), which in DJD 34 is a composite text. Compared to other columns of the document 4Q416 2 ii is a relatively complete column. The column consists of twenty-one lines and is preceded by two fragmentary lines of 4Q416 2 i which help set the first lines of 4Q416 2 ii in context. This column may be generally summarised as containing instruction regarding the addressee's relation to a creditor and the consequences of debt. Poverty is a particularly recurrent idea throughout this column. The implications of poverty, borrowing and debt in these lines are serious and have at times spiritual consequences. A detailed description and analysis of the context where 'shame' occurs is provided here:

1) פתח רח]מיו   למל]א[98] כל מח]סורי אוטו ולתת טרף [

2) לכל חי ואין [∘   ואם [י]קפוץ ידו[ונאספה רוח כול [

3) בשר אל תק[ח   תמשול[99] בה ו]בחרפת[ה] תכסה פניכה ובאולתו

4) מאסיר[101] כמה] בהון ישכה[100] הנושה בו   מהר]שלם ואתה תשוה בו כי כיס

15) [ ] ואתה דמה לו לעבד משכי]ל וגם אל תשפל נפשכה לאשר לא ישוה בכה ואז תהי]ה[

16) [לו לאב[102] ∘]   לאשר אין כוחכה אל תגע פן תכשל וחרפתכה תרבה מאודה

17) [אל תמ]כור נפשכה בהון טוב היותכה עבד ברוח וחנם תעבוד נוגשיכה ובמחיר

18) אל תמכור כבודכה ואל תערבהו בנחלתכה פן יוריש גויתכה אל תשביע לחם

19) *vacat*   ואין כסות אל תשת יין ואין אכל אל תדרוש תענוג ואתה

20) *vacat*   חסר לחם אל תתכבד במחסורכה ואתה רוש פן

21) *vacat*   תבוז חייכה וגם אל תקל כלי [ח]יקכה

---

[98] TIGCHELAAR, *To Increase Learning*, pp. 46-47 does not reconstruct למל]א.

[99] Reconstruction mine. The editors suggest this alternate reconstruction to כשיל. If the concept of 'shame' is related to Gen 3 then the notion that one 'has dominion over her' may have more merit. TIGCHELAAR, *To Increase Learning*, pp. 46-47, does not reconstruct the word.

[100] GARCÍA MARTÍNEZ and TIGCHELAAR omit the word ישכה here, pp. 849-50. TIGCHELAAR, *To Increase Learning*, pp. 46-47 reconstructs: כמה] אם בהון הנושה.

[101] It is difficult to decipher between a *yod* and *waw*, the difference between the two here being 'prisoner' or 'imprisonment'.

[102] The editors reconstruct these lines from the small fragment 4Q418a 19 line 3 (תהיה לו לאב). This fragment also preserves traces of the word חרפתכה (l. 4). The ligature of the *waw* of לו is not visible in the photograph.

(1) He opened His mer[cies…   ]
to fill all the lacking of His אוט[103]
to give nourishment (2) to each living being
and there is not […
if] He closes His hand *then* will be gathered *in* the spirit of all (3) flesh
do not [take…
       … and you will rule over *her/it*]
in *his* shame cover *your* face
and (also) in his folly (4) of *captivity* (?)
much wealth the creditor lent *him*
quickly] pay and you will be equal/similar with him
because your hidden purse/treasure

(15) but be to him like an understanding servant
and also do not humble/lower your life for one
    who is not similar/equal to you
and then you will be (16) [a father to that one…   ]
for one who does not have your strength
do not touch lest you (*cause her to*) stumble
and your shame you greatly multiply
(17) [do not se]ll your life for wealth
it is good to be a servant in the spirit
freely serve your task-master
for a price (18) do not sell your honour/glory
and do not *pledge/mortgage* your inheritance
    lest it dispossess your body
do not be full with bread (19)
vacat when there is no covering do not drink wine
when there is not food do not seek luxuries
and you (20)
vacat lacking bread be not honoured in your lacking
--and you are poor--
    lest (21) *vacat* you despise/despoil your life
and also do not dishonour the 'vessel' of your bosom[104]

Attempts to decipher and explicate this column are hindered not only by
physical damage to the various manuscripts but also by the occurrences of
obscure terms and phrases. While the subject matter is often related to motifs
of wealth and poverty, it is presented in a less than predictable manner.

   The column begins (ll. 1-2) with God's mercy extended to fill the
deficiencies of (מחסורי) His אוט (perhaps 'secret' or 'storehouse'). If one
understands this as God filling the lacking of his *secret*(*s*), the addressee

---

[103] See fn. 90 above, the translation of this word is not certain. The editors translate here
'secrets', as plural although here it is singular, but are themselves not convinced of the
meaning. אוטו occurs in line 12 of 4Q416 2 ii in the construct חכמת אוטו ('wisdom of His
אוט').
[104] Translation and divisions are mine.

himself is described as lacking and poor; however, his lacking in *Musar leMevin* is not material on every occasion, but is a lacking of wisdom. The addressee is consistently portrayed as lacking an understanding of the רז נהיה, and thus is exhorted to pursue it, and the 'spirit of flesh' does not know it at all (4Q417 1 i 17-18). It is not the רז נהיה in *Musar leMevin* that is lacking, but rather the elect addressee and especially the spirit of flesh. The addressee is described as one who tires and struggles with diligent pursuit of learning. Therefore, this אוש should by no means be identified with the mystery (רז) since here it is the אוש itself which lacks.[105] Furthermore, in line 12 of this column אושו occurs in the construct 'wisdom (חכמת) of His אוש' and should not be translated as 'wisdom of His *secret*'.[106]

As discussed in chapter 4, in the following column (4Q416 2 iii) the addressee is poor and yet has been seated among angels (נדיבים). Removing one from poverty and filling up lacking are similar ideas. 'To fill His אוש' is best understood in light of the following phrase 'to give provision to all of life' (ll. 1b-2a). The word 'to fill' is reconstructed by the editors because it complements לתת in the following colon. If one assumes synonymy between the two phrases, חי would explain, perhaps insufficiently, the preceding אוש. Therefore, all of humanity, regardless of their identity as 'flesh' or 'spirit', are sustained by God. אוש could be understood to imply 'material creation' and 'worldly beings' as distinct from the entire created cosmos.[107]

Lines 2-3 confirm that if God did not fill this lacking, the 'spirit of all flesh' would be gathered in and condemned. Line 3 holds a possible allusion to Genesis 3 in the phrase 'you will rule over her'; however, the editors prefer to read כשיל בה ('stumble in it') instead. In the same line the terms '[his] shame' (חרפ[תו]) and 'his folly' (אולתו) occur, but it is difficult to make sense of the pronominal suffixes. The editors suggest a translation of these lines as:

---

[105] MURPHY, *Wealth*, pp. 170-71, comments on this line, 'note that it is not God's mercies or creation itself which are labeled deficient, but rather God's secrets, which by definition humans lack. If the secrecy rather than the mere privacy of God's "business" is conveyed by the term אוש, then the weight of explanation for the present lack lies not in acts of divine deprivation but rather in the nature of divine revelation. Thus the author deftly avoids attributing deficiency directly to God'.

[106] The editors translate line 12 as 'wisdom of His *secrets*', however, they comment in their introduction that the translation 'secret' is not at all certain, *DJD XXXIV*, pp. 31; 93. How one makes sense of a description of אוש as both 'lacking' and 'wise' has a parallel with the description of (angelic/heavenly) hosts lacking in 4Q416 1 line 6 (מחסור צבאם) and yet pursuing understanding without becoming weary.

[107] 4Q418 81 line 16 reads: אוש לכול הלכי אדם ומשם תפקוד טרפכה [...] ('[...] אוש for all the *ways of man* and from there you will *seek* for your food') and suggests a connection between אוש and earthly sustenance as well. The preceding line 15 (4Q418 81 15) has the phrase 'if he has given you authority over חכמת ידים' which might be related to חכמת אושו in 4Q416 2 ii line 12. חכמת ידים is likely to be understood as 'manual skill' (e.g. Sir 9.17).

[thou shalt not make the poor] stumble *at* it (sc. At his poverty) and (nor) from him shalt thou in his shameful condition (actions) hide thy face, and at his foolish acts (turn away thy face) from the prisoner'.[108]

This extensive supplementation to these lines is forced due to the odd assortment of suffixes, and is a projection of sapiential instruction about poverty and borrowing.[109] However, attention to the polyvalent use of themes in the document and the use of metaphors derived from creation allusions elsewhere suggest that these lines may allude to wives and husbands.[110]

4Q416 2 ii lines 3-4 indicate that issues of poverty and folly are associated with 'shame'. Here, the proper response to another's shame is to cover one's face.[111] An argument may be made for interpreting חרפה here as 'nakedness'. This is a theme that may occur in line 19 of the same column where it states 'when there is no covering (כסות), do not drink wine'. In line 4, one might understand the phrase בחרפת[ה] תכסה פניכה as 'and when he is naked, cover your face'. Given the immediately preceding preposition with the feminine pronominal suffix (בה) it would make sense of this line if [ה]בחרפת could be reconstructed, giving us a command to not look upon a woman's nakedness. This would conflict with the suffix of the following ובאולתו and the evidence of 4Q417 2 i line 5. The reconstruction and sense of the entire phrase that

---

[108] *DJD XXXIV*, p. 95. GARCÍA MARTÍNEZ and TIGCHELAAR translate these lines: (2) And there is not […if] he closes his hand, the spirit of all flesh [will be gather]ed in. (3) Do not ta[ke…in it. And] at [his] reproach you will cover your face, and at the folly (4) of imprisonment, how […also with money, and the one who has lent him…quickly] repay, and you will be even with him.

[109] For instance, the editors suggest that 4Q418 8 line 2 may preserve פניה ('her face'), *DJD XXXIV*, p. 91. 4Q416 2 ii does not preserve the pronominal suffix of בחרפת[ן, 4Q417 2 i line 5 reads [תו   ]   ן בה ה [יל thus making certain that this manuscript read 'and in *his* shame'. 4Q416 2 ii theoretically could have read ובחרפת[ה ('in *her* shame'), since the space available is identical for either ה- or ו-.

[110] In this column the general content has been summarised as the relationship between creditor and borrower and the repaying of debts. 'Exchanging your holy spirit' (l. 6); or pledging one's inheritance resulting in the dispossession of the body (l. 18) may relate to issues of monetary debt, but may also transcend it (especially since 'inheritance' is used metaphorically elsewhere). Issues of lacking and hunger are at the same time related to the obscure term אוש (l. 1). The debtor/creditor relationship is described in terms of 'father' and 'firstborn'; MURPHY, *Wealth*, p. 183, finds a parallel in other sapiential literature (Prov 17.2; 27.18) to the idea that a debtor could become like a firstborn son to a creditor; however the combination of similes (depiction as both father and son) seems unusual. 4Q418 81 line 5 also contains language of 'firstborn' alongside the multiplication of glory.

[111] MURPHY, *Wealth*, pp. 169-70, assuming the reconstruction and supplementation of the editors, comments that 'as the writer hopes God will not shut his hand, so too the maven is not to hide his face from the poor man or cause him to stumble by aggravating his shame. The preceding lines indicate that hiding one's face or aggravating the poor man's shame are euphemisms for providing food…'.

follows is unclear. A scenario in which lacking could include the dispossession of a covering is difficult to imagine in line 4.

In line 16, the occurrence of חרפה does not appear to be associated with 'nakedness', which also casts doubt on such an interpretation in line 4. The term חרפה in line 16 occurs in the phrase, 'and your shame you greatly multiply'. The increase of the addressee's shame in the latter half of this line is said to result in the case of causing someone else to stumble. The editors suggest a possible reading of פן תכשל as 'lest you cause her to stumble'.[112] They summarily justify this translation:

> In sum, one could read, in accord with 4Q416's orthographic practices and the meanings of each *binyān*, either a 3rd fem. *Nip'al* or a 2nd masc. *Pi'el*; the former, however, is highly unlikely in view of the suffixes and the preceding stich, but a residual ambiguity between תכשֵׁל and תכשִׁל and between תַרבֶּה (2nd masc. *Hip'il*) and תַרבֶּה (*Qal* 3rd fem.) is difficult to resolve definitely. A decision between תרבה and תרבה will depend (a) on the form and sense of the idiom חרפה + רבה √, (b) on the subject of פן תכשל (as found in the preceding sentence), and (c) on whether there are any parallels, sapiential or other, to the notion of the shame of fighting with women…in that case, one could supply לה as well as לו as the missing retrospective suffixed preposition.[113]

In view of these comments and given a case for reading the term 'shame' in light of a tradition from Genesis 2-3, sense can be made of this line as an exhortation not to touch (תגע; 'smite' ?) a woman, which would multiply one's shame. The opposite of increasing one's shame is to multiply one's glory. 4Q418 81 line 5 describes the multiplication of glory as similar to being a firstborn (בכור). In 4Q416 2 ii line 13 one becomes a firstborn (בכור) by finding favour and perhaps advising about חכמת אוטו ('worldly wisdom' ?).

The first two words of 4Q416 2 ii line 16 are reconstructed from 4Q418a 19 line 3. The addressee becomes a father to someone who is not equal to him.[114] In line 16 the subject is again about equality, only this time the person is not of equivalent strength. It is possible that women are in view in lines 15-16 (see §5.2), several other (possible) references to women would support this interpretation. First, line 3 may be reconstructed with the phrase 'and you will rule over her'. Second, line 21 contains the statement 'do not dishonour the vessel of your bosom'. Third, the following columns of this fragment (4Q416 2 iii-iv) contain significant allusions to the woman in Genesis 2-3. Additionally, the suggestion that a woman relates to her husband as a father (4Q415 2 ii) has already been proposed. The perception of a weaker female form (1 Peter 3.7) could fit well with the statement 'do not touch one who

---

[112] Recall the possible reconstruction of תכשול in line 3. Distinguishing between *kof* and *mem* is as difficult at times as between *waw* and *yod*.

[113] *DJD XXXIV*, p. 105.

[114] 4Q415 9 line 5 is the occurrence of equality/inequality in a context related to women.

does not have your strength'. If this were the case, חרפה would occur in relation to instruction about women as is the case in 4Q416 2 iv.

4Q416 2 ii lines 3 and 16 each have an occurrence of the term חרפה. The term is used in a context that is concerned with the addressees relation to a creditor and taskmaster; however, the subject matter does not always strictly relate to this theme. In the case of line 3, the addressee is said to cover (כסה) his face on account of shame and this shame could be related in the same sentence to folly (אולת). Unfortunately, the surrounding context is too fragmentary to provide an adequate description of the sense of 'shame' here and admittedly the likelihood that it is related to women is uncertain.

4Q417 2 i (par. 4Q416 2 i) lines 23 and 26 contain the last two occurrences of the term חרפה. As a composite text, it is among the lengthier columns in the document. The column as a whole is concerned with issues of poverty, lacking, borrowing, repaying, sin, salvation, forgiveness and relations with an associate. With regard to the theme of lacking and borrowing, this column is similar to 4Q416 2 ii; however, in 4Q417 2 i the motif of 'sin' is present (ll. 4 and 14): ואל תעבור על פשעיכה ('do not disregard your own sins'). In line 7, the author cautions the addressee not to accept help from a 'man of iniquity' and line 8 provides assurance of punishment upon the wicked. In line 11 the addressee is exhorted to comprehend the birth-times of salvation and to know who will inherit glory and toil. Line 15 speaks of the abating of God's anger towards sin and the judgements of God. Line 17 is concerned with the subject of poverty and lacking, a circumstance that is eased by sharing things in common.

Line 21 addresses the issue of borrowing money from others while in the state of impoverishment. The addressee is urged to allow no sleep for himself until he repays the debt. Lines 22-23 then command that one should not lie to their creditor 'lest you bear guilt'. 4Q417 2 i lines 22b-26 read as follows:

(22) ....אל מכוב
(23) לו למה תשה עון וגם מחרפה לנ[ה]115   ולוא האמין ע[וד לרעהו
(24) ובמחסורכה יקפץ ידו כחכה]   וכמוהו לוה ודע מא[ן]116   [
(25) ואם נגע יפגשכה יא[ן]118   °אב אל תסתר מנ[גע]117 בכה]
(26) פן יגלה חר[פ]תכה ה[ן]   מושל בו ואז]

---

115 *DJD XXXIV*, p. 173 reconstruct לנ[ושה בכה] here. TIGCHELAAR, *To Increase Learning*, p. 55 and GARCÍA MARTÍNEZ and TIGCHELAAR do not reconstruct לנ[ושה בכה. This reconstruction is difficult and even the editors do not attempt to translate בכה.

116 *DJD XXXIV*, p. 173 reconstructs א[ן ג]ר and translate 'payment'.

117 TIGCHELAAR, *To Increase Learning*, p. 55, reads here מנושה ('from your lender').

118 Reconstruction mine.

22) ....Do not lie

23) to him lest you bear guilt and also from shame for/to [and you can no longer trust] his neighbour

24) and in your lacking He closes His hand, your strength [and like him borrow and know

25) and if calamity should meet you *it will hurry* [do not hide from that which plagues you]

26) lest it uncover your shame [rule over it and then]

A few similarities between lines 22-26 and 4Q416 2 ii occur in relation to the term חרפה. First, the preceding context in lines 2-3 of 4Q416 2 ii warn that God will close his hand on all flesh (יקפוץ ידו ונאספה רוח כול בשר), while here in line 24 a similar idea is expressed that one (creditor or God) will close his hand. Second, the term כוחכה (defective כחכה) occurs in both texts in close proximity to 'shame' (4Q416 2 ii 16 אל תגע כוחכה אין לאשר; 4Q417 2 i 24). Third, the term נגע occurs in close relationship to 'shame'. Fourth, the idea of covering, uncovering and concealing is tightly interwoven with 'shame' (4Q416 2 ii תכסה פניכה ובאולתו; 4Q417 2 i 25). Finally, there is the possibility of reading the phrase מושל בה in 4Q416 2 ii line 3 which could correspond in some way with מושל בו here (l. 26). Although the sense of these lines is not always clear this shared vocabulary suggests strong similarities in how מחסור (l. 26) is used in *Musar leMevin*.

4Q417 2 i line 26 states 'lest it uncover your shame'. The phrase יגלה חרפתכה, the antithesis of כסה חרפתכה, indicates further that shame is something that ideally should be covered. The threat of one's shame being uncovered occurs in a פן ('lest') clause. Consequential warnings with פן are abnormally frequent (22x) in *Musar leMevin*. Excluding overlaps and occurrences in highly damaged contexts, they are:

4Q415 2 ii line 4 – lest you (f.) neglect a holy covenant
4Q416 2 ii line 16 – lest you cause her to stumble
4Q416 2 ii line 18 – lest it (the loss of glory?) dispossess your body (יורש גויתכה)[119]
4Q416 2 ii line 20 – lest you despise your life and dishonour your *wife*
4Q416 2 iii line 4 – lest you be scorched and your body (גויתכה) burnt by its fire
4Q416 2 iii line 6 – lest you *add* to your poverty
4Q416 2 iii line 8 – lest you displace your boundary [seeking more than your inheritance]
4Q417 2 i line 10 – lest you toil (תעמל) in your life time
4Q417 2 i line 26 – lest it uncover your shame
4Q423 5 line 1a – lest you give it back to Levi the priest

---

[119] גויה ('body') occurs 12x in Qumran literature, 5x in *Musar leMevin*, and 2x in lest clauses in 4Q416 2 ii-iii. It also occurs in 4Q415 11 line 6 (par. 4Q418 167a+b) in an address about one's daughter: 'all her faults tell him and in her bodily defects (ובגויתיה) let [him] understand'. The last occurrence is in 4Q418 127 line 3, lines 2b-3a read: 'buried, it (Sheol) shall cov[er...]...your body (גו[י]תכה)....'

It is not conceivable that shame here could be a description of being physically uncovered. חרפה as 'nudity' does not fit within the context of 4Q417 2 i or the document as a whole.[120] However, this does not imply that 'shame' is not derived from an allusion to Eden. Language of shame may derive from a negative aspect of anthropology as found in some Eden accounts. As discussed throughout, shame is found on a few occasions in *Musar leMevin* in association with women and Genesis allusions. Shame may partially be understood as related to 'lacking'. *Displacing one's boundary marker* by seeking more than one's allotted inheritance may be similar to *uncovering one's shame* by going usury (cf. 4Q416 2 iii 6 above). Poverty, as a multivalent theme, relates also to a metaphorical inheritance. One consequence of not living rightly in relationship to poverty and inheritance is described with imagery from Eden (i.e. shame is uncovered).

4.3 Conclusions Concerning 'Shame'

The two compelling reasons that 'shame' in *Musar leMevin* may be linked to Genesis 2-3 are the combination of the following factors: (1) in 4Q416 2 iv there are two occurrences of the similar phrases 'wife of your bosom and shame' within a context of multiple allusions to Genesis 2-3; and (2) in 4Q418 177-178 there is the unique occurrence of the phrase 'cover your shame' which is also attested in the book of *Jubilees'* Eden narrative. A possible allusion to Job 26.6 in fragment 4Q418 177 may serve to orient the phrase 'cover your shame' closer to Genesis 2-3. The same phrase occurs in 4Q418 178 in a context that refers to a woman. More often than not, references to women in the document are found in an allusion to Genesis.

Occurrences of the term חרפה elsewhere in *Musar leMevin* are more difficult to evaluate. While one might conjecture that one or two of the other occurrences (4Q416 2 ii 3; 4Q417 2 i 26) could connote a sense of 'nudity', this is likely not the sense of the word. One cannot, for example, 'greatly multiply' their 'nakedness' but can their 'shame' (4Q416 2 ii 16). However, this does not negate the term's use as stemming from conceptions of 'nudity' and 'shame' that were a consequence of eating from the tree of knowledge. Shame in *Musar leMevin* would not be understood as a result of knowing good and evil, but rather a negative quality or aspect of the addressee and/or his wife.

The addressee's state or possession of shame is indicated in almost every reference to the term in the document. In order to 'cover your shame' or 'uncover your shame' the addressee must have shame. To increase one's shame exceedingly necessitates the present possession or state of 'shame'. If

---

[120] The closest parallel in the DSS to חרפתכה is found in CD v 10-11 regarding laws of incest that apply equally for males and females: ואם תגלה בת האח את ערות אחי אביה ('the daughter of a brother who uncovers the nakedness of the brother of her father').

we recall that the addressee is also counted among the 'people of spirit', which is distinguished from the 'spirit of flesh' and is in possession of a mysterious revelation (i.e. רז נהיה), this shame is all the more significant. It coheres with motifs already discussed, such as being poor but seated with angels, or possessing and seeking knowledge as fatigable beings. The addressee enjoys a unique status among humankind, but it is by no means one of being in a state of perfection.

The plausible reconstruction of the phrase אל תרב[ה] חרפתכה in 4Q416 2 iv line 10 was previously suggested. The phrase 'do not multiply your shame' is associated with both allusions to Numbers 30 and Genesis 2-3. The allusion to Numbers 30 and the husbands authority to nullify his wife's vows is related to dominion over a woman passing from father to husband. The multiplication of 'shame' could be linked to a failure to properly rule over one's wife as set forth in Genesis 2. The first woman in Genesis is portrayed as disobeying divine instruction and the curse on woman is that her husband will rule over her. Furthermore, the occurrence in line 13 of 'wife of your bosom and shame[', as related to the 'shame' associated with the woman's actions in Eden, could allow one to read conceptions of vows in this light.

Knowing the difference between good and evil in *Musar leMevin* divides humanity into two categories. Those who fail to distinguish between good and evil are part of the 'spirit of flesh' and those who do differentiate are part of the 'people of spirit'. The addressee metaphorically dwells in an Edenic garden where every tree offers fruit to make one wise. However, the task of tending the garden (i.e. increasing one's understanding) is burdensome and the addressee tires in the task. The addressee is also imperfect and is depicted and reminded he is poor and has shame.

Shame in *Musar leMevin* is increased when the addressee fails to behave properly (as is poverty; 4Q416 2 iii 6 'lest you add to your poverty'). Correct behaviour and ethics are derived from reflection on creation, both the order of the cosmos and the allotment to each being is understood from interpretations of the Genesis narrative. One interpretive tradition of this narrative describes Adam and Eve as ashamed and covering their shame. The author(s) of *Musar leMevin* do not conceive of humanity as poor or having shame because they partook of the tree of knowledge, but rather because they are imperfect learners. The proper conduct of the addressee in relation to the created order (e.g. how he relates to his wife) may be to cover his shame. The act of covering his shame may be an act of instructing his wife. Even though Eve was the first to eat of the tree of knowledge, *Musar leMevin* does not credit her for her role as the first to eat of its fruit. Instead the document focuses on creation to understand how the sexes should relate to one another. In *Musar leMevin*, shame and improper behaviour may be related at times to woman and her, oddly, improper actions in Eden.

5. Remaining Fragments about Women

Many of the large fragments that preserve *Musar leMevin* mention women at some point (4Q416 2; 4Q417 1, 4Q423 1, 2). Among important fragments for understanding instruction to women are 4Q415 9 and 4Q415 11 (par. 4Q418 167). These fragments provide the addressee with teaching about how he is to relate to women, wives and daughters. In addition to these fragments, 4Q418 126 i-ii will be considered in this section. 4Q418 126 i-ii and the phrase 'sons of Eve' was discussed briefly in chapter three. This phrase may be re-examined in light of discoveries made in this chapter and Eve may be seen as a character who acted outside of her prescribed role.

5.1 4Q415 11

4Q415 11 was mentioned briefly in relation to 4Q418 178 where it was suggested that the two fragments may share the same subject matter. A close examination of this column will raise issues and observations that relate to allusions to woman in Genesis 2-3 elsewhere in the document. These lines read as follows:

(4 [   ] [רו]חמה[121] ליפי מראיה   [רו]חמה[121] ליפי מראיה
(5 [ ]מבינים כי לפיא רוחות ית[כ]נו   תכנתה ביחד רוחמה
(6 [כ]ול מומיה ספר לו ובגויתיה הבינה[ו
(7 נגף באפלה[122]   [ל[123]] [תהיה לו כמכשול לפניו]
(8 [ ]כ[שלון[124] ו[נגפו וחרה אפו בס]ן
(9 עם משקל תכינה רוחם בש]
(10 ל[ו]א יכשול בה ואם ינגף ב]ה[125]
(11 ואם נפרדה בהריתכה קח מו[ן]לדיה
(12 התהלכה התבונן מואדה אם זכר[126]
(13 מכוניה לוא תמצא באלה בחנהה[ן   א[○○]

---

[121] *DJD XXXIV*, pp. 57-58, the editors consider two possible reconstructions of חמ[. Although they reconstruct רו[חמה they also consider חמה ('the sun'). רוחמה would then occur three times in this fragment.

[122] The editors reconstruct כיא נגף at the end of line 6, TIGCHELAAR reconstructs נגף באפלה at the end of line 7 from 4Q418 167a 7, *To Increase Learning*, pp. 36-37.

[123] The editors reconstruct באופל ('darkness' or 'iniquity') as the first word of this line, TIGCHELAAR, *To Increase Learning*, p. 37, raises a number of convincing reasons why this reconstruction is problematic. See also comments in *DJD XXXIV*, pp. 58, 61.

[124] The editors reconstruct שלח נגפו 'he sends forth His blow' here.

[125] Reconstruction mine.

[126] *DJD XXXIV*, p. 58 reconstruct אם זכר[ן ואם נקבה. In the photographs the *kaf* and part of the *resh* are visible, however, there is no *zion*. If זכר is reconstructed, which is uncertain, another suitable translation would be 'if he remembers'. The editors translate 'if male or female' based partly on their reconstruction זכר את נ]קבה in 4Q415 9 line 7.

4) that are not together[*their spirit* to the beauty of *her* appearance [

5) understanding one, for according to spirits they will be est[ablished   you established them together *by*[127] their spirit[

6) all her faults tell him and in her *bodily defects* let [him] understand[

7) [   ], she will be an obstacle before him[stumbling in her iniquity

8) they staggered and stumbled and his anger burned against[

9) with a weight their spirit is established [

10) he will not stagger in her and if he stumble[in her

11) and when she is separated in your *instruction* (?), understand [her] origins

12) her *way of* going understand exceedingly, if a male[

13) her *foundations* you will not find, in these examine her[128]

According to Qimron, as the editors quote in DJD 34, this fragment 'can be interpreted as having one common theme, giving advice to the addressee (cf. l. 6) on one subject, namely on his marrying off his daughter'.[129] One point of comparison is found with 1QS ix lines 12-16 where the maven weighs the sons of Zadok 'according to their spirits' as is the case of the woman here.[130] The phrase תכן ביחד רוחם, Qimron suggests in light of 1QS ix, should be understood as referring to a public examination of the would be bride. Another parallel is with 4Q271 3 lines 7-9, a fragment of the *Damascus Document* that is inspired by Deuteronomy 27.18, and reads 'if [a man gives his daughter to someone], he should recount all her blemishes to him, lest he bring upon himself judgement'. The details of her blemishes (מומיה) in the following lines of 4Q271 3 are related to sexual promiscuity and a bad reputation before marriage.[131]

Several issues may be raised about Qimron and the editors' interpretation of this column. First, the phrase תכן ביחד רוחם (l. 5) should not be taken as a reference to a *public* examination of the would-be bride (i.e. the addressee's daughter), but rather read 'you established them together'. The editors note the usage at times of the term ביחד meaning 'in public assembly', but the most

---

[127] Perhaps 'established them together, their spirit' .

[128] Compare with the translation in *DJD XXXIV*; p. 59: (4) which are not *together*...And *their spirit* to the beauty of its appearance...(5) understanding ones, For *according to* the spirits will they be me[asured *out*...Thou has measured out *their* spirit in *public* (?)...(6) [A]ll *her* blemishes recount thou to *him*, And make [him] understand *her bodily defects. And it will be when he stubs his foot* (7) in the da[rk]ness, [The]n *she* will (not?) be for him like a stumbling block in front of him...[And God] (8) [will] *send forth[*]His *blow*, And His anger will burn *against*...(9) with a *weight* their spirit *will be meted out* in[...(10) he will n[o]t stumble *against it*. And if *he* stub *against*[...(11) If *she be divided* (?) when she is pregnant for thee, Take thou *the offs[pring of her*...(12) her *walking* consider very diligently. If male or female...(13) *her* foundations thou shalt not find. *By* these things test *her*....

[129] *DJD XXXIV*, p. 59.

[130] The closest and only substantial parallel is: 1QS ix 14 לפי רוחום (l. 5 לפיא רוחות).

[131] The editors comment that 'to read מומיה "her blemishes or faults" does not at first glance improve the parallelism with גויתיה "corpses", but a later meaning of גויות "her bodily defects" (recorded by Jastrow), produces an excellent parallel'; *DJD XXXIV*, p. 60.

common use of the term is as 'together'.[132] The term ביחד also occurs in line 4 ('not together') preceding a statement about their spirit and the 'beauty of her appearance' (cf. 4Q415 9 line 7 יחד ממשל זכר את נ]קבה). It could be that lines 4-5 are concerned with how a husband and wife are established together: (1) line 4 addresses issues of the physical beauty of the would be wife (מראיה); and (2) line 5 underscores that it is according to their spirits they are established together. Line 6 then could be understood as an exhortation to a father to tell a future son-in-law about the imperfections of his daughter.[133]

Line 7 could then be read as a warning to the would be son-in-law that his wife will be an obstacle to him. Line 8 may be read as recounting an interpretation of Eden, that man and woman staggered and stumbled because of the woman's deficiency (l. 6). Women are faulted and their character construed based upon a misogynistic reading of the woman in the garden. The end of line 8 recounts the anger of perhaps man or God.

Line 9 repeats the idea of a husband and wife being established (together?) in the statement 'with a weight their spirit is established'. The imagery of weights occurs only two other times in *Musar leMevin*. 4Q418 127 6 uses weights and 'establishment' together as does this column:

5) ...כי אל עשה כול חפצי אוט ויתכנם באמת]

6) ...כ]י במוזני צדק שקל כול תכינם[134] ובאמת]ו

5) ...for God made all the delights of אוט and He established them in truth[

6) ...f]or by righteous measures He weighs all of their establishment and by truth[

Both in line 9 and 4Q418 127 6 the language of weighing and establishing has the connotation of formation and creation.

Line 10 continues with language of staggering and stumbling. The preceding line may have provided instruction that would prevent the addressee from being hindered by his wife. Line 10b would then envision circumstances in which a wife could be a stumbling block.

Line 11 speaks of the woman's separation (נפרדה)[135] from, perhaps, her parents to her husband and is followed by the obscure term בהריתכה. The

---

[132] The word יחד occurs nine times in *Musar leMevin* adverbially, but never as a noun that could be understood as a reference to a sectarian community.

[133] Her faults and defects could be related to perceived weaknesses of the female, this could pertain to issues of purity laws that are more exhaustive for females than males (e.g. 4Q266 2 ii; 4Q284; 4Q265; 4Q274; 11Q19 xlviii 14-17).

[134] *DJD XXXIV*, p. 257 reconstruct תכונם. הכין as 'preparing' or תכן meaning to 'establish' or 'arrange'.

[135] The editors suggest the word פרח ('bloom' or 'fly') as an alternative reading, however the word does have a *niph'al* form (נפרחה). TIGCHELAAR states that the *dalet* of the word is 'certain'; *DJD XXXIV*, p. 38.

notions of being established together and separated could possibly reflect the woman's separation from her parents and joining with her husband (Gen 2.20-25). The description of a woman leaving her parents and becoming one flesh with her husband has already been noted in the document. This is undoubtedly the case in 4Q416 2 iii line 21 where we read בהתחברכה יחד ('in your being joined together').

The editors question whether the term בהריתכה should go with the preceding or following colon and question how the term should be rendered. The editors read הרה√ ('conceive', 'be pregnant'), however, קח מולדיה should not be understood as 'take her offspring', but rather 'understand her birth-times'. If this is the case, might not הוריה√ ('instruction', 'decision') be preferred in this context?[136] The editors translate the term in the infinitive and reconstruct the following 'קח מון' as קח מון]לדיה ("when she is pregnant for thee, Take thou the offspring of her"). The reconstruction of מולדי is likely given that the 2nd masculine singular imperative קח occurs on three other occasions with the term מולדי in *Musar leMevin*. The three other occurrences of this combination of קח מולדי indicate that a better translation is 'comprehend the origins/birth-time of' (see esp. 4Q415 2 ii 9 and 4Q416 2 iii 20; also 4Q417 2 i 11: וקח מולדי ישע ודע מי נוחל כבוד ועמל; cf. 4Q418 202 1; 4Q416 2 iii 9). The context in 4Q415 11 itself suggests understanding מולדים as a reference to birth-times.

The word הרה√ occurs seven times in *Musar leMevin* almost every time in a context related to women. Excluding 4Q416 9 line 1 which is a single word fragment and two occurrences that overlap (4Q416 2 iii 17; 4Q418 9 18) the remaining five occurrences are translated by Harrington and Strugnell as follows:

4Q415 9 2 'that thy (masc.) womb (i.e. wife) should conceive for you'
4Q415 9 2 להורות בטנכה לכ]ה

4Q415 11 11 'If *she be divided* (?) when she is pregnant for thee'
4Q415 11 11 ואם נפרדה בהריתכה

4Q416 2 iii 17 'they are "the womb that was pregnant with thee"'
4Q416 2 iii 17 המה כור הוריכה

4Q416 9 1 '*on her that is pregnant. . .*'
4Q416 9 1 [בהורת]

4Q423 1, 2 i 5 '...and all the compassion of her that is pregnant'
4Q423 1, 2 i 5 [י]לדה וכל רחמי הורת

4Q423 3 3 'On His word every [womb will bear]'
4Q423 3 3 ועל פיהו הרתה כל] רחם

---

[136] See also GARCÍA MARTÍNEZ and TIGCHELAAR, p. 847, they render the word on most occasions as הוריה. *DJD XXXIV*, p. 62 comment that the two substantive options are 'your pregnant wife' or 'your mother' and the infinitive renderings. In translating the term בהריתכה as an infinitive, they comment '(understanding a 3rd fem. sing. subject from נפרדה), could mean either "when she becomes pregnant with thee" (masculine suffix of a direct object) or better "when she becomes pregnant for thee"'

The form of √הרה is not clear in most of these passages. The suffix -כה is particularly difficult, note in 4Q415 11 line 11 and 4Q416 2 iii line 17 the struggle to translate 'for thee' and 'with thee'. 4Q415 9 line 2, discussed below, could be translated 'to instruct your wife for['. Perhaps forms of both √הרה and הוריה√ occur in *Musar leMevin*.

Line 13 of the column informs the addressee that he will not find the woman's 'foundations' (מכוניה) and exhorts him to test her.[137] The term מכון could be variously rendered as 'place', 'habitation', 'foundation', 'fixed place', or 'establishment'. This could be an expression of how elusive an understanding of the nature of women is for the addressee. Despite being unable to find her elusive foundations the addressee is nonetheless encouraged to understand the nature of women and even examine her. The occurrence of the female's foundations touches again upon the motif of woman's creation and nature.

4Q415 11 is fundamentally concerned with instructing the addressee as a father or would be son-in-law how to deal with a situation of giving away a daughter or taking a wife. Instruction is derived from meditation on the woman in Eden traditions and takes up themes related to establishment of woman (and man together) and her separation from her parents and joining with her husband. Women are also negatively portrayed as posing a potential risk to their husbands and men are cautioned and informed about this possibility.

5.2 4Q415 9

Fragment 4Q415 9, discussed previously in reference to male dominion over the female, shares several motifs that arise in 4Q415 11. This small fragment reads:

(1) [ ] [תתממהמה]

(2) להורות בטנכה לכ]ה

(3) שומ[ן [תרב]

(4) אנשים *vacat* [

(5) עם אולת לוא תשוה לרישן כה[138]

(6) בה הכינה כיא היאה תכון]

(7) יחד ממשל זכר את נ]קבה

(8) רוחה המשל בה כ]ן

(9) ומחסורמה זה מז]ן]ה

---

[137] Though *Musar leMevin* is not to be located among 'Essene' and 'sectarian documents' a statement made by Josephus that the Essenes 'put their wives to the test for a period of three years' (*Bellum* 2 161) is suggestive of the occurrence 'testing' here.

[138] The editors read 'רוש[ן' ('leader') here; *DJD XXXIV*, p. 54.

ולפי זה [(10
נקבה וכמוני[(11

1) [ ] you will delay [
2) to instruct your wife for [
3) --
4) men *vacat* [
5) with foolishness do not compare [your] poverty
6) on it he has established her for it is the foundation[
7) together, male ruling fe[male
8) her spirit, male having dominion over the f[emale
9) and in their lacking, one from anoth[er
10) and according to this [
11) female, and as the scales of [

Similarities between 4Q415 9 and 4Q415 11 are: (1) the occurrence of the term √הרה or √הוריה (frg. 9 l. 2; frg. 11 l. 11); (2) the occurrence of 'foundations' in both (frg. 9 l. 6 תכון; frg. 11 l. 5 תכנתה and יתן]כנו); (3) the use of the term √יחד in reference to male and female; (4) the use of the term √רוח (רוחה frg. 9 l. 8; רוחות/רוחמה frg. 11 ll. 4-5 and 9); (5) the possible occurrence of זכר in both (frg. 9 l. 7; frg. 11 l. 12); and (6) the use of language related to measurements in both (frg. 9 l. 11 כמוני; frg. 11 l. 1 כמוני, l. 3 משקל, l. 9 לאיפה ואיפה לעומר ועומר).

In 4Q415 9 line 9 is the occurrence of מחסור, which suggests a rendering of ריש ('poverty') in line 5 rather than רוש.[139] Furthermore, the most extensive allusions to Genesis 2-3 and woman in *Musar leMevin* are introduced with comments regarding poverty (4Q416 2 iii ll. 19-20 ואם רש אתה; אשה לקחתה ברישכה). Harrington and Strugnell translate line 5 as 'a foolish *people thou shalt* not treat as equal to a leader'. עם as 'with', √שוה as 'compare', and ריש as poor allow: 'with folly you will not compare [your] poverty'.[140] In this case, the phrase זה מזה following מחסור in line 9 continue in the same stream of thought as the exhortation to 'not compare' in line 5.

Line 6 expresses the laying of women's establishment. Dominion of the male over the female in lines 7-8 are expressed in relationship to the nature of the female. However, how does the theme of male ruling over female and the establishment of women relate to the surrounding theme of comparing one's poverty? Both men and women could be portrayed as being anthropologically impoverished. The negative portrayal of women, especially in 4Q415 11, indicates that women could lack even more than men. Lines 5 and 9 may be

---

[139] 4Q415 6 line 3 has the identical term רישכה, which is preceded in line 2 by the phrase אביון אתה ומלכים.

[140] In regard to the term אולת here, an interesting use of this word occurs in 4Q418 243 line 2]ורבת אולת[('*woman* abounding in folly').

exhortations not to foolishly compare the degree of negative differences that
exist between males and females. If this is indeed the case, and shame is
related to poverty, the description of a wife in 4Q416 2 iv as 'wife of your
bosom, for she is the flesh of your ערוה ('shame')' and 'wife of your bosom
and your shame' is better understood.

The translation of line 2 as 'to instruct your wife' has implications for
reading 4Q415 2 ii. How is one to understand instruction to a woman in the
2nd person feminine singular? One option is that some women either listened
to *Musar leMevin* being read aloud or perhaps even read it themselves. A
more likely possibility is that the address to a woman in 4Q415 2 ii is an
example of how the addressee was to instruct his wife, that is: *teach your wife
thusly*.[141] The issues that 4Q415 2 ii, 4Q415 9 and 4Q415 11 are concerned
with are similar. They are concerned with how men relate to women. The
behaviour expected of each is derived from reflecting on certain aspects of an
interpretation of Genesis creation narratives.

5.3 4Q418 126 i-ii

4Q418 126 i-ii is a somewhat obscure fragment that has received almost no
comment outside of DJD 34.[142] This fragment survives in 16 lines with
substantial damage to the left side and none of the lines survive intact. As a
whole, the column addresses issues of condemnation and judgement of the
wicked and redemption and attainment for the poor. In general the column
would appear to depict a division that will take place between 'children of
life' (רוח חיים, l. 8) and 'workers of iniquity' (l. 6). Line 9 opens with the
phrase כול בני חוה ('all the children of Eve'). Comprehending what this phrase
might possibly denote is complicated by several factors. First, the surrounding
context, both the immediately preceding and following lines, are not entirely
certain. Second, the phrase does not occur elsewhere in either the Hebrew
Bible or Dead Sea Scrolls. Lastly, it may even be possible to read the final
word of the phrase as the noun חיה ('life') rather than חוה. More important
than investigating what is meant by the phrase is adjudicating the likelihood
that this is a reference to 'Eve' and therefore an allusion to the first woman in
Genesis.

The Hebrew name 'Eve' (חוה) occurs only twice in the Hebrew Bible (Gen
3.20; 4.1) and nowhere else in early Jewish Hebrew literature.[143] Likewise,

---

[141] Or perhaps daughter. In 4Q415 2 ii 3 the phrase 'in his bosom', could use the 3rd
masculine suffix as a reference to the would-be husband if the father is addressing his
daughter about marriage.

[142] See A. CAQUOT, 'Les textes de Sagesse de Qoumrân (Aperçu Préliminaire),' in *RHPR*
76 (1996): 1-34.

[143] There is one occurrence in *Hekhalot* literature (א66 v §79 line 7) 'you reveal this
mystery to the son of man born of woman... they have been created: heaven and earth, sea
and dry land, mountains and hills, rivers and springs and their sources and fire and hail and

neither the phrase 'sons of life' or 'sons of Eve' occur in the Hebrew literature. In the Septuagint 'Eve' is translated with two terms: Ζωη (Gen 3.20) and Ευαν (Gen 4.1). In the New Testament and Apocrypha 'Eve' is spoken of only by the name Ευα (2 Cor 11.3; 1 Tim 2.13; Tob 8.6). The closest parallel to 'sons of Eve' is likely in the *Similitudes of Enoch* (62.7).[144] In the *Similitudes* the Ethiopic expression '*walda 'eg^wula- 'emmaheyyāw*' is used. Although this expression is used generally of a human being or 'Son of Man', similar to the Ethiopic term '*walda sab'e*', it literally means 'offspring of the mother of the living'. Isaacs comments that the 'first person to be described as "the mother of the living" in the Bible is Eve, so Eth[iopic] grammarians sometimes interpret the expression "offspring of Eve"'.[145] If the expression in *Similitudes* 62.7, referring to the Son of Man, and 4Q418 126 i-ii line 9 are comparable, the implication might be that this singular occurrence of 'sons of Eve' in *Musar leMevin* could be rendered similarly to *1 Enoch* as 'person' or 'son of people'.

If 4Q418 126 i-ii line 9 is translated as 'sons of Eve' (בני חוה) rather than 'sons of life' (בני חיה) it may also have negative connotations. Preceding lines 7-9 are reconstructed, supplemented and translated by Harrington and Strugnell as:

7) And to shut (the door) on (i.e. imprison) the wicked, But to raise up the head of the poor, [*And to show forth His faithfulness to them, And His mercies*]

8) In glory everlasting and peace eternal, and to separate the spirit of life (רוח חיים) [*from every spirit of darkness*]

9) all the children of *Eve*. And on the might of God and the abundance of His glory Together with His bounty [*they shall muse*][146]

These lines contrast two types of people. Line 7 sets the wicked opposite of the poor. Line 8 may portray the 'spirit of life' against a group such as the '*spirit of darkness*'. In line 8 there may have been an occurrence of a designation for a group of people that the 'children of Eve' were set against. It is unknown whether 'sons of Eve' was considered a negative or positive label. It may, for instance, be synonymous with the 'spirit of life' in line 8. Another

---

the garden of Eden and the tree of life and fashioned in it were Adam and Eve (חוה) and beasts and creatures of the field and birds of the sky…' (translation mine). The traditions surrounding Eve that could be considered relevant here are very limited. *The Life of Adam and Eve*, *Genesis Apocryphon* and *Eve's Testament* in the *Apocalypse of Moses* are by far the most extensive works from early Judaism that include Eve, however they contain almost nothing from the first three chapters of Genesis. Eve is also mentioned in *1 Enoch* 69.6; *2 Enoch* 31.6; *Apoc. Abraham* 23.1; *b. Td. Yeb.* 103b; *Ab. Zar.* 22b; and *Shab.* 146a. Secondary literature devoted solely to Eve in early Judaism is almost non-existent.

[144] See CAQUOT, 'Les texts,' pp. 1-9.

[145] J. H. CHARLESWORTH (ed.), *The Old Testament Pseudepigrapha: Volume One* (New York: Doubleday, 1983) p. 43.

[146] *DJD XXXIV*, p. 352. The supplements italicised in brackets are offered only in English.

possibility is that the author(s) conceived of the first woman negatively in some respects. In this case, the epithet 'sons of Eve' could be a description of humanity similar to the wicked of line 7 and the '*spirit of darkness*' in line 8.

6. Conclusions

The portrayal of the female in *Musar leMevin* is largely based upon allusions to Genesis 2-3. It has been suggested that issues of the woman's origin, 'shame', her analogous association with angels, and her subjugation to her husband all aid in establishing relations between wives and husbands as well as other family members in the document. Sapiential instruction in the document is framed within a context of cosmological and anthropological concerns, both for the male addressee and the female addressee. Among the documents from the Dead Sea Scrolls that address the ethics and conduct of women[147] *Musar leMevin* is unique in that it offers this particularly nuanced basis for behaviour. The manner in which both wives and husbands live with and think about one another is derived from the nature of their creation. Conceptions of 'shame' originate with Eden stories and at times reflect the anthropology of women and men. Categories such as 'origins', 'shame' and even 'poverty' spill over into broader cosmological concerns and issues for the addressee. The implications of these observations could affect an understanding of other motifs in the document, such as exhortations to pursue the רז נהיה.

Allusions to Genesis 1-3 provide a foundation for instructing the addressees how to behave generally. In the case of 4Q416 2 iii it is connected to honouring one's parents. In 4Q416 2 iv and elsewhere, it serves to elaborate upon relations between man and woman. The cosmos has been established in a certain way and more general instruction need not at every point allude directly to creation traditions from Genesis. The רז נהיה is conceivably a mystery that stems from notions of cosmology and, therefore, creation. The universe, its origins and function, serve as a basis for which more general instruction might be constructed.

The רז נהיה could point back to everything that God has established and alluding to Genesis 2-3 for female and male relations and the origin of woman is indicative of the assumption that the רז נהיה is the 'mystery of existence'. Issues regarding the female open a window to larger concerns within the document. The instruction of the author(s) is not negotiable; God has set up the universe in a specific way and proper behaviour must follow this pattern.

---

[147] See for example CD iv 20-21; v 9-11; vii 6-7, xi 1-2; 4Q271 3 7-15; 1QM viii 3ff.; 1QSa; 11Q19 lvii 17-19; 4Q159 2-4; 4Q397 5 lines 1-5; 4Q513 2 ii; 4Q251 7; 4Q284 and 4Q502.

In the case of the woman, she is to act according to her creation and origins and likewise the man. In seeking the mystery of existence, the truth and wisdom surrounding creation, one might manifest on earth the proper conduct revealed therein. The multiple allusions to Genesis in *Musar leMevin* provide valuable insight into the רז נהיה and reveal that cosmology, anthropology and creation are part of the very fabric of wisdom in the document.

Sapiential instruction in *Musar leMevin* is concerned with worldly wisdom based upon a heavenly order of the cosmos. This wisdom, more specifically, is often derived from reflections on creation traditions. The addressees are repeatedly exhorted to seek the רז נהיה, which is a meditation on creation. How the addressees conceive of their relationship with angels, for instance, stems from the role angelic beings played in human creation. Likewise, women are to reflect on their own creation based upon their own birth-times. However, women are also participants in the act of creation, which, it may be argued, is analogous to angelic participation in the creation of humankind. The origin of women is used to exhort the male addressee on how he is to relate to his wife as well.

As we have seen, *Musar leMevin* has in mind addressees who are burdened with difficult issues of usury and debt. The insistence on the poverty of the addressees, though at times in a context concerned with material poverty, may be seen against a heavenly reality. Poverty is multivalent. The impoverishment of the addressees is presupposed first on the basis of a more general anthropological lacking, in terms of wisdom, and second on the basis of economic hardship. Exhortations to pursue the mystery of existence is foundational for overcoming this lacking. One comes closer to understanding the mystery when one comprehends how created beings relate one to the other. Even in terms of agricultural language and instruction in the document, the addressee dwells metaphorically in an Edenic garden. Just as poverty language transcends the material, so too practical advice to the farmer. Just as sapiential and apocalyptic are interwoven in *Musar leMevin*, some motifs may be understood in a straightforward earthly manner or a somewhat esoteric and otherworldly way.

7. Excurses: Implications for the New Testament

Observations and conclusions on the female in *Musar leMevin* might further elucidate three New Testament passages referred to in the preceding discussion on women in *Musar leMevin* (1 Tim 2; Eph 5; 1 Cor 11). On the one hand, the significance of *Musar leMevin* for these passages may be as simple as providing an earlier exegetical tradition that these later New Testament authors preserve. A particular exegesis of the first woman Eve in the document serves as a foundation for providing instruction for behaviour. Familial codes, the proper place of parents, fathers, mothers, husbands, wives, and children in the document are organised around their creation. Likewise, on a few occasions in the New Testament a similar tradition based upon Genesis 2 is the basis for instructing families, especially men and women. On the other hand, instruction for and about women based upon Genesis 2-3 in *Musar leMevin* might serve to suggest an exegetical tradition that provides details that clarify or enhance analogies, metaphors or illustrations at play in the New Testament.

The following is a brief expansion upon similar and dissimilar motifs that occur in the New Testament passages and *Musar leMevin*.

1 Timothy 2.11-15. A comparison between 1 Timothy 2 and *Musar leMevin* reveals that their exegesis of Genesis 2 is more dissimilar than similar in regard to details. However, a few significant general similarities can be observed. First, both refer to the origin and sequence of the genders to instruct on proper relations between male and female (1 Tim 2.13 'Adam was formed first and then Eve'). Second, similar in both is the authority of men over women based upon Genesis 2 (cf. 1 Tim 2.12; 4Q415 9 7-8; 4Q418a 18 4). Third, both attribute a certain fault or negative quality to women for Eve's role in Eden ('wife of your bosom and shame' 4Q416 2 iv 13), in the case of 1 Timothy 'transgression' (2.14): 'Adam was not deceived but the woman was deceived and became a transgressor' (δὲ γυνὴ ἐξαπατηθεῖσα ἐν παραβάσει γέγονεν). Neither 1 Timothy nor *Musar leMevin* present an entirely positive view of the female in their use of Genesis 2, however, this does not suggest that 'shame' and 'transgression' are similarly understood by the two works.

1 Timothy 2.15 describes the salvation, due to her deception and transgression, of females as coming from child bearing, faith, love, holiness and modesty. However, *Musar leMevin* does not conceive of salvation, but rather of humanity as divided already into two groups ('people of spirit' and 'spirit of flesh'); one group already stands condemned and the other will inherit glory (each varying in degree). *Musar leMevin* instead exhorts the addressee not to 'despise [אל תבוז] the wife of your bosom' and to live properly with her.

In regard to dissimilarities between 1 Timothy 2 and *Musar leMevin*, 1 Timothy's 'transgression' in relation to the woman's deception in Genesis 2 and subsequent fall of humanity is a wholly inadequate and inappropriate idea to use related to *Musar leMevin*. Conversely, 1 Timothy 2.14 likely envisages a fall as indicated in his use of the terms 'deception' and 'transgression'. Therefore, while a similarity exists between the two in attributing something negative to women based upon a Genesis tradition, whether 'shame' or 'transgression', the actual fault of woman is conceived of in different ways. It is not clear that the fault of Eve in *Musar leMevin* is disobedience or transgression, she may be understood as in some way hindering the addressees in pursuing and acquiring mysteries and learning.

Ephesians 5.21-33. The contribution of *Musar leMevin* to the background of Ephesians 5.21-33 is twofold: (1) the extent to which a form critical analysis of household codes in Greco-Roman literature should be seen as influencing verses 21-33 may be reconsidered; and (2) the ongoing debate on how to interpret the metaphor between Adam and Eve, and Christ and church in these verses may be elucidated by the observations made above. Though much could be said in relation to both of these points, the comments below only summarise possible contributions.

Martin Dibelius first suggested that Greco-Roman *Haustafeln* were adopted by New Testament authors.[148] Particularly, the writings of Aristotle, Plutarch and Seneca preserve a form of household codes that provide conventional advice to heads of households (husbands and masters). New Testament authors, unlike Graeco-Roman authors, adapt this form to include subordinates (e.g. wives, children and slaves) in their addresses. Since Dibelius, others have taken up this theory and argued that New Testament household codes have their origin, with various nuances, in Graeco-Roman sources.[149] *Musar leMevin* provides new evidence for a background to the household code in Ephesians 5. In both Ephesians and *Musar leMevin* exegetical traditions are preserved that reflects upon creation as a source for instructing various subordinates how to conduct themselves. *Musar leMevin* does not necessarily reflect a dependence upon the Graeco-Roman *Haustafeln* form for instructing husbands and wives. Ephesians 5, though sharing similarities with the *Haustafel* form, has far more in common with *Musar leMevin* and it is reasonable to speculate that Paul was familiar with a Jewish tradition such as we find here. Therefore, in the case of Ephesians, based upon instruction found in *Musar leMevin*, an alternative background in early Jewish literature may be proposed.

Second, the language about the body in Ephesians 5.21-33 draws on an analogy based directly upon notions of the first man Adam and his wife Eve. This relationship illuminates the relationship between Christ and the church as derived from Genesis 2.24-3.1. Interpretations of this metaphor have been the

---

[148] M. DIBELIUS, *An die Kolosser, Epheser, an Philemon, 3rd revised edition*, (ed.), H. GREEVEN (Tübingen: Mohr, 1953).

[149] J. A. D. WEIMA, 'What does Aristotle have to do with Paul? An Evaluation of Rhetorical Criticism,' in *BBR* 5 (1995): 177-198; M. GIELEN, *Tradition und Theologie neutestamentlicher Haustafelethik* (BBB 75; Frankfurt am Main: Anton Hain, 1990); D. BALCH, *Let Wives be Submissive: The Domestic Code in 1 Peter* (Chico: Scholars Press, 1981); J. E. CROUCH, *The Origin and Intention of the Colossian Haustafel* (FRLANT 109; Göttingen: Vandenhoeck & Ruprecht, 1972).

subject of much scholarly discussion.[150] If Paul is drawing upon a tradition similar to *Musar leMevin* the implications for interpreting Ephesians 5.21-33 would be significant. For instance, one heavily contested issue is the rendering of the term κεφαλή in 5.23 as either 'source' or 'authority over'.[151] If Ephesians 5 is located in a history of traditions that emphasises the beginning of woman from man at creation, and subsequently instructs husbands and wives on this basis, then reading the term 'head' as 'source' would likely be the sense here. Since man is the *source* of woman, so also Christ is the *source* of the church.[152] While the debate has centred exclusively upon issues of language, *Musar leMevin* provides a tradition history that Ephesians 5.23 may be viewed against.

Another contribution of *Musar leMevin* to Ephesians 5.21-33 may be for understanding the great μυστήριον in verse 32.[153] In verse 28 husbands are exhorted to love their wives as 'their own bodies' and in verse 29 'for no one ever hated his own flesh'. Then in verse 30 the analogy between the source of Eve coming from Adam is likened to the church coming from Christ: 'for we [the church] are part of his body [Christ], part of his flesh and bone'. In verse 31 is a direct quotation of Genesis 2.25. The 'great mystery' of this is debatable; however, in light of *Musar leMevin* we may reflect on creation and

---

[150] See for example the works of G. W. DAWES, *The Body in Question: Metaphor and Meaning in the Interpretation of Ephesians 5:21-33* (BIS 30; Leiden: Brill, 1998); K. H. FLECKENSTEIN, *Ordnet euch einander unter in der Furcht Christi: Die Eheperikope in Eph. 5,21-33: Geschichte der Interpretation, Analyse und Aktualisierung des Textes* (Würzburg: Echter Verlag, 1994); S. F. MILITIC, *'One Flesh': Eph 5.22-24, 5.31: Marriage and the New Creation* (Rome: Pontifical Biblical Institute, 1988); J. P. SAMPLEY, *"'And the Two Will Become One Flesh': A Study in Eph 5.21-33* (SNTSMS 16; Cambridge: Cambridge University Press, 1971).

[151] For example see: R. S. CERVIN, 'Does κεφαλή Mean "Source" or "Authority Over" in Greek Literature,' in *TJ* (1989): 85-112; C. C. KROEGER, 'The Classical Concept of *Head* as "Source",' in G. G. HULL (ed.), *Equal to Serve* (London: Scripture Union, 1987) pp. 267-83; W. GRUDEM, 'Does κεφαλή ("Head") Mean "Source" or "Authority Over" in Greek Literature? A Survey of 2336 Examples,' in *TJ* (1985): 38-59; S. BADALE, 'The Meaning of κεφαλή in the Pauline Epistles,' in *JTS* (1954): 211-15.

[152] See my 'Reconsidering an Aspect,' article for implications of dual creators on Christ and God in 1 Cor 8.5.

[153] Too many works have been written on Eph 5.32 to mention here. Commentators have variously looked at Eph 3.9 and 6.19 for the background of 5.32 as well as the in Qumran literature (cf. 1QpH vii 1-5). See for example: M. N. A. BOCKMUEHL, *Revelation and Mystery in Ancient Judaism and Pauline Christianity* (WUNT2 36; Tübingen: J. C. B. Mohr Paul Siebeck, 1990) p. 204; F. F. BRUCE, *The Epistle to the Colossians, to Philemon and the Ephesians* (Grand Rapids: Eerdmans, 1984) pp. 394-95; C. C. CARAGOUNIS, *The Ephesian 'Mysterion': Meaning and Content* (CBNTS 8; Upsala: CWK Gleerup, 1977); M. BARTH, *Ephesians* (New York: Doubleday, 1974) p. 643; J. COPPENS, '"Mystery" in the Theology of St. Paul and its Parallels at Qumran', in J. MURPHY-O'CONNOR (ed.), *Paul at Qumran: Studies in New Testament Exegesis* (London: Chapman, 1968) p. 146; J. CAMBIER, 'Le grand mystère concernant le Christ et son Eglise: Ephesians 5,22-33,' in *Biblica* 47 (1966): 43-90.

derivations of both women and men in relation to the רז נהיה ('mystery of existence'). The division of male and female as well as the union between them (i.e. the female being separated for man and then reunited) based upon Genesis 2 could, in and of itself, be a mystery in *Musar leMevin*. The use of this mystery in an analogy with Christ and the church may deepen the sense of the mystery but is not necessarily the mystery itself. The term 'mystery' occurs in Ephesians 3.9 and 6.19 as well. While 6.19 may be of little help in deciphering the intent of Paul in 5.32, in 3.9 it is: 'to make everyone see what is the plan of the mystery hidden for ages in God who created all things'.

1 Corinthians 11.2-16. The contributions of reading 1 Corinthians 11.2-16 in light of *Musar leMevin* are: (1) the background of the metaphor of male and female creation as derived from Genesis may be more broadly elucidated;[154] (2) reading the term 'head' in 11.3-4 may be better understood as 'source';[155] (3) subsequently, the sense of the term ἐξουσία may be understood as 'authority over'; (4) the term 'shame' may be considered in light of 'shame' in *Musar leMevin*; and (5) the phrase 'on account of the angels' may, possibly, be read in light of angelology and creation in the document.[156] *Musar leMevin* shares a number of thematic overlaps with 1 Corinthians 11.2-16 and, like Ephesians 5, may hold keys to a fresh interpretation of these verses.

---

[154] The overwhelming number of works that attempt to explicate these verses are too many to list here. For a selection of works, outside of commentaries, that deal specifically with 1 Cor 11.2-16 see: J. M. GUNDRY-VOLF, 'Gender and Creation in 1 Cor. 11:2-16: A Study in Paul's Theological Method,' in J. ADNA, S. J. HAFEMANN and O. HOFIUS (eds.), *Evangelium, Schriftauslegung, Kirche : Festschrift für Peter Stuhlmacher* (Göttingen: Vandenhoeck & Ruprecht, 1997) pp. 151-71; D. B. MARTIN, *The Corinthian Body* (New Haven: Yale University Press, 1995) pp. 229-49; L. A. JERVIS, '"But I Want You to Know...": Paul's Midrashic Intertextual Response to the Corinthian Worshippers (1 Cor. 11:2-16),' in *JBL* 112 (1993): 231-46; G. P. CARRINGTON, 'The "Headless Woman": Paul and the Language of the Body in 1 Cor. 11:2-16,' in *PRS* 18 (1991): 223-31; J. MURPHY-O'CONNOR, 'Sex and Logic in 1 Cor. 11:2-16,' in *CBQ* 42 (1980): 482-500; W. O. WALKER, '1 Cor. 11:2-16 and Paul's Views Regarding Women,' in *JBL* 94 (1975): 94-110; L. COPE, '1 Cor. 11:2-16: One Step Farther,' in *JBL* 97 (1978): 435-36; B. K. WALTKE, '1 Cor. 11:2-16: An Interpretation,' in *BSac* 135 (1978): 46-57; A. FEUILLET, 'L'Homme "gloire de Dieu" et la femme "gloire de l'homme" (1 Cor. XI:7b),' in *RB* 81 (1974): 161-82; W. J. MARTIN, '1 Cor. 11:2-16: An Interpretation', in W. W. GASQUE and R. P. MARTIN (eds.), *Apostolic History and the Gospel: Presented to F. F. Bruce* (Exeter: Paternoster, 1970) pp. 231-41.

[155] See: A. C. PERRIMAN, 'The Head of a Woman: The Meaning of in 1 Cor. 11:3,' in *JTS* 45 (1994): 602-22; J. A. FITZMYER, 'Another Look at κεφαλή in 1 Cor. 11:3,' in *NTS* 35 (1989): 503-11; P. S. FIDDES, '"Woman's Head is Man": A Doctrinal Reflection upon a Pauline Text,' in *Baptist Quarterly* 31 (1986): 370-83.

[156] See: R. S. CARLÈ, *Because of the Angels: Unveiling 1 Cor. 11:2-16* (Paraparaumu Beach: Emmaus, 1998); J. A. FITZMYER, 'A Feature of Qumran Angelology and the Angels of 1 Cor. 11:10,' in *NTS* 4 (1957-58): 48-58. FITZMYER's analysis of Qumran Angelology does not take into account the angelology of *Musar leMevin*.

1 Corinthians 11 is more explicit than *Musar leMevin*, 1 Timothy or Ephesians in detailing the origins of woman in contrast to the current order of creation. This theme is used to exhort men and women how to behave, here it is in regard to their manner of appearance when praying. The relations between men and women based upon Genesis 2.23-25 (and 1.26-27), like Ephesians 5, hold an analogy with Christ. However, in 1 Corinthians 11 it is a different analogy: Christ is the head of man in the same way man is the head of woman (in contrast to the metaphor in Eph that Christ = man, and church = woman). The analogy is that just as woman comes from man, so man comes from Christ, Christ from God (vs. 3) and everything ultimately from God (vs. 12). In *Musar leMevin* the formation of humanity in the image and likeness of God and angels is used to structure anthropological and cosmological conceptions (4Q417 1 i 15-18; 4Q416 2 iii 15-18). Likewise, the creation of woman plays a significant role in defining her present relationship to men.

Paul's argument in 1 Corinthians 11 assumes the audience possesses knowledge of an interpretive tradition, one which is not entirely known to the modern reader. While *Musar leMevin* cannot solve this puzzle it might add one piece; 1 Corinthian 11, like *Musar leMevin*, addresses the origin of woman and exhorts women to be covered. Perhaps the interrelated motifs of angels, men and women in *Musar leMevin* are distantly related to the tradition Paul alludes to and assumes of his readership.

While much more may be said about the relationship between these New Testament passages and *Musar leMevin*, the overwhelming literature surrounding these passages prevents a developed conversation here. This brief sketch of similarities between the New Testament and *Musar leMevin* reveals one significant point: *exegetical traditions of Genesis 1-3 were widespread in the first few centuries BCE and were a source for instructing various communities on how men and women should relate to one another as well as, at times, to God and angelic beings.* Most persistent in the literature reviewed is the use of Genesis 2.25 as a source of reflection on women. The creation and nature of women and wives, within the context of these allusions, may have subsequently been used in Ephesians and Corinthians in a metaphor with Christ and the church.

CHAPTER 6

Conclusions

The analysis of this study has led to several theological contributions. Theological observations made were done so from a sustained examination of creation traditions. The identification of non-explicit uses of traditions often entails a certain amount of imprecision and efforts have been made to broaden the discussion to more clearly identify non-explicit usages of traditions in *Musar leMevin*. The author(s) allude to known and unknown interpretations of Genesis 1-3. In order to recognise themes interrelated to these creation allusions issues of reconstruction and translation were addressed. Similar to identifying the use of non-explicit literary traditions, reading and rendering these fragments entails an element of speculation. However, despite these challenges, significant progress has been made in viewing how this document used creation traditions to formulate instruction.

Musar leMevin is attested by multiple manuscripts which survive in hundreds of fragments. Additionally, it has been suggested by others that there are various literary strata in *Musar leMevin* or that certain columns were composed separately from the remainder of the document. This study is concerned with reading the surviving fragments as representing a theologically cohesive document. Smaller more obscure fragments have been related to the larger and more discussed fragments. In so doing, some progress has been made in understanding how these fragments may relate to themes discussed in connection with Creation.

Attention to Genesis traditions in *Musar leMevin* offers several important insights regarding the angelology in the document. The participation of angelic beings in the creation of humanity in 4Q417 1 i lines 15-18 is a significant motif. It not only occurs in 4Q417 1 i, but also in 4Q416 2 iii lines 15-18. The addressees are expected to conceive of their relationship with angels in several ways: (1) they are to understand themselves as bearing a spiritual likeness with the angels and to act in accordance with it; (2) they venerate the angels as co-creators with God and as paradigmatic figures who seek and gain knowledge untiringly; (3) they have a share in an inheritance similar to that of the angels, an inheritance which is both present and future

(4Q416 2 iii); and (4) it is possible they conceive of the relationship between husband and wife on occasion as analogous to God and angels.

Musar leMevin is exceptional in its presentation of angelology. The document may be viewed as one of the most substantial works from early Judaism that displays a venerative attitude towards angelic beings (esp. 4Q418 81). The addressees conceive of themselves as presently relating to the angels in the heavenly realm and yet not sharing in their perfect state. The particular character of angel veneration in the document is found in providing reasons for this attitude: (1) angelic beings participated in creation; and (2) angelic beings presently serve as superior models of beings who pursue understanding. Whereas a document such as *Shirot 'Olat ha-Shabbat* envisages human and angelic worshippers coming together in the act of Sabbath praise, *Musar leMevin* conceives of the angels somewhat more distantly. While the addressees relate to angelic beings on one level, they are never seen as participating in a human event (e.g. as co-worshippers or as participants in a final eschatological battle; e.g. in *Sefer haMilhamah*).

Musar leMevin also applies unique language for angels. Both the terms אדנים and נדיבים have been seen to be used as terms for angelic beings. In the case of the term אדנים, *Musar leMevin* offers new evidence against which the Greek term κύριοι in early Judaism and nascent Christianity may be read. The identification of this term as an epithet for angels is cause for reconsidering the use of the title *kyrios* in some New Testament passages as a designation for angels.

Musar leMevin's witness to a tradition where members of a community venerated angelic beings is significant for ongoing discussions in early Angel Christology. Theories of angel veneration as the background for early Angel Christology are further substantiated by this study. While it is beyond the scope of this work to relate angelology to the larger discussion of Angel Christology, there can be little doubt of its importance for research taking place in this field.

Another important theological contribution of this research concerns the understanding of women. We have seen that instruction to husbands and their wives, daughters, and mothers are grounded in the text's allusions to creation. It may even be speculated that the woman's beginning from the side of man in *Musar leMevin* has an analogy with angelic beings and God. The derivative nature of the female from the male reflects on the cosmic created order, which is encapsulated by the expression רז נהיה. It may be that the רז נהיה serves as a replacement for traditional 'wisdom' and this-worldly sapiential instruction can itself be derived from this mystery.

Allusions to Genesis 2.25 as the foundation for instructing wives and husbands in *Musar leMevin* may be seen as a background for Ephesians 5 and 1 Corinthians 11. The use of a metaphor derived from the creation of woman in Genesis 2 in these New Testament passages has long been the focus of debate. *Musar leMevin* represents one interpretive tradition that suggests that the exegetical emphasis in the New Testament may be on understanding men as the source of women for establishing how they relate to one another.

Equally as important as creation allusions for establishing instruction for men and women in *Musar leMevin* is the address to a woman in 4Q415 2 ii. It may be questioned whether this address presupposes literacy on the part of females in the community. In this case the contribution of this column is not only theological, but historical as well. If we are to understand that 4Q415 2 ii was read by female members of a religious community then it is an exceptional discovery for studies on women in late antiquity. More likely, however, is that husbands were to instruct their wives who are perceived to be potential obstacles to their ultimate of goal of learning and grasping the 'mystery of existence'. 4Q415 2 ii may have been prefaced with instruction for the addressee to speak to his wife in this manner: 'you (f.) will not remove[... etc.'

The distribution of allusions to Genesis creation traditions in *Musar leMevin* is relatively widespread. Not only are allusions broadly distributed, but they are not limited in use to one concern. 4Q416 1, very likely the opening column of the document, uses creation to frame cosmology. 4Q417 1 i, which should be located within the first few columns of the document, alludes to creation for issues pertaining to the female (ll. 8-9) and for angelic participation in the creation of humanity (ll. 15-18). 4Q416 2 ii-iv, columns which are to be located at or near the beginning columns of the document, hold numerous allusions to creation traditions as well. 4Q423 fragments (esp. 1, 2 i and 5), likely to be located in the last columns of the document, are concerned with the Garden of Eden as well as agricultural motifs. Many of the fragments proposed to hold allusions to Genesis 1-3 have not been located. It may be that remaining allusions were distributed from beginning to end throughout *Musar leMevin*, but unfortunately there is simply not enough material to determine if this was the case. Furthermore, throughout the document there are multiple addresses (fem. sing; masc. sing.; and plural) and yet creation motifs appear in each context.

Although scholars have been generally aware of the significance of Genesis creation traditions in *Musar leMevin*, until now no sustained attention has been given to the topic. Nor, for that matter, has any work focused exclusively on angelology or anthropology in the document. Sustained attention yields important results. Creation traditions are operative in a number of passages and it appears to be an underlying thread in the document and not just a topic that arises in one specific context in connection to a given theme.

This study, however, is only one endeavour to understand biblical traditions in *Musar leMevin*. Before one can assert any predominance of creation traditions in *Musar leMevin*, it would be further necessary to explore biblical traditions throughout the document and not just traditions stemming from Genesis 1-3. Throughout this study, caution has been taken not to force a creation grid on the document. A proper analysis would require documenting and discussing the occurrence of *all* biblical traditions in *Musar leMevin*, and this study is just one step in this larger task. Therefore, creation provides at least one important framework within which the coherence of the document may be ascertained.

There are a large number of documents that allude to or quote creation traditions but are not founded upon creation traditions (e.g. *Hodayot*, 1QS, or Sirach). We see in *Musar leMevin* that creation is a significant tradition that surfaces repeatedly. It should be delineated, then, whether creation traditions should be seen as: (1) foundational for the document; or (2) merely frequent. In order to determine which of these two options best describes the role of creation in *Musar leMevin*, it is important to revisit the רז נהיה and the significance of creation for this motif in the document.

Unlike traditional sapiential literature such as Proverbs (or Sirach, Wisdom of Solomon, 4Q185), where an exalted view of wisdom occurs, *Musar leMevin* does not reflect such a view. Rather, the רז נהיה functions as a substitute for exalted wisdom and sapiential instruction in the document falls under its umbrella. No other topic in *Musar leMevin* is as significant as the רז נהיה. Therefore, if this mystery is to be identified with creation, then allusions to Genesis 1-3 are to be seen as foundational.

Much of the research on *Musar leMevin* has concentrated on a source critical rather than on a narrative approach. Not surprisingly, therefore, studies on the רז נהיה have not paid much attention to the larger networks of biblical traditions that might go with it. A narrative approach to *Musar leMevin*, such has been attempted in parts of chapters four and five, explores the document on a level that relates disparate parts to one another. The רז נהיה, when interpreted in relation to the multiple allusions to creation in the document, may be understood as referring in part to the mystery of creation.

The רז נהיה is preserved approximately 28 times in *Musar leMevin*. More often than not, the phrase occurs in fragments that are too small or damaged to determine the context of the phrase (e.g. 4Q415 6 4; 24 1; 4Q416 17 3; 4Q418 17 4; 77 2, 4; 190 2; 219 2).[1] However, and importantly: *the vast majority of the time, the phrase* רז נהיה *occurs in those fragments which contain allusions*

---

[1] An occurrence of the רז נהיה in a fragment that may questionably hold an allusion to creation is 4Q418 123 i-ii 2-4: for the coming forth of times and the going out of times [ ] all that has been, which was and will be [ ] its seasons which he revealed to the ear of the understanding ones in the רז נהיה.

to creation (4Q416 2 ii 9; 2 iii 9, 14, 18, 21; 4Q417 1 i 2, 8, 13, 18, 21, 25; 4Q418 177 7). Such occurrences of the רז נהיה in creation contexts, I suggest, presuppose a link between this mystery and creation.

In chapter one various opinions on the interpretation of the רז נהיה were reviewed. It is unlikely that this mystery refers to an actual composition (e.g. Hagi or Haguy). Therefore, three interpretative options remain: (1) it is an eschatological mystery; (2) it is a mystery of creation; or (3) it is a mystery that encompasses everything from creation to judgement. If the mystery is to be associated with a meditation on the nature and order of creation (both cosmic and worldly), the relevance of this mystery for judgement would not be negated. This mystery likely coordinates *Urzeit* with *Endzeit*. Instruction in the document, and exhortations to pursue understanding by means of the mystery, is understood as consonant with the created order. The mystery itself might be discerned, in part, behind a number of distinctions drawn at the time of creation: (1) heavens, earth and seasons; (2) the 'spiritual people' and the 'spirit of flesh'; (3) humanity and angelic beings; and (4) male and female. This understanding derives from creation; it is the basis for sapiential teachings in the present, and transgression against this order will lead (or has led to) condemnation.

Musar leMevin repeatedly instructs the addressees to pursue the רז נהיה. As this study has attempted to demonstrate, wisdom instruction in the document is often found within the context of allusions to Genesis 1-3. Furthermore, the interrelated motifs of usury, poverty and lacking are prominent. While the notion of 'lacking' in the document may be seen to be a description of material poverty on some occasions, it is suggested throughout that this is a multivalent concept in *Musar leMevin*, among other multivalent themes, and also reflects on anthropology and even angelology (4Q416 1). The twin emphases of the document on the רז נהיה and instruction conceptually based on creation traditions – especially those instructions which are concerned with how the addressees should understand themselves – help establish that the notion of 'lacking' has an anthropological aspect. The motif of 'lacking' in *Musar leMevin* is one example of how the 'mystery of existence', as demonstrated in relation to angelic beings and women, combines apocalyptic elements with sapiential instruction. The רז נהיה is not so much concealed from the addressees as it is revealed within the instruction of the document. The addressee is exhorted to persevere in grasping the mystery and is to live according to it.

Selected Bibliography

1. Primary Sources and Reference Works

Alexander, P., and Vermes, G., *Discoveries in the Judean Desert XXVI: Qumran Cave 4. XIX: 4QSerekh Ha-Yahad* (Oxford: Clarendon, 1998).

Allegro, J. M., *Discoveries in the Judean Desert V: Qumran Cave 4. I (4Q158-4Q186)* (Oxford: Clarendon, 1969).

Baillet, M., *Discoveries in the Judean Desert VII: Qumran grotte 4. III (4Q482-4Q520)* (Oxford: Clarendon, 1982).

Barthelémy, D., and Milik, J. T., *Discoveries in the Judean Desert I: Qumran Cave 1* (Oxford: Clarendon, 1955).

Baumgarten, J. M., *Discoveries in the Judean Desert 18: Qumran Cave 4: The Damascus Document* (Oxford: Clarendon, 1996).

Beyer, K., *Die aramäischen Texte vom Toten Meer* (Göttingen: Vandenhoeck & Ruprecht, 1994).

Black, M., *Apocalypsis Henochi Graece* (PVTG 3; Leiden: E. J. Brill, 1970).

_____, *The Book of Enoch or I Enoch: A New English Edition with Commentary and Textual Notes* (SVTP 7; Leiden: E. J. Brill, 1985).

Charles, R. H. (ed.), *The Apocrypha and Pseudepigrapha of the Old Testament in English*, 2 vols. (Oxford: Clarendon Press, 1913).

Charlesworth, J. H., *et al.* (ed.), *Graphic Concordance to the Dead Sea Scrolls* (Tübingen: J.C.B. Mohr (Paul Siebeck), 1991).

_____, *The Old Testament Pseudepigrapha*, 2 vols. (Garden City: Doubleday, 1983 -1985).

Colson, F. H. and Whitaker, G. H., *Philo*, 10 vols. (LCL ; London: Heinemann, 1929-1943).

Eisenman, R. H. and Robinson, J. M. (eds.), *Fascimile Edition*, 2 vols. (Washington, D. C.: Biblical Archaeology Society, 1991).

Elgvin, T., Kister, M., Lim, T., Nitzan, B., Pfann, S, Qimron, E., Schiffman, L. H., Steudel, A., *Discoveries in the Judean Desert XX: Qumran Cave 4. XV: Sapiential Texts, Part 1* (Oxford: Clarendon, 1997)

Eshel, H., Eshel, E., Newsom, C., Nitzan, B., Schuller, E. and Yardeni, A. (eds.), Discoveries in the Judean Desert XI: Poetical and Liturgical Texts, Part 1 (Oxford: Clarendon, 1998).

Freedman, H. and Simon, M. (trs. eds.), *The Midrash Rabah* (New York: Soncino, 1983).

García Martínez, F., *The Dead Sea Scrolls Translated: The Qumran Texts in English,* English translation by W. G. E. Watson (Leiden: E. J. Brill, 1994).

García Martínez, F., Tigchelaar, E. J. C., *The Dead Sea Scrolls Study Edition*, 2 vols. (Leiden: E. J. Brill, 1997-1998).

Gaster, T. H*., The Dead Sea Scriptures* (Garden City: Doubleday, 1976).

Ginzberg, L., *Legends of the Jews* (Philadelphia: The Jewish Publication Society of America, 1909).

Grossfeld, B., *The Targum Onqelos to Genesis* (Edinburgh: T & T Clark, 1988).

Harrington, D. J., Strugnell, J., and T. Elgvin, *Discoveries in the Judean Desert XXXIV: Qumran Cave 4. XXIV: Sapiential Text, Part 2 4QInstruction (Mūsār l^eMēvîn): 4Q415ff.* (Oxford: Clarendon, 1999).

Hatch, E. and Redpath, H. A., *A Concordance to the Septuagint and the Other GreekVersions of the Old Testament, Including the Apocryphal Books* (Grand Rapids: Baker Books, 1998).

Jastrow, M., *A Dictionary of the Targumim, the Talmud Babli and Yerushalmi, and Midrashic Literature* (Brooklyn: P. Shalom, 1967).

Knibb, M. A., *The Ethiopic Book of Enoch: A New Edition in the Light of Aramaic Dead Sea Fragments*, 2 vols. (Oxford: Clarendon, 1978).

Licht, J. מגילת הסרכים (Jerusalem: Bialik, 1965).

Maher, M., *Targum Pseudo-Jonathan: Genesis* (Edinburgh: T & T Clark, 1992).

Margolioth, M. (ed.), *Sepher ha-Razim: A Newly Recovered Book of Magic from the Talmudic Period, Collected from Genizah Fragments and Other Sources* (Jerusalem: American Academy for Jewish Research, 1966). Hebrew.

McNamara, M., *Targum Neofiti 1: Genesis* (Edinburgh: T & T Clark, 1992).

Newsom, C., *Songs of the Sabbath Sacrifice: A Critical Edition* (HSS 27; Atlanta: Scholars Press, 1985).

Qimron, E., and Strugnell, J., *Discoveries in the Judean Desert X: Qumran Cave 4. V: Miqsat maʻaśe ha-Torah* (Oxford: Clarendon, 1994).

Rahlfs, A. (ed.), *Septuaginta*, 2 vols. in 1 (Stuttgart: Deutsche Bibelgessellschaft, 1935).

Schäfer, P. (ed.), *Geniza-Fragmente zur Hekhalot-Literatur* (TSAJ 6; Tübingen: J. C. B. Mohr [Paul Siebeck], 1984).

_____, *Synopse zur Hekhalot-Literatur* (TSAJ 2; Tübingen: J. C. B. Mohr [Paul Siebeck],1981).

_____, *Übersetzung der Hekhalot-Literatur* (TSAJ 17, 22, 29, 46; Tübingen: J. C. B. Mohr [Paul Siebeck], 1987-1991).

Schiffman, L. H., VanderKam, J. C. (eds.), *Encyclopedia of the Dead Sea Scrolls* (Oxford: Oxford University Press, 2000).

Strugnell, J., 'The Angelic Liturgy at Qumran – 4QSerek Šîrôt 'Olat Haššabat', in *Congress Volume: Oxford 1959* (VTS 7; Leiden: E. J. Brill, 1960) pp. 318-45.

Tanzer, S. J., '424: 4QInstruction-like Composition B' in S. J. Pfann *et al.* (eds.), *Discoveries in the Judean Desert XXXVI, Qumran Cave 4 XXVI. Cryptic Texts and Miscellanea, Part 1.* (Oxford: Clarendon, 2000) pp. 333-46.

Vermes, G., *The Complete Dead Sea Scrolls in English* (London: Penguin, 1997).

Wacholder, B. Z., and Abegg, M. G., *A Preliminary Edition of the Unpublished Dead Sea Scrolls: The Hebrew and Aramaic Texts from Cave 4* (Fasc. 2; Washington, D.C.: Biblical Archaeological Society, 1991-1992).

_____, *A Preliminary Edition of the Unpublished Dead Sea Scrolls. The Hebrew and Aramaic Texts from Cave 4, Fasc. 4: Concordance of Fascicles 1-3* (Washington DC: Biblical Archaeology Society, 1996).

Yadin, Y., 'The Masada Fragment of the Qumran Songs of the Sabbath Sacrifice', in *IEJ* 34 (1984): 77-88.

_____, *The Temple Scroll* (Jerusalem: Israel Exploration Society, 1983). Zuckermandel, M. S. (ed.), *Tosephta* (Jerusalem: Wahrmann Books, 1963).

2. Secondary Sources

Abegg, M., 'Messianic Hope and 4Q285: A Reassessment,' in *JBL* 113 (1994): 81-91.

Aitken, J. K., 'Apocalyptic, Revelation and Early Jewish Wisdom Literature,' in P. J. Harland and R. Hayward (eds.), *New Heaven and New Earth: Prophecy and the Millennium. Essays in Honour of Anthony Gelston* (SVT 77; Leiden: E. J. Brill, 1999) pp. 181-93.

Achtemeier, P. J., *1 Peter* (Minneapolis: Fortress Press, 1996).

Albani, M., Frey, J. and Lange, A. (eds.), *Studies in the Book of Jubilees* (TSAJ 65; Tübingen: J. C. B. Mohr Siebeck, 1977).

Allison, D. C., *The New Moses: A Matthean Typology* (Edinburgh: T & T Clark, 1993).

Anderson, G. A., *The Genesis Perfection: Adam and Eve in Jewish and Christian Imagination* (Louisville: Westminster/John Knox, 2001).

Anderson, H., 'The Old Testament in Mark's Gospel,' in J. M. Efird (ed.) *The Use of the Old Testament in the New and Other Essays: Studies in Honor of W. F. Stinespring* (Durham: Duke University Press, 1972) pp. 280-306.

Badale, S., 'The Meaning of κεφαλή in the Pauline Epistles,' in *JTS* (1954): 211-15.

Balch, D., *Let Wives be Submissive: The Domestic Code in 1 Peter* (Chico: Scholars Press, 1981).

Barr, J., 'Adam: Single Man or All Humanity?' in J. Magness and S. Gitin (eds.), *Hesed Ve-Emet: Studies in Honor of Ernest S. Frerichs* (BJS 320; Atlanta: Scholars Press, 1998) pp. 3-12.

Barth, M., *Ephesians* (New York: Doubleday, 1974).

Baumgarten, J. M., On the Testimony of Women in 1QSa,' in *JBL* 76 (1957): 266-69.

_____, '4Q502, Marriage or Golden Age Ritual?' in *JJS* 34 (1983): 125-35.

Beale, G. K., *The Right Doctrine from the Wrong Texts? Essays on the Use of the Old Testament in the New* (Grand Rapids: Baker, 1994).

Becker, J. C., 'Echoes and Intertextuality: On the Role of Scripture in Paul's Theology,' in C. A. Evans and J. A. Sanders (eds.), *Paul and the Scriptures of Israel* (JSNTSup 83; Sheffield: Sheffield Academic Press, 1993) pp. 64-69.

Bernstein, M., 'Contours of Genesis Interpretation at Qumran: Contents, Context, and Nomenclature,' in J. L. Kugel (ed.), *Studies in Ancient Midrash* (Cambridge: Harvard University Center for Jewish Studies, 2001) pp. 57-85.

Black, M., 'The Theological Appropriation of the Old Testament by the New Testament,' in *SJT* 39 (1986): 1-17.

Boccaccini, G., *Beyond the Essene Hypothesis: the Parting of the Ways Between Qumran and Enochic Judaism* (Grand Rapids: Eerdmans, 1998).

Bockmuehl, M. N. A., *Revelation and Mystery in Ancient Judaism and Pauline Christianity* (Grand Rapids: Eerdmans, 1990).

_____, Revelation and Mystery in Ancient Judaism and Pauline Christianity (WUNT2 36; Tübingen: J. C. B. Paul Mohr Siebeck, 1990).

Borgen, P., *Philo of Alexandria: An Exegete for His Time* (SNT 86; Leiden: E. J. Brill, 1997).

Bowker, J. *The Targums and Rabbinic Literature: An Introduction to Jewish Interpretations of Scripture* (Cambridge: Cambridge University Press, 1969).

Brawley, R. L., *Text to Text Pours Forth Speech: Voices of Scripture in Luke-Acts* (Bloomington: Indiana University Press, 1995).

Brewer, D. I., *Techniques and Assumptions in Jewish Exegesis Before 70 CE* (Tübingen: Mohr Siebeck, 1992).

Brin, G., 'Studies in 4Q424, Fragment 3,' in *VT* 46 (1996): 271-95.

_____, 'Studies in 4Q424 1-2,' in *RevQ* 18 (1997): 21-42.

Brooke, G. J., 'Qumran Pesher: Towards the Redefinition of a Genre,' in *RevQ* 10 (1979-1981): 483-503.

_____, *Exegesis at Qumran: 4QFlorilegium in its Jewish Context* (JSOTSup 29; Sheffield: Sheffield Academic Press, 1985).

_____, '4Q500 1 And the Use of Scripture in the Parable of the Vineyard,' in *DSD* 2 (1995): 268-94.

_____, 'Miqdash Adam, Eden and the Qumran Community,' in B. Ego *et al.* (eds.), *Gemeinde ohne Tempel* (Tübingen: Mohr Siebeck, 1999) pp. 285-301.

_____, 'Biblical Interpretation in the Wisdom Texts from Qumran,' in C. Hempel, A. Lange, H. Lichtenberger (eds.), *The Wisdom Texts from Qumran and the Development of Sapiential Thought* (Leuven: Peeters-Leuven University Press, 2002) pp. 201-22.

Broshi, M., 'Matrimony and Poverty: Jesus and the Essenes,' in *RevQ* 19 (2000): 629-34.

Brown, R. E. *The Semitic Background of the Term 'Mystery' in the New Testament* (BS 21; Philadelphia: Fortress Press, 1968).

Brownlee, W. H., 'Biblical Interpretation in the Dead Sea Scrolls,' in *BA* 14 (1951): 54-76.

Bruce, F. F., *Biblical Exegesis in the Qumran Texts* (London: Tyndale Press, 1959).

_____, The Epistle to the Colossians, to Philemon and the Ephesians (Grand Rapids: Eerdmans, 1984).

Buchanan, G. W., 'The Old Testament Meaning of the Knowledge of Good and Evil,' in *JBL* 75 (1956): 114-20.

Burkes, S., 'Wisdom and Apocalypticism in the Wisdom of Solomon,' in *HTR* 95 (2002): 21-44.

Burns, J. E., 'Practical Wisdom in 4QInstruction,' in *DSD* 11 (2004): 12-42.

Callaway, P., 'Remarks on Some Sapiential Texts from Qumran,' in *The Qumran Chronicle* 8 (1998): 121-27.

Callender, D. E. Jr., *Adam in Myth and History: Ancient Israelite Perspectives on the Primal Humans* (HSS 48; Winona Lake: Eisenbrauns, 2000).

Cambier, J., 'Le grand mystère concernant le Christ et son Eglise: Ephesians 5,22-33,' in *Biblica* 47 (1966): 43-90.

Campbell, J., *The Use of Scripture in the Damascus Document 1-8, 19-20* (BSAW 228; Berlin : Walter de Gruyter, 1995).

Caquot, A., 'Les text de sagesse de Qoumrân (Aperçu préliminaire),' in *RHPhR* 76 (1996): 1-34.

Caragounis, C. C., *The Ephesian 'Mysterion': Meaning and Content* (CBNTS 8; Upsala: CWK Gleerup, 1977).

Carlè, R. S., *Because of the Angels: Unveiling 1 Cor. 11:2-16* (Paraparaumu Beach: Emmaus, 1998).

Carmignac, J., *Les texts de Qumran: traduits det annotés* (Paris: Letouzey et Ané, 1961).

Carrington, G. P., 'The "Headless Woman": Paul and the Language of the Body in 1 Cor. 11:2-16,' in *PRS* 18 (1991): 223-31.

Cathcart, K. J., 'Numbers 24:17 in Ancient Translations and Interpretations,' in J. Krasovec (ed.), *The Interpretation of the Bible: The International Symposium in Slovenia* (JSOTSup 289; Sheffield: Sheffield Academic Press, 1998) pp. 511-20.

Cervin, R. S., 'Does κεφαλή Mean "Source" or Authority Over" in Greek Literature,' in *TJ* (1989): 85-112.

Charles, R. H., *The Book of Jubilees or the Little Genesis* (London: A & C Black, 1972).

Charlesworth, J. H., 'The Portrayal of the Righteous as an Angel,' in J. J. Collins and G. W. E. Nicklesburg (eds.), *Ideal Figures in Ancient Judaism: Profiles and Paradigms* (SBLSCS 12; Chico: Scholars Press, 1980) pp. 135-51.

_____, 'The Pseudepigrapha as Biblical Exegesis,' in C. A. Evans and W. F. Stinespring (eds.), *Early Jewish and Christian Exegesis: Studies in Memory of William Hugh Brownlee* (Atlanta: Scholars Press, 1987) pp. 139-52.

Chazon, E., 'The Creation and Fall of Adam in the Dead Sea Scrolls,' in J. Frishman and L. Van Rompay (eds.), *The Book of Genesis in Jewish and Oriental Christian Interpretation: A Collection of Essays* (Leuven: Peeters-Leuven University Press, 1997) pp. 13-24.

Ciampa, R. E., *The Presence and Function of Scripture in Galatians 1 and 2* (WUNT2 102; Tübingen: Mohr Siebeck, 1998).

Collins, J. J., *Apocalyptic Imagination* (New York: Crossroad, 1984).

_____, *Daniel* (Minneapolis: Fortress Press, 1993).

_____, Wisdom, Apocalypticism and Generic Compatibility,' in L. J. Perdue, B. B. Scott and W. J. Wiseman (eds.), *In Search of Wisdom in honor of John G. Gammie* (Louisville: Westminster, 1993) pp. 165-85.

_____, *Jewish Wisdom in the Hellenistic Age* (Edinburgh: T & T Clark, 1997).

_____, 'Wisdom, Apocalypticism and the Dead Sea Scrolls,' in *Seers, Sybils and Sages in Hellenistic-Roman Judaism* (JSJS 54; Leiden: E. J. Brill, 1997) pp. 369-83.

_____, 'Wisdom Reconsidered in Light of the Scrolls,' in *DSD* 4 (1997): 265-81.

_____, 'In the Likeness of the Holy Ones: The Creation of Humankind in a Wisdom Text from Qumran,' in D. W. Parry and E. Ulrich (eds.), *The Provo International Conference on the Dead Sea Scrolls: Technological Innovations, New Texts, and Reformulated Issues* (STDJ 30; Leiden: E. J. Brill, 1999) pp. 609-18.

_____, 'The Eschatologizing of Wisdom in the Dead Sea Scrolls', (handout, Orion International Symposium, Mount Scopus, Jerusalem, 20-22 May 2001).

_____, 'The Mysteries of God: Creation and Eschatology in 4QInstruction and the Wisdom of Solomon,' in F. García Martínez (ed.), *Wisdom and Apocalypticism in the Dead Sea Scrolls and in the Biblical Tradition* (BETL 168; Leuven: Peeters-Leuven University Press, 2003) pp. 287-306.

Collins, R. F., ' "This is the Will of God: Your Sanctification" (1 Thess 4:3),' in *LTP* 39 (1983): 27-53.

Cope, L., '1 Cor. 11:2-16: One Step Farther,' in *JBL* 97 (1978): 435-36.

Coppens, J., '"Mystery" in the Theology of St. Paul and its Parallels at Qumran,' in J. Murphy-O'Connor (ed.), *Paul and Qumran: Studies in New Testament Exegesis* (London: Chapman, 1968) pp. 132-58.

Coulot, C., 'L'image de Dieu dans les écrits de sagesse 1Q26, 4Q415-418, 4Q423,' in F. García Martínez (ed.), *Wisdom and Apocalypticism in the Dead Sea Scrolls and in the Biblical Tradition* (BETL 168; Leuven: Peeters-Leuven University Press, 2003) pp. 171-181.

Crouch, J. E., *The Origin and Intention of the Colossian Haustafel* (FRLANT 109; Göttingen: Vandenhoeck & Ruprecht, 1972).

Davidson, M. J., *Angels at Qumran: A Comparative Study of 1 Enoch 1-36, 72-108 and Sectarian Writings from Qumran* (JSPSup 11; Sheffield: Sheffield Academic Press, 1992).

Davies, W. D., '"Knowledge" in the Dead Sea Scrolls and Matthew 11:25-30,' in *HTR* 46 (1953): 113-39.

_____, 'Paul and the Dead Sea Scrolls: Flesh and Spirit,' in K. Stehndahl (ed.), *The Scrolls and the New Testament* (New York: Harper, 1957) pp. 157-82, 276 82.

Davila, J. R., 'A Wedding Ceremony? (4Q502),' in *Liturgical Works* (Grand Rapids: Eerdmans, 2000) pp. 181-201.

_____, *Descenders to the Chariot: The People Behind the Hekhalot Literature* (JSJS 70; Leiden: E. J. Brill, 2001).

Dawes, G. W., *The Body in Question: Metaphor and Meaning in the Interpretation of Ephesians 5:21-33* (BJS 30; Leiden: E. J. Brill, 1998).

Dibelius, M., An die Kolosser, Epheser, an Philemon, 3rd revised edition, (ed.), H. Greeven (Tübingen: Mohr, 1953).

Dimant, D., 'Qumran Sectarian Literature,' in M. E. Stone (ed.), *Jewish Writings of the Second Temple Period* (CRINT 2.2; Philadelphia: Fortress Press, 1984) pp. 483-548.

_____, 'Use and Interpretation of Mikra in the Apocrypha and Pseudepigrapha,' in M. J. Mulder and H. Sysling (eds.), *Mikra: Text, Translation, Reading and Interpretation of the Hebrew Bible in Ancient Judaism and Early Christianity. Compendia Rerum Iudaicarum ad Novum Testamentum*, II 1 (Philadelphia: Fortress Press, 1988) pp. 379-419.

_____, 'Men as Angels: The Self-Image of the Qumran Community,' in A. Berlin (ed.), *Religion and Politics in the Ancient Near East* (Bethesda: University Press of Maryland, 1996) pp. 93-103.

_____, 'Noah in Early Jewish Literature,' in M. E. Stone and T. A. Bergen (eds.), *Biblical Figures Outside the Bible* (Harrisburg: Trinity Press, 1998) pp. 123-50.

_____, '4QInstruction (Mussar la-mevin) – A Sectarian Wisdom,' (handout, Orion International Symposium, Mount Scopus, Jerusalem, 20-22 May 2001) 5 pages.

Dochhorn, J., '«Sie wird dir nicht ihre Kraft geben» – Adam, Kain und der Ackerbau in 4Q423 2 3 und Apc Mos 24,' in C. Hempel, A. Lange, H. Lichtenberger (eds.), *The Wisdom Texts from Qumran and the Development of Sapiential Thought* (Leuven: Peeters-Leuven University Press, 2002) pp. 351-66.

Dodd, C. H., *According to the Scriptures: The Sub-structure of New Testament Theology* (London: Nisbet, 1953).

Dupont, J. 'Les πτωχοὶ τῷ πνεύματι de Matthieu 5,3 et les 'nwy rwh de Qumrân,' in J. Blinzler, O. Kuss, F. Mussner (eds.) Neutestamentliche Aufsätze: Festschrift für Prof. Josef Schmid (Regensburg: Pustet, 1963) pp. 53-64.

Ego, B., 'Der Strom der Tora – zur Rezeption eines tempeltheologischen Motivs in frühjüdischer Zeit,' in B. Ego et al. (eds.), *Gemeinde ohne Tempel* (WUNT 118; Tübingen: Mohr Siebeck, 1999) pp. 205-14.

Elgvin, T., 'Admonition Texts from Qumran Cave 4,' in M. O. Wise *et al.* (eds.), *Methods of Investigation of the Dead Sea Scrolls and the Khirbet Qumran Site. Present Realities and Future Prospects* (ANYAS 722; New York: The New York Academy of Sciences, 1994) pp. 179-94.

_____, 'The Reconstruction of Sapiential Work A (*),' in *RevQ* 16 (1995): 559-80.

_____, Wisdom, Revelation, and Eschatology in an Early Essene Writing,' in *SBLSP* (1995): 440-63.

_____, *An Analysis of 4QInstruction* (Ph.D. dissertation submitted to Hebrew University, 1997).

_____, 'To Master His Own Vessel, 1 Thess 4:4 in Light of New Qumran Evidence,' in *NTS* 43 (1997): 604-19.

_____, 'The Mystery to Come: Early Essene Theology of Revelation,' in F. H. Cryer and Th. L. Thompson (eds.), *Qumran Between the Old and New Testaments* (JSOTSSup 290; Copenhagen International Seminar 6; Sheffield, 1998) pp. 113-50.

_____, 'Early Essene Eschatology: Judgment and Salvation According to *Sapiential Work A,*' in D. W. Parry and E. Ulrich (eds.), *The Provo International Conference on the Dead Sea Scrolls: Technological Innovations, New Texts, and Reformulated Issues* (STDJ 30; Leiden: E. J. Brill, 1999) pp. 126-65.

_____, 'Wisdom and Apocalypticism in the Early Second Century BCE: The Evidence of 4QInstruction,' in L. H. Schiffman, E. Tov, and J. C. VanderKam (eds.), *The Dead Sea Scrolls: Fifty Years after Their Discovery. Proceedings of the Jerusalem Congress, July*

20-25, 1997 (Jerusalem: Israel Exploration Society in cooperation with the Shrine of the Book, Israel Museum, 2000) pp. 226-47.

_____, 'Wisdom With and Without Apocalyptic,' in D. K. Falk, F. García Martínez, E. M. Schuller (eds.), *Sapiential, Liturgical and Poetical Texts from Qumran. Proceedings of the Third Meeting of the International Organization for Qumran Studies Oslo 1998. Published in Memory of Maurice Baillet* (STDJ 35; Leiden: E. J. Brill, 2000) pp. 15-38.

_____, 'Priestly Sages? The Milieus of Origin of 4QMysteries and 4QInstruction' (handout, Orion International Symposium, Mount Scopus, Jerusalem, 20-22 May 2001).

Elliot, J. H., *1 Peter* (New York: Doubleday, 2000).

Endres, J. C., *Biblical Interpretation in the Book of Jubilees* (Washington D. C.: Catholic Biblical Association of America, 1987).

Evans, C. A., 'Listening for Echoes of Interpreted Scripture,' in C. A. Evans and J. A. Sanders (eds.), *Paul and the Scriptures of Israel* (JSNTSup 83; Sheffield: Sheffield Academic Press, 1993) pp. 47-51.

Evans, C. A. (ed.), *The Interpretation of Scripture in Early Judaism and Christianity: Studies in Language and Tradition* (JSPSup 33; Sheffield: Sheffield Academic Press, 2000).

Feuillet, A., 'L'Homme "gloire de Dieu" et la femme "gloire de l'homme" (1 Cor. XI:7b),' in *RB* 81 (1974): 161-82.

Fiddes, P. S., '"Woman's Head is Man": A Doctrinal Reflection upon a Pauline Text,' in *Baptist Quarterly* 31 (1986): 370-83.

Finkel, A., 'The Pesher of Dreams and Scriptures,' in *RevQ* 4 (1963-1964): 357-70.

Fish, S., *Is There a Text in This Class?* (Harvard: Harvard University Press, 1980).

Fishbane, M., 'The Qumran Pesher and Traits of Ancient Hermeneutics,' in *PWJCS* 6 (1977) I: 97-114.

_____, *Biblical Interpretation in Ancient Israel* (Oxford: Clarendon, 1988).

_____, 'Use, Authority and Interpretation of Mikra at Qumran,' in M. J. Mulder and H. Sysling (eds.), *Mikra: Text, Translation, Reading and Interpretation of the Hebrew Bible in Ancient Judaism and Early Christianity. Compendia Rerum Iudaicarum ad Novum Testamentum*, II 1 (Philadelphia: Fortress Press, 1988) pp. 339-77.

_____, 'The Well of Living Water: A Biblical Motif and its Ancient Transformations,' in M. Fishbane and E. Tov (eds.), *Sha'arei Talmon: Studies in the Bible, Qumran, and the Ancient Near East* (Winona Lake: Eisenbrauns, 1992) pp. 3-16.

Fisk, B. N., *Do You Not Remember: Scripture, Story and Exegesis in the Rewritten Bible of Psuedo-Philo* (JSPS 37; Sheffield: Sheffield Academic Press, 2001).

Fitzmyer, J. A., 'A Feature of Qumran Angelology and the Angels of 1 Cor. 11:10,' in *NTS* 4 (1957-58): 48-58.

_____, 'The Use of Explicit Old Testament Quotations in Qumran Literature and in the New Testament,' in *NTS* 7 (1960-1961): 297-333.

_____, *The Genesis Apocryphon of Qumran Cave 1: A Commentary* (BibOr 18a; Rome: Biblical Institute Press, 1971).

_____, 'Another Look at κεφαλή in 1 Cor. 11:3,' in *NTS* 35 (1989): 503-11.

Fleckenstein, K. H., *Ordnet euch einander unter in der Furcht Christi: Die Eheperikope in Eph. 5,21-33: Geschichte der Interpretation, Analyse und Aktualisierung des Textes* (Würzburg: Echter Verlag, 1994).

Fletcher-Louis, C. H. T., *Luke-Acts: Angels, Christology and Soteriology* (WUNT2 94; Tübingen: Mohr Siebeck, 1997).

_____, 'Some Reflections on Angelomorphic Humanity Texts Among the Dead Sea Scrolls,' in *DSD* 7 (2000): 292-312.

Flint, P. W., *The Dead Sea Scrolls and the Book of Psalms* (STDJ 17; Leiden: E. J. Brill, 1997).

_____, *All the Glory of Adam: Liturgical Anthropology in the DSS* (Leiden: E. J. Brill, 2002).

Flusser, D., 'He Has Planted it as Eternal Life in Our Midst,' in *Tarb* 58 (1988-1989): 147-53.

Fox, M. V. 'Words of Wisdom,' in *ZAH* 6 (1993): 149-69.

_____, 'Words for Folly,' in *ZAH* 10 (1997): 4-15.

Fraade, S. D., *Enosh and his Generation: Pre-Israelite Hero and History in Post-biblical Interpretation* (SBLMS 30; Chico: Scholars Press, 1984).

Frey, J., 'Die paulinische Antithese von "Fleisch" und "Geist" und die palästinisch-jüdische Weisheitstradition,' in *ZNW* 90 (1999): 45-77.

_____, 'The Notion of "Flesh" in 4QInstruction and the Background of Pauline Usage,' in D. Falk *et al.* (eds.), *Sapiential, Liturgical and Poetical Texts from Qumran: Proceedings of the Third Meeting of the International Organization for Qumran Studies, Oslo 1998* (STDJ 35; Leiden: E. J. Brill, 2000) pp. 197-226.

_____, 'Flesh and Spirit in the Palestinian Jewish Sapiential Tradition and in the Qumran Texts: An Inquiry into the Background of Pauline Usage,' in C. Hempel, A. Lange, H. Lichtenberger (eds.), *The Wisdom Texts from Qumran and the Development of Sapiential Thought* (Leuven: Peeters-Leuven University Press, 2002) pp. 367-404.

García Martínez, F., 'Wisdom at Qumran: Worldly or Heavenly?' in F. García Martínez (ed.), *Wisdom and Apocalypticism in the Dead Sea Scrolls and in the Biblical Tradition* (BETL 168; Leuven: Peeters-Leuven University Press, 2003) pp. 1-16.

Gielen, M., *Tradition und Theologie neutestamentlicher Haustafelnethik* (BBB 75; Frankfurt am Main: Anton Hain, 1990).

Gieschen, C. A., *Angelmorphic Christology: Antecedents and Early Evidence* (Leiden: E. J. Brill, 1998).

Goff, M. J., *The Worldly and Heavenly Wisdom of 4QInstruction* (Ph.D. dissertation submitted to University of Chicago, 2002).

_____, 'The Mystery of Creation in 4QInstruction,' in *DSD* 10 (2003): 1-24.

_____, *The Worldly and Heavenly Wisdom of 4QInstruction* (STDJ 50; Leiden: Brill, 2003).

_____, 'Reading Wisdom at Qumran: 4QInstruction and the Hodayot,' in DSD 11 (2004): 263-88.

Gordis, R., 'The Knowledge of Good and Evil in the Old Testament and the Qumran Scrolls,' in *JBL* 76 (1957): 122-38.

Gottstein, M. H., 'Bible Quotations in the Sectarian Dead Sea Scrolls,' in *VT* 3 (1953): 79-82.

Grudem, W., 'Does κεφαλή ("Head") Mean "Source" or "Authority Over" in Greek Literature? A Survey of 2336 Examples,' in *TJ* (1985): 38-59.

Gundry-Volf, J. M., 'Gender and Creation in 1 Cor. 11:2-16: A Study in Paul's Theological Method,' in J. Adna, S. J. Hafemann and O. Hofius (eds.), *Evangelium, Schriftauslegung, Kirche : Festschrift für Peter Stuhlmacher* (Göttingen: Vandenhoeck & Ruprecht, 1997) pp. 151-71.

Halpern-Amaru, B., 'The First Woman, Wives, and Mothers in Jubilees,' in *JBL* 113 (1994): 609-26.

Halperin, D. J., *The Faces of the Chariot: Early Jewish Responses to Ezekiel's Vision* (Tübingen: Mohr Siebeck, 1988).

Hannah, D. D., *Michael and Christ: Michael Traditions and Angel Christology in Early Christianity* (WUNT2 109; Tübingen: Mohr Siebeck, 1999).

Harrington, D. J., 'Wisdom at Qumran,' in E. Ulrich and J. C. VanderKam (eds.), *The Community of the Renewed Covenant: The Notre Dame Symposium on the Dead Sea Scrolls* (Notre Dame: University of Notre Dame Press, 1994) pp. 137-52.

_____, 'The Rāz Nihyeh in a Qumran Wisdom Text (1Q26, 4Q415-418, 423),' in *RevQ* 17 (1996): 549-53.

_____, *Wisdom Texts from Qumran* (London: Routledge, 1996).

_____, 'Ten Reasons Why the Qumran Texts are Important,' in *DSD* 4 (1997): 245-54.

_____, 'Two Early Jewish Approaches to Wisdom. Sirach and Qumran Sapiential Work A,' in *JSP* 16 (1997): 25-38.

_____, 'Wisdom and Apocalyptic in 4QInstruction and 4 Ezra,' in F. García Martínez (ed.), *Wisdom and Apocalypticism in the Dead Sea Scrolls and in the Biblical Tradition* (BETL 168; Leuven: Peeters-Leuven University Press, 2003) pp. 343-56.

Harrington, H. K., *The Purity Systems of Qumran and the Rabbis* (SBLDS 143; Atlanta: Scholars Press, 1993).

Hays, R., *Echoes of Scripture in the Letters of Paul* (New Haven: Yale University Press, 1989).

_____, 'On the Rebound: A Response to Critiques of *Echoes of Scripture in the Letters of Paul*,' in C. A. Evans and J. A. Sanders (eds.), *Paul and the Scriptures of Israel* (JSOTSup 83; Sheffield: Sheffield Academic Press, 1993) pp. 70-73.

Hayward, C. T. R., 'The Figure of Adam in Pseudo-Philo's Biblical Antiquities,' in *JSJ* 23 (1992): 1-20.

Hempel, C., 'The Qumran Sapiential Texts and the Rule Books,' in C. Hempel, A. Lange, H. Lichtenberger (eds.), *The Wisdom Texts from Qumran and the Development of Sapiential Thought* (BETL 168; Leuven: Peeters-Leuven University Press, 2002) pp. 277-96.

_____, 'Kriterien zu Bestimmung „essenischer Verfasserschaft" von Qumrantexten,' in J. Frey and H. Stegemann (eds.), *Qumran kontrovers: Beiträge zu den Textfunden vom Toten Meer* (Bonifatius: Paderborn, 2003) pp. 71-88.

Holm-Nielsen, S., *Hodayot: Psalms from Qumran* (Aarhus: Universitetsforlaget, 1960).

Horgen, M. P., *Pesharim: Qumran Interpretation of Biblical Books* (CBQMS 8; Washington D. C.: Catholic Biblical Association, 1979).

Horton, F. L., 'Formulas of Introduction in the Qumran Literature,' in *RevQ* 7 (1969-1971): 505-14.

Huppenbauer, H., בשר "Fleisch" in den Texten von Qumran,' in *Theologische Zeitschrift* 13 (1957): 298-300.

Hurtado, L. W., *One God, One Lord: Early Christian Devotion and Ancient Jewish Monotheism* (London: SCM, 1988).

Ibba, G., 'Il "Libro dei Misterei" (1Q27, F. 1): Testo escatologico,' in *Henoch* 21 (1999): 73-84.

Jefferies, D. J., *Wisdom at Qumran: A Form-Critical Analysis of the Admonitions in 4QInstruction* (Ph.D. dissertation; University of Wisconsin-Madison, 2001).

_____, *Wisdom at Qumran: A Form-Critical Analysis of the Admonitions of 4QInstruction* (Gorgias Dissertations NES 3; Piscataway: Gorgias Press, 2002).

Jervell, J., *Imago Dei: Gen 1,26f. im Spätjudentum, in der Gnosis und in den paulinischen Briefen* (FRLANT 76; Göttingen: Vandenhoeck & Ruprecht, 1960).

Jervis, L. A., '"But I Want You to Know...": Paul's Midrashic Intertextual Response to the Corinthian Worshippers (1 Cor. 11:2-16),' in *JBL* 112 (1993): 231-46.

Jobes, K. H., 'Jerusalem, Our Mother: Metalepsis and Interextuality in Gal. 4:21-31,' in *WTJ* 55 (1993): 299-320.

de Jonge, M. and Tromp, J., *The Life of Adam and Eve and Related Literature.* (GAP; Sheffield: Sheffield Academic Press, 1997).

Kampen, J. 'The Diverse Aspects of Wisdom at Qumran,' P. W. Flint and J. C. Vanderkam (eds.), *The Dead Sea Scrolls After Fifty Years*, vol. 1 (Leiden: E. J. Brill, 1998) pp. 211-43.

Kandler, H. J., 'Die Bedeutung der Armut im Schrifttum von Chirbet Qumran,' in *Judaica* 13 (1957): 193-209.

Keck, L. E., 'The Poor among the Saints in Jewish Christianity and Qumran,' in *ZNW* 57 (1966): 54-78.

Kelly, J. N. D., *The Epistle of Peter and of Jude* (New York: Harper & Row, 1969).

Kimball, C. A., *Jesus' Exposition of the Old Testament in Luke's Gospel* (JSNTSup 94; Sheffield: Sheffield Academic Press, 1994).

Kister, M., 'A Qumranic Parallel to 1 Thess 4:4? Reading and Interpretation of 4Q416 2 II 21,' in *DSD* 10 (2003): 365-71.

Kittel, B. P., *The Hymns of Qumran* (SBLDS 50; Chico: Scholars Press, 1981).

Klijn, A. F. J., *Seth in Jewish, Christian and Gnostic Literature* (SNT 46; Leiden: E. J. Brill, 1977).

Kroeger, C. C., 'The Classical Concept of *Head* as "Source",' in G. G. Hull (ed.), *Equal to Serve* (London: Scripture Union, 1987) pp. 267-83.

Küchler, M., *Frühjüdische Weisheitstradition* (OBO 26; Freiburg: Universtätsverlag, 1979).

Kugel, J. L., *In Potiphar's House: The Interpretive Life of Biblical Texts* (Cambridge, Harvard University Press, 1990).

_____, *The Bible As It Was* (Cambridge: Harvard University Press, 1997).

_____, *Traditions of the Bible: A Guide to the Bible as it was at the Start of the Common Era* (Cambridge: Harvard University Press, 1999).

Kuhn, K. G. (ed.), *Kondordanz zu den Qumrantexten* (Göttingen: Vandenhoeck & Ruprecht, 1960).

Lange, A., *Weisheit und Prädestination: Weisheitliche Urordnung und Prädestination in den Textfunden von Qumran* (STDJ 18; Leiden: E. J. Brill, 1995).

_____, 'Wisdom and Predestination in the Dead Sea Scrolls,' in *DSD* 2 (1995): 340-54.

_____, 'In Diskussion mit dem Tempel. Zur Auseinandersetzung zwischen Kohelet und weisheitlichen Kreisen am Jerusalemer Tempel,' in A. Schoors (ed.), *Qohelet in the Context of Wisdom* (BETL 136; Leuven: Peeters-Leuven University Press, 1998) pp. 113-59.

_____, 'The Determination of Fate by the Oracle of the Lot in the Dead Sea Scrolls, The Hebrew Bible and Ancient Mesopotamian Literature,' in D. K. Falk, F. García Martínez, E. M. Schuller (eds.), *Sapiential, Liturgical and Poetical Texts from Qumran. Proceedings of the Third Meeting of the International Organization for Qumran Studies Oslo 1998. Published in Memory of Maurice Baillet* (STDJ 35; Leiden: E. J. Brill, 2000) pp. 39-48.

_____, 'Die Weisheitstexte aus Qumran: Eine Einleitung,' in C. Hempel, A. Lange, H. Lichtenberger (eds.), *The Wisdom Texts from Qumran and the Development of Sapiential Thought* (Leuven: Peeters-Leuven University Press, 2002) pp. 3-30.

_____, 'Kriterien essenischer Texte,' in J. Frey and H. Stegemann (eds.), *Qumran kontrovers: Beiträge zu den Textfunden vom Toten Meer* (Bonifatius: Paderborn, 2003 pp. 59-69.

Lange, A., and Lichtenberger, H., 'Qumran,' in *TRE* vol. 28 (1997) pp. 45-79.

Lehmann, M. R., 'Midrashic Parallels to Selected Qumran Texts,' in *RevQ* 3 (1961-1962): 545-51.

Levison, J. R., *Portraits of Adam in Early Judaism: From Sirach to 2 Baruch* (JSPSS 1; Sheffield: JSOT Press, 1988).

Licht, J. 'The Plant Eternal and the People of Divine Deliverance,' in C. Rabin and Y. Yadin (eds.), *Essays on the Dead Sea Scrolls in Memory of E. L. Sukenik* (Jerusalem: Hekhal ha-Sefer, 1961) pp. 67-69.

_____, *The Rule Scroll: A Scroll from the Wilderness of Judea*. Hebrew (Jerusalem: The Bialik Institute, 1965).

Bibliography

Lichtenberger, H., 'Eine weisheitliche Mahnrede in den Qumranfunden (4Q185),' in M. Delcor (ed.), *Qumrân, sa piété, sa théologie et son milieu* (BETL 46; Paris: Duculot, 1978) pp. 151-62.

_____, *Studien zum Menschenbild in Texten der Qumrangemeinde.* (SUNT 15; Göttingen: Vandenhoeck & Ruprecht, 1980).

Lipscomb, W. L. and Sanders, J. A., 'Wisdom at Qumran,' in J. G. Gammie *et al.* (eds.) *Israelite Wisdom: Theological and Literary Essays in Honor of Samuel Terrien* (Missoula: Scholars Press, 1978) pp. 277-85.

Longenecker, R., *Biblical Exegesis in the Apostolic Period* (Grand Rapids: Eerdmans, 1975).

Lucassen, B., Steudel, A., 'Aspekte einer vorläufigen materiellen Rekonstruktion von 4Q416-4Q418,' handout *Forschungsseminar: Die Weisheitstexte aus Qumran, Tübingen, 22-24 Mai; 20-21. Juni 1998.*

Lührmann, 'The Beginning of the Church at Thessalonica,' D. L. Balch, E. Ferguson and W. A. Meeks (eds.), *Greeks, Romans and Christians: Essays in Honor of Abraham J. Malherbe* (Minneapolis: Fortress Press, 1990) pp. 237-49.

Luttikhuizen, G. P. (ed.), *Eve's Children: The Biblical Stories Retold and Interpreted in Jewish and Christian Traditions* (Leiden: E. J. Brill, 2003).

Mach, M. *Entwicklungsstadien des jüdischen Engelglaubens in vorrabbinscher Zeit* (TSAJ 34; Tübingen: J. C. B. Mohr [Paul Siebeck], 1992).

Margalioth, M. *Sepher Ha-Razim* (Jerusalem: Yediot Achronot, 1966).

Martin, D. B., *The Corinthian Body* (New Haven: Yale University Press, 1995).

Martin, W. J., '1 Cor. 11:2-16: An Interpretation,' in W. W. Gasque and R. P. Martin (eds.), *Apostolic History and the Gospel: Presented to F. F. Bruce* (Exeter: Paternoster, 1970) pp. 231-41.

Maxwell, J. M., 'In the "Image" and "Likeness" of God,' in *JBL* 91 (1972): 289-304.

McGehee, M., 'A Rejoinder to Two Recent Studies Dealing with 1 Thess 4.4,' in *CBQ* 51 (1989): 82-89.

Metso, S., *The Textual Development of the Qumran Community Rule* (STDJ 21; Leiden: E. J. Brill, 1997).

Metzger, B. M., 'The Formulas Introducing Quotations of Scripture in the New Testament and the Mishnah,' in *JBL* 70 (1951): 297–307.

Michaels, J. R., *1 Peter* (Waco: Word Books, 1988).

Michaelis, W., *Zur Engelchristologie im Urchristentum. Abbau der Konstruktion Martin Werners* (GBTh 1; Basel: Majer, 1942).

Michel, D., 'Weisheit und Apocalyptik,' in A. S. van der Woude (ed.), *The Book of Daniel in the Light of New Findings* (BETL 106; Louvain: University Press, 1993) pp. 413-34.

Militic, S. F., *'One Flesh': Eph 5.22-24, 5.31: Marriage and the New Creation* (Rome: Pontifical Biblical Institute, 1988).

Miller, M. P., 'Targum, Midrash, and the Use of the Old Testament in the New Testament,' in *JSJ* 2 (1971): 29-82.

Morgan, M. A., *Sepher Ha-Razim: The Book of Mysteries* (Chico: Scholars Press, 1983).

Morgenstern, M., 'The Meaning of מולדים בית in the Qumran Wisdom Texts,' in *JJS* 51 (2000): 141-44.

Moyise, S., *The Old Testament in the Book of Revelation* (Sheffield: Sheffield Academic Press, 1995).

_____, 'Intertextuality and the Study of the Old Testament in the New Testament,' in S. Moyise (ed.), *The Old Testament in the New Testament: Essays in Honour of J. L. North* (JSNTSup 189; Sheffield: Sheffield Academic Press, 2000) pp. 14-41.

Murphy, C. M., *Wealth in the Dead Sea Scrolls and in the Qumran Literature* (STDJ 40; Leiden: E. J. Brill, 2001).

Murphy, R. E., '*Yeser* in the Qumran Literature,' in *Biblica* 39 (1958): 334-44.

_____, 'Wisdom and Creation,' in *JBL* 104 (1985): 3-11.

_____, *The Tree of Life: An Exploration of Biblical Wisdom Literature* (2nd ed.; Grand Rapids: Eerdmans, 1996).

Murphy O'Connor, J., 'Sex and Logic in 1 Cor. 11:2-16,' in *CBQ* 42 (1980): 482-500.

Newsom, C., 'The Sage in the Literature of Qumran: The Function of the Maskil,' in J. G. Gammie and L. G. Perdue (eds.), *The Sage in Ancient Israel and the Ancient Near East* (Winona Lake: Eisenbrauns, 1990) pp. 101-20.

Nickelsburg, G. W. E., 'Revealed Wisdom as a Criterion for Inclusion and Exclusion: From Jewish Sectarianism to Early Christianity,' in J. Neusner and E. S. Frerichs (eds.), *To See Ourselves as Others See Us: Christians, Jews, and 'Others' in Late Antiquity* (Chico: Scholars Press, 1985) pp. 73-91.

_____, 'Wisdom and Apocalypticism in Early Judaism: Some Points for Discussion,' in *Society of Biblical Literature Seminar Papers 1994* (SBLSP 33; Atlanta: Scholars Press, 1994) pp. 715-32.

Niehr, H., 'ערם, ערום, ערמה,' in G. J. Botterweck and H. Ringgren (eds.), *Theologisches Wörterbuch zum Alten Testament VI*, (Stuttgart: Kohlhammer, 1989) pp. 387-92.

_____, 'Die Weisheit des Achikar und der musar lammabin im Vergleich,' in C. Hempel, A. Lange and H. Lichtenberger (eds.), *The Wisdom Texts from Qumran and the Development of Sapiential Thought* (BETL 159; Leuven: Peeters-Leuven University Press, 2002) pp. 173-86.

Nitzan, B., 'The Idea of Creation and Its Implications in Qumran Literature,' in H. G. Reventlow and Y. Hoffman (eds.), *Creation in Jewish and Christian Tradition* (Sheffield: Sheffield Academic Press, 2002) pp. 240-64.

Osten-Sacken, P., *Gott und Belial. Traditionsgeschichtliche Untersuchungen zum Dualismus in den Texten aus Qumran* (StUNT 6; Göttingen: Vandenhoeck & Ruprecht, 1969).

Paul, S., 'Heavenly Tablets and the Book of Life,' in *JANESCU* 5 (1973): 345-53.

Perdue, L. G., 'Cosmology and the Social Order in the Wisdom Tradition,' in J. G. Gammie and L. G. Perdue (eds.), *The Sage in Israel and the Ancient Near East* (Winona Lake: Eisenbrauns, 1990) pp. 457-78.

_____, *Wisdom and Creation: The Theology of Wisdom Literature* (Nashville: Abingdon, 1994).

Perriman, A. C., 'The Head of a Woman: The Meaning of in 1 Cor. 11:3,' in *JTS* 45 (1994): 602-22.

Piper, O. A., 'The "Book of Mysteries" (Qumran I 27): A Study in Eschatology,' in *JR* 38 (1958): 95-106.

Puech, É., 'Apports des Textes Apocalyptiques et Sapientiels de Qumrân : À l'eschatologie du Judaïsme Ancien,' in F. García Martínez (ed.), Wisdom and Apocalypticism in the Dead Sea Scrolls (BETL 168 ; Leuven : Peeters-Leuven University Press, 2003) pp. 133-70.

Puech, É., Steudel, A., 'Un nouveau fragment du manuscrit *4QInstruction* (XQ7 = 4Q417 ou 4Q418),' in *RevQ* 19 (2000): 623-27.

Qimron, E., *The Hebrew of the Dead Sea Scrolls* (HSS 29; Atlanta: Scholars Press, 1986).

Rabinowitz, I. L., 'The Qumran Author's spr hhgw/y,' in *JNES* 20 (1961): 109-14.

_____, 'Pesher/Pittaron: Its Biblical Meaning and Significance in the Qumran Literature,' in *RevQ* 8 (1972-1975): 219-32.

Reicke, B., 'The Knowledge Hidden in the Tree of Paradise,' in *JSS* 1 (1956): 193-201.

Roberts, B. J., 'Bible Exegesis and Fulfillment in Qumran,' in P. R. Ackroyd and B. Lindars (eds.), *Words and Meaning: Essays Presented to David Winton Thomas* (Cambridge: Cambridge University Press, 1968) pp. 195-207.

Rofé, A., 'Revealed Wisdom: From the Bible to Qumran,' in G. Sterling and J. J. Collins (eds.), *Sapiential Perspectives: Wisdom Literature in Light of the Dead Sea Scrolls. Proceedings of the Sixth International Symposium of the Orion Center, 20-22 May 2001* (Leiden: E. J. Brill, forthcoming).

Rosner, B. S., Paul, *Scripture and Ethics: A Study of 1 Corinthians 5-7* (Leiden: E. J. Brill, 1994).

Ruiten, J. van, 'The Garden of Eden and Jubilees 3.1-31,' in *Bijdragen: Tijdschrift voor Filosofie en Theologie* 57 (1996a): 305-17.

Runia, D. T., *Philo of Alexandria and the Timaeus of Plato* (Leiden: E. J. Brill, 1986).

Sampley, J. P., "'And the Two Shall Become One Flesh': A Study in Eph 5.21-33* (SNTSMS 16; Cambridge: Cambridge University Press, 1971).

Sanders, J. A., 'Habakkuk in Qumran, Paul and the Old Testament,' in *JR* 39 (1959): 232-44.

_____, 'Intertextuality and Canon,' in S. L. Cook and S. C. Winter (eds.), *On the Way to Nineveh* (Atlanta: Scholars Press, 1999) pp. 300-29.

Sanders, J. A. with Charlesworth, J. H. and Rietz, H. W. L., 'Hymn to the Creator,' in J. H. Charlesworth *et al.* (eds.), *Princeton Theological Seminary Dead Sea Scrolls Project volume 4A* (Tübingen: Mohr Siebeck/Louisville: Westminster John Knox Press, 1998) pp. 198-99.

Sawyer, J. F. A., 'The Meaning of אלהים בצלם ('In the Image of God') in Genesis I-XI,' in *JTS* 25 (1974): 418-26.

Schiffman, L. H., 'Women in the Scrolls,' in *Reclaiming the Dead Sea Scrolls* (Philadelphia: The Jewish Publication Society, 1994) pp. 127-44.

_____, 'Laws Pertaining to Women in the Temple Scroll,' in P. W. Flint and J. C. VanderKam (eds.), *The Dead Sea Scrolls After Fifty Years: A Comprehensive Assessment* (Leiden: E. J. Brill, 1999) pp. 210-28.

_____, 'Halakhic Elements in the Sapiential Texts,' (handout, Orion International Symposium, Mount Scopus, Jerusalem, 20-22 May 2001)

Scholem, G. G., *Major Trends in Jewish Mysticism*, 3rd ed. (New York: Schocken, 1954).

Schoors, A., 'The Language of the Qumran Sapiential Works,' in C. Hempel, A. Lange, H. Lichtenberger (eds.), *The Wisdom Texts from Qumran and the Development of Sapiential Thought* (Leuven: Peeters-Leuven University Press, 2002) pp. 61-98.

Schuller, E. M., 'Women in the Dead Sea Scrolls,' in M. O. Wise, N. Golb, J. J. Collins and D. G. Pardee (eds.), *Methods of Investigation of the Dead Sea Scrolls and the Khirbet Qumran Site: Present Realities and Future Prospects* (New York: New York Academy of Sciences, 1994) pp. 115-31.

Schwartz, M. D., *Mystical Prayer in Ancient Judaism: An Analysis of Ma'aseh Merkavah* (Tübingen: JCB Mohr [Paul Siebeck], 1992).

Schwemer, A. M., 'Gott als König in den Sabbatliedern,' in M. Hengel and A. M. Schwemer (eds.), *Königsherrschaft Gottes und himmlischer Kult im Judentum, Urchristentum und in der Hellenistischen Welt* (WUNT2 55; Tübingen: Mohr Siebeck, 1991) pp. 81-100.

Scott, J. M., 'Korah and Qumran,' in P. W. Flint (ed.), *The Bible at Qumran. Text, Shape, and Interpretation* (SDSSRL; Grand Rapids: Eerdmans, 2001) pp. 182-202.

Sekki, E. *The Meaning of ruah at Qumran* (SBLDS 110; Atlanta: Scholars Press, 1989).

Shum, Shiu-Lun, *Paul's Use of Isaiah in Romans* (WUNT2 156; Tübingen: Mohr Siebeck, 2002).

Shupak, N., *Where can Wisdom be Found?* (OBO 130; Göttingen: Vandenhoeck & Ruprecht, 1993).

Slomovic, E., 'Towards an Understanding of the Exegesis in the Dead Sea Scrolls,' in *RevQ* 7 (1969-1971): 3-15.

Sommer, B. D., 'Exegesis, Allusion and Intertextuality in the Hebrew Bible: A Response to Lyle Eslinger,' in *VT* 46 (1996): 479-89.

Stanley, C. D., *Paul and the Language of Scripture: Citation Technique in the Pauline Epistles and Contemporary Literature* (Cambridge: Cambridge University Press, 1992).

Stegemann, H., 'Die Bedeutung der Qumranfunde für die Erforschung der Apokalyptik,' in D. Hellholm (ed.), *Apocalypticism in the Mediterranean World and the Near East: Proceedings of the International Colloquium on Apocalypticism Uppsala, August 12-17, 1979* (Tübingen: Mohr Siebeck, 1989) pp. 495-530.

_____, 'Methods for the Reconstruction of Scrolls from Scattered Fragments,' in L. H. Schiffman (ed.), *Archaeology and History in the Dead Sea Scrolls. The New York University Conference in Memory of Yigael Yadin* (JSPSup 8; JSOT/ASOR Monographs 2; Sheffield: JSOT Press, 1990) pp. 189-220.

Steinmetz, D., 'Sefer heHago: The Community and the Book,' in *JJS* 52 (2001): 40-58.

Stone, M. E., 'Lists of Revealed Things in the Apocalyptic Literature,' F. M. Cross *et al.* (eds.), *Magnalia Dei: The Mighty Acts of God* (Garden City: Doubleday, 1976) pp. 414-51.

_____, 'The Parabolic Use of Natural Order in Judaism of the Second Temple Age,' in S. Shaked, D. Shulman, G. G. Stroumsa (eds.), *Gilgul. Essays on Transformation, Revolution and Permanence in the History of Religions Dedicated to R. J. Zwi Werblowsky* (SHR 50; Leiden: E. J. Brill, 1987) pp. 298-308.

Stordalen, T., *Echoes of Eden: Genesis 2-3 and Symbolism of the Eden Garden in Biblical Hebrew Literature* (Leuven: Peeters-Leuven University Press, 2000).

Strugnell, J., 'More on Wives and Marriage in the Dead Sea Scrolls (4Q416 2 ii 21 [Cf. 1 Thess 4:4] and 4QMMT §B),' in *RevQ* 17 (1996): 537-47.

_____, 'The Sapiential Work 4Q415ff and Pre-Qumranic Works from Qumran: Lexical Considerations,' in D. W. Parry and E. Ulrich (eds.), *The Provo International Conference on the Dead Sea Scrolls. Technological Innovations, New Texts, and Reformulated Issues* (STDJ 30; Leiden: E. J. Brill, 1999) pp. 595-608.

_____, 'The Smaller Hebrew Wisdom Texts Found at Qumran: Variations, Resemblances, and Lines of Development,' in C. Hempel, A. Lange, H. Lichtenberger (eds.), *The Wisdom Texts from Qumran and the Development of Sapiential Thought* (Leuven: Peeters-Leuven University Press, 2002) pp. 31-60.

Stuckenbruck, L. T., *Angel Veneration and Christology* (WUNT2 70; Tübingen: Mohr Siebeck, 1995).

_____, '4QInstruction and the Possible Influence of Early Enochic Traditions: An Evaluation,' in C. Hempel, A. Lange, H. Lichtenberger (eds.), *The Wisdom Texts from Qumran and the Development of Sapiential Thought* (Leuven: Peeters-Leuven University Press, 2002) pp. 245-62.

_____, '"Angels" and "God": Exploring the Limits of Early Jewish Monotheism', in L. T. Stuckenbruck and W. S. North (eds.), *Exploring Early Jewish and Christian Monotheism* (JSNTSS 263; London/New York: T & T Clark International, 2004) pp. 45-70.

Sullivan, K. P., Wrestling with Angels: A Study of the Relationship Between Angels and Humans in Ancient Jewish Literature and the New Testament (AGAJU 55; Leiden: E. J. Brill, 2004).

Tigchelaar, E. J. C., 'הבא ביחד' in *4QInstruction* (4Q418 64 = 199 = 66 par 4Q417 1 i 17-19) and the Height of the Columns of 4Q418,' in *RevQ* 18/4 (1998): 589-93.

_____, 'Eden and Paradise The Garden Motif in Some Early Jewish Texts,' in P. G. Luttikhuizen (ed.), *Paradise Interpreted: Representations of Biblical Paradise in Judaism and Christianity* (Leiden: E. J. Brill, 1999) pp. 37-57.

_____, 'More Identifications of Scraps and Overlaps,' in *RevQ* 19 (1999): 61-68.

_____, 'The Addressees of 4QInstruction,' in D. K. Falk, F. García Martínez, E. M. Schuller (eds.), *Sapiential, Liturgical and Poetical Texts from Qumran. Proceedings of the Third Meeting of the International Organization for Qumran Studies Oslo 1998. Published in Memory of Maurice Baillet* (STDJ 35; Leiden: E. J. Brill, 2000) pp. 62-75.

_____, *To Increase Learning for the Understanding Ones: Reading and Reconstructing the Fragmentary Early Jewish Sapiential Text 4QInstruction* (STDJ 44; Leiden: E. J. Brill, 2001).

_____, 'Towards a Reconstruction of the Beginning of 4QInstruction (4Q416 Fragment 1 and Parallels),' in C. Hempel, A. Lange, H. Lichtenberger (eds.), *The Wisdom Texts from Qumran and the Development of Sapiential Thought* (BETL 168; Leuven: Peeters-Leuven University Press, 2002) pp. 99-126.

Tiller, P. A., 'The "Eternal Planting" in the Dead Sea Scrolls,' in *DSD* 4 (1997): 312-35.

Tobin, T. H., *The Creation of Man: Philo and the History of Interpretation* (CBQMS 14; Washington D. C.: The Catholic Biblical Association, 1983).

Trever, J. C., 'The Qumran Covenanters and Their Use of Scripture,' *Per* 39 (1958): 127-38.

_____, 'The Qumran Interpretation of Scripture in its Historical Setting,' in G. Vermes (ed.), *Post Biblical Jewish Studies* (Leiden: E. J. Brill, 1975) pp. 37-49.

VanderKam, J. C., 'The Interpretation of Genesis in 1 Enoch,' in P. W. Flint (ed.), *The Bible at Qumran: Text, Shape, and Interpretation* (Grand Rapids: Eerdmans, 2001) pp. 129-48.

_____, *The Book of Jubilees* (Sheffield: Sheffield University Press, 2001).

Vermes, G., 'Genesis 1-3 in Post-Biblical Hebrew and Aramaic Literature before the Mishnah,' in *JJS* 43 (1992): 221-25.

Walker, W. O., '1 Cor. 11:2-16 and Paul's Views Regarding Women,' in *JBL* 94 (1975): 94-110.

Waltke, B. K., '1 Cor. 11:2-16: An Interpretation,' in *BSac* 135 (1978): 46-57.

Watson, F., *Paul and the Hermeneutics of Faith* (London: T & T Clark, 2004).

Weima, J. A. D., 'What does Aristotle have to do with Paul? An Evaluation of Rhetorical Criticism,' in *BBR* 5 (1995): 177-98.

Weitzman, S., 'Allusion, Artifice, and Exile in the Hymn of Tobit,' in *JBL* 115 (1969): 49-61.

Werman, C., 'What is the Book of Hagu?' in G. Sterling and J. J. Collins (eds.), *Sapiential Perspectives: Wisdom Literature in Light of the Dead Sea Scrolls. Proceedings from the Sixth International Symposium of the Orion Center, 20-22 May 2001* (Leiden: E. J. Brill, forthcoming).

Wernberg-Møller, P., 'Some Reflections on the Biblical Material in the Manual of Discipline,' in *ST* 9 (1955): 40-66.

Werner, M., *Die Entstehung des christlichen Dogmas* (Tübingen: Katzmann-Verlag KG, 1941).

Whitton, J., 'A Neglected Meaning of *skeuos* in 1 Thessalonians 4:4,' in *NTS* 28 (1982): 142-43.

Williams, H. H. D. III, *The Wisdom of the Wise: The Presence and Function of Scripture within 1 Cor. 1:18-3:23* (AGAJU 49; Leiden: E. J. Brill, 2001).

Wold, B. G., 'Reconsidering an Aspect of the Title *Kyrios* in light of Sapiential Fragment 4Q416 2 iii,' in *ZNW* 95 (2004): 149-160.

_____, 'Reconstructing and Reading 4Q416 2 II 21: Comments on Menahem Kister's Proposal,' in *DSD* 12 (2005): 205-11.

Wright, B. G., 'Wisdom and Women at Qumran,' in *DSD* 11 (2004): 240-61.

_____, 'The Categories of Rich and Poor in the Qumran Sapiential Literature,' in G. Sterling and J. J. Collins (eds.), *Sapiential Perspectives: Wisdom Literature in Light of the Dead Sea Scrolls. Proceedings from the Sixth International Symposium of the Orion Center, 20-22 May 2001* (Leiden: E. J. Brill, forthcoming).

Yarbrough, O. L., *Not Like the Gentiles: Marriage Rules in the Letters of Paul* (SBLDS 80; Atlanta: Scholars Press, 1985).

Index of References

Hebrew Bible

Genesis
1	149
1-3	1, 24, 42, 43, 48, 49, 65, 68, 75, 77, 79–80, 81, 82
1.1	88
1.2	90
1.3	90
1.7	107–108
1.9-10	88
1.11	83, 107
1.12	83, 107
1.14-20	90
1.15	90
1.16	107
1.18	90
1.20	112
1.25	107
1.26	88, 94, 101–102, 107, 124, 132, 141–150, 184, 206, 208
1.26-27	180, 211, 240
1.27	134, 136, 139
1.28	112, 115, 120
1.26-27	132–134
1.26-28	112
1.29	83
1.31	107
2	88, 95, 97, 149
2.2	107
2.3	107

2-4	35, 38
2.4	105–107
2.7	88, 143
2.9	114–115, 204, 205, 211
2.15-16	115, 121
2.16-17	115
2.19-20	90
2.18	95, 107, 111, 113
2.18-20	187
2.20	187, 189–190
2.20-25	88, 91, 97, 99, 150, 187, 202–204, 216, 229
2.21	200
2.21-24	96
2.23	187, 190, 201, 212
2.23-24	188, 240
2.24	75, 96, 188, 203
2.24-25	191
2.25	100, 191, 209, 238, 240, 242
2.25-3.1	110, 237
3.1	100, 199
3.5	136–137
3.6	114–115, 204, 211
3.16	75, 96–97, 100, 112, 116, 186, 188, 198, 200, 203–205
3.17-18	188
3.18	83, 116, 204
3.20	232–233
3.22	136, 205, 207

4	130, 204	3.1	105
4.1	232–233	8.14	169
4.6-7	116	11.21	50
4.7	188	16	120
4.12	116, 188	16.9	169
4.26	127, 129–130, 139, 130	18.20	163–164, 169
5.1	105	20	60
5.3	130	24.17	129–131, 135
6.9	105	30	189, 225
10.1	105–106	30.6-9	188
11.7	143	30.6-15	75
11.10	105	30.15-17	96
11.28	105	30.17	97
16.5	189		
17.5	140	*Deuteronomy*	
25.12	106	4.16-18	132
25.19	105	10.8-9	169–170
36.1	105–106	10.17	152
36.9	105	13	189
37.2	105	13.7	74–75, 189, 194
48.15	144	18.16	140
48.15-16	176	22.9	75
48.16	144	27.18	227
49	63	28.20	29
		28.54	75, 189, 194
Exodus		31.34	63
6.16	167		
7.50	167	*1 Samuel*	
17	60	2.8	156
20.12	150–151	21.6	194
23.33	167		
27.30	83–84	*2 Samuel*	
29.1	167	7.10	140
28.42	190	12.8	189
31.11	167	15	59
33.22	60	19.13	187
Leviticus		*1 Kings*	
27.30	83–84	6.16	167
		22.17	152
Numbers		19	58
1.20	106		

2 Kings
16.10	126
22.17	152

Isaiah
19.4	152
26.13	152
28.11	67
37.30	84
44.13	132
47.8	140
58.13	167

Jeremiah
17.27	167
23.4	140

Ezekiel
8.3	132
10.8	132
14.44ff.	128
16.3	86, 200
16.36	210
16.38	210
17.6	213
21.35	200
22.10	210
23.10	210
23.18	210
23.29	210
28.12-19	213
29.14	200
31.8-13	212–213
44.11	153
46.20	167
47.1ff.	164

Hosea
14.14	67

Haggai
1.6	29

Zechariah
3	70
8.12	84
13.1	166

Malachi
1.6	151
2.2	30
2.14	201
3.6-12	30
3.9	30
3.13-21	30
3.16	30, 152

Psalms
2	62, 68
2.10	62
21.11	84
22	67
31	67
34.10	132, 173
36.10	164
42	67
46.5	164
51.15	170
59.12	170
63.3	170
71.23	170
65.10	164
88.12	110
104	67
107.37	84
119.171	170
136.3	152

Proverbs
1.23	74
2.17	201
8.15	63
15.11	110
17.2	220
27.18	220

27.20	110	*Lamentations*	
28.27	29	5.10	213
Job		*Qohelet*	
1.1	64	5.5	72
1.2-3	64	6.8-11	72
1.4-19	64		
1.10	70	*Daniel*	
2.3	64	2.18	20
2.7-8	64	2.19	20
2.9	64	2.27	20
3	64	2.30	20
3.10	195	2.47	20
19.17	195	4.6	20
24.20	140	7.10	101
26.6	110, 214–215, 224	10.21	101
28.22	110	11.39	115
31.10	64, 110	12	128
38.7	143	12.1	101
42.11-15	64		
42.16-17	64	*Nehemiah*	
		13.22	167
Canticles			
7.11	188	*1 Chronicles*	
		17.9	140
Ruth			
4.18	105	*2 Chronicles*	
		4.22	167
		18.16	152
		29.17	167

New Testament

Matthew		*John*	
2.9-11	143	19.34	60
5.3	181		
		Acts	
Mark		9.5	154
1	58	10.3ff.	154
6.20	181		

Romans
5.12-14   148
9.21-23   196

1 Corinthians
1-3   61
8.5   154, 238
10.4   50, 60
11   235, 242
11.2-16   201, 239–240
11.7-12   190
11.12   190
15.45ff.   148

2 Corinthians
4.7   196
11.3   233

Ephesians
1.21   154
3.9   239
5   235, 242
5.21-33   201, 237–240
5.28   202
5.29   203
5.31   203
5.32   239
6.19   239

Philippians
1.19   52

Colossians
1.16   154

1 Thessalonians
4.4   191, 194, 196–197

1 Timothy
2   235
2.11-15   236–239
2.13   190, 233

2 Timothy
2.20-25   196

Hebrews
6.8   204

1 Peter
3.7   196–197, 221

2 Peter
2.10   154

Jude
8   154
14   45

Apocalypse of John
3.18   210
9.1   142
12.4   142
16.15   210

Apocrypha

1 Maccabees
3.3-9   171–172

2 Maccabees
7.34   160

4 Maccabees
18.6-8   118
18.7   190

Sirach (Ben Sira)

1.6-12	64
1.13	64
1.15-20	64
1.16-17	64
2.1-6	64
2.2-5	64
2.9-10	64
2.11-14	64
4.21	211
5.14	211
6.1	211
9.1	189
9.17	219
14.2-3	64
14.11-12	64
15.4	211
16.25	74
17.7	84, 116, 133
20.22	211
20.23	211
20.26	211
24.22	211
25.24	118
26.8	211
26.25	211

29.14	211
36.24	187
41.16	211
42.1	211
42.14	211
44-50	172
49.16	138
50	171

Tobit

8.6	233
8.6-7	187
8.15	177
11.14	176
11.14-15	177
12.12-15	177

Wisdom of Solomon

18.15-16	171

Psalm 154

	44

Syriac Psalm 2

	44

Pseudepigrapha

Apocalypse of Moses

	130, 213, 216
20.4	210
24.1-2	188, 210

Ascension of Isaiah

	154

1 Enoch:

1-36 (Book of the Watchers)

1.9	101

2-5	90
8.2-9.4	152
12.2	101
14.23	101
32.6	210

37-71 (Similitudes)

41.10	154
43.1-4	143
47.3	101
62.7	109
69.6	233

72-82 (Astronomical Book)
78-79   90
80   90
81.5   101

85-90 (Animal Apocalypse)
81-83   90
84.6   117
86.1-6   143
90.20-27   143

92-108 (Epistle of Enoch)
101.1   160
108.3   101

*93.1-10 + 91.11-17 (Apocalypse of
Weeks)*
93.1-2   101
93.5   117
93.10   117

2 Enoch
131.6   233

4 Ezra
                 154
4.29-30   84
8.5   84

Joseph and Aseneth
15.11-12   177
22   171

Jubilees
                 214
1.9   209
2.14   115
3.16   209
3.21-31   110
3.22   209
3.27-31   110
3.30   209
3.31   209–210
30.20-22   101
30.20-25   109

Letter Sent to Adam by God
1.1   1

Life of Adam and Eve
                 233
10-11   109

Testament of Levi
5.5-6   177

Testament of Naphtali
8.6   187

Testament of Solomon
20.14-17143

Qumran and Related Literature

CD (Cairo Damascus Document)
        12
i 7   117
ii 2-3   15
ii 10   22
iv 20-21   234

v 9-11   224, 234
vii 6-7   234
vii 21   130
xi 1-2   234
xiff.   15
xvi 2-4   45

xx 8	101
1QpHab (Pesher Habakkuk)	
	12
viii 5-14	15
xi 4-8	10
1Q19 (Book of Noah)	
2	152
2 i	160
1QapGen (Genesis Apocryphan)	
	233
1Q26 (Musar leMevin)	
1	32, 204–206
2	22
2 2-4	32
1Q27 (Book of Mysteries)	
	15, 21, 72
1 i 4	12
1 ii 3	72–73
6 2-3	72–73
1QS (Serekh haYahad)	
	12
iii 15	22
iii 13	106
iii 13-iv 26	15, 133–134
iii 17-18	101, 115, 136, 139
iii 18ff.	143
iv 22	159
iv 26	116
iv 28	171
vi 7-8	166
vii 12-14	194
viii-xi	171
viii 5	168
ix 9	126
ix 12-16	227
ix 14	227

ix 18	20
ix 26-xi 22	126
x 1ff.	90
x 8	128
x 6	170
x 12	164
xi	22, 165, 178
xi 3	164–165, 167
xi 4-7	129
xi 5-6	129
xi 6	164
xi 6-7	170
xi 7-8	160
xi 8	101, 117, 159, 168
xi 22	186
1QSa (Book of Meditation)	
	234
1QSb (Messianic Rule)	
	12
i 3	164–165
i 6	164
iii-iv	101
iv 28	171
1QM (Sefer haMilhama)	
	12
iv 4	126
vi 6	101
viii 3ff.	234
x 10	132
x 12	101
xi 6	130
xi 8ff.	90
xii 1	101
xiv 7	181
xvi 1	101
1Q34 (Liturgical Prayers)	
3 i 1-2	211
3 i 3	208

1QH^a (Hodayot)

	12, 47–48, 60, 65–71
i	15
ii 18	167
ii 20-30	69
ii 21	70
iii 22	159
iv 21	164
iv 37	126
v 30	126–127
v 30-36	126
vi 15	168
vii 6-25	70
vii 34ff.	126
viii 6	168
viii 21	167
ix 21	20, 164
ix 22	164
ix 25-26	90
ix 27-31	170
x 9	208
x 18	164–165
x 27-28	13
x 31	167
x 33-34	208
xi 19	167
xi 21-23	160
xii 30ff.	126
xiii 6-7	211–212
xiii 35	212
xiv 17-18	164–165
xv 4	212
xvi	107, 166
xvi 4	164
xvi 6	83, 117
xvi 8	83, 164
xvi 7	83
xvi 11	83
xvi 10	83
xvi 12	83
xvi 13	83
xvi 14	83

xvi 15	117
xvi 20	83
xvi 25	204
xvi 30	83, 212
xviii 10	167
xix 21	212
xx 7ff.	90
xx 25	164
xx 29	164–165
xxiii 10	164
xxiii 12	164
xxiii 13	164
xxvi 4	165
xxvi 8	165
xxvi 11	160

4Q88 (Psalms^f)

viii	44
ix	44
x	44

4Q159 (Ordinances A)

2-4	234

4Q166 (Hosea Pesher)

i 12-13	213

4Q171 (Psalms Pesher)

	50

4Q174 (Florilegium)

	50

4Q177 (Eschatological Midrash)

	50

4Q180 (Ages of Creation A)

1 1-15	15

4Q181 (Ages of Creation B)

1 ii 2	159-160

4Q185 (Sapiential Work)
i 13-15   75

4Q186 (Horoscope)
2 i 4   187

4Q200 (Tobit^e)
1 i 3   208
1 ii 1   208

4Q202 (Aramaic Enoch^b)
iii   152

4Q249 (Midrash Sefer Moshe)
                    50

4Q251 (Halakhah A)
7   234

4Q255-263 (Serekh haYahad^{a-i})
                    12

4Q265 (Serekh)
                    228

4Q266-273 (Damascus Document^{a-h})
                    12
266 6 ii   228
271 3 7-9   227
271 3 7-15   234

4Q274 (Purification Rule)
                    228
1 i 6   101

4Q284 (Liturgical Text)
                    228, 234

4Q285 (Sefer haMilhamah)
                    12, 174

4Q286 (Blessings^a)
3 2   153

4Q287 (Blessings^b)
2 9-12   153

4Q299-301 (Book of Mysteries^{a-c})
                    12, 15, 21, 72
299 1 4   86, 95, 187
299 3a ii-b 13   86, 187
299 3 ii   87, 107
299 3 ii 7-9   88
299 3 ii 12   88
299 3 ii 15   20
299 5   87, 90, 107
299 5 1-2   88
299 5 5   86, 187
299 6 i 7   88
300 1 ii 2   20
300 3 2   116
300 3-4   20
300 8 5   20
301 1 1   74
301 3 6   115

4Q303 (Meditation on Creation A)
                    113, 117–118
8-9   116
9   118
10   95, 150

4Q304 (Meditation on Creation B)
                    117

4Q305 (Meditation on Creation C)
                    113, 117-118
2 2   116

4Q381 (Apocryphal Psalm B)
1 6-8   115

4Q394-398 (Miqsat Ma'aseh haTorah^(a-e))
394 8 i 11-12   212
397   212
397 5 1-5   234

4Q400-405 (Shirot 'Olat haShabbat^(a-f))
                   101
400 1 i 4-7   127, 153
400 1 ii 7   132
400 1 ii 14   160
400 2   174
400 2 1   175
400 2 2   132
400 2 7   158
400 3 ii 2   160
401 1 i 1   160
401 1 i 10   160
401 1 i 21   160
401 14 i 6   174
402 1 4   153
403 1 i 21   153
403 1 i 24   126
403 1 i 31b-33a   176
403 1 i 34   126
403 1 i 43ff.   126
403 1 ii 3   126, 132
405 13 2-5   160
405 13 7   160
405 20 ii 8   132
405 23 i 3-6   153

4Q413 (Sapiential Text)
                   20

4Q415 (Musar leMevin)
                   138, 155
1   31
1 ii + 2 i   169
2   85
2 i + 1 ii   82–84, 122, 155
2 i + 1 ii 5-6   26

2 ii   3, 41, 85–86, 88–89,
                   94–95, 122, 183, 185,
                   196, 199, 205, 221,
                   232, 243
2 ii 1   93
2 ii 3   189, 193, 201, 232
2 ii 4   223
2 ii 9   187
6 2   24, 27–29, 156
6 4   244
9   94, 185, 226, 230–231
9 2   195, 229–230
9 5   221, 231
9 7   226, 228–229
9 7-8   203, 236
9 8   112
9 9   24, 231
11   31, 37, 94, 185, 216,
                   226, 229, 231
11 6   223
11 11   86, 94–95, 187, 229–
                   230
11 11-13   96
11 12   216
11 13   86, 215
24 1   244

4Q416 (Musar leMevin)
                   86
1   3, 19, 28, 31, 33, 36–
                   38, 41, 79, 84, 121, 89–
                   91, 161, 243, 245
1-2   79
1 1-9   121
1 2-7   34
1 3   104
1 6   24, 219
1 8   104
1 8-10   34
1 11-16   34
1 12   127, 135
1 14   104

1 16-19	34	2 iii 9-10	160
2 i-iv	3	2 iii 9-12	30
2 i	32–33, 34, 37, 91, 95, 97	2 iii 9-14	180
		2 iii 10	172
2 i 21-ii 3	33	2 iii 10-11	120
2 ii	32, 34, 37, 91, 95, 97	2 iii 11	108, 155, 157
2 ii 1	24, 28	2 iii 11ff.	156, 158, 160
2 ii 2-3	135	2 iii 11-12	29, 155–156
2 ii 3	186, 208, 222–224	2 iii 11-14	156
2 ii 3-4	188, 220	2 iii 12	24, 26, 29, 112, 180
2 ii 3-18	33	2 iii 13-21	22
2 ii 9	245	2 iii 14	21, 245
2 ii 12	87, 219	2 iii 15	172
2 ii 13	221	2 iii 15-18	91, 94, 122, 149–150, 180, 185, 202, 206–207, 240, 241
2 ii 16	186, 221–224		
2 ii 18	120, 172		
2 ii 18-iii 3	33	2 iii 15b-16	149, 151, 200
2 ii 7-15	25	2 iii 15-21	92, 97, 150
2 ii 16	186, 208	2 iii 15-iv 13	34
2 ii 18	223	2 iii 16	93, 150, 154
2 ii 20	24, 26, 29, 202, 223	2 iii 16-18	200
2 ii 20-21	28	2 iii 17	112, 120, 154–155, 203, 229–230
2 ii 21	71, 74-76, 86, 94, 186, 189, 191–202, 216	2 iii 18	21, 155, 172, 245
		2 iii 19	29, 92, 231
2 iii	27–28, 32, 34, 39, 83, 88, 91, 95, 91, 93, 95, 97, 110, 112, 122, 149, 150–152, 155–156, 163, 177, 180, 195, 199, 242	2 iii 20	86, 88, 94, 85, 192, 201–202, 229, 231
		2 iii 21	95–96, 111, 113, 229, 245
		2 iii 20-21	8
2 iii-iv	75	2 iv	32, 37, 88, 91, 94–95, 97, 100, 110, 112, 195, 199
2 iii 2	26, 29, 180, 198		
2 iii 2-14	92	2 iv 1	96, 150, 188
2 iii 3-6	33	2 iv 2	112, 188
2 iii 4	215, 223	2 iv 3	116, 188
2 iii 6	157, 223–225	2 iv 4	188
2 iii 6-8	33	2 iv 5	76, 85–86, 88, 189–190, 193, 208
2 iii 8	26, 29, 180, 223		
2 iii 8-9	193	2 iv 6	112
2 iii 8-15	34	2 iv 6-9	75, 97
2 iii 9	21, 86, 92, 95, 105, 187–188, 202, 229, 245	2 iv 7	112, 201

2 iv 8-10	188		150, 154, 179, 181,
2 iv 10	225		240, 241
2 iv 13	85–86, 88, 110, 189,	1 i 16	71, 76, 152
	191, 193, 208, 236	1 i 16-17	107, 145
2 iv 16	188	1 i 17	107, 120, 137–140, 155
3	34	1 i 17-18	116, 219
3 2	26	1 i 18	245
3 3	104	1 i 21	245
3 4	104	1 i 25	245
4	34	1 i 27	3
4 1	37	1 ii	35, 97
4 3	26	2 i	3, 21, 33–32, 36
4 11-12	129	2 i 4	222
7	104	2 i 5	220
7 1-3	32	2 i 6	21
9 1	229	2 i 7	21, 204
17 3	244	2 i 10	223
		2 i 10-11	23
4Q417 (Musar leMevin)		2 i 10-12	22-23
1-2	103	2 i 11	86, 105, 187, 229
1 i	3, 6, 15–18, 21, 33–34,	2 i 14	222
	36–37, 39–40, 79, 84,	2 i 17	24
	94, 97–102, 119, 121,	2 i 19	24
	243	2 i 21	24
1 i 1-14	22	2 i 22b-26	222
1 i 2	156, 245	2 i 23	141, 208, 222
1 i 6	21	2 i 24	24, 223
1 i 7	104	2 i 25	223
1 i 7-8	21	2 i 26	208, 222–224
1 i 8	245	2 ii	32, 34, 36–37, 73
1 i 8-9	189	2 ii 25	192-193
1 i 8-12	196–198, 201, 203	2 ii + 23	217
1 i 9	85–86, 100, 191, 203–	2 ii + 23 3	24
	204	2 ii + 23 5	208
1 i 7-17	23	2 ii + 23 21	188
1 i 8-12	185	5	35
1 i 10-11	21	20 5	172
1 i 13	23, 172, 245		
1 i 15-16	30	*4Q418 (Musar leMevin)*	
1 i 15-17	44		97
1 i 15-18	76, 94, 102, 104, 119,	1	31
	121, 124–141, 147–	2	31

4	31
7	32, 34
7b 7	24
8	32, 34, 217
8 2	208, 220
8 13	87
9	34, 93, 151, 155
9 8	86, 187
9-10	32
9 12	172
9 13	26
9 17	91
9 18	229
10	34, 95, 189
12 1	24
14 1	24
16 3	24
17 4	244
21	32
22	32
43	98
43, 44, 45	32-33, 37
55	3, 35, 39, 89, 103, 124, 146, 157, 160, 163, 177–178, 180–181
55 8-9	158
55 8-12	157
55 9	181
55 10	13, 179, 181
55 10-11	158
55 11	129, 131, 160
69	3, 32, 39, 89, 103, 122, 124, 146, 158, 177–178, 180–181
69 8	135
69 10-15	159
69 12-13	160
69 14	104, 172
69 ii + 128	35
77	32, 104–106
77 2	21, 131, 244
77 3	129
77 4	94, 202, 244
81	3, 17, 31–32, 35, 39, 83, 106–107, 122, 124, 127, 161–78, 242
81 1	40, 172
81 1b-2a	181
81 2	165, 178
81 1-3	108
81 2	107
81 3	112, 120, 131, 163
81 4	168
81 5	164, 220–221
81 9	112, 180
81 10	168
81 11	120, 172
81 12	172
81 13	84, 104, 168
81 14	116
81 15	112, 219
81 16	219
81 17	178
81 18	24
81 20	120
86 1	200
87 6	24
81 + 103	35
88 5	24
88 8	26
97 2	24
103	3, 37, 106, 113
103 ii	35
103 ii 7-9	74
107 3	24
119	201
122 i	7
123 i	32
123 i-ii 2-4	244
123 ii 3-4	22
123 ii 2-8	22-23
126	3, 108–109, 122, 226, 232
126 1-10	30

126 3-4	25
126 6	26
126 9	233
126 ii 8	107
126 ii 13	24
127	3, 35, 215
127 1	24
127 3	223
127 6	228
128 ii	35
138 3	106
243 2	231
148 ii 4	26
148 ii 6	99
149	155
159 ii 5	24
167	106, 226
167a + b	37, 223
172 5-13	26
167	31
167 7	226
168 3	200
177	84, 109–110, 122, 155, 191, 214–215
177 2	110, 214
177 3	208, 210, 214, 224
177 4	105
177 5	24, 26–28, 106, 155–156
177 7	245
178	109–111, 113, 122, 191, 214
178 3	216
178 4	111, 208, 210, 216, 224, 226
186	96
187	96
188	32
190 2	244
201	121
202 1	86, 187, 229
206	111–112, 203

207 + 69	35
213	33
219 2	244
221 4	107
221 5	149
222+221+220	74
228	201, 203
229	89
234 1	26
237 3	26
240 3	24
249	26
251	26
251 1	131
286	31
286 3	104
296	31

4Q418a (Musar leMevin)

1	37
2	37
3	37
4	37, 113
5	37
6	37
7	37
8	37
9 2	37
10	37
11	32, 36–37
12	37
15	31, 37
16	37
16b+17	91, 112, 122
16b+17 3	111, 187, 204, 216
17	37, 113
18	201
18 1-4	37
19	32
19 3	221, 217
19 1-4	37
18 4	204, 236

22	32, 36
22 1-5	37
25 2	106

4Q422 (*Paraphrase of Genesis and Exodus*)

1 9	112
1 9-11	205

4Q423 (*Musar leMevin*)

	79
1, 2 i	3, 35, 79, 83–84, 103, 110, 112, 121, 122, 137, 179, 204, 226, 243
1, 2 i 1	115
1, 2 i 1-2	113-119
1, 2 i 2	115, 203
1, 2 i 3	188
1, 2 i 5	94, 229
1, 2 i 7	117
3	22, 32, 195
3a	195
3 2-4	32
3 3	229
4	32, 205
4 1-2	205
5	36–37, 120, 122, 243
5 1	120, 223
5 2	120
5 3	120
5 5	104
8	32, 106
8 1-4	31
8 2	131
9	32
9 1-4	32
13 4	131
22 2	191

4Q424 (*Sapiential Text*)

1 6	215

4Q481 (*Narrative H*)

3	208

4Q491-496 (*Sefer haMilhama[a-f]*)

8-10 i 12	20

4Q500 (*'Planting'*)

	213

4Q501 (*Apocryphal Lamentation B*)

1	213
5	208, 212–213

4Q502 (*Marriage Ritual*)

	234

4Q504-506 (*Words of the Luminaries[a-c]*)

	15
1-2 v 2	164
8 6	106, 112, 115, 118

4Q508 (*Liturgical Prayers*)

1	208

4Q511 (*Against Demons*)

35	171
35 4	153
52	164
54-55	164
57-59	164
63 iii 1	164
63+64 iii 1-2	170

4Q513 (*Ordinances B*)

2 ii	234

4Q525 (*Beatitudes*)

14 ii 8	208
15 7-9	208

4Q545 (*Visions of Amram[e]*)

9 18	168

5Q11 (Serekh haYahad)
                    12

6Q18 (Hymn)
ii 4   186

11Q5 (Psalms^a^)
                    15
xviii   44
xix   44

11Q11 (Apocryphal Psalm)
                    44

11Q13 (Melchizedek)
                    59
ii 5   157

ii 10   132

11Q14 (Sefer haMilhamah)
                    174
1 ii 2-6   177
1 ii 5-6   172

11Q17 (Shirot 'Olat haShabbat)
ix 4   126
v-vi 2   132

11Q19 (Temple Scroll)
                    14
xlviii 14-17   228
li 4-5   212
liv 20   189
lvii 17-19   234

Josephus

Bellum
2 161   230

8 148   194

Philo

De confusione linguarum
68-70   144
171-174   102
171-178   143

De ebrietate
55   197

De fuga et inventione
65-70   102
65-70   144

De gigantibus
                   143
8   143

29ff.   141

Legum allegoriae
2 63-64   97
3 77-106   143

De migratione Abrahami
193   197

De mutatione nominum
27-34   145
27-34   102
33   149

De opificio mundi
23   142
72-76   102
72-77   142, 144
179-181   144

De plantatione
12   143

De somniis

1 135   143
1 26   197

Questiones et solutiones in Genesin
1 27   190, 200, 205

De virtutibus
198-210   143
198-210 143

Rabbinic and Hekhalot Sources

Avodah Zarah
22b   233

Genesis Rabbah
1.26   102, 148
14:3   132
19:4   206–207
21.5   133

Exodus Rabbah
30:16   133

Numbers Rabbah
19.25-1650

Qohelet Rabbah
11:2   195

Esther Rabbah
1:11   195

B. Megillah
12b   195

B. Mezi'a
84b   195

Pirqe Avot
5.6   50

B. Sanhedrin
38b   102, 147

Shabbat
35a   50
146a   233

Y. Shabbat
10.6   195

Hekhalot:

א34 588§ (N8128)
          153-154
ב13 277§ (N8128)
          153-154

Targumic Sources

Neofiti:

Genesis
1-3	206-208
2.23	190
2.25	209
3.5	207

Deuteronomy
28.54	189

Onqelos:

Deuteronomy
28.54	189

Pseudo Jonathan:

Genesis
1-3	206–208
1.26	102, 147, 206
2.23	190
2.25	208
3.4-5	205, 207
3.6-7	209
3.10	209
3.22	207

Deuteronomy
28.54	189

Malachi
1.6	151

Greek and Roman Literature

Plato's Symposium
189-191 190

Index of Authors

Abegg, M.   4, 125–126, 174
Aitken, J. K.   4, 20, 24, 29–30
Achtemeier, P. J.   196
Albani, M.   209
Allison, D. C.   57–60, 77
Anderson, H.   47
Badale, S.   238
Baillet, M.   212
Barr, J.   131
Barth, M.   238
Barthelémy, D.   4, 152
Baumgarten, J. M.   184
Beale, G. K.   60
Becker, J. C.   47
Beyer, K.   152
Black, M.   47, 83, 184
Boccaccini, G.   16
Bockmuehl, M. N. A.   238
Borgen, P.   142
Bowker, J.   147
Brawley, R. L.   47
Brewer, D. I.   46, 60
Brooke, G. J.   6, 39, 46, 71–76, 96, 130–131, 138, 147, 188, 213
Brownlee, W. H.   46
Burns, J. E.   4
Callender, D. E. Jr.
Cambier, J.   238
Campbell, J.   60
Caquot, A.   232–233
Caragounis, C. C.   238
Carlè, R. S.   239
Carmignac, J.   69
Carrington, G. P.   239
Cervin, R. S.   238
Charles, R. H.   209
Charlesworth, J. H.   46, 83, 233
Chazon, E.   118
Ciampa, R. E.   55

Collins, J. J.   1, 3–8, 16, 19, 23, 39–40, 94, 101–102, 124, 131–141, 145, 156, 173, 184, 195
Cope, L.   239
Coppens, J.   238
Coulot, C.   7, 126, 135, 155
Crouch, J. E.   237
Davidson, M. J.   38
Davila, J. R.   153, 184
Dawes, G. W.   238
Dibelius, M.   237
Dimant, D.   6, 19, 62–65, 77–78
Dochhorn, J.   6, 116, 188, 210
Dodd, C. H.   60
Dupont, J.   181
Ego, B.   164
Elgvin, T.   1–2, 4, 6, 8, 16–19, 22–23, 30–33, 35–37, 82, 85, 89, 91, 95, 97, 103–104, 106, 108–109, 111–113, 115–117, 120–122, 125–129, 131, 135, 138, 162, 166–167, 171, 191, 194–196, 205
Elliot, J. H.   196
Endres, J. C.   209
Evans, C. A.   46–47, 55–56
Feuillet, A.   239
Fiddes, P. S.   239
Finkel, A.   46
Fish, S.   57
Fishbane, M.   44, 46
Fisk, B. N.   46
Fitzmyer, J. A.   1, 46, 177, 239
Fleckenstein, K. H.   238
Fletcher-Louis, C. H. T.   5, 39–40, 119, 157–158, 163, 170–172, 176
Flusser, D.   117
Fraade, S. D.   127
Frey, J.   5, 6, 9, 126, 141, 167, 209

García Martínez, F.   5–6, 20, 109, 125, 129, 215, 220, 222, 229
Gielen, M.   237
Gieschen, C. A.   39
Goff, M. J.   3, 5, 7, 18–19, 24, 28 30, 39, 65, 119, 135–140, 145, 156–157
Gottstein, M. H.   46
Grudem, W.   238
Gundry-Volf, J. M.   239
Halpern-Amaru, B.   209
Halperin, D. J.   153
Harrington, D. J.   1, 5, 6, 7, 12–13, 15–16, 19–23, 25, 30–32, 36, 86–87, 90, 93, 96, 99, 109–111, 113, 125, 137–138, 162, 167–168, 184, 186, 194–197, 205, 215, 229, 231, 233
Hays, R.   45, 47, 49–57, 59, 61, 67, 77–79
Hempel, C.   6, 8–9, 13, 15
Holm-Nielsen, S.   60, 65–69, 72, 77
Horton, F. L.   46
Hurtado, L. W.   38–39
Ibba, G.   5
Jastrow, M.   227
Jefferies, D. J.   7, 19
Jervis, L. A.   239
Jobes, K. H.   55
Kelly, J. N. D.   196
Kimball, C. A.   48
Kister, M.   5, 191–193
Kittel, B. P.   65, 69–72, 77
Klijn, A. F. J.   130
Knibb, M. A.   83
Kroeger, C. C.   238
Kugel, J. L.   46
Lange, A.   5–7, 9, 11, 15, 19, 21–22, 72, 73, 85, 87, 98, 100, 125–129, 131–132, 138–140, 163–167, 170–171, 197, 209
Licht, J.   105, 117
Lichtenberger, H.   6, 9
Longenecker, R.   47
Lucassen, B.   31–33, 35–36, 82, 85, 89, 91, 95, 97, 103–104, 106, 108–109, 111–113, 120–121
Lührmann   197
Luttikhuizen, G. P.   109, 113
Maher, M.   206–207
Martin, D. B.   239
Martin, W. J.   239

McGehee, M.   197
McNamara, M.   207
Metzger, B. M.   46
Michaels, J. R.   196
Michaelis, W.   154
Milik, J. T.   4, 20, 22, 30, 152
Militic, S. F.   238
Miller, M. P.   47
Morgenstern, M.   5, 86, 187
Moyise, S.   43-44, 47
Murphy, C. M.   5–6, 24–28, 30, 84, 156, 192, 219–220
Murphy O'Connor, J.   238–239
Newsom, C.   39
Niehr, H.   6
Perdue, L. G.   8
Perriman, A. C.   239
Puech, É.   5-6
Qimron, E.   192, 227
Rabinowitz, I. L.   46
Roberts, B. J.   46
Rosner, B. S.   47
Ruiten, J. van   209
Runia, D. T.   102
Sampley, J. P.   238
Sanders, J. A.   43–44, 46–47, 55
Schäfer, P.   153
Schiffman, L. H.   5–6, 14, 32, 183–184
Scholem, G. G.   153
Schoors, A.   15, 72
Schuller, E. M.   5, 184, 200
Schwartz, M. D.   193
Schwemer, A. M.   174, 176
Shum, Shiu-Lun   47, 77–78
Slomovic, E.   46
Stanley, C. D.   47
Stegemann, H.   9, 32
Strugnell, J.   1, 4–5, 13–16, 19–20, 25, 30–32, 36, 74, 86–87, 93, 96, 99, 109–111, 113, 125, 137–138, 162, 167–168, 186, 191, 194–197, 205, 215, 229, 231, 233
Stuckenbruck, L. T.   6, 8, 17, 38, 157, 162, 170–171, 173–178,
Steudel, A.   31–33, 35–36, 82, 85, 89, 91, 95, 97, 103–104, 106, 108–109, 111–113, 120–121
Sullivan, K. P.   38–39
Tigchelaar, E. J. C.   5, 8, 17–18, 24, 28, 303–32, 35–38, 73, 79, 82, 85, 87, 89,

ʳ

91–92, 95, 97, 103–104, 106, 108–
109, 111–113, 115, 120, 122, 125,
129, 156–157, 161, 165, 167–170,
172, 190, 213, 215, 217, 220, 222,
226, 228–229

Tiller, P. A.   17, 117, 168
Tobin, T. H.   102, 133, 141
Trever, J. C.   46
VanderKam, J. C.   5, 209
Vermes, G.   19, 46, 209
Wacholder, B. Z.   4, 20, 125
Walker, W. O.   239
Waltke, B. K.   239

Watson, F.   56
Weima, J. A. D.   237
Weitzman, S.   46
Wernberg-Møller, P.   22
Werner, M.   154
Whitton, J.   194
Williams, H. H. D. III   45, 61–62, 77
Wold, B. G.   5, 154, 238
Wright, B. G.   6, 24, 27–28, 30, 156,
183–184
Yadin, Y.   32, 117, 189
Yarbrough, O. L.   195

Index of Subjects and Key Terms

Abaddon   109–110, 214

Adam   26, 94, 101, 102, 104–105, 109–
110, 112, 115, 117–119, 121, 131–134,
136–137, 139, 171, 179, 187, 190–191,
200, 204–205, 207–212, 225, 236–238

Agriculture   24, 82–84, 119, 121–122,
206, 235, 243

אות   28, 108, 113–114, 172, 214–215,
217–219, 220–221, 228

אישה   85, 91, 98–99, 197–199

אלהים   10, 93, 105, 107, 114, 124, 132–
133, 136, 149, 187, 207–208

Angels/angelic beings   11, 19, 29, 35,
38–41, 84, 89, 90, 94, 101–102, 105,
107, 109, 116, 119, 124, 126–128,
132–134, 136–150, 152–161, 163, 166,
168, 170, 172–182, 184–185, 202,
206–208, 210, 214, 219, 225, 234–235,
239–240, 241–243, 245

Angelmorphology   39, 119, 172, 173

Anthropology   39–41, 81, 89, 101–102,
109, 136–138, 146, 160, 163, 168, 180,
182, 184, 224, 231, 234–235, 240, 243,
245

Apocalyptic   3, 7-8, 16, 19–20, 23, 28,
30, 101, 128, 134–137, 141, 159, 166,
179, 235, 245

Behaviour   21, 24–25, 75, 88, 91, 128,
134–137, 141, 159, 166, 179, 184, 225,
232, 234, 236

בטן   195, 203, 229–230

Body   186, 190, 194, 196–197, 202, 215,
218, 223, 237–238

Bosom   74, 76, 85–86, 92, 94, 96–97,
122, 186, 189–194, 199, 201–204, 213,
218, 221, 224–225, 232, 236

Boundary   92, 97, 109, 155, 186, 223–
224, 193

Christology   39–40, 242

Citation   44, 46–50, 52–53, 57–58, 62,
66, 68–69, 71, 77–79, 203

כלי   86, 97, 186, 189, 191–197, 199, 202,
217

(un)Cover   92, 109–111, 185, 191, 194,
208–216, 218, 220–226, 240

Cosmology   41, 89–90, 121, 173, 184,
234–235

Daughter   86, 95–97, 183–184, 186, 200,
203, 216, 223–224, 226–228, 230, 232,
242

Decalogue   74, 93, 150–151, 195, 200

Deeds   98–100, 120, 126, 159–160, 166,
197–199, 205

Distinguish, to   20–21, 23, 84, 90, 100–
101, 107–108, 112, 119, 121, 131, 133,
135, 137, 140, 166, 169, 185, 192, 206,
211, 225

Dualism   11, 14, 16, 101–102, 128–129,
133–137, 139, 141–145, 152

Establish/ment   33–34, 86–87, 90, 103–
104, 109, 111, 113, 165, 216, 227–231,
234

Eve   109, 185, 187, 190, 205–207, 209–
211, 216, 225–226, 232–238

the 'Fall'   119, 140–141, 148, 204, 209,
236

Fashioning 92–93, 98–100, 103–104, 107, 120–122, 128, 137, 141, 144, 146, 148, 159, 185, 190–191, 197–198, 233

Father 22, 71, 74, 85, 92–93, 96–97, 120, 130, 144, 149–151, 154–155, 161, 172, 180, 184, 186–187, 191, 195, 199–201, 203, 206, 210, 216, 218, 221, 225, 228, 230, 236

Farmer 24, 35, 38, 115, 121, 235

First-Born 107, 162–163, 168, 170, 179, 195

Free-Narrative 64, 77, 81, 111

Garden 24, 35, 38, 45, 48, 82–83, 100, 110, 104, 106, 114–122, 137, 166, 179, 190, 199, 204–211, 213, 225, 228, 235, 243

Glory 13, 21, 23, 29, 34, 39, 107–109, 126, 129, 156, 162–163, 172, 175–176, 208, 210–211, 218, 220–223, 233, 236

Good and Evil, knowledge of 3, 21, 84, 88, 90, 93, 98–100, 116–122, 133, 136–137, 139–141, 143–144, 148–149, 156, 180–181, 185, 198, 204–205, 211, 224–225

Haguy 23, 33, 35, 98–99, 125, 137, 139, 141, 146, 245

Halakha 11, 71, 74, 76

Head 91–92, 108, 155, 233, 237–240

Helper 92, 95, 111, 113, 118, 186–188, 190, 204, 216

Hermeneutical Event 52–53, 56, 59–61, 79

Holy Ones 39–40, 128, 132–137, 139, 145–146, 148–150, 152, 154, 161–63, 165–67, 170–173, 175, 178–179, 181

Holy Spirit 99–102, 107, 121, 211, 220

Honour 13, 21–22, 34–35, 39, 71, 74, 85, 92–93, 107, 131, 149–151, 155–156, 158, 162, 172, 175, 178–181, 186–187, 191, 194–196, 199–203, 205, 218, 221, 223, 234

Host, angelic 28, 89–90, 108–109, 151, 153, 157, 160, 219

House Hold Codes (*Haustafeln*) 237

Humanity 3, 11, 20, 22, 33, 35, 41, 68, 76, 94, 98–102, 104–107, 112, 116, 119, 121, 124, 127, 129–154, 156–158, 160–161, 163, 165, 169–170, 178–181, 184–185, 196–197, 203–204, 206–207, 211, 219, 225, 234, 236, 240, 241, 243, 245

Husbands 85, 88, 95–99, 112, 184, 196, 202–203, 206, 208, 220, 225, 230, 234, 236–238, 242–243

Immortal/ality 134–135, 140, 143

Inheritance/Heritage 13, 17, 21, 26–27, 29–30, 33–34, 60, 76, 83–84, 92, 98, 107, 112, 120, 128, 137, 139–140, 155–158, 160–163, 171, 174, 179–180, 186, 205, 211–212, 218, 220, 223–224, 241

Joy 287

Likeness of 33, 35, 39–40, 83, 91, 93, 102, 105, 121, 132–137, 139, 146–148, 154, 179–181, 185, 198, 206, 240, 241

Marriage 195, 201, 216, 227, 232

Midrash 49–50, 59, 67, 133, 148

מחסור 4, 14, 24, 41, 89, 161, 193, 215, 217–218, 222–223, 230–231

Mother 22, 71, 74–75, 92–93, 96, 149–150, 154, 161, 180, 184, 186–187, 190–191, 195, 206, 208, 210, 233, 236, 242

נדיבים 26–27, 29, 41, 82–83, 92, 109–110, 155–156, 160, 180, 214, 219

Nudity 100, 110, 191, 195, 208–211, 213, 216, 224

Offspring 82, 87, 93–96, 150, 164, 187, 195, 229, 233

One flesh, become 75, 96, 186, 188, 191, 203, 229, 238

Origins/Birth-Times 34, 86–88, 92, 94–95, 105–106, 142, 155, 160, 185–187, 199, 201–203, 222, 227, 229,

234–235, 240

Parents   12, 21, 74, 93, 95, 122, 149–
     150, 154–155, 184, 187, 187, 203, 206,
     228–230, 234, 236

Planting   17, 84, 114, 116–117, 166,
     168, 173, 179

Poverty/Lacking   3, 4, 6, 23–30, 33–34,
     41, 81, 89, 90–94, 98–99, 108, 119,
     149, 155–156, 157–158, 160–161, 180,
     186–187, 193, 201, 204, 215, 217–220,
     222–225, 231–235, 245

Pregnant   93, 96, 227, 229

Priest/ly   8, 10–11, 39, 153, 163–173,
     175–176, 178–179, 223

Provenance, of document   6–9, 11, 13,
     15, 18, 20, 26, 103, 157

קדושים   124–128, 132–133, 136–140,
     149, 152, 161–162, 164, 167–168,
     170–172, 174–175, 177–178

רוח בשר   98, 101

רז נהיה   1, 3, 12, 14, 16, 20–25, 40–41,
     81, 91–95, 98–100, 104–106, 120, 125,
     139, 141, 146, 149–150, 155–156, 158,
     161, 165, 172, 179–180, 184–186,
     197–198, 202, 205, 214, 219, 225,
     234–235, 239

Reading Mechanism   53

Revelation   3, 10, 23, 25, 40–41, 101,
     119, 128, 135–136, 139–141, 149,
     179–180, 219, 225, 238

Re-written (Bible)   45–46, 48, 56–57,
     64, 111, 113, 142

Ruling   99, 100, 112, 120, 131, 188, 199,
     204, 231

Seasons   82, 84, 89, 90, 104, 108, 120–
     121, 244–245

Sectarian/Monastic, community   7–9,
     11–19, 26, 132, 160, 168, 183–184,
     228, 230

Separation   96, 99–100, 108, 119, 170,
     185, 197–199, 202, 228–230

Serpent   190–191, 199, 206–207, 209–

210

Shame   33–34, 96–97, 109–111, 185–
     186, 188–189, 191, 195, 205, 208–225,
     232, 234, 236, 239

Sheol   110, 214–215, 223

Sheth   71, 76, 131, 135

Sitz im Leben   25

'Sons of Seth'   127, 129–131, 139

Spring   40, 107, 129, 143, 148, 150, 162,
     164–165, 167, 179, 215

Temple   10–11, 15, 39, 86, 88, 153,
     164–167, 172

Transgression   204, 211, 236–237, 245

Unity/Unification   92, 95–96, 191, 206

Urzeit/Endzeit   99, 245

Veneration   92–93, 146, 149–150, 155–
     156, 158, 163, 170, 172–178, 180–181,
     241–242

Vessel   74, 76, 86, 186, 191–192, 194–
     197, 202–203, 210, 218, 221

ועוד לא   98, 119, 125, 129, 135–136,
     138, 140

Wealth   6, 23–25, 27–29, 73, 84, 92,
     156, 166

Wife/Wives   12, 34–35, 74–75, 85–86,
     88, 91–92, 94–97, 110, 112, 118, 122,
     150, 186–192, 194–197, 199–209,
     212–213, 223–225, 228–232, 235–237,
     242–243

Womb   93, 195, 203, 229

עם רוח   98, 101, 125, 133

ערם   87, 110, 191, 195, 208–209, 213–
     214

Wissenschaftliche Untersuchungen zum Neuen Testament

Alphabetical Index of the First and Second Series

Ådna, Jostein: Jesu Stellung zum Tempel. 2000. *Volume II/119.*

Ådna, Jostein and *Kvalbein, Hans* (Ed.): The Mission of the Early Church to Jews and Gentiles. 2000. *Volume 127.*

Alkier, Stefan: Wunder und Wirklichkeit in den Briefen des Apostels Paulus. 2001. *Volume 134.*

Anderson, Paul N.: The Christology of the Fourth Gospel. 1996. *Volume II/78.*

Appold, Mark L.: The Oneness Motif in the Fourth Gospel. 1976. *Volume II/1.*

Arnold, Clinton E.: The Colossian Syncretism. 1995. *Volume II/77.*

Ascough, Richard S.: Paul's Macedonian Associations. 2003. *Volume II/161.*

Asiedu-Peprah, Martin: Johannine Sabbath Conflicts As Juridical Controversy. 2001. *Volume II/132.*

Avemarie, Friedrich: Die Tauferzählungen der Apostelgeschichte. 2002. *Volume 139.*

Avemarie, Friedrich and *Hermann Lichtenberger* (Ed.): Auferstehung – Ressurection. 2001. *Volume 135.*

Avemarie, Friedrich and *Hermann Lichtenberger* (Ed.): Bund und Tora. 1996. *Volume 92.*

Baarlink, Heinrich: Verkündigtes Heil. 2004. *Volume 168.*

Bachmann, Michael: Sünder oder Übertreter. 1992. *Volume 59.*

Bachmann, Michael (Ed.): Lutherische und Neue Paulusperspektive. 2005. *Volume 182.*

Back, Frances: Verwandlung durch Offenbarung bei Paulus. 2002. *Volume II/153.*

Baker, William R.: Personal Speech-Ethics in the Epistle of James. 1995. *Volume II/68.*

Bakke, Odd Magne: 'Concord and Peace'. 2001. *Volume II/143.*

Balla, Peter: Challenges to New Testament Theology. 1997. *Volume II/95.*

– *The Child-Parent Relationship in the New Testament and its Environment. 2003. Volume 155.*

Bammel, Ernst: Judaica. Volume I 1986. *Volume 37.*

– Volume II 1997. *Volume 91.*

Bash, Anthony: Ambassadors for Christ. 1997. *Volume II/92.*

Bauernfeind, Otto: Kommentar und Studien zur Apostelgeschichte. 1980. *Volume 22.*

Baum, Armin Daniel: Pseudepigraphie und literarische Fälschung im frühen Christentum. 2001. *Volume II/138.*

Bayer, Hans Friedrich: Jesus' Predictions of Vindication and Resurrection. 1986. *Volume II/20.*

Becker, Michael: Wunder und Wundertäter im früh-rabbinischen Judentum. 2002. *Volume II/144.*

Bell, Richard H.: Provoked to Jealousy. 1994. *Volume II/63.*

– No One Seeks for God. 1998. *Volume 106.*

Bennema, Cornelis: The Power of Saving Wisdom. 2002. *Volume II/148.*

Bergman, Jan: see *Kieffer, René*

Bergmeier, Roland: Das Gesetz im Römerbrief und andere Studien zum Neuen Testament. 2000. *Volume 121.*

Betz, Otto: Jesus, der Messias Israels. 1987. *Volume 42.*

– Jesus, der Herr der Kirche. 1990. *Volume 52.*

Beyschlag, Karlmann: Simon Magus und die christliche Gnosis. 1974. *Volume 16.*

Bittner, Wolfgang J.: Jesu Zeichen im Johannesevangelium. 1987. *Volume II/26.*

Bjerkelund, Carl J.: Tauta Egeneto. 1987. *Volume 40.*

Blackburn, Barry Lee: Theios Anēr and the Markan Miracle Traditions. 1991. *Volume II/40.*

Bock, Darrell L.: Blasphemy and Exaltation in Judaism and the Final Examination of Jesus. 1998. *Volume II/106.*

Bockmuehl, Markus N.A.: Revelation and Mystery in Ancient Judaism and Pauline Christianity. 1990. *Volume II/36.*

Bøe, Sverre: Gog and Magog. 2001. *Volume II/135.*

Böhlig, Alexander: Gnosis und Synkretismus. Teil 1 1989. *Volume 47* – Teil 2 1989. *Volume 48.*

Böhm, Martina: Samarien und die Samaritai bei Lukas. 1999. *Volume II/111.*

Böttrich, Christfried: Weltweisheit – Mensch-heitsethik – Urkult. 1992. *Volume II/50.*

Bolyki, János: Jesu Tischgemeinschaften. 1997. *Volume II/96.*

Bosman, Philip: Conscience in Philo and Paul. 2003. *Volume II/166.*

Bovon, François: Studies in Early Christianity. 2003. *Volume 161.*

Brocke, Christoph vom: Thessaloniki – Stadt des Kassander und Gemeinde des Paulus. 2001. *Volume II/125.*

Brunson, Andrew: Psalm 118 in the Gospel of John. 2003. *Volume II/158.*

Büchli, Jörg: Der Poimandres – ein paganisiertes Evangelium. 1987. *Volume II/27.*

Bühner, Jan A.: Der Gesandte und sein Weg im 4. Evangelium. 1977. *Volume II/2.*

Burchard, Christoph: Untersuchungen zu Joseph und Aseneth. 1965. *Volume 8.*

– Studien zur Theologie, Sprache und Umwelt des Neuen Testaments. Ed. von D. Sänger. 1998. *Volume 107.*

Burnett, Richard: Karl Barth's Theological Exegesis. 2001. *Volume II/145.*

Byron, John: Slavery Metaphors in Early Judaism and Pauline Christianity. 2003. *Volume II/162.*

Byrskog, Samuel: Story as History – History as Story. 2000. *Volume 123.*

Cancik, Hubert (Ed.): Markus-Philologie. 1984. *Volume 33.*

Capes, David B.: Old Testament Yaweh Texts in Paul's Christology. 1992. *Volume II/47.*

Caragounis, Chrys C.: The Development of Greek and the New Testament. 2004. *Volume 167.*

– The Son of Man. 1986. *Volume 38.*

– see *Fridrichsen, Anton.*

Carleton Paget, James: The Epistle of Barnabas. 1994. *Volume II/64.*

Carson, D.A., O'Brien, Peter T. and Mark Seifrid (Ed.): Justification and Variegated Nomism.
Volume 1: The Complexities of Second Temple Judaism. 2001. *Volume II/140.*
Volume 2: The Paradoxes of Paul. 2004. *Volume II/181.*

Ciampa, Roy E.: The Presence and Function of Scripture in Galatians 1 and 2. 1998. *Volume II/102.*

Classen, Carl Joachim: Rhetorical Criticsm of the New Testament. 2000. *Volume 128.*

Colpe, Carsten: Iranier – Aramäer – Hebräer – Hellenen. 2003. *Volume 154.*

Crump, David: Jesus the Intercessor. 1992. *Volume II/49.*

Dahl, Nils Alstrup: Studies in Ephesians. 2000. *Volume 131.*

Deines, Roland: Die Gerechtigkeit der Tora im Reich des Messias. 2004. *Volume 177.*

– Jüdische Steingefäße und pharisäische Frömmigkeit. 1993. *Volume II/52.*

– Die Pharisäer. 1997. *Volume 101.*

– and *Karl-Wilhelm Niebuhr (Ed.):* Philo und das Neue Testament. 2004. *Volume 172.*

Dettwiler, Andreas and *Jean Zumstein (Ed.):* Kreuzestheologie im Neuen Testament. 2002. *Volume 151.*

Dickson, John P.: Mission-Commitment in Ancient Judaism and in the Pauline Communities. 2003. *Volume II/159.*

Dietzfelbinger, Christian: Der Abschied des Kommenden. 1997. *Volume 95.*

Dimitrov, Ivan Z., James D.G. Dunn, Ulrich Luz and *Karl-Wilhelm Niebuhr* (Ed.): Das Alte Testament als christliche Bibel in orthodoxer und westlicher Sicht. 2004. *Volume 174.*

Dobbeler, Axel von: Glaube als Teilhabe. 1987. *Volume II/22.*

Du Toit, David S.: Theios Anthropos. 1997. *Volume II/91*

Dübbers, Michael: Christologie und Existenz im Kolosserbrief. 2005. *Volume II/191.*

Dunn , James D.G. (Ed.): Jews and Christians. 1992. *Volume 66.*

– Paul and the Mosaic Law. 1996. *Volume 89.*

– see *Dimitrov, Ivan Z.*

Dunn, James D.G., Hans Klein, Ulrich Luz and *Vasile Mihoc* (Ed.): Auslegung der Bibel in orthodoxer und westlicher Perspektive. 2000. *Volume 130.*

Ebel, Eva: Die Attraktivität früher christlicher Gemeinden. 2004. *Volume II/178.*

Ebertz, Michael N.: Das Charisma des Gekreuzigten. 1987. *Volume 45.*

Eckstein, Hans-Joachim: Der Begriff Syneidesis bei Paulus. 1983. *Volume II/10.*

– Verheißung und Gesetz. 1996. *Volume 86.*

Ego, Beate: Im Himmel wie auf Erden. 1989. *Volume II/34*

Ego, Beate, Armin Lange and Peter Pilhofer (Ed.): Gemeinde ohne Tempel – Community without Temple. 1999. *Volume 118.*

Eisen, Ute E.: see *Paulsen, Henning.*

Ellis, E. Earle: Prophecy and Hermeneutic in Early Christianity. 1978. *Volume 18.*

– The Old Testament in Early Christianity. 1991. *Volume 54.*

Endo, Masanobu: Creation and Christology. 2002. *Volume 149.*

Ennulat, Andreas: Die 'Minor Agreements'. 1994. *Volume II/62.*

Ensor, Peter W.: Jesus and His 'Works'. 1996. *Volume II/85.*

Eskola, Timo: Messiah and the Throne. 2001. *Volume II/142.*

– Theodicy and Predestination in Pauline Soteriology. 1998. *Volume II/100.*

Fatehi, Mehrdad: The Spirit's Relation to the Risen Lord in Paul. 2000. *Volume II/128.*

Feldmeier, Reinhard: Die Krisis des Gottessoh-nes. 1987. *Volume II/21.*

– Die Christen als Fremde. 1992. *Volume 64.*

Feldmeier, Reinhard and *Ulrich Heckel* (Ed.): Die Heiden. 1994. *Volume 70.*

Fletcher-Louis, Crispin H.T.: Luke-Acts: Angels, Christology and Soteriology. 1997. *Volume II/94.*

Förster, Niclas: Marcus Magus. 1999. *Volume 114.*

Forbes, Christopher Brian: Prophecy and Inspired Speech in Early Christianity and its Hellenistic Environment. 1995. *Volume II/75.*

Fornberg, Tord: see *Fridrichsen, Anton.*

Fossum, Jarl E.: The Name of God and the Angel of the Lord. 1985. *Volume 36.*

Foster, Paul: Community, Law and Mission in Matthew's Gospel. *Volume II/177.*

Fotopoulos, John: Food Offered to Idols in Roman Corinth. 2003. *Volume II/151.*

Frenschkowski, Marco: Offenbarung und Epiphanie. Volume 1 1995. *Volume II/79* – Volume 2 1997. *Volume II/80.*

Frey, Jörg: Eugen Drewermann und die biblische Exegese. 1995. *Volume II/71.*

– Die johanneische Eschatologie. Volume I. 1997. *Volume 96.* – Volume II. 1998. *Volume 110.*

– Volume III. 2000. *Volume 117.*

Frey, Jörg and *Udo Schnelle (Ed.):* Kontexte des Johannesevangeliums. 2004. *Volume 175.*

– and *Jens Schröter* (Ed.): Deutungen des Todes Jesu im Neuen Testament. 2005. *Volume 181.*

Freyne, Sean: Galilee and Gospel. 2000. *Volume 125.*

Fridrichsen, Anton: Exegetical Writings. Edited by C.C. Caragounis and T. Fornberg. 1994. *Volume 76.*

Garlington, Don B.: 'The Obedience of Faith'. 1991. *Volume II/38.*

– Faith, Obedience, and Perseverance. 1994. *Volume 79.*

Garnet, Paul: Salvation and Atonement in the Qumran Scrolls. 1977. *Volume II/3.*

Gemünden, Petra von (Ed.): see *Weissenrieder, Annette.*

Gese, Michael: Das Vermächtnis des Apostels. 1997. *Volume II/99.*

Gheorghita, Radu: The Role of the Septuagint in Hebrews. 2003. *Volume II/160.*

Gräbe, Petrus J.: The Power of God in Paul's Letters. 2000. *Volume II/123.*

Gräßer, Erich: Der Alte Bund im Neuen. 1985. *Volume 35.*

– Forschungen zur Apostelgeschichte. 2001. *Volume 137.*

Green, Joel B.: The Death of Jesus. 1988. *Volume II/33.*

Gregory, Andrew: The Reception of Luke and Acts in the Period before Irenaeus. 2003. *Volume II/169.*

Gundry, Robert H.: The Old is Better. 2005. *Volume 178.*

Gundry Volf, Judith M.: Paul and Perseverance. 1990. *Volume II/37.*

Hafemann, Scott J.: Suffering and the Spirit. 1986. *Volume II/19.*

– Paul, Moses, and the History of Israel. 1995. *Volume 81.*

Hahn, Johannes (Ed.): Zerstörungen des Jerusalemer Tempels. 2002. *Volume 147.*

Hannah, Darrel D.: Michael and Christ. 1999. *Volume II/109.*

Hamid-Khani, Saeed: Relevation and Con-cealment of Christ. 2000. *Volume II/120.*

Harrison; James R.: Paul's Language of Grace in Its Graeco-Roman Context. 2003. *Volume II/172.*

Hartman, Lars: Text-Centered New Testament Studies. Ed. von D. Hellholm. 1997. *Volume 102.*

Hartog, Paul: Polycarp and the New Testament. 2001. *Volume II/134.*

Heckel, Theo K.: Der Innere Mensch. 1993. *Volume II/53.*

– Vom Evangelium des Markus zum viergestal-tigen Evangelium. 1999. *Volume 120.*

Heckel, Ulrich: Kraft in Schwachheit. 1993. *Volume II/56.*

– Der Segen im Neuen Testament. 2002. *Volume 150.*

– see *Feldmeier, Reinhard.*

– see *Hengel, Martin.*

Heiligenthal, Roman: Werke als Zeichen. 1983. *Volume II/9.*

Hellholm, D.: see *Hartman, Lars.*

Hemer, Colin J.: The Book of Acts in the Setting of Hellenistic History. 1989. *Volume 49.*

Hengel, Martin: Judentum und Hellenismus. 1969, ³1988. *Volume 10.*

– Die johanneische Frage. 1993. *Volume 67.*

– Judaica et Hellenistica.
  Kleine Schriften I. 1996. *Volume 90.*
– Judaica, Hellenistica et Christiana.
  Kleine Schriften II. 1999. *Volume 109.*
– Paulus und Jakobus.
  Kleine Schriften III. 2002. *Volume 141.*
Hengel, Martin and *Ulrich Heckel* (Ed.): Paulus
  und das antike Judentum. 1991. *Volume 58.*
Hengel, Martin and *Hermut Löhr* (Ed.):
  Schriftauslegung im antiken Judentum und
  im Urchristentum. 1994. *Volume 73.*
Hengel, Martin and *Anna Maria Schwemer:*
  Paulus zwischen Damaskus und Antiochien.
  1998. *Volume 108.*
– Der messianische Anspruch Jesu und die
  Anfänge der Christologie. 2001. *Volume 138.*
Hengel, Martin and *Anna Maria Schwemer*
  (Ed.): Königsherrschaft Gottes und himm-
  lischer Kult. 1991. *Volume 55.*
– Die Septuaginta. 1994. *Volume 72.*
Hengel, Martin; Siegfried Mittmann and *Anna
  Maria Schwemer* (Ed.): La Cité de Dieu /
  Die Stadt Gottes. 2000. *Volume 129.*
Herrenbrück, Fritz: Jesus und die Zöllner. 1990.
  Volume II/41.
Herzer, Jens: Paulus oder Petrus? 1998.
  Volume 103.
Hoegen-Rohls, Christina: Der nachösterliche
  Johannes. 1996. *Volume II/84.*
Hofius, Otfried: Katapausis. 1970. *Volume 11.*
– Der Vorhang vor dem Thron Gottes. 1972.
  Volume 14.
– Der Christushymnus Philipper 2,6-11. 1976,
  ²1991. *Volume 17.*
– Paulusstudien. 1989, ²1994. *Volume 51.*
– Neutestamentliche Studien. 2000. *Volume 132.*
– Paulusstudien II. 2002. *Volume 143.*
Hofius, Otfried and *Hans-Christian Kammler:*
  Johannesstudien. 1996. *Volume 88.*
Holtz, Traugott: Geschichte und Theologie des
  Urchristentums. 1991. *Volume 57.*
Hommel, Hildebrecht: Sebasmata. Volume 1 1983.
  Volume 31 – Volume 2 1984. *Volume 32.*
Hvalvik, Reidar: The Struggle for Scripture and
  Covenant. 1996. *Volume II/82.*
Johns, Loren L.: The Lamb Christology of the
  Apocalypse of John. 2003. *Volume II/167.*
Joubert, Stephan: Paul as Benefactor. 2000.
  Volume II/124.
Jungbauer, Harry: „Ehre Vater und Mutter".
  2002. *Volume II/146.*
Kähler, Christoph: Jesu Gleichnisse als Poesie
  und Therapie. 1995. *Volume 78.*
Kamlah, Ehrhard: Die Form der katalogischen
  Paränese im Neuen Testament. 1964. *Volume 7.*

Kammler, Hans-Christian: Christologie und
  Eschatologie. 2000. *Volume 126.*
– Kreuz und Weisheit. 2003. *Volume 159.*
– see *Hofius, Otfried.*
Kelhoffer, James A.: The Diet of John the
  Baptist. 2005. *Volume 176.*
– Miracle and Mission. 1999. *Volume II/112.*
Kieffer, René and *Jan Bergman (Ed.):* La Main de
  Dieu / Die Hand Gottes. 1997. *Volume 94.*
Kim, Seyoon: The Origin of Paul's Gospel.
  1981, ²1984. *Volume II/4.*
– Paul and the New Perspective. 2002.
  Volume 140.
– "The 'Son of Man'" as the Son of God.
  1983. *Volume 30.*
Klauck, Hans-Josef: Religion und Gesellschaft
  im frühen Christentum. 2003. *Volume 152.*
Klein, Hans: see *Dunn, James D.G..*
Kleinknecht, Karl Th.: Der leidende Gerechtfer-
  tigte. 1984, ²1988. *Volume II/13.*
Klinghardt, Matthias: Gesetz und Volk Gottes.
  1988. *Volume II/32.*
Koch, Michael: Drachenkampf und Sonnenfrau.
  2004. *Volume II/184.*
Koch, Stefan: Rechtliche Regelung von
  Konflikten im frühen Christentum. 2004.
  Volume II/174.
Köhler, Wolf-Dietrich: Rezeption des Matthäus-
  evangeliums in der Zeit vor Irenäus. 1987.
  Volume II/24.
Köhn, Andreas: Der Neutestamentler Ernst
  Lohmeyer. 2004. *Volume II/180.*
Kooten, George H. van: Cosmic Christology in
  Paul and the Pauline School. 2003.
  Volume II/171.
Korn, Manfred: Die Geschichte Jesu in
  veränderter Zeit. 1993. *Volume II/51.*
Koskenniemi, Erkki: Apollonios von Tyana in
  der neutestamentlichen Exegese. 1994.
  Volume II/61.
Kraus, Thomas J.: Sprache, Stil und historischer
  Ort des zweiten Petrusbriefes. 2001.
  Volume II/136.
Kraus, Wolfgang: Das Volk Gottes. 1996.
  Volume 85.
– and *Karl-Wilhelm Niebuhr* (Ed.): Früh-
  judentum und Neues Testament im Horizont
  Biblischer Theologie. 2003. *Volume 162.*
– see *Walter, Nikolaus.*
Kreplin, Matthias: Das Selbstverständnis Jesu.
  2001. *Volume II/141.*
Kuhn, Karl G.: Achtzehngebet und Vaterunser
  und der Reim. 1950. *Volume 1.*
Kvalbein, Hans: see *Ådna, Jostein.*
Kwon, Yon-Gyong: Eschatology in Galatians.
  2004. *Volume II/183.*

Laansma, Jon: I Will Give You Rest. 1997. *Volume II/98.*

Labahn, Michael: Offenbarung in Zeichen und Wort. 2000. *Volume II/117.*

Lambers-Petry, Doris: see *Tomson, Peter J.*

Lange, Armin: see *Ego, Beate.*

Lampe, Peter: Die stadtrömischen Christen in den ersten beiden Jahrhunderten. 1987, ²1989. *Volume II/18.*

Landmesser, Christof: Wahrheit als Grundbegriff neutestamentlicher Wissenschaft. 1999. *Volume 113.*

– Jüngerberufung und Zuwendung zu Gott. 2000. *Volume 133.*

Lau, Andrew: Manifest in Flesh. 1996. *Volume II/86.*

Lawrence, Louise: An Ethnography of the Gospel of Matthew. 2003. *Volume II/165.*

Lee, Aquila H.I.: From Messiah to Preexistent Son. 2005. *Volume II/192.*

Lee, Pilchan: The New Jerusalem in the Book of Relevation. 2000. *Volume II/129.*

Lichtenberger, Hermann: see *Avemarie, Friedrich.*

Lichtenberger, Hermann: Das Ich Adams und das Ich der Menschheit. 2004. *Volume 164.*

Lierman, John: The New Testament Moses. 2004. *Volume II/173.*

Lieu, Samuel N.C.: Manichaeism in the Later Roman Empire and Medieval China. ²1992. *Volume 63.*

Lindgård, Fredrik: Paul's Line of Thought in 2 Corinthians 4:16-5:10. 2004. *Volume II/189.*

Loader, William R.G.: Jesus' Attitude Towards the Law. 1997. *Volume II/97.*

Löhr, Gebhard: Verherrlichung Gottes durch Philosophie. 1997. *Volume 97.*

Löhr, Hermut: Studien zum frühchristlichen und frühjüdischen Gebet. 2003. *Volume 160.*

– see *Hengel, Martin.*

Löhr, Winrich Alfried: Basilides und seine Schule. 1995. *Volume 83.*

Luomanen, Petri: Entering the Kingdom of Heaven. 1998. *Volume II/101.*

Luz, Ulrich: see *Dunn, James D.G.*

Mackay, Ian D.: John's Raltionship with Mark. 2004. *Volume II/182.*

Maier, Gerhard: Mensch und freier Wille. 1971. *Volume 12.*

– Die Johannesoffenbarung und die Kirche. 1981. *Volume 25.*

Markschies, Christoph: Valentinus Gnosticus? 1992. *Volume 65.*

Marshall, Peter: Enmity in Corinth: Social Conventions in Paul's Relations with the Corinthians. 1987. *Volume II/23.*

Mayer, Annemarie: Sprache der Einheit im Epheserbrief und in der Ökumene. 2002. *Volume II/150.*

McDonough, Sean M.: YHWH at Patmos: Rev. 1:4 in its Hellenistic and Early Jewish Setting. 1999. *Volume II/107.*

McGlynn, Moyna: Divine Judgement and Divine Benevolence in the Book of Wisdom. 2001. *Volume II/139.*

Meade, David G.: Pseudonymity and Canon. 1986. *Volume 39.*

Meadors, Edward P.: Jesus the Messianic Herald of Salvation. 1995. *Volume II/72.*

Meißner, Stefan: Die Heimholung des Ketzers. 1996. *Volume II/87.*

Mell, Ulrich: Die „anderen" Winzer. 1994. *Volume 77.*

Mengel, Berthold: Studien zum Philipperbrief. 1982. *Volume 8.*

Merkel, Helmut: Die Widersprüche zwischen den Evangelien. 1971. *Volume 13.*

Merklein, Helmut: Studien zu Jesus und Paulus. Volume 1 1987. *Volume 43.* – Volume 2 1998. *Volume 105.*

Metzdorf, Christina: Die Tempelaktion Jesu. 2003. *Volume II/168.*

Metzler, Karin: Der griechische Begriff des Verzeihens. 1991. *Volume II/44.*

Metzner, Rainer: Die Rezeption des Matthäusevangeliums im 1. Petrusbrief. 1995. *Volume II/74.*

– Das Verständnis der Sünde im Johannesevangelium. 2000. *Volume 122.*

Mihoc, Vasile: see *Dunn, James D.G..*

Mineshige, Kiyoshi: Besitzverzicht und Almosen bei Lukas. 2003. *Volume II/163.*

Mittmann, Siegfried: see *Hengel, Martin.*

Mittmann-Richert, Ulrike: Magnifikat und Benediktus. *1996. Volume II/90.*

Mournet, Terence C.: Oral Tradition and Literary Dependency. 2005. *Volume II/195.*

Mußner, Franz: Jesus von Nazareth im Umfeld Israels und der Urkirche. Ed. von M. Theobald. 1998. *Volume 111.*

Niebuhr, Karl-Wilhelm: Gesetz und Paränese. 1987. *Volume II/28.*

– Heidenapostel aus Israel. 1992. *Volume 62.*

– see *Deines, Roland*

– see *Dimitrov, Ivan Z.*

– see *Kraus, Wolfgang*

Nielsen, Anders E.: "Until it is Fullfilled". 2000. *Volume II/126.*

Nissen, Andreas: Gott und der Nächste im antiken Judentum. 1974. *Volume 15.*

Noack, Christian: Gottesbewußtsein. 2000. *Volume II/116.*

Noormann, Rolf: Irenäus als Paulusinterpret. 1994. *Volume II/66.*

Novakovic, Lidija: Messiah, the Healer of the Sick. 2003. *Volume II/170.*

Obermann, Andreas: Die christologische Erfüllung der Schrift im Johannesevangelium. 1996. *Volume II/83.*

Öhler, Markus: Barnabas. 2003. *Volume 156.*

Okure, Teresa: The Johannine Approach to Mission. 1988. *Volume II/31.*

Onuki, Takashi: Heil und Erlösung. 2004. *Volume 165.*

Oropeza, B. J.: Paul and Apostasy. 2000. *Volume II/115.*

Ostmeyer, Karl-Heinrich: Taufe und Typos. 2000. *Volume II/118.*

Paulsen, Henning: Studien zur Literatur und Geschichte des frühen Christentums. Ed. von Ute E. Eisen. 1997. *Volume 99.*

Pao, David W.: Acts and the Isaianic New Exodus. 2000. *Volume II/130.*

Park, Eung Chun: The Mission Discourse in Matthew's Interpretation. 1995. *Volume II/81.*

Park, Joseph S.: Conceptions of Afterlife in Jewish Insriptions. 2000. *Volume II/121.*

Pate, C. Marvin: The Reverse of the Curse. 2000. *Volume II/114.*

Peres, Imre: Griechische Grabinschriften und neutestamentliche Eschatologie. 2003. *Volume 157.*

Philip, Finny: The Originis of Pauline Pneumatology. *Volume II/194.*

Philonenko, Marc (Ed.): Le Trône de Dieu. 1993. *Volume 69.*

Pilhofer, Peter: Presbyteron Kreitton. 1990. *Volume II/39.*

– Philippi. Volume 1 1995. *Volume 87.* – Volume 2 2000. *Volume 119.*

– Die frühen Christen und ihre Welt. 2002. *Volume 145.*

– see *Ego, Beate.*

Plümacher, Eckhard: Geschichte und Geschichten. Aufsätze zur Apostelgeschichte und zu den Johannesakten. Herausgegeben von Jens Schröter und Ralph Brucker. 2004. *Volume 170.*

Pöhlmann, Wolfgang: Der Verlorene Sohn und das Haus. 1993. *Volume 68.*

Pokorný, Petr and *Josef B. Souček:* Bibelauslegung als Theologie. 1997. *Volume 100.*

Pokorný, Petr and *Jan Roskovec* (Ed.): Philosophical Hermeneutics and Biblical Exegesis. 2002. *Volume 153.*

Porter, Stanley E.: The Paul of Acts. 1999. *Volume 115.*

Prieur, Alexander: Die Verkündigung der Gottesherrschaft. 1996. *Volume II/89.*

Probst, Hermann: Paulus und der Brief. 1991. *Volume II/45.*

Räisänen, Heikki: Paul and the Law. 1983, ²1987. *Volume 29.*

Rehkopf, Friedrich: Die lukanische Sonderquelle. 1959. *Volume 5.*

Rein, Matthias: Die Heilung des Blindgeborenen (Joh 9). 1995. *Volume II/73.*

Reinmuth, Eckart: Pseudo-Philo und Lukas. 1994. *Volume 74.*

Reiser, Marius: Syntax und Stil des Markusevangeliums. 1984. *Volume II/11.*

Rhodes, James N.: The Epistle of Barnabas and the Deuteronomic Tradition. 2004. *Volume II/188.*

Richards, E. Randolph: The Secretary in the Letters of Paul. 1991. *Volume II/42.*

Riesner, Rainer: Jesus als Lehrer. 1981, ³1988. *Volume II/7.*

– Die Frühzeit des Apostels Paulus. 1994. *Volume 71.*

Rissi, Mathias: Die Theologie des Hebräerbriefs. 1987. *Volume 41.*

Roskovec, Jan: see *Pokorný, Petr.*

Röhser, Günter: Metaphorik und Personifikation der Sünde. 1987. *Volume II/25.*

Rose, Christian: Die Wolke der Zeugen. 1994. *Volume II/60.*

Rothschild, Clare K.: Luke Acts and the Rhetoric of History. 2004. *Volume II/175.*

Rüegger, Hans-Ulrich: Verstehen, was Markus erzählt. 2002. *Volume II/155.*

Rüger, Hans Peter: Die Weisheitsschrift aus der Kairoer Geniza. 1991. *Volume 53.*

Sänger, Dieter: Antikes Judentum und die Mysterien. 1980. *Volume II/5.*

– Die Verkündigung des Gekreuzigten und Israel. 1994. *Volume 75.*

– see *Burchard, Christoph*

Salier, Willis Hedley: The Rhetorical Impact of the Sēmeia in the Gospel of John. 2004. *Volume II/186.*

Salzmann, Jorg Christian: Lehren und Ermahnen. 1994. *Volume II/59.*

Sandnes, Karl Olav: Paul – One of the Prophets? 1991. *Volume II/43.*

Sato, Migaku: Q und Prophetie. 1988. *Volume II/29.*

Schäfer, Ruth: Paulus bis zum Apostelkonzil. 2004. *Volume II/179.*

Schaper, Joachim: Eschatology in the Greek Psalter. 1995. *Volume II/76.*

Schimanowski, Gottfried: Die himmlische Liturgie in der Apokalypse des Johannes. 2002. *Volume II/154.*
– Weisheit und Messias. 1985. *Volume II/17.*
Schlichting, Günter: Ein jüdisches Leben Jesu. 1982. *Volume 24.*
Schnabel, Eckhard J.: Law and Wisdom from Ben Sira to Paul. 1985. *Volume II/16.*
Schnelle, Udo: see *Frey, Jörg.*
Schröter, Jens: see *Frey, Jörg.*
Schutter, William L.: Hermeneutic and Composition in I Peter. 1989. *Volume II/30.*
Schwartz, Daniel R.: Studies in the Jewish Background of Christianity. 1992. *Volume 60.*
Schwemer, Anna Maria: see *Hengel, Martin*
Scott, James M.: Adoption as Sons of God. 1992. *Volume II/48.*
– Paul and the Nations. 1995. *Volume 84.*
Shum, Shiu-Lun: Paul's Use of Isaiah in Romans. 2002. *Volume II/156.*
Siegert, Folker: Drei hellenistisch-jüdische Predigten. Teil I 1980. *Volume 20* – Teil II 1992. *Volume 61.*
– Nag-Hammadi-Register. 1982. *Volume 26.*
– Argumentation bei Paulus. 1985. *Volume 34.*
– Philon von Alexandrien. 1988. *Volume 46.*
Simon, Marcel: Le christianisme antique et son contexte religieux I/II. 1981. *Volume 23.*
Snodgrass, Klyne: The Parable of the Wicked Tenants. 1983. *Volume 27.*
Söding, Thomas: Das Wort vom Kreuz. 1997. *Volume 93.*
– see *Thüsing, Wilhelm.*
Sommer, Urs: Die Passionsgeschichte des Markusevangeliums. 1993. *Volume II/58.*
Souček, Josef B.: see *Pokorný, Petr.*
Spangenberg, Volker: Herrlichkeit des Neuen Bundes. 1993. *Volume II/55.*
Spanje, T.E. van: Inconsistency in Paul? 1999. *Volume II/110.*
Speyer, Wolfgang: Frühes Christentum im antiken Strahlungsfeld. Volume I: 1989. *Volume 50.*
– Volume II: 1999. *Volume 116.*
Stadelmann, Helge: Ben Sira als Schriftgelehrter. 1980. *Volume II/6.*
Stenschke, Christoph W.: Luke's Portrait of Gentiles Prior to Their Coming to Faith. *Volume II/108.*
Sterck-Degueldre, Jean-Pierre: Eine Frau namens Lydia. 2004. *Volume II/176.*
Stettler, Christian: Der Kolosserhymnus. 2000. *Volume II/131.*
Stettler, Hanna: Die Christologie der Pastoralbriefe. 1998. *Volume II/105.*

Stökl Ben Ezra, Daniel: The Impact of Yom Kippur on Early Christianity. 2003. *Volume 163.*
Strobel, August: Die Stunde der Wahrheit. 1980. *Volume 21.*
Stroumsa, Guy G.: Barbarian Philosophy. 1999. *Volume 112.*
Stuckenbruck, Loren T.: Angel Veneration and Christology. 1995. *Volume II/70.*
Stuhlmacher, Peter (Ed.): Das Evangelium und die Evangelien. 1983. *Volume 28.*
– Biblische Theologie und Evangelium. 2002. *Volume 146.*
Sung, Chong-Hyon: Vergebung der Sünden. 1993. *Volume II/57.*
Tajra, Harry W.: The Trial of St. Paul. 1989. *Volume II/35.*
– The Martyrdom of St.Paul. 1994. *Volume II/67.*
Theißen, Gerd: Studien zur Soziologie des Urchristentums. 1979, ³1989. *Volume 19.*
Theobald, Michael: Studien zum Römerbrief. 2001. *Volume 136.*
Theobald, Michael: see *Mußner, Franz.*
Thornton, Claus-Jürgen: Der Zeuge des Zeugen. 1991. *Volume 56.*
Thüsing, Wilhelm: Studien zur neutestamentlichen Theologie. Ed. von Thomas Söding. 1995. *Volume 82.*
Thurén, Lauri: Derhethorizing Paul. 2000. *Volume 124.*
Tolmie, D. Francois: Persuading the Galatians. 2005. *Volume II/190.*
Tomson, Peter J. and *Doris Lambers-Petry* (Ed.): The Image of the Judaeo-Christians in Ancient Jewish and Christian Literature. 2003. *Volume 158.*
Trebilco, Paul: The Early Christians in Ephesus from Paul to Ignatius. 2004. *Volume 166.*
Treloar, Geoffrey R.: Lightfoot the Historian. 1998. *Volume II/103.*
Tsuji, Manabu: Glaube zwischen Vollkommenheit und Verweltlichung. 1997. *Volume II/93*
Twelftree, Graham H.: Jesus the Exorcist. 1993. *Volume II/54.*
Urban, Christina: Das Menschenbild nach dem Johannesevangelium. 2001. *Volume II/137.*
Visotzky, Burton L.: Fathers of the World. 1995. *Volume 80.*
Vollenweider, Samuel: Horizonte neutestamentlicher Christologie. 2002. *Volume 144.*
Vos, Johan S.: Die Kunst der Argumentation bei Paulus. 2002. *Volume 149.*
Wagener, Ulrike: Die Ordnung des „Hauses Gottes". 1994. *Volume II/65.*

Wahlen, Clinton: Jesus and the Impurity of Spirits in the Synoptic Gospels. 2004. *Volume II/185.*

Walker, Donald D.: Paul's Offer of Leniency (2 Cor 10:1). 2002. *Volume II/152.*

Walter, Nikolaus: Praeparatio Evangelica. Ed. von Wolfgang Kraus und Florian Wilk. 1997. *Volume 98.*

Wander, Bernd: Gottesfürchtige und Sympathisanten. 1998. *Volume 104.*

Watts, Rikki: Isaiah's New Exodus and Mark. 1997. *Volume II/88.*

Wedderburn, A.J.M.: Baptism and Resurrection. 1987. *Volume 44.*

Wegner, Uwe: Der Hauptmann von Kafarnaum. 1985. *Volume II/14.*

Weissenrieder, Annette: Images of Illness in the Gospel of Luke. 2003. Volume II/164.

–, *Friederike Wendt* and *Petra von Gemünden* (Ed.): Picturing the New Testament. 2005. *Volume II/193.*

Welck, Christian: Erzählte ‚Zeichen'. 1994. *Volume II/69.*

Wendt, Friederike (Ed.): see *Weissenrieder, Annette.*

Wiarda, Timothy: Peter in the Gospels. 2000. *Volume II/127.*

Wifstrand, Albert: Epochs and Styles. 2005. *Band 179.*

Wilk, Florian: see *Walter, Nikolaus.*

Williams, Catrin H.: I am He. 2000. *Volume II/113.*

Wilson, Walter T.: Love without Pretense. 1991. *Volume II/46.*

Wischmeyer, Oda: Von Ben Sira zu Paulus. 2004. *Volume 173.*

Wisdom, Jeffrey: Blessing for the Nations and the Curse of the Law. 2001. *Volume II/133.*

Wold, Benjamin G.: Women, Men, and Angels. 2005. *Volume II/2001.*

Wright, Archie T.: The Origin of Evil Spirits. 2005. *Volume II/198.*

Wucherpfennig, Ansgar: Heracleon Philologus. 2002. *Volume 142.*

Yeung, Maureen: Faith in Jesus and Paul. 2002. *Volume II/147.*

Zimmermann, Alfred E.: Die urchristlichen Lehrer. 1984, ²1988. *Volume II/12.*

Zimmermann, Johannes: Messianische Texte aus Qumran. 1998. *Volume II/104.*

Zimmermann, Ruben: Christologie der Bilder im Johannesevangelium. 2004. *Volume 171.*

– Geschlechtermetaphorik und Gottesverhältnis. 2001. *Volume II/122.*

Zumstein, Jean: see *Dettwiler, Andreas*

Zwiep, Arie W.: Judas and the Choice of Matthias. 2004. *Volume II/187.*

For a complete catalogue please write to the publisher
Mohr Siebeck • P.O. Box 2030 • D–72010 Tübingen/Germany
Up-to-date information on the internet at www.mohr.de